EXPLORING IBM CLIENT/SERVER COMPUTING

Other titles of interest from Maximum Press

Marketing on the Internet: Mathiesen, 1-885068-01-8

Real World Client/Server: Krantz, 0-9633214-7-1

Exploring IBM's New Age Mainframes: 1-885068-05-0, Young

Exploring the IBM PC Power Series: Hoskins, Bradley; 0-9633214-5-5

Exploring the PowerPC Revolution! Second Edition: Hoskins, 1-885068-02-6

Exploring the IBM AS/400 Advanced 36: Hoskins, Dimmick; 1-885068-00-X

IBM AS/400, A Business Perspective, Sixth Edition: Hoskins, 0471-048089

Exploring the IBM RISC System/6000 Model 41, MaxFacts™ Special Report: Hoskins, 0-9633214-8-X

IBM RISC System/6000, A Business Perspective, Sixth Edition: Hoskins, 0471-129593

IBM Personal Computers, A Business Perspective, Eighth Edition: Hoskins, 0471-04795-3

What About ProductManager? Curtis, 0-9633214-4-7

For more information, visit our Internet World Wide Web site at: http://www.maxpress.com/books/maxpress/435

EXPLORING IBM
CLIENT/SERVER
COMPUTING

David Bolthouse

MAXIMUM PRESS
605 Silverthorn Road
Gulf Breeze, FL 32561
(904) 934-0819

Publisher: Jim Hoskins

Manager of Finance/Administration: Donna Tryon

Production Manager: ReNae Grant

Marketing/Public Relations Manager: Gina C. Matson

Cover Design: Lauren Smith Designs

Compositor: Type-Write Publications

Copyeditor: Andrew Potter

Proofreader/Indexer: Janis Paris

Printer: Malloy Lithographing

All photographs courtesy of International Business Machines Corporation.

This publication is designed to provide accurate and authoritative information in regard to the subject matter covered. It is sold with the understanding that the publisher is not engaged in rendering professional services. If legal, accounting, medical, psychological, or any other expert assistance is required, the services of a competent professional person should be sought. ADAPTED FROM A DECLARATION OF PRINCIPLES OF A JOINT COMMITTEE OF THE AMERICAN BAR ASSOCIATION AND PUBLISHERS.

Recognizing the importance of preserving what has been written, it is a policy of Maximum Press to have books of enduring value published in the United States printed on acid-free paper, and we exert our best efforts to that end.

Library of Congress Cataloging-in-Publication Data

Bolthouse, David, 1961-

  Exploring IBM client/server computing / by David Bolthouse.

   p. cm.

  Includes index.

  ISBN 1-885068-04-2

  1. Client/server computing. I. Title.

QA76.9.C55B65 1996

004'.36—dc20   96-10079
                                         CIP

Trademarks

1-2-3	Lotus Development Corporation
Adobe	Adobe Systems Incorporated
AdvanceNet	Hewlett-Packard Company
AFS	Transarc Corporation
Andrew File System	Transarc Corporation
Apple	Apple Computer, Incorporated
AppleTalk	Apple Computer, Incorporated
ARDIS	The ARDIS Company
AT&T	American Telephone and Telegraph
Banyan	Banyan Systems Incorporated
Bay Networks	Bay Networks Incorporated
Bell Laboratories	American Telephone and Telegraph
Bellcore	Bell Communications Research, Incorporated
BeyondMail	Beyond Corporation
Burroughs	Unisys Corporation
cc:Mail	Lotus Development Corporation
Certified Novell Engineer	Novell, Incorporated
Cisco Systems	Cisco Systems Incorporated
Compaq	Compaq Computer Corporation
DaVinci	ON Technology Corporation
DCE	Open Software Foundation, Incorporated
DEC	Digital Equipment Corporation
DECdns	Digital Equipment Corporation
DECdts	Digital Equipment Corporation
DECnet	Digital Equipment Corporation

Delta	Delta Air Lines, Incorporated
Digital	Digital Equipment Corporation
Digital Network Architecture	Digital Equipment Corporation
Distributed Computing Environment	Open Software Foundation, Incorporated
DNA	Digital Equipment Corporation
Encina	Transarc Corporation
Ethernet	Xerox Corporation
Ford	Ford Motor Company
Freelance Graphics	Lotus Development Corporation
Galileo	Galileo International
Gartner Group	Gartner Group, Incorporated
Hayes	Hayes Microcomputer Products, Incorporated
Hertz	Hertz Corporation
Hewlett-Packard	Hewlett-Packard Company
HP	Hewlett-Packard Company
HP-UX	Hewlett-Packard Company
Hyatt	Hyatt Corporation
Informix	Informix Software, Incorporated
Ingres	Computer Associates, Incorporated
Intel	Intel Corporation
IPX	Novell, Incorporated
Kalpana	Cisco Systems, Incorporated
Kodak	Eastman Kodak Company
LAT	Digital Equipment Corporation
LocalTalk	Apple Computer, Incorporated
Lotus	Lotus Development Corporation
Macintosh	Apple Computer, Incorporated
MacOS System 7	Apple Computer, Incorporated
Marriott	Marriott International, Incorporated
Microsoft	Microsoft Corporation
Motif	Open Software Foundation, Incorporated
MS	Microsoft Corporation
MS-DOS	Microsoft Corporation
NCR	NCR Corporation
NCS	Hewlett-Packard Company
NetWare	Novell, Incorporated
NetWare Loadable Module	Novell, Incorporated
Network Computing System	Hewlett-Packard Company
Network File System	Sun Microsystems, Incorporated
NFS	Sun Microsystems, Incorporated
NLM	Novell, Incorporated
NLSP	Novell, Incorporated
Notes	Lotus Development Corporation
Novell	Novell, Incorporated
OMEGAVIEW	Candle Corporation
ONC	Sun Microsystems, Incorporated

Open Network Computing	Sun Microsystems, Incorporated
Open Software Foundation	Open Software Foundation, Incorporated
OpenVMS	Digital Equipment Corporation
Oracle	Oracle Corporation
OSF	Open Software Foundation, Incorporated
PCL	Hewlett-Packard Company
Pentium	Intel Corporation
PostScript	Adobe Systems Incorporated
Proteon	Proteon Incorporated
Radio Shack	Tandy Corporation
RUMBA	Wall Data Corporation
SABRE	AMR Corporation
SCO	The Santa Cruz Operation, Incorporated
Seiko	Seiko Epson Corporation
SINIX	Siemens Nixdorf Informationssysteme AG
Solaris	Sun Microsystems, Incorporated
Sperry	Unisys Corporation
Sprint	Sprint Communications Company, L.P.
SPX	Novell, Incorporated
SQL Server	Sybase, Incorporated
Sun	Sun Microsystems, Incorporated
Sun Microsystems	Sun Microsystems, Incorporated
SunOS	Sun Microsystems, Incorporated
Sybase	Sybase, Incorporated
Taligent	Taligent, Incorporated
Tandem	Tandem Computers Incorporated
Toyota	Toyota Motors
Transarc	Transarc Corporation
UNIX	Licensed exclusively by X/Open Company, Ltd.
VAX	Digital Equipment Corporation
VINES	Banyan Systems Incorporated
VMS	Digital Equipment Corporation
Volvo	The Volvo Group
VT	Digital Equipment Corporation
Wang	Wang Laboratories, Incorporated
WANGnet	Wang Laboratories, Incorporated
Wellfleet Communications	Bay Networks Incorporated
Windows	Microsoft Corporation
Windows 95	Microsoft Corporation
Windows NT	Microsoft Corporation
WordPerfect	Novell, Incorporated
WordPro	Lotus Development Corporation
X Window System	X Consortium
X/Open	X/Open Company, Ltd.
Xerox	Xerox Corporation
Xerox Network System	Xerox Corporation

The following list includes trademarks and registered trademarks of International Business Machines Corporation.

3090
3745 Communications Controller
Advanced 36
Advanced Peer-to-Peer Networking
Advanced Program-to-Program Communications
AFP
AIX
AnyNet
APPC
Application System/400
APPN
Aptiva
AS/400
Audio Visual Connection
C Set ++
CICS
Common User Access
CommonPoint Application System for AIX
CommonPoint Application System for OS/2
CUA
Customer Information Control System
DATABASE 2
Database/2
DataGuide
DataJoiner
DataPropagator
DB/2
DB2
DB2/2
DB2/400
DB2/6000
Distributed Database Connection Services
Distributed Relational Database Architecture
DOS LAN Requester
DRDA
Enterprise System/9000
Enterprise Systems Connection Architecture
ES/9000
ESCON
ESCON XDF
EtherStreamer
FlowMark

FormTalk
IBM
IBM Personal Computer (PC)
IMS
IMS
Info Warehouse
Information Management System
Intelligent Printer Data Stream
IPDS
LAN Distance
LAN Server
Language Environment
LANStreamer
LPDA
MO:DCA
MQSeries
Multiple Virtual System
MVS
Mwave
NetDoor
NetView
NetView
NetView Distribution Manager
Nways
OfficeVision/MVS
OfficeVision/VM
Open Blueprint
OpenEdition
Operating System/2
Operating System/400
OS/2
OS/390
OS/400
Parallel Sysplex
PeerMaster
PM
Portmaster
POWER
POWERparellel
PowerPC
PR/SM
Presentation Manager
Print Services Facility

Processor Resource System Management
PSF
PSF/2
PSF/6000
RACF
RISC System/6000
RXR/2
SAA
SNA
SOM
SP
SQL/DS
Sysplex TImer
System Object Model
System/3
System/36
System/360
System/38
Systems Network Architecture
SystemView

ThinkPad
TrackPoint
TURBOWAYS
Ultimedia
Virtual Machine
Virtual Telecommunications Access Method
VisualAge
VisualGen
VisualLift
VM
VM/ESA
VRPG CLIENT
VSE/ESA
VTAM
WAVERUNNER
WebConnection
WebExplorer
WIN-OS2
X-Station

Disclaimer

The purchase of computer software, hardware, and services is an important and costly business decision. While the author and publisher of this book have made reasonable efforts to ensure the accuracy and timeliness of the information contained herein, the author and publisher assume no liability with respect to loss or damage caused or alleged to be caused by reliance on any information contained herein and disclaim any and all warranties, expressed or implied, as to the accuracy or reliability of said information.

This book is not intended to replace the suppliers' documentation or personnel in determining the specifications and capabilities of the products mentioned in this book. The suppliers' documentation should always be consulted, as the specifications and capabilities of computer hardware, software, or services are subject to frequent modification. The reader is solely responsible for the choice of computer hardware, software, or services. All configurations and applications of computer hardware, software or services should be reviewed with the manufacturer's representatives prior to choosing or using any computer hardware and software. If you do not agree with this disclaimer, you may return this book to the publisher for a full refund.

Table of Contents

Chapter 2:
Client/Server Computing: A New Approach 45

Chapter 3:
Networking: The Foundation Of
Client/Server Computing   90

Chapter 4:
IBM Hardware For Client/Server Computing   174

Chapter 5:
Software For Building Client/Server Applications   285

Introduction

What This Book Is

Over the last five years, the frenzy of hype surrounding networked, small computers reached fever pitch. First, consultants and pundits told us large, shared computers were dinosaurs, lumbering beasts with no future. Then, Wall Street analysts cast networked personal computers as mammals, flexible survivors with an infinitely bright future. Compaq advertised their largest, fastest personal computers as "your next mainframe." Many managers and executives adopted these views, causing rifts and layoffs in the industry as revenues shifted. Microsoft, Intel, Cisco Systems, and Oracle have spoken. We are mammals. Only the small, the fast, and the nimble survive. Buy our stuff; join our herd now, and you will survive too. Nonsense.

In the IBM North American Open Systems Center, we see the survivors and the casualties alike. We design, build, and integrate new multivendor client/server systems for some of our clients. For others, we perform triage upon broken systems that do not meet their technical or business goals. We like building new, successful systems more, but working the emergency room keeps us on our toes.

Our clients can be large or small firms. Only a few build new client/server systems using only small computers. The others use existing large computers, along with small computers, to transform how they conduct business. All use their existing investments in hardware, software, and people, forging them into powerful levers to open new business opportunities.

To succeed today, your firm must be both nimble and reliable. So must your systems. Client/server computing helps you to succeed by building revenues, improving quality, or shortening product cycles. It can help you become more flexible. Client/server computing can increase your costs, because building reliability into a networked system of computers and humans isn't trivial, but client/server computing makes up for these costs in productivity and new opportunity.

This book is about understanding, building, and operating flexible, dependable client/server systems. These systems contain four main parts: networks, hardware, software, and people. This is also a book about the world's largest and broadest supplier of client/server computing products. Its name may surprise you: IBM.

The core of any computer system is software. You can buy software, build it, and integrate it into useful, productive computing systems. When you turn the system over for normal use, you must operate it effectively. As your needs change, it should change as well. Software can distinguish your firm from its rivals. Applied badly, it becomes a hole in your financial dike, through which your cash gushes. Applied well, it gives you a competitive edge. Client/server computing gives you a chance to harness the flexible power of small computer systems to the reliability of larger, shared computers.

Understanding software technologies—both old and new techniques—gives you an edge in defining, buying, building, or integrating a successful application. It lets you choose which techniques are most applicable to the task at hand. You can also manage your staff and your contractors more carefully. Finally, when the first revision is complete, you must operate what you have built while planning your next steps. Software well understood, well planned, and reliably operated underpins a successful client/server computing application.

This is a book about networks. Networks expand your reach globally, touching customers, shareholders, regulators, employees, and suppliers. You can use networks within a building, across town, nationwide, or globally. Networks can help you lower transaction costs, increase product quality, and open new markets. Without networks, client/server computing would be considered an academic curiosity.

Because networks have no purpose without devices and software attached to them, I also examine computer hardware, networking hardware, and networking software. Different kinds of computers and networks behave differently in a client/server system. Understanding these differences helps you to know the costs, performance, and predictability of a client/server system.

This book is about enabling your staff. People design, build, and operate client/server systems. They solve problems for those who use the system. They ensure the integrity of the data the system contains. They change the system's applications as your business changes. Without their experience, their ingenuity, and their discipline, a client/server system doesn't stand a chance. By automating some of their tasks, you can increase the system's reliability, reduce frustration, and increase profits.

Finally, this book attempts to find some clarity in an industry filled with obfuscation. It tries to make complex undertakings simpler. I assume that you know how to use a personal computer, but if you don't have that experience, I still try to make client/server techniques approachable. I have structured these materials in a way that should be simple to use. If you find that you are familiar with some of the material, you should be able to skip parts as needed. If you gain a greater understanding of client/server computing, and IBM's approach to it, then I will have succeeded.

What This Book Is Not

If you're looking for the latest hot technology, please don't come here. Everything discussed in this book exists, with a few clearly marked exceptions. You can put your hands on it, buy it, and even get support for it if something goes awry. You won't get any inklings of Wall Street's next hot Initial Product Offering here. If you want a Theoretical Discussion of Vaporous Possibilities, this isn't the right book for you. I hate hype, and refuse to contribute to it as a matter of principle.

If you want to understand Oracle's client/server computing products, this isn't the right book. The same holds for Microsoft, Hewlett-Packard, Cisco Systems, or any other firm besides IBM and Lotus. Other people can write those books; this one covers a broad enough expanse.

If you need detailed knowledge about individual products such as IBM's Application System/400, the IBM RISC System/6000, or IBM's Operating System/2, this is the wrong book. I don't have enough room to tell you everything that touches client/server computing. Maximum Press, this book's publisher, and others have published books covering these subjects.

About the Author

Because any book reflects its author, you should know a little about me. I am an IBMer in the North American Open Systems Center; however, this book is not sponsored by the IBM Corporation. When I joined IBM seven years ago, my computer systems background was not in IBM equipment, but in Digital Equipment Corporation products. This is like others in our group, most of whom joined IBM due to their knowledge of various non-IBM products. Although we work mostly with North American clients, over the years my work has taken me to four continents.

I demand much from computer systems, both large and small. Unpredictability frustrates me; I expect informative, responsive systems that work whenever I want to use them. I expect equivalent function, but not equivalent performance, when I use computer systems from my office, my home, or a hotel room. I use whatever software or network is available to me to meet my clients' needs. When necessary, I write programs, using conventional or object oriented languages. Within the Open Systems Center, I mostly design, build, and diagnose large, multiple-vendor networks.

Designing new applications and networks is the most useful work I do. It's particularly satisfying for me to see work done years ago still performing reliably. Triage is challenging and fun, but it's an expensive thrill for my clients. By the time I'm brought in, a failure or poor performance has cost thousands, even millions of dollars in lost productivity.

Daily, I use an IBM ThinkPad laptop computer, configured as a help desk's nightmare. It runs IBM's OS/2 Warp operating system for my production purposes. I also have Microsoft's MS-DOS, Windows, and Windows 95 installed for client needs. I use OS/2 Warp by itself or I tie it to our lab's network. For personal productivity, I use Lotus Freelance Graphics for Windows, Lotus Notes, Lotus 1-2-3, and WordPerfect for DOS. These tools helped me to write this book.

Our lab's network attaches products from IBM, Hewlett-Packard, Digital, Sun, Apple, and other computer vendors. We use it for production, testing, and teaching others how to build multivendor networks. It uses products from IBM, Bay Networks, Cisco Systems, 3-Com, and other suppliers. It isn't uncommon for us to build prototype systems and stress test client/server systems for clients that contain products from dozens of vendors. We regularly build and test such prototypes next to production systems, without causing unpredictable interactions between them.

How This Book Is Organized

Chapter 1 describes how computers and their software are traditionally built. It covers all of the main kinds of computers, from personal computers to room filling mainframe computers. It also relates how and why different styles of software evolved.

Chapter 2 characterizes client/server computing. Here, I define the terms "client" and "server," and how they interact using a network. I also examine the six most common architectural models for client/server computing. Although I don't discuss specific products here, I set out a series of examples that we'll discuss in more detail later in the book.

Chapter 3 is an overview of a complex field, computer networking. To operate an effective client/server system, you'll need a cost-effective, reliable network. Unfortunately, for many managers and business owners, networking is a black art. We'll demystify it for you.

Chapter 4 discusses the hardware IBM provides for use in client/server systems. Most of the chapter describes IBM's four main computer families, the operating systems available for each, and how to attach them to networks. The last part of the chapter considers IBM's hardware for building networks, such as switches, routers, and communications controllers.

Chapter 5 looks at the software tools developers use to build client/server systems. Your staff might use them, or someone else might provide them to you as part of a package. Either way, understanding how your client/server software is developed will help you to operate your system more effectively.

Chapter 6 focuses on designing and operating client/server systems. I introduce you to client/server computing's 800-pound gorilla: support costs. Then, I discuss ways to reduce costs and improve service using systems integration services and operational support software. Finally, Chapter 7 reconsiders the six examples introduced in Chapter 2. These are not actual case studies but we in the Open Systems Center have found them typical of real projects. They should be useful to you as you buy or build your own systems.

If you are considering buying or building a client/server computing system, I hope this book helps you and your firm to become more prosperous. Perhaps you can avoid the pitfalls others have discovered. Maybe you'll gain a few ideas from my text to smooth your path. Perhaps you'll make more informed decisions. If so, then I am pleased to have helped.

Acknowledgements

All photographs used within this book are copyright of the IBM Corporation, and are used with permission. They are reproduced courtesy of International Business Machines Corporation.

Few authors complete a book without much help and encouragement. Many IBMers helped me write this book; I can't acknowledge them all here. Ron Clipp, Bob Hilbish, Rick Kingsley, Sandra Ambrose, Paul Marchesseault, and Mike Jones encouraged me, read early drafts of chapters and contributed useful suggestions to improve the book. Sandra Ambrose helped immensely with Chapter 5; without her, this book wouldn't be in your hands now. Maggie Archibald was a font of information regarding database products, Patricia Carando helped me understand object oriented technologies better, Art Cannon clarified the RISC System/6000 product line, and Paul Marchesseault led me to appreciate the AS/400 and OS/400. My director, Margaret Potter, encouraged me and helped me find people within IBM who could provide "raw material" for the manuscript. Stan Kimer, of IBM's Networking Division, advised me as IBM announced new networking products. Dale Rogers and Len Hand kept the Open Systems Center's networks and servers running smoothly; I found the lab's stability invaluable in the wee hours of the morning.

People outside of IBM contributed as well. Dr. Alan Roth read early drafts, and reminded me of what computer users care about. Jim Hoskins and Andrew Potter helped me structure my thoughts more clearly, corrected poor prose, and contributed many ideas. Specifically, the six client/server computing sample applications were Jim's idea. My clients might see a little of themselves in these pages; our work together has focused my views of what works well and what will fail. The music of Mahler, Brahms, Bach, Messiaen, and Saint-Saens bouyed me between the last few hundred pages of the manuscript. Finally, my best friend and wife, Colleen, fueled me with cappuccino and bagels, endured over a year of boring weekends, and kept our household going during my "absence." Thanks.

1

How We Came to
Where We Are Today

If you read computer newspapers or magazines, you've undoubtedly seen articles about client/server computing. Perhaps you're trying to understand how this trend fits your organization's needs. Perhaps you're confused about varying definitions and claims made by writers about client/server computing. Within the computer industry today, client/server computing means different things to different people. Our view, explained more fully in Chapter 2, is simple: Client/server computing is an effective way to design and build computer programs that run on multiple computers. So, to understand client/server computing, we hope to help you understand how people build systems from computers, networks, and programs. In this chapter, we set the stage. First, we chronicle the most important ideas used to develop computer systems over the past 30 years. We look at both single and multiple computer systems. Also, we discuss some of the reasons for each new idea in computer systems design. If you're an "old hand," and you know how computers, programs, and networks have worked together in multiple-user computer systems, skip the sections you already understand.

Figure 1.1. An IBM System/360 mainframe computer.

Computers for Corporations: Mainframes

Early Computers Automate Individual Tasks

As seen in Figure 1.1, the first electronic computers filled a room. Now, tiny chips of silicon do the same work faster. Others have documented this quick development of **hardware**. **Software**, the stored sequences of instructions that tell the hardware what to do, is equally important. It made the first computers different from other machines. Then, most machines had a single purpose. One computer, using different software, could manage a large firm's accounting, monitor inventories, or calculate materials needed for a week's production. Although software has not developed at the same breakneck pace as hardware, without software even the best hardware is a useless pile of elegant circuitry.

In the first computers, a person called an **operator** loaded software instructions, called **programs**, and data into the computer's memory. The program then ran. The next program loaded into memory wrote over any earlier programs or data.

Operators first loaded, or **input**, programs and data by hand using switches. Naturally, these programs were small. Results, called **output**, went to printers or to **keypunch** machines. A keypunch made holes in paper cards. Some computers used **card readers** to interpret these holes back into alphabetic or numeric data, loading it into memory. Similarly, **tape drives** stored and retrieved data using magnetic tapes. Soon, punched cards and magnetic tapes replaced switches. Operators loaded tapes and stacks of punched cards, kept the printers filled with paper, and pressed the "run button" to run programs.

Only one program could run at a time. While the program ran, the tapes, printers, and keypunches waited for work. While the printer ran, the next program couldn't use the processor. Compared with today's computers, this seems inefficient, but it was better than using mechanical ways to calculate, sort, and store data.

Since only one program ran at a time, each program included instructions to control the simplest operations, such as how to position a punched card in the card reader. This caused problems when any of the computer's hardware changed: People would need to rewrite the software to adapt to the new hardware.

Automating Scheduled Tasks with Batch Jobs

The earliest computers were expensive, and the firms using them wanted to get as much work as possible from them. Idle components wasted both time and money. The first **operating systems** improved the use of the computer's parts by overlapping operations. Now, a computer could calculate, read a program, and print a report simultaneously. These first operating systems also ended the need for each program to understand everything about the hardware being used. The distinction between operating systems and application programs became more clear. **Applications** did "useful work." Operating systems did **I/O (Input/Output)**, allocated hardware usage fairly, ensured data integrity, and maintained security. Operating systems also requested human help when needed—say, to mount a tape.

Soon, operating systems defined a **job**, several related programs run one right after another. Data for these programs was collected, or **batched**, until the time came for the job to run. The **batch job** would process the entire batch of data when it ran. Operators scheduled jobs based on business needs. A job that calculated a firm's daily balance sheet, for example, would probably run nightly, whereas the job that printed paychecks might run weekly. The key idea here is the batched data: Computing your accounting position immediately, for example, is difficult with this approach.

When newer, more capable computer systems could run jobs either serially or in parallel, firms found they could automate many business processes. For example, one job could update and age accounts receivable files. This job might produce a file listing overdue accounts that needed reminder notices. The next job might take that list, print the notices, and add a note to the accounts receivable file saying the notice was sent. It might also print a report for management so they could take remedial actions such as reducing a customer's credit line. You can probably imagine similar ways to automate payroll, sales tax, and other scheduled processing.

Many of today's practices derive from software designed using these techniques. When designers and programmers built these applications, they mirrored the way businesses worked. Managers scheduled factory output days or weeks in advance, ordered any required materials, and stocked inventory. If the firm predicted demand incorrectly, it might stock finished goods awaiting sale. For a business like that, batch jobs fit well for everything from payroll to production scheduling. Software using batch jobs serves many firms well even today.

Batch jobs can change simply and quickly. Often one system does all of the processing for a job. Thousands of programmers understand batch programming. Operations such as writing payroll checks or producing reports required by governmental agencies fit well within batched operations: The nature of both the data and the business process fits the batched processing method. Finally, some batched software written in the 1960s still runs—a stunning achievement given the short lifetime of earlier software.

In this discussion, though, you may note an absence of one common group of people: the computer's users. In a batched environment, the notion of a user really doesn't exist. Input comes from tapes or punched cards, and output goes to tapes, cards, or printers. People who use information from batch jobs have printed reports delivered to them. If someone only needs a few lines of data from a report, he or she still gets the whole report. If several people need different parts of the same report, they might ask for new jobs to be programmed. They can't just change jobs themselves, because a change would affect other users simultaneously.

Getting Instant Answers: Transaction Processing

Batch processing doesn't work well for people such as travel agents and customer service reps. They need answers quickly; their customer wants an answer immediately. They need their information readily at hand, or **online**. Time sharing systems and transaction processing monitors help software designers build applications that give people responses to their requests in seconds instead of minutes or hours.

A **Transaction Processing monitor** (**TP monitor**) is software that resides "between" the application program and the operating system. It's not part of either the application program or the operating system. You might think of it as an extension of the operating system. The TP monitor invokes or "calls" a transaction, but it maintains a degree of control over the transaction as it runs. A program might contain several transactions, each of which runs independently under the control of the TP monitor.

People use **terminals**, made up of a video display and a keyboard, to interact with the TP monitor. So, a system with a TP monitor has users, unlike a batch system. Automated devices such as modern cash registers, automatic teller machines, or gasoline pumps can also provide input to transactions. Usually, a TP monitor's user types in a transaction name (or makes a choice from a menu), completes a form shown on their screen, and presses the Enter key to start the transaction. The TP monitor then takes over and calls part of the application program. When that part of the program has run, it returns control to the TP monitor. The key idea in a TP monitor is this: The TP monitor maintains the integrity of each transaction so that application programs don't have to worry about all these details.

Transactions are simple, such as looking up a balance in a savings account, or complex, such as updating available parts balances when finished goods leave an assembly line. A transaction must be "**atomic**": All computations and I/Os it contains must complete successfully. If anything fails, the whole transaction is "rolled back"; partially completed transactions are forbidden. A TP monitor also provides locking services for programs. If only one seat is available on a flight and two buyers want it, a TP monitor can avoid contention. The first buyer should get a confirmed seat. The second buyer might receive a standby ticket.

A common example where a TP monitor might be used is with an automatic teller machine. Maintaining the integrity of the transaction is crucial here. Before it gives you cash, the ATM finds your bank and checks your account balance. Then, your bank's ATM support software might tentatively apply the withdrawal to your account. Next, the machine gives you the cash you so desperately need. Finally, the ATM tells the main computer that the transaction is complete. Now, the main computer must finish all of the accounting. Let's say the teller machine has no cash because someone needs to refill it. When that portion of the transaction fails, the data on the main computer should be rolled back. The TP monitor should ensure that the earlier record of the aborted withdrawal is erased.

TP monitors are fast and efficient. Often, less than one second passes between when a user presses the Enter key and when the screen displays the results. Today, TP monitors service thousands of users at a time. They are the mainstays of business computing, supporting everything from inventory control systems to travel reservation systems.

Along with batch jobs, transaction processing software encompasses much of the software written for large, shared computers, often called **mainframe computers**. This software has a vast value to organizations worldwide: In its 1994 annual report, IBM estimated the value of software written for its mainframe systems alone at one trillion U.S. dollars.

Files and Databases Organize Your Data

In the first computers, organizations stored their data on punched cards. A card usually contained 80 columns, or characters, of data. You could think of one or more cards as a **record**, perhaps of a financial transaction. Similarly, a line of text on a printed report is considered a record. Collections of similarly structured records are called **files**. Physically, you could think of a box of punched cards as a file. Conceptually, files have no specified size, so they can grow or shrink as needed. You could also put files onto magnetic tapes. Because magnetic tapes had a greater capacity than boxes of punched cards, it became common over time to store many files on a single tape.

At first, programs processed a file's records sequentially. Punched cards and magnetic tapes were considered **offline** data storage, because the correct files or tapes had to be loaded before they could be processed. This fits well with batch processing techniques, but not with online processing, such as transaction processing.

In the late 1950s, IBM invented another data storage medium, the **Direct Access Storage Device (DASD)**. A DASD contains one or more platters, each of which looks rather like a compact disc. These platters spin at high speeds. For each platter, a magnetic read/write head, an extremely sensitive, sophisticated version of the head found in a tape player, reads and writes zeros and ones on the surface of the DASD. These heads, usually mounted on a pole, resemble a comb between the platters. The comb is capable of swinging across the platters. Because of this, any part of any platter is accessible quite quickly. Today, most people call DASDs **disks**, because that's what the platters resemble. Besides, disk is easier to pronounce than DASD.

Disks were a great step forward because they allowed both sequential and direct, or nonsequential, access to the data stored on them. You could program the disk's supporting electronics to retrieve a specific record, say, from the middle of a file, without reading all of the records before it. Also, the storage was continuously available, or online. This improved storage access times considerably, because you didn't have to wait for the operator to load a tape. Although they were more expensive than other storage media, disks caught on quickly because of these advantages.

So now you could retrieve records from files quickly and easily, once you'd located the record you needed. As online data grew dramatically, finding required records quickly became a pressing issue. Vendors responded at first with a variety of schemes to structure files with indexes. The idea was to define one or more unique "keys" into each record and to place these keys into a index. Since the index was smaller than the whole file, you could search them much more quickly. Sorting keys was also faster than sorting complete records. Unfortunately, customers outgrew this technology as well.

In the 1970s and 1980s, vendors supplied customers with software designed to manage large quantities of records more easily. **Database** software defined how records were interrelated. IBM invented today's most commonly used database technique, the **relational database**, in 1975. Relational databases store all of their records in tables, which operate according to strict mathematical rules. Soon, with the advent of structured files and database software, most firms put their current information online, using disks to store it. Today, offline data storage is used mostly for backup and archival purposes.

How Large Computers Affected Organizations

The first computers were large, complex, and expensive. They generated lots of heat, so firms put them in special, air-conditioned rooms. These rooms also had false floors to keep people from tripping over the cables between the computer's various parts. Sometimes, they had large windows onto hall-ways, to allow proud officials to show the new machine on a facilities tour. Eventually, the computer room and the surrounding staff facilities became known as a **data center**. Probably in honor of the large windows, some people also call data centers "**glass houses.**"

Early computers required a large supporting staff. Three shifts of operators made sure that the machine was "well and truly fed." They fixed unforeseen problems, such as changing the processing schedule when someone stumbled and scattered a box of punched cards across the computer room floor. They copied important business data to magnetic tape. One backup copy stayed onsite in case users accidentally deleted data, and other copies went to other facilities, guarding against fire or natural disaster. If the data storage hardware failed, or if a fire destroyed the data center, valuable business records would exist elsewhere.

Systems programmers set up and changed the operating system and its supporting **subsystems**, such as TP monitors and batch job processors. They defined policies for how the computer was used, and worked with operational staff to verify the integrity of daily operations. They tested new versions of software and software for compatibility with existing programs. Sometimes, they designed enhancements to existing programs, exploiting new operating system capabilities. They also arranged for orderly changes to occur, to avoid inconveniencing users if possible.

If someone needed a new or changed program, **applications program-mers** would create or modify programs, transactions, or jobs. They changed how output was printed when forms changed. When government regulations changed, they altered programs to fit the new requirements. When a report was insufficiently detailed, or if a screen was hard to understand, they worked with users to find a better answer.

Database administrators managed the structure of online information on disks. They optimized the performance of I/Os to files and databases, designed procedures to ensure the integrity of the data entrusted to them, and worked with systems programmers and applications programmers to ensure that the design of a new program or subsystem would work smoothly with the existing data.

Eventually, a department or division, called Data Processing or Information Systems, evolved. At first, it generally serviced "back office" operations such as accounting rather than manufacturing or distribution. Most firms today have an **Information Systems or Information Services (I/S)** organization providing centralized information services to the firm. It usually resides at a firm's headquarters or at the data center, manages the data center's computers, and mediates between the system and those who need information.

A culture developed along with the I/S organization. I/S groups often have a distinctly "corporate" viewpoint. They abhor chaos or risk, particularly when sensitive business records may be exposed to loss, corruption, or theft. They try to find economies of scale, where possible, among departments or divisions of a firm. They know how to reduce costs by efficiently using computers and networks. They think strategically more than tactically. Many of these "old hands" have seen technologies endlessly hyped, and they maintain a healthy skepticism. Usually, they are well disciplined and professional, and they take their responsibilities to the firm seriously.

Users, though, sometimes find the I/S culture stodgy and onerous. Some I/S organizations deserve this opinion, responding slowly to changing market and business conditions. Others are simply overburdened maintaining older software while simultaneously responding to changes in technology and new requests for service.

These users may believe they can perform the I/S function better than the I/S group. Sometimes, these users may not value the discipline that ensures the integrity and security of a firm's information assets. They might want to cut costs, taking risks with backups or other operational procedures. In extreme cases, some users may resent the I/S group's almost monopolistic power in managing the firm's data.

Minicomputers for Departments and Small Businesses

During the rise of I/S, smaller businesses and departments of large firms needed computers too. By themselves, they couldn't justify large machines that needed a large staff. For example, a manufacturing company might need a computer to monitor and schedule a plant's production, or a business might need a computer for a regional processing center that tracks inventories and sales in dozens of stores. In these cases, a large, specialized staff is impossible to justify. Overly expensive hardware, software, and maintenance expenses would also wipe out the savings automating simple processes would bring.

Computer vendors noticed these evolving needs and developed other kinds of hardware and software better suited to smaller needs. A **minicomputer**, shown in Figure 1.2, usually runs similar, but less complex, software than its larger counterparts. Minicomputers don't have the processing speed

Figure 1.2. An IBM System/3 minicomputer.

or the raw I/O capacity of the largest computers available at any given time. Where some mainframe computers can support ten thousand or more transaction processing users at once, minicomputers typically might support dozens to hundreds of active users.

Time Sharing Operating Systems

Many programs do not need transaction processing's discipline to be effective. Consider a small simulation program that several users can run at once. If these users aren't trying to change the same data simultaneously, transaction processing's disciplines probably aren't needed. A department of programmers sharing a computer to develop software doesn't need transaction processing discipline. Neither does a typing pool. These users need a simple, highly interactive environment to improve their personal and organizational productivity. Computers using **time sharing operating systems** provide them with these simple, responsive services.

Digital Equipment Corporation (DEC) developed and shipped the first commercial time sharing system in the early 1960s. Others, including IBM, followed. As in transaction processing systems, a person uses a terminal to interact with a time sharing system. The operating system divides available hardware resources, such as processor time and main memory storage, between the users who are actively using the system. It tries to allocate resources fairly among active users. Time sharing fits applications where users need responsive interaction but the business process doesn't need the disciplines transactions provide.

Usually, time sharing systems don't worry about "wall clock time" when scheduling system resources. In batch systems, getting jobs done on time may be more important than being temporarily unfair to one job or another. If the CEO wants a report at 8:00 A.M. daily, allocating hardware resources to that job may well be the most important task the batch system can do at 7:30. Most time sharing systems don't try to get jobs done at a particular time.

Over time, vendors added many capabilities to time sharing systems. Most systems include a simple file management system. For most minicomputer users, this is adequate, because the problem they need to solve isn't huge. If simple approaches are insufficient, you can buy database software to organize your data. Other vendors developed transaction processing software, layered upon the basic time sharing system. Today, some minicomputers even include a rudimentary batch processing capability. Overall, though, time sharing systems continue to provide a simple, highly interactive environment for textual applications.

How Organizations Assimilated Minicomputers

Minicomputers quickly developed a following because they empowered smaller organizations. They seemed more personal and responsive than the big, centralized systems controlled by I/S. Minicomputers were good for such tasks as automating the typing pool or encouraging collaboration among a department of engineers. You could also use them to run a small or medium-sized business. Some people grew emotionally attached to minicomputers and the empowered feelings they provided.

Minicomputers, and later, mainframes, with time sharing systems also provided services to firms that didn't own a computer. Instead, these firms leased time on a computer owned by others. Time sharing operating systems provide an interactive, textual interface to users. Because different users have differing data access needs, time sharing systems also provide a rudimentary security facility. So, it wasn't inconceivable for a small company to lease time, sharing a system with another firm. Of course, a firm that owns a minicomputer still requires a staff. Since minicomputer software is usually less complex than its larger brothers, each staff could be smaller. They could also make changes more quickly because a change might only affect a department or two rather than a whole firm. At first, this flexibility proved valuable to the departments that bought these machines.

Over time firms bought more minicomputers and hired more staff. In the mid-1980s, some firms noticed that they could support their minicomputers more effectively if they consolidated these staffs. After all, why should a company support duplicated skills in several places around the firm? As firms consolidated their staff, they followed two main paths. Either they consolidated the staff into their existing I/S group, or they built a separate, parallel I/S group for minicomputer support. Today, in most large firms, I/S supports both mainframe computers and minicomputers.

Back to the Future: Standalone Personal Computers

When the earliest personal computers, or **microcomputers**, came onto the marketplace in the 1970s, they were programmed just like their larger grand-fathers: by hand, usually with toggle switches. Compared with today's mod-els, the first **Personal Computers (PCs)** were expensive and very limited. It was unusual to have 4000 characters of main memory, and existing mini-computer and mainframe programs would take hundreds of times as much space. So, PC programmers started anew.

How Early PC Software Worked

Soon, programmers with sore fingertips placed system software into a sili-con chip called **Read Only Memory (ROM)**. This ROM contained only the simplest software for talking with the computer's hardware. Applications talked to the ROM. This was unproductive: Personal computers needed an operating system before software developers could be more productive.

Successful microcomputers, including the **IBM Personal Computer (IBM PC)** shown in Figure 1.3, supported one or more operating systems. Usually, the operator—now the owner/user—would reset the hardware to load the new operating system into memory. When you turned the PC's power on, the ROM verified the correct operation of the hardware. Then it tried to load an operating system from an I/O device, usually a cassette tape or a small, magnetic **diskette**. Over time, the popularity of cassette tape waned dramatically, and after about 1982 or so, diskette drives became standard equipment for microcomputer systems.

Let's say a software program for your IBM PC needed IBM's **Personal Computer Disk Operating System (PC-DOS)** operating system to run. Let's also say you had already loaded and used a different operating system. You would restart the machine, load the proper diskette into the drive, and read the new operating system from it. You could then start and run your appli-cation program, usually from another diskette. While your program was running, no other program could run. When you finished using the pro-

Figure 1.3. The Original IBM Personal Computer.

gram, you could load another program, which then overwrote the first program in the PC's memory.

Remember the first large computer operating systems? A person loaded a program into memory, ran it, and then overwrote it when the next program was loaded. If you replace the punched cards and the tape drives with diskettes, you've essentially got the early versions of PC-DOS. Today, PC-DOS (and Microsoft's equivalent, **MS-DOS**) still runs one program at a time, provides no systematic protection against programs with mistakes (**bugs**), and supports one user at a time. Several companies, including Microsoft, with its **Windows** software, have tried to extend PC-DOS and MS-DOS, but these operating systems remain primitive compared to their larger and more capable cousins. With PC software, we went back to the future.

How the PC Affected Software

Despite the limitations of PC-DOS and MS-DOS, the PC's hardware spawned a generation of standalone software that redefined the phrase "ease of use." Because these machines supported only one person at a time, the computer responded quickly and consistently to each keystroke or to each movement or a joystick or a mouse. New firms like Lotus prospered by supplying PC software that provided personal productivity at a much lower initial cost than mainframe or minicomputer alternatives.

More important, new forms of software emerged, such as business graphics software, spreadsheets, and desktop publishing software, and as people bought PCs to use at home, they bought computer games to entertain and educate. You can even use your PC to manipulate still or moving images. If your children want to "morph" a photograph of Newt Gingrich into a Jurassic Park–sized Bill the Cat, your PC can do it. Parental discretion is advised.

Because the potential market for PC software is huge, the PC is important to software developers. Today, you can buy tens of thousands of applications for the PC. In this way, the PC has become a flexible, responsive tool: The same computer that can play chess with you can graph anomalies in the stock market, send and receive facsimiles of legal documents, or show you a photo and statistics about your favorite tennis players. Programmed well, the PC is a vehicle of flexibility and aesthetic design because it can manipulate images and sounds along with words.

How PCs Affected Organizations

Like empowered minicomputer users, people can become attached to their PCs. These machines enable them to work better and smarter. With a personal computer, the user or owner is also the machine's I/S department. However, most such empowered users don't follow traditional I/S disciplines. Almost everyone has heard a story about how someone has lost data due to a personal computer failure. Sometimes, rogue programs called **viruses** attack machines, wiping out data or making a PC temporarily unusable. In a large firm, it is both inconvenient and unproductive to have all employees maintain their own PCs. Most often, needed safeguards simply aren't taken.

Although many people embraced PCs, others worked in fear of them. Because PCs appeared to increase personal productivity, firms encouraged workers to use them. Companies funded information centers that helped PC users to understand their machines and their software more. They conducted training, answered questions, and evaluated new hardware and software. Over time, information centers often became the focus of PC hardware and software knowledge.

Inevitably, however, firms discovered that having multiple, separate organizations proved expensive over time. After people became more comfortable with PCs, information centers began to be consolidated into regional or centralized **help desks**. Help desk staff would help people with many questions. If users had problems using Lotus 1-2-3 or their mainframe software didn't work as expected, the help desk usually received the call. If the help desk staff couldn't assist, they called in others with more specialized knowledge. As with minicomputer staffs, I/S often absorbed the responsibility for the help desk. Eventually, I/S often became a firm's one stop for help with computers and software of any sort. Of course, exceptions to this rule exist as well.

From an organization's viewpoint, one crucial problem with these marvelous tools is inherent to early personal computers. Unlike their larger cousins, they weren't shared. To share data with colleagues, you had to store it on a diskette or a tape and deliver it to them. This was a little faster and easier than printing a report and delivering it, because the recipient didn't need to type in any relevant data, but it still wasn't as easy as sending an electronic copy on a shared computer system.

The Downsizing Phenomenon

PCs affected organizations in another profound way. People began to use networked PCs to perform tasks earlier done by larger computers. Sometimes they succeeded. They almost always started with a lower hardware and software cost. The computer industry media noticed and began hyping these success stories.

Downsizing is the idea of taking software written for shared systems, such as mainframes and minicomputers, and redeploying it on smaller computers, usually PCs. Others took the same notion and applied it differently: **Rightsizing** is finding your true costs of computing and assigning the most economical hardware, network, and support staff to do the job. Downsizing and rightsizing are aimed at reducing overall computing costs for existing business processes.

Properly applied, rightsizing makes sense. Sometimes, rightsizing means changing from one kind of shared system to another. Sometimes, it involves using a larger, centralized system instead of several smaller computers. Rightsizing helps you to understand your costs of computing over several years. Then, you make decisions that reduce those costs while providing equivalent capabilities.

For many, though, especially journalists, downsizing means "Let's use personal computers for everything and get rid of our mainframes and minicomputers." Lower initial hardware and software costs justify the idea at first. Over time, though, blindly downsizing can prove costly.

According to studies by the Gartner Group and others, moving software from shared systems to networks of personal computers is about 40% more costly. Some studies conclude that as many as 65 cents of every dollar spent on downsized systems goes to support costs. Also, depending upon the software used and the supporting staff's discipline, groups of PCs can prove less reliable than older, shared systems.

Those who rightsize typically keep their existing software portfolio. They simply decide to change their hardware. Perhaps a newer generation of hardware is faster or more cost-effective. Maybe you can save money by centralizing support staff and using faster network links to users. Maybe you can standardize more or buy some prewritten software for the new hardware, changing your remaining applications to fit.

However, if your software is inadequate or inappropriate to your business processes, cost savings don't help. You'd be doing the wrong thing more efficiently. Downsizing inadequate software is akin to putting a 30-year-old engine into a new Formula One racer. It may save money at first, but it won't do the job nearly as well as a new design.

Building Software for Networks of Computers

When software designers considered multiple systems, the basic techniques of building software still applied. Companies designed and built hardware and software that tied many computers into **networks**. These networks could support batch processing, transaction processing, and time sharing, whether the users were in a different part of the building or across the country. Sometimes, the workload for an application would be split across several networked computers. Each major computer systems vendor developed its own networking architecture, and optimized it to support the kinds of work their customers most commonly processed on their machines.

Batch Processing Networks

In batch processing systems, operators outside the main computer room used **Remote Job Entry (RJE)** hardware to transfer programs and batches of data to the main system. The RJE hardware usually sent data over telephone lines specially conditioned to reduce transmission errors. The large computer saw an **RJE station** as a special combination of a punched card reader, keypunch, and printer. The application software didn't change much: A batch program usually didn't care if the user submitted it via the main console or from an RJE station in another country. The RJE station also provided error detection and correction capabilities.

RJE is sometimes called a **master/slave** system, because a large computer system is the master and the RJE station responds to its requests. The computer regularly polls the RJE station to see if it has any work to be done. Master/slave systems are suited to centralized computers, since most data traffic comes from or goes to the main machine anyway. Today, you can buy software packages for minicomputers or PCs that lets them emulate an RJE station.

Later, **Network Job Entry** (**NJE**) software let computers send programs and data to one another. NJE is a **peer-to-peer** system. Each machine in an NJE network can initiate and respond to data transfer requests. Because of this design, any system running NJE can send and receive data as needed. NJE is also more convenient to use for file transfers because, unlike RJE, it can handle almost any kind of file. Although both RJE and NJE can enter batch jobs and transfer files, NJE is more capable. Like RJE, several vendors supply NJE software.

Networks of Terminals

In time sharing and transaction processing systems, firms first needed to connect remote terminals to shared systems. People across town, or even around the world, needed to use large computer systems. Like RJE and NJE, networks of terminals used special telephone lines designed to reduce transmission errors. Unlike batch job entry, with terminal access the application did need to know how to move data to and from terminals. So, many different software programs again needed to understand how remote and local terminals worked.

Terminal access networks typically support many users per telephone line. Given suitable electronics, the input and output needs of these terminal users could be **concentrated** or **multiplexed** onto a single telephone line. Sometimes, one **multidropped** telephone line could provide services to multiple sites. Since these lines were (and often still are) costly compared to electronic devices, **communications controllers** became popular.

Each major computer and communications vendor came up with its own approach for concentrating or multiplexing data traffic. Some techniques are more efficient than others. Your design choices can still make a big difference in the operational cost and the perceived responsiveness of a computer system or a software application today.

The type of communications controller that fit a company's needs depended heavily on the terminals used. Three terminal types evolved: character mode, line mode, and block mode. **Character mode** terminals send one character at a time to the main computer. A **line mode** terminal collects characters until the user presses the Carriage Return key, then it sends the entire line to the main computer. **Block mode** terminals send and receive large blocks of characters, up to a full screen at a time. Along with their communications controllers, they contain the intelligence to interpret these blocks of data, displaying it correctly. They also encode efficiently the information they send to the main computer. Today, most people use either block mode or character mode terminals.

Most early terminal networks used block mode terminals. Block mode streamlines processing on the main computer, since the system spends less time being interrupted by incoming characters. Also, it takes a long time for electronic pulses to go through the telephone network. Using block mode to reduce the number of "chunks" transmitted through the network improves perceived responsiveness. Finally, block mode uses telephone lines more efficiently, sharing a costly service more effectively among users.

Hierarchical Networking

Terminal access networks and job entry systems laid the foundation for hierarchical networks. These networks contained telephone lines, communications controllers, and large computers, which resided at the top of the hierarchy. Although vendors used different techniques, IBM introduced the most widely accepted hierarchical networking approach in 1974, **Systems Network Architecture (SNA)**. Hierarchical SNA supported 1974's dominant hardware: block mode terminals, line mode terminals, printers, and RJE workstations. SNA also allowed connections suited for simple communications between applications, not just between programs and hardware devices. As a result, an SNA network can support terminal access, batch job entry, and communications between computers on the same telephone lines. As we mentioned earlier, with older forms of terminal networking, each application needed to include appropriate instructions to transfer data to and from the user's terminal. With SNA, IBM introduced a **Virtual Telecommunications Access Method (VTAM)**. VTAM hid many hardware details from the application. The application still needed to know if the terminal had 25 lines or 43 lines, or if it supported color or graphics. With VTAM, though, the application didn't care if the terminal sat in the computer room or halfway across the world. Nor did it care how many communications controllers were between the mainframe and terminal.

In 1974, SNA was a significant achievement. It let IBM's large computer customers reduce their ongoing telephone line costs. At the same time, it simplified the task of creating new applications programs. Finally, it opened the door to let users run many different applications on different systems on the same terminal. IBM's customers responded enthusiastically, and today SNA is still widely used.

Networking Between Peer Computers

Hierarchical networks, like SNA, met the needs of large computer system users for many years. Minicomputer vendors and their customers faced a different problem: How should many smaller machines communicate, and how should programs talk with each other? It took IBM until the early 1980s to answer this question clearly. IBM then introduced **Advanced Program-to-Program Communications** (**APPC**), allowing application programs to converse with each other. Later, IBM defined **Advanced Peer-to-Peer Networking** (**APPN**) to provide networking services between peer computers. APPC became available in the early 1980s, and IBM introduced APPN to customers on its System/36 and System/38 minicomputers in the mid-1980s.

In defining APPC and APPN, IBM viewed them as extensions to SNA, providing existing SNA users with a path into peer networking. This is increasingly important today, as even personal computers can run APPC and APPN. APPC is also important because it explicitly supports the notion of a secure, networked transaction. This is unique among commonly used networking approaches. As a result, programmers who use APPC can simplify their transaction processing programs dramatically.

Digital Equipment Corporation developed a different peer-to-peer network, their **Digital Network Architecture** (**DNA**). DNA emerged in phases in the late 1970s and early 1980s, along with Digital's **DECnet** series of products. Xerox also developed an approach called the **Xerox Network System** (**XNS**). Their products and techniques influenced network developers, and they maintain significant market share today. Other vendors did the same: Wang developed WANGnet, Hewlett-Packard designed and built AdvanceNet, and Burroughs developed its Burroughs Network Architecture.

As before, vendors and customers used telephone lines, usually leased, conditioned lines, to interconnect machines in different locations. The exception to this was XNS, which used a new kind of network, a LAN. We'll discuss LANs in more detail later.

The Internet

While SNA, APPN, and other approaches became important in business networks, the United States Defense Advanced Research Projects Agency (DARPA) built a research network. The network, called the **ARPANET** for many years, started in 1969 and has been in operation since. At first, it connected several universities and a few companies together.

Much has changed about this network since its beginning: Even the network's name and "ownership" have changed. Mostly, this came about because the ARPANET became a useful tool for people at universities. One school, the University of California at Berkeley, packaged and sold inexpensive networking software derived from the ARPANET. Many computer vendors, especially young firms like Sun Microsystems, bought this software and incorporated it into their offerings. As these vendors' products grew in popularity, so did this included networking software. It became known as **TCP/IP**, from the initials of its major components.

As the ARPANET grew, it became the backbone for a collection of independently operated networks. During this time, the National Science Foundation (NSF) took over responsibility for the network. The NSFnet operated at higher speeds and used different equipment than the ARPANET. Most of the attached networks used TCP/IP software, but some used other approaches: For example, the BITNET used NJE. Each network had its own charter: MILNET supported the military, CS-NET supported computer science research, and so forth. As these independently operated networks connected with each other, the resulting worldwide network became the **Internet**. Over time, the government has ceded the operation of the Internet to private companies, although it still owns several important telephone lines and sites on the Internet.

Because the Internet is widely available at universities, several developments ensued. First, several TCP/IP applications grew, without the usual research and development costs. Most often, these applications were sold at a minimal charge to interested parties. Next, the networking software itself improved. Finally, a generation of Internet-aware graduates is now flooding businesses. Today, over 30 million people worldwide have Internet-capable software, and about 4 or 5 million use it regularly. "Netslang," such as "to flame" (verb, to disagree viciously, often profanely with someone else on the network) is entering our vocabulary.

This is a big potential market, so companies are now putting marketing and investor materials onto the Internet. Some even accept orders over the network. Firms also use the Internet as a conduit for their views of fast-breaking events. For example, when IBM bought Lotus Development Corporation, IBM's Internet materials were more current than any other information source. IBM's internal rumor mill talked about Wall Street traders and reporters monitoring these materials, presumably trying to attain seconds of advantage over their rivals. More seriously, the Internet site gave IBM a public way to reassure Lotus employees during a time of personal stress. It also squelched rumors quickly.

The Internet's amount and variety of data staggers and overwhelms beginners: It includes comic strips, investment data, support groups for cancer patients, poetry, satellite weather maps, and restaurant reviews. Most often, you still need to know where to look. Internet "maps" are rare, and much of the information is uncatalogued. The Internet can also be trivial or downright scary. The FBI recently arrested several people for using the Internet to distribute child pornography. On the silly side, in one location, I counted ten people who save the contents of their computer's screens periodically to a file. You can then get that file and look at their screens. Others use small "spy cameras" and load the resulting images onto their Internet attached machines.

Overall, the Internet's data can be productive and sometimes even sublime. University libraries are now coming online: If you want to know if Indiana University's music library has a particular book or manuscript, you can see for yourself. If you want to know about an IBM product, you can check it out yourself, without waiting for a salesperson to call on you or send you literature. If your child is ill, you can ask others for help in understanding a particular treatment. As a society, we don't yet understand how to best use this tool we've created, but we're trying.

Local Area Networks and Networks of PCs

We've already discussed one development of the late 1970s and early 1980s that caused a vast change in how firms built hardware systems: the IBM PC. The second such development is the **Local Area Network (LAN)**. LANs improved network capacity dramatically and thus enabled new kinds of applications.

Early LAN Uses

Until LANs became available from several vendors, businesses built networks using telephone lines. Even networks within the same building used simulated telephone lines if the main computer's I/O conduits couldn't reach the users. Typical AT&T telephone lines in the early 1980s, before divestiture, transmitted between 4800 and 19,200 bits per second (bps). The two most common kinds of LANs today are standardized products that you can buy from many vendors. **Ethernet** was developed by Xerox in the 1970s; it works rather like a telephone party line. Ethernet runs at speeds between 1 and 10 million bps (Mbps), with the most common version running at 10 Mbps. Later, IBM weighed in with the **Token-Ring** LAN. This LAN first ran at 4 Mbps and now commonly runs at 16 Mbps. Dozens or hundreds of devices, such as PCs, could be attached to each kind of LAN.

Companies discovered they could build LANs quickly and administer them easily. Once up, LANs proved much faster and more reliable than emulated telephone lines. They reduced redundant wiring at many sites. Later, LANs became known as the best way to connect personal computers and minicomputers within a facility (and sometimes beyond, but we'll cover that later). LANs also became a part of mainstream network architectures, including SNA among others.

Early PC Networks

The earliest personal computer networking products worked over LANs. In fact, they still work best with LANs. These products used peer techniques, treating each computer on the network as if they were equally capable. The disadvantage to this soon became apparent: If your PC had the department's high-speed printer attached to it, your spreadsheet calculations slowed whenever someone else used that printer. Later PC networking products shared laser printers and large hard disks between workgroup members without impeding anyone's work. Most often, one PC or minicomputer, sometimes called the **server**, housed the more expensive devices and users' machines had smaller disks and an inexpensive printer, if any. The users' systems used the server's disks and printers as if they were their own.

Centralizing disks in a dedicated server simplifies operations. For example, data backups become easier, especially if the server also contains a tape drive. Using server software also enables simpler security administration. Finally, when new versions of software come to market, the network's administrator needs to update only one copy of the software per workgroup. Today, many groups of PCs use centralized disks and printers. The software that provides these services is called a **file server** and a **printer server**, respectively. Most often, the users of these PCs are related, perhaps in the same department. Sometimes, people apply the term **workgroup** to describe this related group of PCs, data, and users.

As PCs became more interconnected, departments appointed network administrators to oversee the shared PC equipment. These would perform traditional I/S functions such as maintaining security, adding users, and monitoring printers. Eventually, many I/S organizations also accepted responsibility for these tasks, adding them to their shared system operations. Sometimes, different departments within a firm chose different ways to support their networked PCs.

As PCs began to proliferate throughout firms, users wanted to connect them to existing shared systems. Interconnecting PCs to minicomputers and mainframes began when networking vendors developed and marketed **terminal emulators**. These emulators typically included hardware and software that made a PC behave like a block mode or character mode terminal. Vendors usually included a simple file transfer method as well. At the same time, though, networks of PCs became more capable.

PC Networks Expand and Become More Sophisticated

In the late 1980s, networks of PCs typically expanded beyond a particular department or site. Usually, firms connected file and print servers together using WAN links. Loading software into the server machine allowed it to **route** traffic destined from one site to another. This new PC WAN usually existed alongside minicomputer networks and mainframe networks. Often, the costs were funded by departments or divisions, not by corporate I/S. For a while, people with PC backgrounds operated these networks.

An entire subindustry grew up around building and operating these PC networks. **Novell**, in particular, threw their corporate weight behind these developments. They trained thousands of Certified Novell Engineers, who worked for consulting firms, computer dealers, and businesses worldwide. These networks enabled connectivity to file and print servers across an entire business. Suddenly, using PC-based networks became the popular way to connect.

When companies introduced PC-based **electronic mail (e-mail)**, it enabled people to send spreadsheets, word processor documents, and similar PC files easily to others. (Mainframes and minicomputers have e-mail software, but it is harder to use these packages to send PC files.) As firms added PCs, the capability to "point, click, and transmit" files throughout an organization became increasingly valuable.

Lotus is currently the PC e-mail market leader with its **cc:Mail** software. This program typically uses file servers to store e-mail and can use PC networks to forward messages between users. So, e-mail bolstered the role of networked PC-based file servers in most organizations. Today, e-mail is one of the most heavily used productivity applications on any network.

How Programmers Create Software

Over time, software creation has evolved from flipping switches on a system's front panel to manipulating symbols that represent instructions and data. As time passed, more of the software development process became automated. We'll trace this evolution briefly here.

Hardware-Dependent First- and Second-Generation Languages

In the early days of computing, a programmer entered instructions into the computer manually, using switches. These programs were small, and it was easy for a programmer to make a mistake. Later, someone came up with the idea of using symbols or mnemonics to represent each instruction. These symbols were easier to remember than binary bit patterns. This **assembler language** was cryptic, but it was also a significant improvement. Now, programmers could see more easily how their instructions related to each other. The **assembler** would translate the textual program into the same bits previously entered manually. The resulting instruction stream is small and runs very efficiently.

Simple assembler languages might be considered **first-generation languages**. Over time, programmers noticed they tended to repeat common sequences of symbols frequently. For example, one sequence might fill a table with integers. Instead of writing many redundant instructions, they developed a different kind of assembler. This assembler let programmers define a **macroinstruction** to do some of the work for them. Macroinstructions expand a small number of symbols into a larger number. After expansion is complete, the assembler works like older assemblers, translating symbols into machine instructions. Some call languages like this **second-generation languages.**

Firms valued the small size and efficiency of programs created in assembler languages. When computers were expensive, small, fast programs were important. Today, some businesses still maintain many assembler language programs on large, shared systems. Sometimes, where size or speed is crucial, programmers will use an assembler language for PC programs as well. Using assembler languages causes some difficulties, though. First, programs tend to be long and hard to understand. Also, programs written in one assembler language can't run on other hardware; the language is inherently hardware dependent. Finally, skilled assembler programmers are costly and hard to find.

Third-Generation Languages Enable Abstractions

The biggest problem with assembler languages was the one-to-one relationship between language symbols and machine instructions. To be more productive, programmers needed languages that could be used as a kind of shorthand, where one language expression could expand into dozens, or even thousands, of hardware instructions. Macroinstructions helped, but they were insufficiently flexible, so computer scientists developed new computer languages. Many of these languages fall into a category called **third-generation languages.**

These languages hid the hardware even more. Some, like the **COmmon Business Oriented Language (COBOL)**, were meant to resemble English, for business use. Others, like **FORmula TRANslation (FORTRAN)**, were better for mathematicians or scientists. Third-generation languages (3GLs) define syntax for common programming constructions. For example, a common construction is the decision (IF something is true, then do A, otherwise, do B). Most 3GLs have an IF statement that expresses such a decision. Using a 3GL, the programmer creates textual **source code.** Then a language processor, called a **compiler,** translates this source code into those same machine instructions, now called **object code.** When you run the program, the operating system **loads** the instructions into memory for execution. Most businesses have large investments in existing applications written with 3GLs.

Many 3GLs have rules for syntax that are defined by national and international groups. For example, the American National Standards Institute (ANSI) maintains definitions of FORTRAN and COBOL, among others. When compiler vendors follow standards like these, developers can produce portable software. If developers follow the language's rules carefully, and only use constructions allowed by the language's definition, then when they recompile software on a new computer, it should run just as it did on the first machine.

How Programmers Structure Software

Programmers at first designed and wrote applications as one large program that handled everything. This works well for simple problems using a few programmers. However, these programs are inflexible: Even minor changes would sometimes require a complete redesign. They were also difficult to fix, or **debug**, when errors were found.

In the mid-1970s businesses realized that due to these problems, most of their software budgets went to maintain or enhance existing programs. Also, as more powerful hardware became available, applications became more complex. This complexity resulted in bigger teams of programmers to create the applications. Larger teams need better communications and more structure for development to succeed. To make programs easier to understand and develop, designers used a technique called **top-down design**. Also, to make programs easier to change, programmers used a new way to write applications called **structured programming**.

As shown in Figure 1.4, top-down design takes a high-level representation of a problem and gradually breaks it down into a hierarchy of components. This example represents part of a car dealer's application: selling a car. To sell the car, the dealer must check a potential customer's credit, and the dealer must check their inventory. Checking the customer's credit requires gathering information about that person and validating their credit. The dealer would also need to check their stock. If the desired car was not available, then the dealer would order it from the factory.

So, each component represents a function required to solve the problem. Each of these functions acts upon some data. This model fits well with 3GLs: The hierarchy defines the programs, subprograms, and subroutines needed to create the system. A **subroutine**, sometimes called a **function**, is a distinct section of code; a program can invoke, or **call**, it any number of times to do a specific function. Breaking down the problem this way also works well with large teams because the subroutines can be assigned to individuals. Then, as long as the subroutines have well-defined inputs and outputs, these parts should all work together. Using this technique, teams of programmers could create libraries of common subroutines. Then, they could

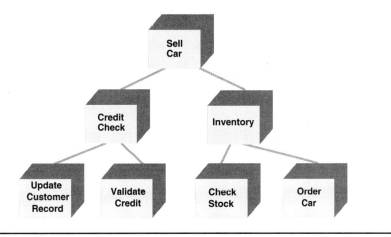

Figure 1.4. Top-down structured programming.

reuse them in other applications, decreasing development time. Sometimes, vendors package subroutine libraries for sale.

Fourth-Generation Languages Simplify Programming Further

Soon a new generation of languages appeared: the **fourth-generation languages**, or 4GLs. These are more sophisticated but less efficient than their predecessors because they use an even higher level of abstraction. This helps programmers to be more productive. A simple task such as "read a record from a file" might require hundreds of machine instructions, dozens of assembler statements and macros, several 3GL statements, and one or two 4GL statements.

Two kinds of 4GLs exist, differing in how they produce output. Some 4GLs produce 3GL source code as output; others use a proprietary intermediate language. Unlike 3GLs, most 4GLs are not standardized; each 4GL remains largely proprietary to its vendor. A 4GL's type influences a system's cost to develop and deploy.

The top diagram in Figure 1.5 shows a 4GL that generates 3GL source code. 4GLs like this make it easier to develop an application on one system and move it to another for execution, enabling some **portability**. Since different computers have different machine instructions, your staff must compile the resulting intermediate 3GL program for each processor. This generates the correct instructions for each system.

The bottom diagram in Figure 1.5 shows a 4GL that generates code in a proprietary intermediate language. These 4GLs are also portable, but only to other systems that the vendor supports, because a runtime component, or **interpreter** must exist for each system. This **runtime environment** interprets the intermediate language, generating and executing the appropriate machine instructions. Using an interpreter also implies that execution will be slower, because the interpreter does more work.

Many of today's software development tools, including 4GLs, contain two main components: one to develop applications and one to run the resulting applications. Only programmers need the development component. This reduces cost somewhat. However, every system running the resulting applications must have the runtime component. This may increase your costs to deploy an initial application. Additional applications can take advantage of any existing runtime components already in place.

Tools That Support Traditional Software Development

We've already discussed the most important tools developers use: programming languages. However, programmers use other tools as well. Good tools can make a software development group more productive. Without them, software would be more expensive and less reliable.

To a programmer, a good program to edit text is crucial. Programmers use editors to produce textual information, such as 4GL or 3GL source code. Some editors, called **language sensitive editors**, can be customized for a particular programming language. Language sensitive editors speed programming and prevent common mistakes.

An executable program can consist of hundreds or even thousands of separately compiled components. Library tools and version control tools ensure that the correct revision of the correct source file is compiled. **Linkers** take these components and link them together into a single file, ready for execution. **Loaders** take these files and load them into memory when required by a batch job, a transaction, or a user.

Programmers also use testing tools extensively. The most commonly used testing tool, a **debugger**, helps programmers to find simple errors. Another common testing technique is **regression testing**. In regression testing, whenever a bug is discovered, testers develop scripts to force the bug to show itself. Then, after a new version is built, they run these scripts to see if the bugs are still present. Tools also exist to measure software's performance.

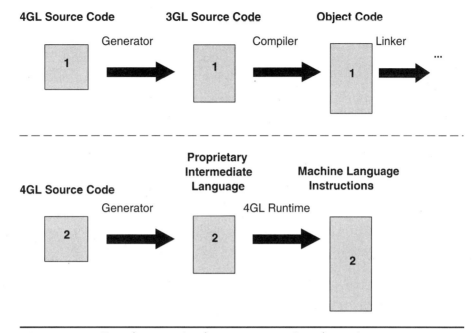

Figure 1.5. Fourth-generation language generation alternatives.

Changes in Software Development

Recent advances in software development tools make the software process easier. New tools also provide more capabilities for the programmer. **Graphical User Interfaces (GUIs)** and object orientation are two new technologies changing how software is built.

Graphical User Interfaces and Visual Programming

For new and changed PC applications, most buyers insist on GUIs. A consistent GUI reduces training costs and reduces errors; people familiar with one application can quickly learn another that looks and feels similar. Graphical applications are also easier to learn than their textual counterparts that use terminals. GUI specifications make this fast adaptation possible. They also enable the creation of programming tools to enforce these standards.

IBM and other vendors use IBM's **Common User Access (CUA) '91** specification to standardize how users interact with applications. For example, CUA '91 specifies how windows appear and move, how function keys should work, and how pointing devices (a mouse, trackball, or pen) point and click. Another important GUI specification is the Open Software Foundation's **Motif**.

Visual programming tools can provide a common GUI by enforcing specifications such as Motif or CUA '91. As a programmer creates an interface, these tools show exactly how it will look. For example, suppose the developer wants the user to click on a button to open a file. Using a visual programming tool, the developer drags a symbol representing a button into the window and places it where the user should click. Then the developer associates the action of opening a file with clicking on the button. This approach is much better than using a text editor and hundreds of cryptic commands to generate the same window.

Tools that simply assist with the creation of the GUI are sometimes referred to as GUI builders. Besides presenting the interface, some visual programming tools also help the programmer to visualize relationships between parts of the program. A programmer could create new components or reuse previously developed components. Such reused components might be subroutines or entire programs, created and tested before. Again, by promoting reuse, these more sophisticated tools let developers create programs more quickly and productively.

Object Orientation

If your firm wants to develop software components for internal use or for sale, **object oriented computing** holds great promise. We'll discuss object oriented computing in more depth in another chapter, but we'll cover it briefly now.

Object oriented programming techniques were first developed during the 1960s. Some software developers, theorists, and writers have given them greater focus because they can help to improve how software is developed. This focus has sharpened since Xerox developed the **Smalltalk** programming language in the 1970s and early 1980s.

Seeing the World Objectively

Using objects requires managers, programmers, and designers familiar with top-down design to see the world differently. Whereas top-down design is oriented toward tasks, an **object** represents both data and the actions, called **methods**, associated with that data. Figure 1.6 depicts a person object. Here, a person object includes a name, address, phone number, and Social Security number. A particular person is an **instance** of a person object.

An object may have many instances; each instance behaves identically. Objects come from object **classes**; think of them as "object factories." Programmers usually design hierarchies of object classes, defining new objects based on existing object classes. This is like building several products in a single, modular factory. Reusing object classes makes ongoing development easier, faster, and more accurate.

As a more concrete example, consider a sales application for car dealers. A sale involves the customer, the sales associate, and the sales manager. All are similar, but slightly different. In Figure 1.7, our person class now has three **subclasses**: manager, sales associate, and customer.

Figure 1.8 shows how customer objects **inherit** names, addresses, phone numbers, and Social Security numbers, and methods from the person object. The customer object also has additional data, such as the vehicle identification number (VIN) of the car purchased. Similarly, our sales associate object inherits from the person object. It also retains the value of cars sold this month so that the dealership knows how much to pay the associate, and it has an additional method to record a sale.

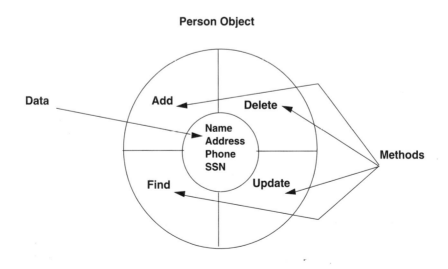

Figure 1.6. An example of an object.

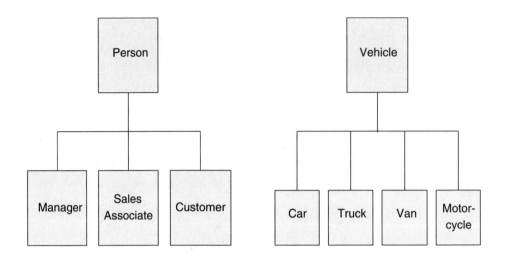

Figure 1.7. Object classes and subclasses.

Objects talk with each other, usually with **messages**, to perform complex tasks. Let's say a customer wants to buy a car. So, in Figure 1.9, a customer object sends a message to a sales associate object to buy the red Porsche for an agreed sum. This message invokes the sales associate's selling method. The selling action increases the associate's total sales. This is just one part of the total transaction, but it does show how objects work with each other.

Finally, a person object's "Find" method finds a person's name from a Social Security number. Sales associates and customers inherit it. However, to pay sales associates, the manager must find their monthly sales totals, so a programmer extended the sales associate's Find method. When a manager sends a Find message with a Social Security number to a sales associate, the Find method returns both a name and total sales. If a manager sends the same message to a customer, the customer uses the inherited method, and returns only a name. The same message invokes different methods depending on the receiving object, hence the name **polymorphism** (many forms).

Objects embody three important techniques: **encapsulation, inheritance,** and polymorphism. Of these, only encapsulation is possible using traditional techniques. Objects encapsulate automatically, because one object cannot change another object's data. Inheritance and polymorphism encourage programming teams to extend existing software. Together, encapsulation, polymorphism, and inheritance reduce ongoing development and maintenance costs.

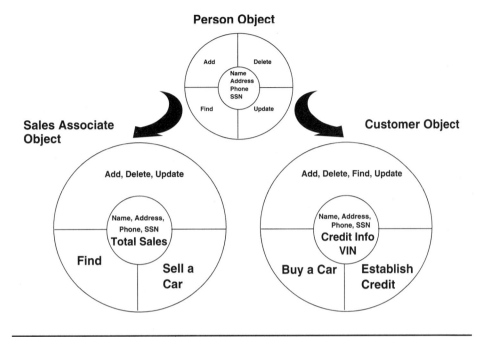

Figure 1.8. Inheritance.

Figure 1.9. Interaction of objects.

Object Oriented Programming Languages

Newer design techniques incorporate object oriented ideas, and newer tools help your programmers develop objects. For example, there are **Object Oriented Programming Languages (OOPLs)** such as Smalltalk and **C++**. In addition, vendors supply object oriented extensions for 3GLs such as object oriented Pascal. Standards bodies are defining extensions for other 3GLs, such as COBOL.

A traditional programmer will require several weeks of training to understand object orientation because the terminology and structure of object oriented software is so different from traditional software. Object oriented designers need even more training, because object oriented design techniques are more foreign to traditional designers than the programming languages are to programmers.

Why Are Objects Important?

Object oriented software better represents the real world. In our system, a customer buys a car from a sales associate. That statement represents both what happens in the dealership and what happens in the system. This is important because it makes communicating between a system's users and its developers easier than in the past. The improved communications can help the developers create a complex system that is more suitable to business needs.

Many people hope that object orientation will change programming as dramatically as interchangeable parts changed manufacturing. This will only occur over time and with a considerable investment in training. It will also occur if vendors can supply prewritten collections of objects for others to use.

Most of the savings likely will come from reusing objects. In our example, we defined a person object and used it for our customer, sales associate, and manager subclasses. If the person object was in a library with other object types, then it could also be used for other applications. A car dealer application might use a mechanic object. In the health care industry, a nurse, doctor, and patient might be subclasses of the person object. Of course, each subclass would have additional data associated with it, and additional actions could be performed on it. However, the same basic information and actions could be performed on each. Also, these basic actions would work the same for all persons. If the parent object's methods work correctly, then the inherited behaviors also will be correct.

If you imagine the **class library** growing with more object classes you can see how to achieve significant productivity gains. As the class library grows, programmers and designers can look for objects like those they need, modifying them to achieve the required behavior. Then, after testing, they place the new object into the class library. In this approach, programming by exception becomes the rule. However, the design of the class library is an important task. If the class library is poorly designed, object oriented software may be large, inefficient, and expensive.

A class library designed for a specific group of tasks is called a **framework**. Vendors intend to develop and sell frameworks, so companies can buy objects pertinent to their applications. Then, buyers can build on these existing components.

Computer-Aided Software Engineering

Finally, another genre of tools spans the entire life cycle of software development. These are **Computer-Aided Software Engineering (CASE)** tools. As shown in Figure 1.10, the software life cycle consists of five stages:

- Defining the requirements

- Analyzing these requirements and creating a design

- Developing the software

- Testing the software

- Using the software in production and maintaining it

Upper-CASE tools help with the requirements and analysis/design phases of application development. **Lower-CASE** tools help with the development, testing, and production/maintenance phases. So, upper-CASE tools can model an application, and lower-CASE tools implement that model. Some tools combine both upper- and lower-CASE functions; others provide one of the two. Some lower-CASE tools integrate with 3GLs or 4GLs. So, designers or

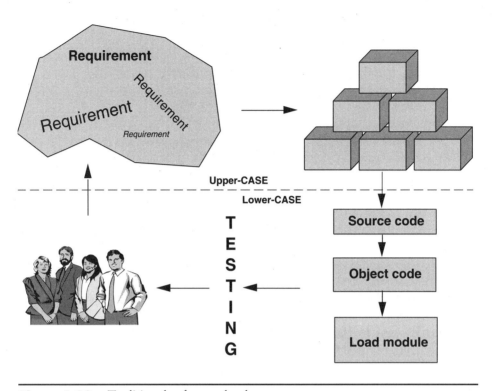

Figure 1.10. Traditional software development.

analysts might use upper-CASE tools to graphically depict the system to be created. A programmer, or a team of programmers, takes that representation and uses a lower-CASE tool, a 3GL, or a 4GL to generate the resulting software.

Software Gives Computers Multiple Personalities

Software designers can give any shared computer system the appearance of several "personalities." For example, they can layer TP monitors and batch job processors onto large time sharing systems. Some departments might use a TP monitor while others use the time sharing system; batch work might be processed overnight. Similarly, designers can add time sharing systems and

TP monitors to job oriented operating systems. How users or operators interact with the shared system depends on how this software presents the system to them.

Because you can change how shared systems interact with their users, a user's view of a system might even change from one terminal to the next. For example, a sophisticated personnel application might restrict transactions related to changing salaries to specific terminals or users, or managers might have different options available to them that their employees can't see. Software makes things seem real, even if they aren't. Software makes computers virtual: The hardware becomes a chameleon.

For example, IBM's **Virtual Machine** (**VM**) system, pretends to be many computer systems. Each VM user appears to have a complete computer; VM schedules the resources of the physical hardware as needed. Within your virtual machine, you can even run a "guest" operating system, which itself might run transaction monitors, job entry systems, and so forth. If one user's VM crashes, perhaps due to a software error, it dosen't affect other VM users.

Originally, VM provided an accurate testing environment for programmers. Before VM, they waited until the wee hours of the morning to get testing time on a physical computer. With VM's virtual machines, these people could again sleep at night and work during the day. Also, their management saved on overtime pay. IBM and its customers still use VM for training, testing, and time sharing computing.

Many ways exist to design and layer software, some more effective or efficient than others. However, time sharing systems, batch systems, and TP monitors exist on almost all shared systems sold today. They, along with standalone processing, are the fundamental ways software designers have built systems for nearly 30 years.

Similarly, PCs are chameleons. At one moment, a user works on a spreadsheet. Next, she electronically mail weekly production figures to colleagues around the world. Then, she might pack up her laptop and play a game of chess on the plane. Software enables these devices of silicon, plastic, and glass to become the flexible tools we've come to know.

Standardizing Software Components: The Open Systems Movement

With software as diverse and as flexible as it is, you can imagine the problems developers face in reusing software parts from one project to another.

Reusing software is one key to improving both programmer productivity and software quality. Reusing software also reduces support costs for vendors and I/S groups alike. Defining and creating standardized, common components is one way software developers have used to improve their productivity and product quality.

The UNIX Time Sharing System

When we discussed minicomputers, we briefly touched upon time sharing systems. One such operating system, **UNIX**, deserves special mention because it has strongly influenced software and operating systems design. Because of how it was designed and built, UNIX came to embody an ideal: software that is independent of any particular brand or kind of hardware. To this way of thinking, UNIX is the first **open system**. Programmers at Bell Laboratories first developed UNIX as a small, time sharing operating system for other programmers to use. It broke new ground not in particular features, but in how its parts worked together. Other programmers easily understood the original design's simplicity and elegance. UNIX lore has it that "the documentation associated with early versions of the operating system was not unreasonably transported in an attache case." Unfortunately, "this deficiency has since been corrected."

UNIX was the first portable operating system. Until UNIX, operating systems and applications were tied to specific computer architectures. You couldn't use IBM's operating systems on a DEC or a Sperry computer. Similarly, you rarely could use applications programs developed for one computer on another without significant changes. The hardware, operating system, and application programs were closely related. Also, a firm's investment in training and staffing were similarly related to the hardware used.

The developers of UNIX chose a different path. They built almost all of UNIX using a 3GL called **C**. This language is processed by software much smaller than an operating system. By adapting the smaller C language processor to a new hardware architecture, it became simpler to transfer, or **port**, UNIX to different hardware. Once programmers adapted the C language processor to the new hardware, they made only small changes to the rest of UNIX. Then, they processed the ported language statements into instructions the new hardware understood.

Because of this porting process, software easily modified for other platforms is called **portable software**. The experience of porting UNIX and

UNIX-based software to many kinds of hardware informed the open systems movement in the 1980s. The principles embodied within UNIX still influence the design of software intended for multiple hardware and operating system platforms today.

Portable Software Increases Developers' Productivity

In the 1980s, the market for computers and software fragmented. The PC made it possible for software developers to reach a huge market with a small investment. What once was an industry with a few dozen suppliers grew to include over 60,000 firms. Eventually, software developers realized they couldn't optimize their profits if their products were tied to only one hardware architecture, so they produced portable software instead. Essentially, the philosophy of portable software provided more efficient production and support processes for them.

Some software developers and large firms believed they could define a common framework of operating system services. This would simplify further the task of building portable software. To this end, several organizations around the world tried to define a standardized, UNIX-like operating system. The task continues today, within several international standards bodies. Today, some people view an "open system" as a computer running an operating system derived from UNIX. Others believe a system is open if they can purchase each component from multiple suppliers. Still others prefer defined specifications for each component of the system. All of them are right, to a point.

An "Open" Automobile

To make an analogy, the open systems idea at its extreme is like defining a completely standard automobile. If such a thing existed, you could build your own car from components. For example, you might take a Ford transmission, bolt it onto a Volvo engine, and install it in a Toyota chassis. With standardized components, you can shop around and compare them based upon price or a narrow range of performance specifications; each component becomes a commodity.

The problem with such an approach is that it discourages innovation in component design. If Volvo developed a sporty, efficient engine that didn't fit the standard, you couldn't use it in your standardized car, no matter how large its benefits to you might be. If the steering wheel standard required narrow spokes and small centers, manufacturers couldn't fit air bags within them.

On the other hand, the open systems idea can also be compared to an automobile's interior. Everyone who knows how to drive a car understands what a steering wheel is for, even if Americans may find it on the "wrong" side in Great Britain or Japan. Replacing steering wheels with, say, a device like an airplane pilot's stick would cause needless trouble. Some tires can be fitted to several different kinds of vehicles, thanks to standardized wheel sizes. A new tire that won't fit on existing wheels won't sell well, no matter how wonderful it is.

Building Systems from Prewritten Building Blocks

As the computer industry fragmented, standards and standardized components became more important to computer system buyers. Often, I/S groups became **systems integrators**, organizations that take common or standard components, building and integrating them into a system. Other, independent, firms also built systems using these techniques. For these groups, buying and integrating systems is quicker and less costly than building new systems from scratch. If little innovation is required within all or part of the system, this approach makes sense.

The rise of the personal computer also hastened the advent of standardized building blocks in computer systems. When buying software for PCs, firms typically purchase prewritten software packages, "shrink-wrapped, off the shelf." With this approach, the firm's focus moves from developing software to configuring and customizing software. People don't think about developing spreadsheet software for their firm; instead, they buy a spreadsheet package from Lotus or another provider and customize it to their needs. Again, the need for systems integration becomes important when combining several packages into a complete system.

Specifications, Recommendations, and Standards

Specifications are important to systems and network designers. Without clearly understood specifications, the compatibility and conformance of the devices and software that comprises the system cannot be proven. Specifications cannot guarantee compatibility, but achieving compatibility without them is nearly impossible.

When many parties agree on a specification, most people call it a **recommendation**. When a formal organization agrees on a specification, it is usually called a **standard**. Most often, worldwide groups, such as organizations that are part of the United Nations, or national groups, such as the American National Standards Institute, publish standards. Vendors and industry consortia typically publish recommendations.

Standards and specifications related to computers first came about in telephone networks. When data networking first began, vendors advanced their own designs, making it difficult for firms to build networks using products from multiple vendors. This seems to be an impediment to the ideal of networking—moving information freely wherever its needs to be—and it is. Ideally, all data networks would be as compatible as a simple telephone system. Today, they are not.

Of course, the worldwide telephone system was not compatible at first, but we've forgotten that. In the 1920s, Los Angeles had six incompatible telephone systems. Over time, national and worldwide organizations grew to define how telephone equipment works across vendor and country boundaries. Now, telephone networks that comply with international standards work together to allow you to call anyone in the world from your phone (even in Los Angeles).

Where do standards help?

Standards make sense when products from several vendors must work together to build a long-lasting network or a system. Widely used standards protect hardware and software investments as such a system grows and changes. Published recommendations and specifications also aid compatibility. Although most vendors follow international standards, some might choose not to follow a particular recommendation or specification, depending on its source. For example, if IBM developed and published a new specification, Microsoft might choose not to use it, even if most vendors do. That's part of the competitive nature of the computer industry. Even in "standard" telephone systems, you can't use Sprint's voice activated calling with your AT&T calling card.

Standardized products can reduce purchasing and staffing costs. If one supplier goes out of business, you should be able to find a second source.

On the other hand, standardized products don't confer significant competitive advantage because everyone, including your competitors, can easily buy and use the same technology. For example, Asian and European auto makers didn't gain market share by using the same tools and methods as their rivals in Detroit.

Standards hold an important place in a well-managed Client/Server system, but they aren't a panacea. Proprietary tools and methods can often help your system and your business become more effective and efficient.

To Be Open, or Not To Be Open?

The open systems movement points out the importance of deciding carefully where to use standard components in a computer system. This is especially true when using hardware, software, and services from several suppliers in a system. Using nonstandard software that adds little value adds needless cost to a system; using standard components where you could build a competitive edge or reduce cost through innovation wastes opportunity. You must make this decision on an application by application basis; your opportunity and costs are unique each time.

So Where Do We Go Now?

Until recently, computer systems design mirrored the people and organizations that bought software. Products designed for the I/S environment ran on shared computers systems and provided for data integrity, security, backup, and high availability. Transaction monitors, batch processors, and time sharing systems remain effective choices for either standalone or networked shared systems. They provide solid services for users in an office or around the world. Change in this environment can only occur slowly, because simple changes can affect other users or production processes. This can limit a firm's opportunities in the marketplace. If a user needs a different "view" of production data, for example, traditional techniques often don't provide sufficient flexibility.

Products designed for PC users emphasized flexibility, ease of use, and responsiveness. Where time to market, flexibility, and responsiveness in service differentiate one provider from another, these are significant advantages. PC software is also less expensive to acquire than its shared system counterpart. However, these products may not accommodate growth easily, and their support costs can chew into a firm's profits. Worse, the temptation exists to ignore operational disciplines, risking data loss or compromise. PC products are useful and productive, but basing fundamental business processes upon them can be risky and expensive.

The software industry needed a way to harness PC software's flexibility, ease of use, and responsiveness to the predictability and discipline of software for shared systems. The approach would provide the following advantages:

- It would preserve the integrity of the firm's data.

- It would provide for secured access to data.

- It would allow for backup and recovery as needed.

- It would be easy for users and operators to learn and use.

- Groups of users could customize the software to their needs.

- When changes were needed, they would be easy and predictable.

- Standardized components could be used where appropriate.

- The system could grow or shrink easily, as needs dictate.

- Operational costs would grow slowly as users were added.

Client/server computing, applied well, meets these needs. That's what all the hype in trade magazines and newspapers is all about: Client/server computing provides flexibility, speed to market, and peace of mind. Although more costly to build and operate than traditional shared system alternatives, client/server computing gives nimble firms an edge in the marketplace, improving revenues, productivity, and market share. Some vendors and firms pursued client/server computing from the "bottom up," trying to grow PC-based computing techniques. Others worked from the "top down," enfolding PCs and their software into more traditional I/S approaches. Depending upon a buyer's priorities, different firms or departments find some approaches more successful than others. We'll examine the different facets of client/server computing next.

2

Client/Server Computing: A New Approach

One of the biggest challenges of client/server computing is defining it clearly. Some authors view client/server computing as a new way to structure business computing. Others see it as a useful method to redesign business processes, using technology more effectively. Some seem to find it a panacea for nearly any computing need. Many equate it to downsizing. Everyone seems to have an opinion. Unfortunately, few try to define client/server computing crisply. In this chapter, we'll define client/server computing, consider several client/server computing models, and review why client/server computing is here to stay.

What Is Client/Server Computing?

In a services business, such as law or accounting, a "client" is someone who requests assistance from a specialized services provider. Lawyers provide legal services to their clients; they do not provide accounting services. Mechanics fix your car. When you request help from a service provider, you find the right kind of provider, or "server" to meet your needs. Often, providers have knowledge you lack or can perform tasks more efficiently because they specialize. Finally, when you tell your mechanic and your accountant what you need done, you must understand at least a little of what they can do. Otherwise, they may not understand your needs properly.

Computing is no different. The key idea is this: The terms "client" and "server" refer to software, not to hardware. A **software client** is a computer program that doesn't know how to do everything. It therefore requests help from other software, the **server software.** Server software is specialized to perform specific tasks effectively. A software server that understands printing probably would not be able to help a client that needs help retrieving a stock quote. Software clients are also like service business clients because software clients must interact with servers using a common language.

What Makes Up a Client/Server Computing System?

Figure 2.1 shows how the parts of a software client and a server relate. A software client usually consists of two pieces. The first piece is the **client application software;** the second is what we'll call "**client enabling software.**" They talk using a carefully specified common language, called an **Application Programming Interface (API).** Because computer programs must be specified precisely, the API determines exactly what interactions are possible

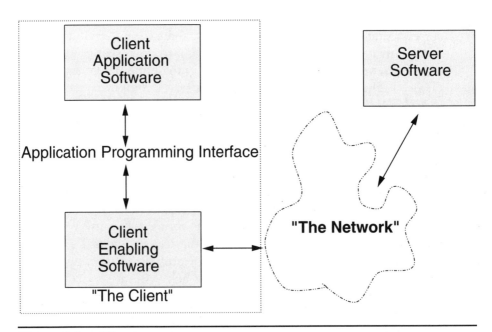

Figure 2.1. Client/server concept.

between the client application software and the rest of the client/server system.

The client enabling software takes any request the client application software makes via the API and verifies it for correctness. It then decodes the request and forwards it to one or more servers for action. Usually, the servers reside somewhere else on a network, so the client enabling software also creates "links" or "sessions" over the network to the servers. When the servers are done, they send the results back to the client enabling software. The client enabling software then interprets these results and gives them back to the client application software via the API.

Client enabling software and server software generally talk using a binary language, using only zeros and ones. Humans cannot easily read a binary language, or **protocol**, but computers interpret it efficiently. A network, usually a LAN, carries the interactions between client enabling software and the servers. The server software can usually accept requests from dozens, hundreds, or even thousands of clients concurrently. Clients may request services from one server or from many servers, depending on the application's needs.

To make another analogy, a client application is like a customer in a restaurant, client enabling software is like a waiter, and the server software is like the chef that prepares the meal. A customer can only order from the menu and passes instructions to the waiter. This interaction works like the API between client application software and client enabling software. The waiter verifies these requests and writes them down, often in a shorthand language, then passes these requests to the chef. Upon completing the meal, the chef notifies the waiter, who delivers the food to the customer.

Client/server computing environments usually encompass personal computers working hand in hand with larger, shared computers. The larger machines may store and retrieve shared data, provide large memories and greater processing power, or provide shared access to costly or specialized I/O devices. Using larger machines can also reduce operational costs.

Users of client/server computing software might work within the same building, using a LAN to communicate, or use client/server software using a **Wide Area Network (WAN)**, which links computer systems across global distances. client/server computing can take place within an organization or between organizational or enterprise boundaries to support a business process.

A Closer Look at the Client Software

Like most software, you can buy prewritten client applications and client enabling software. If you buy software today, you usually don't buy the software itself. Instead, you buy a **license** to use the software from the vendor, according to the terms and conditions of the license agreement. The software itself remains the vendor's property. Depending upon your license, you can buy the right to use the software on one computer, on several computers simultaneously, on any computers within a site, or on all the computers in your organization. Some vendors offer volume discounts instead of, or in addition to, these schemes. Suppliers also offer support services, usually at extra cost, to help you to use their software correctly.

Software vendors often supply server software and client enabling software together. You might be able to purchase a single license for one server and, say, up to 250 clients. This kind of licensing is common with file and print servers, for example. Vendors may also supply client application software for use with their client enablers and their servers. For example, Lotus supplies optional client application software for use with their **Notes** client/server software.

In a client/server system, at least two boundaries, or **interfaces**, exist where you could "bolt together" software from different sources: The API between the client application and the client enabling software defines one clear boundary; the protocol between the client enabling software and the server software defines a second. Most often, the first boundary is specified, but the second, being proprietary to a software vendor, is not. Sometimes, both boundaries are specified, and you can buy each component from more than one source.

Clearly specified, published boundaries enable you to use multiple sources of supply. For example, you may want to write client application software yourself and buy client enabling software and server software from one vendor, or you may want a systems integration firm to supply customized client software while a software vendor supplies prewritten server software. However, you should use caution when using multiple suppliers, including your own staff, because the stability of a client/server system depends heavily upon the stability of the boundaries it uses. If a boundary changes, your suppliers must support the new version. Otherwise, you may have nifty new server software from one vendor that won't work with existing client enabling software from another.

As another example, let's assume you want to use prewritten server and client enabling software and build your own client applications. At that point, your staff becomes one of the suppliers of the client/server computing system. They may use any programming language or tool, as long as their development tools can use the client enablers' APIs correctly.

You'll remember that we discussed the C programming language briefly in Chapter 1. Many APIs today work well with C, partly because C is commonly used. Some compilers, such as IBM's **COBOL/2 (COBOL for Operating System/2)**, understand how to use APIs specified for different programming languages. With COBOL/2, for example, you could build part of your application in COBOL, and part in C. These parts would then work together, forming a single application. Many programming languages today support APIs designed for other languages; this capability isn't just limited to C or COBOL/2.

Using client enabling software is similar. Usually, the API for the client enabling software is specified for one or two programming languages. You could use a different tool or language for your client application software if it understands how to use, or call, components specified in the API's language. For example, suppose you wanted to use a client enabler that works with COBOL. If your 4GL generates COBOL or understands how to call COBOL subroutines, it should work with the client enabler. Of course, if you build your own servers, APIs, and client enablers, you may use any language or technique you wish; you control the entire project.

For the rest of this book, we will refer the combination of the client application program and the client enabling software as the "client." Where it is necessary for our discussion, however, we will make a distinction between client application software and client enabling software.

A Closer Look at the Server Software

Just as in the real world, where lawyers, accountants, mechanics, and architects provide services, many types of software servers exist: file servers, print servers, fax servers, and communications servers, to name a few. Also, industry-specific servers exist. For example, financial services companies might have servers that connect their stock and bond trading floors to financial information providers or to worldwide news feeds. As with clients, you can buy or build servers. Each software server embodies highly specific functions. Just as you would not ask a lawyer to fix your car, it is silly for a client application to ask a file server to send a fax.

Since, like clients, servers are software, they can coexist on a single computer or be set up on separate computer systems. This can provide you flexibility. For example, you can arrange servers on a network to optimize responsiveness, perhaps using several computer systems to serve several departments, or you might choose to centralize servers, reducing operational costs. A common arrangement today is to centralize the computers that house the servers that service a given site or campus. Sometimes it may be best for clients and servers to exist within the same computer system or even within the same software program.

For example, consider a communications server that receives a request to make a connection. It might then ask a security server to authenticate the request. The communications server doesn't need to contain all of the software to maintain security. Instead, it could simultaneously be a client for the security server. The security server might be on the same computer or on a different machine. This approach makes both the communications server and the security server easier to develop, administer, and change.

A Simple Client/Server Example

In a simple client/server environment, you would need client application software, client enabling software, server software, supporting hardware, and a network. In the simplest case, all these pieces of the client/server puzzle might reside in the same place, in a branch office, for example. You would also need someone to spend time attending to the daily care and feeding of your system. That person might do ordinary operational tasks such as backing up data in case of disaster or disk failure, maintaining security, and updating user profiles. He or she might also install and configure new software, tune software for better efficiency, and monitor the system's performance.

Figure 2.2 shows an example of a simple but common client/server environment. Suppose that someone using a word processor, say, **Lotus Word Pro**, running on a PC-DOS system, needs to print a document. A file and printer server, such as IBM's LAN Server, exists on the network. A fast printer connects to hardware on which the server runs. Here, the Client Enabling Software is IBM's **DOS LAN Requester**, which works with LAN Server.

DOS LAN Requester includes software called a **redirector**. The redirector takes requests for printing services from a program and sends them over the network to the server. Word Pro isn't aware of the client/server software. It requests printing services as if the printer were directly attached. This interface is well defined and openly documented. The redirector intercepts these requests and processes them. The redirector talks to the network via an API and a protocol. Here, IBM and Microsoft jointly specified the API, the **Network Basic Input/Output System (NetBIOS)**.

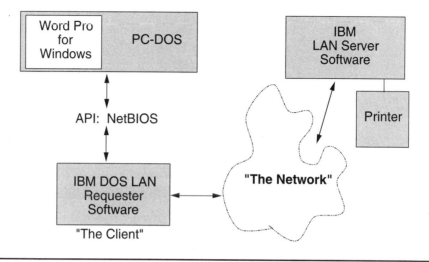

Figure 2.2. A simple client/server environment.

As requests for service come to the redirector, DOS LAN Requester receives them and examines their structure. If a request's syntax is correct, DOS LAN Requester then sends it to the **LAN Server** software. DOS LAN Requester and LAN Server talk over the network using a protocol called the **Server Message Block (SMB)** protocol. Here, the request would be to print the first part of the document. When it prints the requested document part, LAN Server notifies DOS LAN Requester, which then returns the request's status to the Redirector. The redirector tells Word Pro it is ready to receive more data for printing, Word Pro sends the next part of the document, and the cycle continues.

A More Complex Client/Server Example

Figure 2.3 depicts a more complex sample client/server environment. In this example, a client application running in a regional office requests services from multiple servers in sequence. For example, it gets a table from a corporate database server and reads a record from a regional file server. Next, it processes this data and sends the results to a local clerk's display server. Here, you need the client's application software, client enabling software, and server software for each server, and a network connecting your sites. You would also hire or train people to design, build, operate, tune, and update the software and the network.

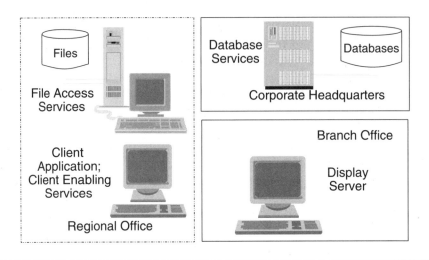

Figure 2.3. A more complex client/server environment.

Often, client application and client enabling software uses specific APIs and services. For example, one enabler may need Novell's NetWare or the **Open Software Foundation's Distributed Computing Environment (OSF DCE)**. Others may require a generic file server. They may not care if you use IBM's LAN Server or another file server. These requirements vary according to the software developer's technical and marketing needs.

If you need multiple client applications or multiple client enablers on the same client hardware, as is becoming more common, your client and network configurations may become complex. As a result, the people who support your client/server system should have a broad understanding of all aspects of your environment. They should also be expert in one or two aspects, such as file server administration or network troubleshooting.

What Do Some Writers Mean by Client/Server Computing?

The term "client/server," as commonly used, seems to have come from the experience of using networks of PCs. As you will recall from our discussions in Chapter 1, some PC networks use a dedicated PC for disk storage. This PC, typically called the server, usually also has printers attached to it.

If a PC user can store and retrieve data from another, dedicated system elsewhere on a network, that system is usually called a file server. This is because of the software running on it, not because of any hardware capability, but some writers don't make this distinction. Similarly, if users can use a printer on a networked system as if the printer were attached to their PCs, the system is called a printer server. You don't need to use separate computers for file and printer serving, as vendors often bundle these capabilities into a single software package, like IBM's LAN Server.

Because of this experience, many writers refer to a dedicated, networked computer simply as a server. It usually runs file and printer server software. It might run other servers as well, such as a fax server, depending upon its capacity and the users' needs. Because others use this terminology, you should be aware of it. To avoid ambiguity, though, we will continue to use the more precise, software-oriented definition of client and server.

Who Is Building Client/Server Systems Today?

The "Grassroots" Approach

The people who design and build client/server computing systems seem to favor different views of computing. The first group views computing more from a workgroup perspective outward. These people have successfully built applications and systems in workgroups and are expanding that successful workgroup model to encompass larger and larger parts of an organization. We'll call this the **grassroots** way to build client/server systems. People who subscribe to this approach think about harnessing better the power of personal computers and scientific workstations. They may believe strongly in using PCs for nearly everything because of the initial hardware cost savings. As budgets move down the organization chart, empowering departments, grassroots approaches have become more common.

The "Corporate" Approach

The second group views client/server computing as a way to enhance corporate data processing by integrating into it the increasing power of small computers. This group, which typically includes a firm's I/S group, espouses top-down views to link a company's data, existing software, and new software into a new, more effective system. We'll call this the **corporate** way to build client/server systems. Those in this group do not believe that large, shared computing systems are dead; they believe the role of these systems is changing. They also know the size and cost of an enterprise's existing investment in software and understand the costs of replacing this investment all at once. They guard your firm's data, and they take I/S disciplines very seriously.

As client/server computing systems process and store more data critical to business operations, grassroots and corporate technologists must find common ground. Indeed, the pioneers who are building corporate client/server systems today believe they need the disciplines of large-scale computing for client/server designs to succeed. It is also fair to say that many client/server computing projects have been completed late and over budget because the designers underestimated the complexities of supporting the new environment reliably. The most successful client/server systems today harness the flexible processing of smaller computers to the disciplined reliability of shared systems to support redesigned business practices.

Common Approaches to Client/Server Computing

Between 1991 and 1993, IBM conducted a study of over 50 customers building client/server systems. The study team published their findings in a white paper titled "Application Reference Designs for Distributed Systems," published in June 1993. An article based on the same work, written by Dr. John Shedletsky and John Rofrano, appeared in the *IBM Systems Journal* (Volume 32, Number 4, 1993). This study identified several broad categories of distributed systems, and by contrast, included a brief discussion of a monolithic approach to building a system. We'll discuss six ways to use client/server Computing:

- Sharing Resources in Workgroups: The Resource Sharing Model

- Automating Process Flows: The Process-Driven Model

- Giving Applications Face Lifts: The Front End Model

- Pointing and Clicking over the Network: The Remote Presentation Model

- Dividing and Conquering: The Distributed Logic Model

- Keeping Replicas of Data Close at Hand: The Data Staging Model

The first two models discussed fit into a grassroots technique, and the last four typically require a corporate approach.

Sharing Resources in Workgroups: The Resource Sharing Model

The first model, the **Resource Sharing Model** (called the "resource-centric reference design" in the IBM Systems Journal article), extends a PC user's access to files, devices, and databases that reside elsewhere in the network. It works well for workgroups, and it can extend beyond the workgroup as well. Figure 2.4 shows the parts of the Resource Sharing Model.

This model covers most of the client/server marketplace today. File servers, printer servers, client/server database software, fax servers, and similar products all fall into this model. Here, client/server software makes remote

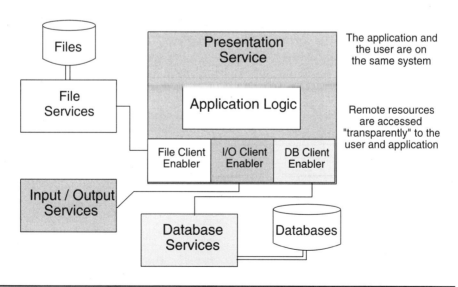

Figure 2.4. The Resource Sharing Model.

devices and data appear local to personal computer applications and users. For example, by using a file server, data stored in files on a server look to the user like data stored in files on a local hard disk. This would be true even if each system used different data storage methods. The file server and its corresponding client enabling software would provide a way of "translating" any differences in formats between the client and the server.

In the Resource Sharing Model, the application software resides on the system closest to the user, which is usually a personal computer. This software is usually not aware that the served resources reside elsewhere on the network. The client enabling software resides on the personal computer as well.

The clearest examples of the model are disk servers and file servers. A computer running PC-DOS usually has one or more long-term storage devices, called hard disks or hard drives. PC-DOS called the first such hard disk the C drive, and the term stuck. IBM's **Operating System/2 (OS/2)** also calls the first hard disk the C drive. When a machine has multiple hard disk drives, the second is the D drive, the third the E drive, and so forth. When the disk server's client enabling software is loaded, usually when the computer is first started, information on the server is "mapped" to local drive letters. For example, if a client's machine has only one hard drive, the C drive may be local, whereas the D, E, and F drives reside on the file server. Some call the drives residing on the file server "served drives."

All access to data on the served drives occurs as if the drives were local to the user's PC. No changes in commands, applications, or other software need occur. Reading and writing data to the served drives may be slower than using a local drive, but everything else works as it does on a single machine. This is an important plus and at the same time a potential problem of using applications with a file server.

Consider, for example, software designed for a personal computer. Since a PC has only one user, many applications do not include logic to prevent simultaneous changes to data. If you need concurrent access to a record, using such software will likely cause corrupted data. Unfortunately, many workgroups use file servers without knowing that their software does not prevent uncoordinated, concurrent access to data. To them, it looks "the same," but it isn't.

Also, consider performance. If the application reads or writes data only a few bytes at a time, the client enabling software must repeatedly transfer small amounts of information over the network. In a standalone PC, this isn't a problem, but in a shared, networked system, it is. Many such requests will visibly decrease software responsiveness by clogging the network and by making the client and the server do more work. This is especially true when the network includes WAN links, which are slower than LANs anyway.

For many workgroups, though, the Resource Sharing Model provides important advantages. Because everything "looks the same," users need little additional training. Existing procedures and support processes may still work. Many more people understand this model compared to other client/server computing models. Finally, some software, especially database software, provides logic to avoid corrupted data. If you choose your software carefully, the Resource Sharing Model can help you provide good service to your PC users at a reasonable cost.

Order Entry Using Networked Resources: Global Plumbing Supplies

We'll use several hypothetical examples throughout this book to illustrate common business problems and how client/server computing can help. Here, we tell you about each business and describe the main problem. We'll also show how the client/server model under discussion might help. Later chapters will cover what IBM products might fit each situation and what design considerations might apply.

Our first company is Global Plumbing Supplies, Inc. (GPSI). GPSI makes and distributes pipe, valves, waterproof electrical supplies, and other materials. It sells in 16 countries, although its main market is in the United States. Its market grows slightly from year to year, but its profit margins lag behind competing firms.

An office in San Francisco houses GPSI's headquarters and an engineering staff of about 750 employees. The New York and Rome sales offices each have about 100 employees. GPSI's plants reside in the United States, Mexico, and Singapore. Customers like GPSI's approach to sales, but they complain GPSI is slow to deliver needed parts, causing them to order parts from GPSI's competitors. GPSI's vendors don't like maintaining extra stock for GPSI's last-minute orders; they want help in reducing their finished goods stocks. Finally, GPSI's CFO has noted an increase in goods shipped to customers who have trouble paying on time.

Until now, GPSI's sales staff used processes with minimal automation. They relied on printed inventory worksheets and experience to tell customers when to expect shipments. GPSI's internal parts catalogs were often out of date, and unusual parts weren't included in them due to printing costs. The sales process was minimally automated: Sales staff gave orders to clerks, who entered the orders into GPSI's mainframe computer. Finally, sales staff had no way to know if a customer wasn't paying its bills.

Today, GPSI's older mainframe, housed in San Francisco, uses homegrown, textual, batch-oriented software. Clerks enter orders as needed. Batch software prints orders every other day, and GPSI then sends them to vendors or to GPSI's manufacturing sites via air courier. The current software would be expensive to change, since some of the programmers who wrote it no longer work for GPSI. GPSI also has a few personal computers scattered throughout the company.

GPSI's Board of Directors, in a meeting four months ago, decided to improve the sales process. They also want GPSI's CEO, Rose Carando, to reduce cycle time by linking sales and fulfillment more tightly to inventory management and procurement. To that end, Rose assigned a team to study these issues. This group then developed a plan to redesign these business processes.

Rose's team discovered that GPSI's software wouldn't support the newly developed processes. For internally sourced parts, the sales staff need correct, online inventory information; for vendor supplied parts, GPSI needs electronic supply links to those vendors. Sales reps should be able to fax images of any part to customers and view these images as they speak with the customers. As parts change, these images and their descriptions should change with little staff effort. The sales rep should be able to check the customer's payment history and credit before accepting an order. The clerks should not be needed; they were to be retrained as additional sales staff.

The CIO, Chris Fu, decided to equip the sales staff with PCs running a new application that communicates with a relational database server. This application handles order entry and updates the customer, order, and inventory databases accordingly. He also decided to provide the sales staff with prebuilt queries for the relational databases. One such query checks a customer's payment history; another checks existing inventory and production schedules for a part. Other parts of the project addressed tighter integration with suppliers, using **Electronic Data Interchange** (EDI).

The requirements for images challenged Chris' staff. They didn't want to put all of the images on each PC, because it would be too hard to make synchronized changes. An image server, along with suitable client software, would meet the sales staff's needs, and it would reduce ongoing administration expenses. The same machine could fax images of parts or marketing information on demand. Figure 2.5 shows how clients and servers relate in GPSI's approach.

Automating Process Flows: The Process-Driven Model

The second model for client/server computing is the **Process-Driven Model**. With it, you may build systems using either grassroots or corporate approaches, perhaps as part of a business process redesign. It fits well with the notion of "business process reengineering," both in a department and throughout a company. However, most of the applications to date are smaller applications, so we encounter this model most often in a grassroots approach.

The Process-Driven Model stems from the idea that a large process can be broken down into smaller processes, with data and status passing between them. A main process path may have several exception paths. Several points may exist where work can enter or exit the process, although a well-designed process tries to reduce these. When work enters the process, it needs to be "told where to go" based upon the business practices the policy supports. A **workflow manager** coordinates the system's activities, shepherding each work item along the correct path. The workflow manager dictates this path, but decisions taken in individual steps of the process can cause the workflow manager to change the path. Figure 2.6 shows this model.

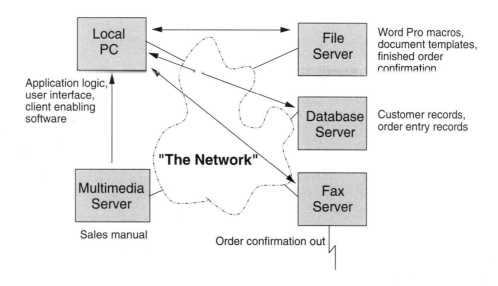

Figure 2.5. Resource sharing at GPSI.

The Process-Driven Model emulates well how people conduct business. For example, in a capital spending justification process, a committee might decide to suspend approval of a request pending further analysis. Someone then goes off and gets the information the committee needs. When the analysis is done, the committee makes a decision. The Process-Driven Model works the same way. It allows people and machines to make decisions based upon the work entering the process. Then, the workflow manager takes the results of these decisions and guides the work item to the next step of the process for that work item.

In this approach, software designers keep the data and the processing for each step together. This differs from the other models. Here, the step itself defines how to distribute functions across computers. Steps 1 through 3 might reside on machine A while step 4 runs on machine B and steps 5 through 7 use machine C. The workflow manager also might reside on one or more machines.

Message passing is usually used to communicate between steps, allowing work to flow through the system "at its own pace." Messages inform the workflow manager of changes in status, send data between process steps, and send constraining information to process steps. The system can send messages immediately or, if it detects a failure, put messages into queues for later retransmission. The workflow manager may thus send messages "reliably," even if immediate delivery is impossible. This approach provides

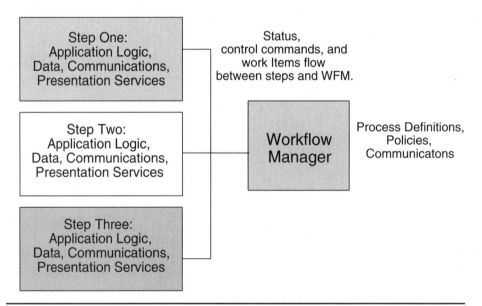

Figure 2.6. The Process-Driven Model.

flexibility in updating pieces of the system at a time. It also allows for downtime on individual computers for needs such as preventive maintenance and software changes. Programmers, though, can find message passing harder to understand at first than other communications techniques, possibly increasing development costs.

A step within the Process-Driven Model may choose to use other client/server techniques, such as resource sharing, if it is convenient. For example, a step to approve expense statements might use a database server to find the approving manager's employee number and electronic mail address. Here, the step avoids keeping track of redundant information. However, if a step uses or changes data local to another step, this breaks with the spirit of the model.

Ordering Office Supplies Using Automated Workflows: Acme Roadrunner Traps

Acme Roadrunner Traps wants to change how it orders and approves small purchases. Acme's owner, Mr. Wiley, benchmarked a number of mail order firms, and found Acme's costs to be above most. While Acme's unique roadrunner trap technologies allow solid profits, Mr. Wiley wants to diversify Acme's products. To do this, Acme's costs must drop. Mr. Wiley decided the pilot application would be to order office supplies. If successful, the application would be expanded to include other low cost purchases.

Acme needs speedy decisions to reduce costs. Today, paper sits on desks for approvals, wasting staff time and increasing administrative work in process. Acme's I/S staff evaluated an application on a shared system and decided it would become inflexible and cumbersome as the system expanded. After looking further, they decided to use a process-driven design.

Figure 2.7 shows this process. It is simple; most would be more complex than this. The process has four main steps and one exception step. The first step, invoked by Fritz Payling, a staff member in Cactus Flats, builds a work item. It asks Fritz to fill out an online form.

When Fritz completes the online form, the newly generated work item reaches the second step, which assesses the size of the request. If the request costs more than $50.00, then Will Warner, Fritz's supervisor, must approve it as an exception. If it costs less than $50.00, the work item goes directly on to the third step. If Mr. Warner approves the item as an exception, the work item also goes on to the third step; otherwise, it goes to the fourth step. Step 3 places the order, and step 4 notifies Fritz of the request's outcome via electronic mail.

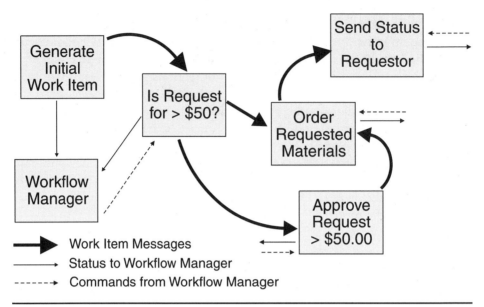

Figure 2.7. Acme Roadrunner Supplies orders office supplies.

Note that we have made no mention so far of the underlying computing technologies used. This process places only two constraints on the underlying technology. First, electronic mail with a consistent addressing scheme must be available to all process users. Second, the underlying software must adapt to substantial delays. Consider, for example, the possibility that Mr. Warner, who approves large requests, is out of the office.

We haven't explicitly documented the workflow manager's role. That's because some workflow managers can be quite flexible in how they operate, even including a special workflow language to help reduce development time. Some workflow managers are more sophisticated than others. For example, if Mr. Warner is away for more than a day, perhaps the workflow manager should reroute the request to Fred Brewer, his administrative assistant, who can approve it. At least, if the request waits for more than a day or so, the workflow manager should let Fritz know its status. A fully featured workflow manager can perform tasks like these automatically.

Giving Applications Face Lifts: The Front End Model

Figure 2.8 shows the next model, the **Front End Model**. This approach provides a graphical **front end** for existing applications. Some call it the "face lift" approach, because the looks improve while everything else remains the same. Because this approach requires no changes to the existing application, it can be done in a grassroots manner. However, the client application software depends upon consistent screens from the existing application. So, it helps to cooperate with the application's owner where possible.

GUIs, like Microsoft's Windows or IBM's OS/2 **Presentation Manager,** have become popular as personal computers have become a ubiquitous business tool. As mentioned briefly in Chapter 1, a GUI simplifies how a user relates to an application. So, using software with a GUI can decrease training time and costs, and can sometimes provide better performance.

The Front End Model increases user productivity and reduces training costs without changing the original software. A front end can also provide an integration point between multiple existing applications by providing "cut and paste" functions between them. For example, the textual output of a transaction could be "massaged" by the front end's application software, turning it into input to another program on a different computer.

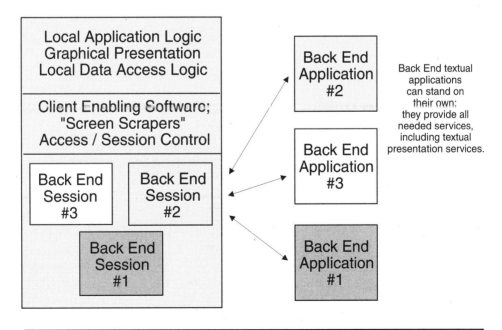

Figure 2.8.   Front End Model.

In the diagram, we show three sessions to three different existing applications. Three is convenient for us; it could be one or more. The user's machine, usually a machine running OS/2, Windows, or Apple's Macintosh operating system, **MacOS System 7**, is on the left. It may contain some local program logic, and it may use local data along with data from the existing applications. The software uses these applications via a network, although we do not show the network in the diagram.

Graphical front end enabling software, along with networking software, starts, maintains, and ends sessions with target applications or subsystems. Front ends also intercept or "scrape" data from these sessions and divert it to the local application program. There, the local program can interact with the user or manipulate the data somehow. Once this is done, the local program "pastes" the resultant information back into the session to the back end application, and sends it over the network. Sometimes, writers and programmers call the client enabling software "**screen scrapers.**"

The back end applications usually work with terminals, not PCs. They are complete; they may provide data access services, transaction services, locking services, and other similar services. The applications already know how to present data to users and accept textual data from users. They format streams of data, most often block mode screens, for output, and they interpret keystrokes as input. Other users may use the same back end applications using block mode or character mode terminals while PC users concurrently use the graphical front end. Either way, the application doesn't know that the data is coming from another program rather than a user typing on a keyboard.

This approach explicitly ties the front end software to the back end application. If the back end application changes the way it sends data to a screen, for example, the front end must adapt to the new format. Let's assume an additional input field is added to one screen of a back end application designed to interact with a block mode terminal. The positions of the existing fields also change to adapt to the new field. When the new version of the back end application goes into production, the front end will probably function incorrectly until it also reflects the new field positions.

A second consequence of this approach is more fundamental: It doesn't change the way you do business unless you combine it with other changes. As a result, building a front end is sometimes the start of a longer journey to redesign business processes and their supporting software. Some people might say, "Where's the server?" in this model. Well, you can look at the existing applications as the server. The protocol between the client enabling software and the server is the data stream the application thinks is going to a terminal. The client simply interprets this data stream differently, giving the application's user a better interface.

Jones' Happy Travel: Improving Productivity with a New Front End

Jones' Happy Travel, a mid-sized travel agency based in Dallas, has a problem because most airlines have capped travel agency commissions. It must either invest to increase sales volume or decide to sell the firm. Fortunately, Jones' Happy Travel has highly satisfied clients because of its personalized service. So, the challenge is to increase volume substantially while maintaining this highly personalized service.

Jones' uses two main computer reservations systems. Some agents have terminals for SABRE; others have terminals for Galileo. These older, single-purpose terminals attach to the main computers via communications controllers at the agency and dedicated telephone lines to each system. All of the terminals and communications hardware belong to the reservation system's owners. Clearly, Jones' Happy Travel can't change the main reservation system.

The agency wants to improve productivity by making common transactions, such as finding the lowest fare in a particular market, simpler to use. It also wants to add profiles for its clients; if Alan Marchesseault likes to fly on Delta, rent a Hertz car, and stay in Marriott hotels, the agency notes this information in Alan's profile. Perhaps Maggie Corder has similar preferences, but only if cheaper alternatives save $100 per trip or less. With the profiles, agents won't waste time researching alternatives Alan and Maggie wouldn't like.

Figure 2.9 shows how Jones' Happy Travel might design their front end. The agency added the profiles to the application by using the Resource Sharing Model. A database server lets any of Jones' agents to use the same profile information. The logic that reads and changes a profile lives in the application software on every agent's PC, but the database server prevents concurrent updates. Using a relational database server also helps the agency's management to fine-tune sales campaigns. Using the information in the relational database, the agency's management might easily target promotions to customers who travel more than 30 times and year and who like, say, Hyatt hotels.

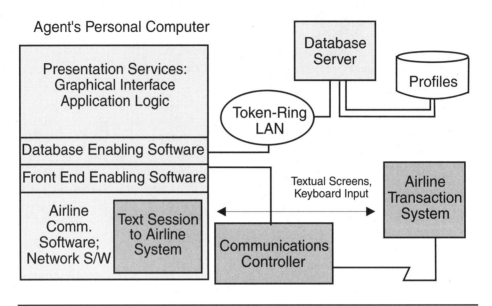

Figure 2.9. A front end for Jones' Happy Travel.

Pointing and Clicking over the Network: The Remote Presentation Model

The **Remote Presentation Model** is conceptually simple. First, visual output generated by an application on one system gets displayed on another. Next, the system that displays the output also takes the user's actions and turns them into input for the application. Several examples of the Remote Presentation Model exist, but two approaches dominate today: the X-Windows System and Web Browsers.

The X-Windows System

The model's first common application is the **X-Windows** windowing system. The X-Windows consortium has defined five releases of their software, sometimes called X11 or simply X. They call the current release X11 Release 5 (X11R5). The Massachusetts Institute of Technology (MIT) first developed the X-Windows system, with funding from IBM and other computer vendors, and has since licensed X-Windows to many vendors. Software that uses X11 can thus be more portable than software that uses a different way to interact with users.

X11 defines a graphical interface server that runs on the user's machine. This is different from most client/server enablers, where the client is closest to the user. UNIX-based application software commonly uses X-Windows, but many other operating systems support X11 as well.

In X-Windows, as shown in Figure 2.10, the application processing is done on the client machines. In the diagram, three client applications have three windows open on the server system; the user interacts with one of these windows (and therefore with one application) at a time. A program may have more than one window open at a time, but we show a one-to-one correspondence between windows and applications to simplify the drawing. The server provides a graphical output device for these client applications. It also takes the user's mouse movements, keystrokes, and menu choices and sends them on to the correct application. Here, the client application doesn't know how to display graphical output or grab mouse movements, so it asks for help from the server. The server and the client enabling software are bound together by a series of events and messages both must understand; these events and messages encode the user's actions and the application's output requirements. Sometimes, writers call the protocol that defines these events and messages **X-Wire**.

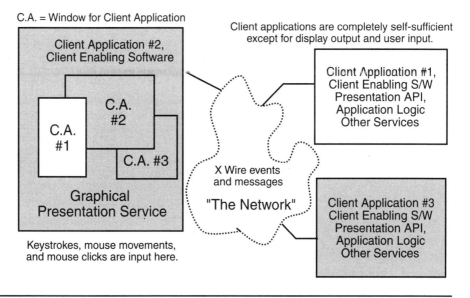

Figure 2.10. The Remote Presentation Model.

The last component of X-Windows is the window manager. It defines how the windows "look and feel." It also dispatches events, making sure all the mouse clicks and other user actions end up being sent to the correct client application. The Open Software Foundation's Motif, mentioned briefly in Chapter 1, is the most commonly used window manager.

X11 contains only openly specified protocols. So, vendors have developed several very different devices that act as X- Windows servers. On some fast, graphical workstations, such as an IBM RISC System/6000, the client application, the client enabler, and the server software can exist on the same system. IBM, among other vendors, also makes low cost devices optimized to run an X-server. These **X-terminals** have a smaller processor and a graphical, PC-like display. IBM calls its device an **X-Station**. If an X-Station user wants to run a client application, X-Windows can direct that program's I/O from the RISC System/6000 to the X-server on the X-Station. The application isn't aware that the user has a different kind of hardware; it only knows that whatever X-server it works with understands the X-Windows system.

Similarly, if an X-server from, say, Hewlett-Packard, uses Motif, then X-Windows and Motif could easily direct the application's output to the HP server. Here, an application, without change, can use the X-Windows system to display output and gather input on vastly different hardware devices.

Surfing the World Wide Web

Another common Remote Presentation application is the **World Wide Web**. The World Wide Web, sometimes called the Web or the WWW, is a way of interacting with data stored on machines attached to the Internet. People use software, called a **browser**, to look around the Internet and to retrieve data, including text, images, and video, from servers located throughout the Internet.

Information developers encode data on a Web server, using a language called **HyperText Markup Language (HTML)**, into **pages**. Figure 2.11 shows a sample page, in this case, IBM's main, or "home" page. A home page usually functions like a table of contents for a firm's information. Each page almost always contains text, and pointers to other pages, especially the firm's home page. Optionally, pages can also contain images, sounds, or video clips.

Web pages are becoming increasingly useful. Some firms use pages on the Web as a product catalog. Some vendors use them to describe simple fixes to common problems, avoiding excessive telephone and warranty costs. Newer versions of the software let people using a Web page type in text. When the industry defines a way to keep financial information such as credit

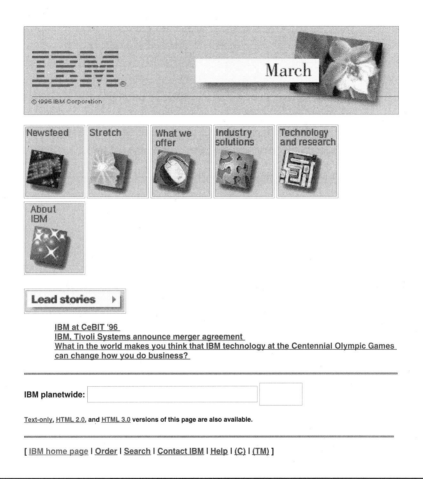

Figure 2.11. IBM's home page on the World Wide Web.

card numbers secure on the Internet, this will open new possibilities. For example, someone browsing through your product catalog could place an order for a particular product.

Browsers use the pointers on a page, called **hypertext links** to move transparently from one page to another. These pages might be on the same server or on different servers. You can also use hypertext links as buttons, to initiate actions. If, for example, you wanted to distribute software updates via the Internet, one way might be to maintain pages that describe the up-dates. If users wanted to get a particular updated package, a click on a button would transfer the files to their computers.

Linking these pages is important: Servers don't contain any logic to verify that a link continues to be valid. Let's say I maintained a Web page that had a hypertext link to someone else's system, A. If system A's owner moved the page to system B, but didn't tell me, my link would continue to look for system A. In that case, if a user clicked on my pointer, the reference would fail, and the user's browser would display an error message.

The linking concept can be quite powerful, as long as the links stay up to date. Without needing any centralized catalog, users can peruse matters of interest to them to any level of depth. You can go off onto tangent after tangent of interest to you. On the other hand, without a centralized catalog or searching facility, the WWW, as the World Wide Web is sometimes called, can be frustrating if you don't know where to look.

Firms also use WWW technology for internal purposes. For example, IBM uses the Web for internal communications. The problems of severed links are also less of a problem when a Web has a single master.

Making Physicians More Productive: Cripple Creek Community Hospital

Cripple Creek Community Hospital is interested in retaining referrals from the best physicians at a time when demand for traditional hospital services is decreasing. One way the hospital can do this is to make physicians' time more productive.

Today, the hospital's physicians use many systems. The Hospital Information System (HIS), runs on an IBM mainframe computer and handles patient information such as insurance, billing, and treatment planning. The pharmacy uses a minicomputer system with a specialized software package, and the radiology lab uses a different minicomputer system for image processing. Today, physicians must find the correct terminals to access these systems and navigate their way through the systems before they can perform "useful" work.

Cripple Creek wanted to eliminate these distractions. At the same time, physicians wanted the system to look "the same," whether they use it from home, from their offices, or from within the hospital. They wanted it to remain simple so that they wouldn't need specialized training.

The hospital decided to use X-Windows. A pilot project discovered that the system responded well within the hospital, but too slowly in a physician's office or home. For this application, the X-Wire protocol is "chatty"; it needs faster lines. So, the local telephone company plans to install upgraded telephone equipment. It will offer the hospital a new, integrated digital telephone service within a year. This new service will make X-Windows feel more responsive, with speeds five or six times faster than CCCH's existing modems. Until then, the system is still faster for physicians than driving to the hospital to review an X-ray or order a prescription.

With the new system, a physician or a nurse walks up to any networked device and enters a username and password to use the system. After authentication is complete, the user sees a personalized desktop. Nurses have a different desktop than physicians. Each desktop has a series of icons that describe the actions the user can take. When a physician clicks on, say, the "order a prescription" icon, it attaches to the pharmacy's computer; when a nurse clicks on the "review treatment plan" icon, it attaches to the HIS computer. Any PC with the appropriate reader and software, whether onsite, in a physician's office, or at a physician's home, can work with this approach.

Dividing and Conquering: The Distributed Logic Model

Our next model, the **Distributed Logic Model**, does what the database vendors did years ago to develop client/server database products. In this approach, neither part of the application can stand on its own. Using the Distributed Logic Model commits a business to using PCs, cash registers, machine tools, and other programmable devices instead of ordinary terminals. This model also maintains its data centrally. This makes it suitable for critical applications and data. It also allows a firm to use distributed TP monitors to safeguard the integrity of business transactions. Figure 2.12 depicts this model's main parts.

Selling Tickets Using Distributed Logic: SpeedyTix Ticket Agency

Consider a ticket brokering company, SpeedyTix in Salt Lake City. SpeedyTix sells seats to arts, sports, and special events at ticket counters in retail outlets. Now, SpeedyTix wants to expand its distribution methods. It wants to use kiosks, devices like automatic teller machines, to sell tickets. These kiosks could reside in shopping malls, hotels, or similar locations. They must be friendly and easily used. For example, the kiosk IBM developed for the Minnesota Twins even shows a customer the view from a selected seat.

The seating data cannot reside inside the kiosk. SpeedyTix' many kiosks, ticket counters, and telesales reps sell seats, so the firm must control seating data carefully. It can't sell the same seat twice or report an event is

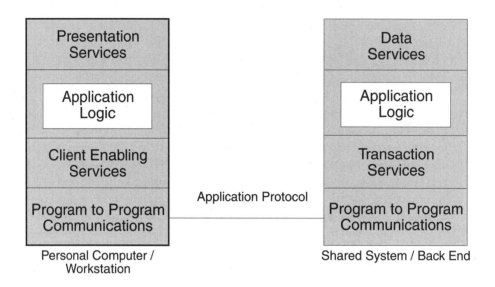

Figure 2.12. The Distributed Logic Model.

sold out when seats really are available. The kiosk's software might also include a transaction monitor, because SpeedyTix must maintain the transaction's integrity if a failure occurs. This application is ideal for the Distributed Logic Model because the transaction's integrity is crucial.

In the kiosk, SpeedyTix could use voice processing or a touch screen to guide a customer through events, dates, and seating charts. At some point, the kiosk's software should have an event, a date, a series of desired seats, and a credit card number. Without these, a ticket sale isn't possible. Then, the kiosk starts a transaction using a local TP monitor that communicates with a transaction server on a central system. This server allocates seats and processes credit card transactions. If seats are available and the credit card is valid, it returns a list of seats closely matching the customer's request. The customer then confirms the seat selections. Next, the kiosk's transaction reports the sale to the central server, which reserves the seats. If the reservation is successful, the kiosk prints the tickets.

Some processing must be local and some centralized for the ticking kiosk to meet both SpeedyTix' and their customers' needs. Without local processing, the kiosk wouldn't be as friendly. The centralized seating inventory allows SpeedyTix to add sales outlets without worrying about corrupting data.

Keeping Replicas of Data Close at Hand: The Data Staging Model

Sometimes, sending all the data needed from a central site using the Resource Sharing Model is too costly or time-consuming. Replicating the data to each PC, though, is also unwieldy in some cases. It might be useful to duplicate the data at several sites, however, if little of the data changes regularly. When these conditions fit, the **Data Staging Model** is a good choice.

Various ways exist to duplicate data to or from a central site. Duplicating data regionally might make sense if headquarters needed to use all data, but one regional office didn't need to use another office's data. Another method "clears" all changes to data through a central site and then distributes regular data updates throughout the organization. This approach works well with a TP monitor; the TP monitor changes the data, then these changes are regularly sent to the other systems. Other policies for distributing duplicated data could be appropriate under other conditions.

Figure 2.13 outlines a data staging environment. It shows updates being propagated to one or more intermediate systems. Part of the diagram might look like the Resource Sharing Model, because these models can work together well. The Resource Sharing part is optional, since the data could be staged to a shared system. To keep the distributed data up to date, a pro-

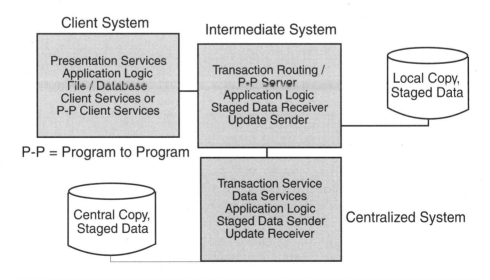

Figure 2.13. The Data Staging Model.

gram, a schedule, or both regularly send data changes to and from the main computer. This program or schedule operates between the middle box in the diagram and the box on the right.

It is fair to say this approach optimizes the costs and performance of a centralized data storage and retrieval design. It retains the elements of centralized control over the data, but it allows access to the data quickly. This makes it suitable for use, given the right conditions, for workgroups and for critical data. Using this approach, a local facility could probably survive a limited central machine or communications failure, since the data resides locally as well.

A Data Staging Example: Customer Information at Five and Dime

As an example of data staging, consider Five and Dime Imports. Five and Dime operates warehouses in several locations throughout the United States, and their main facility is in Newark, New Jersey. They import goods from countries in Europe and the Middle East. Goods typically come via container ship into the Port of Newark. Five and Dime receives the containers and transfers and stores their contents for their clients. Sometimes, a customer wants a full container, but most often, a container's contents go to different customers throughout the country.

Until now, Five and Dime has been a traditional, hierarchically managed firm, with a centralized computer. Senior management, however, engaged a management consultant to study operations for possible improvements. The consultant recommended that Five and Dime decentralize its decision making to make the firm more responsive to customer requests. Also, the consultant advised Five and Dime to make contingency plans for growth, since tariffs between the European Community and the United States may drop over time.

Five and Dime now intends to manage most of its operations regionally, with autonomous teams at each warehouse responsible for sales and inventory management. However, management at headquarters still needs a view of how the whole business is running. That way, they can target promotions and national marketing programs to specific kinds of customers. Also, the firm allows one region to sell goods that reside in another region's warehouse. That way, large accounts receive the best possible service: one-call shopping with the fastest possible delivery. So, each region needs to know the inventory at the other warehouses.

Five and Dime Imports expects to use a TP monitor to enter orders, track shipments, and process arriving containers of goods. Some of this tracking is automated, using bar code readers to drive transactions. Other processing uses clerks, equipped with traditional, textual terminals. The TP monitor uses a relational database for storage.

Each region updates and maintains its own inventory, ordering, financial, and customer data. Then, every hour, the regional system replicates the transactions to the centralized system. With the new approach, no matter how many regions Five and Dime eventually has, each region searches for inventory locally. If goods aren't available locally, the region can check the central site to see if other regions have stock. If so, then the first region can sell inventory from the second as required. That way, the customer receives goods as quickly as possible. All this time, Five and Dime's headquarters also has the data it needs, in a standardized, easily queried format.

Contrast this with a completely centralized approach or a completely decentralized approach. Using only a central system hurts autonomy and might slow transactions down due to network delays. On the other hand, using completely decentralized systems doesn't give headquarters a common view of the firm. It also makes it harder for individual regions to look for inventory elsewhere in the firm. The extracted, staged data solves the dilemma.

We'll discuss the products that Five and Dime uses to achieve this staging and replication in Chapter 5. Here we will just remark that data staging can be simple or complex. Data staging becomes more complex if the ownership of data isn't so easily defined, and sometimes, changes must be propagated in both directions.

Architectures for Client/Server Applications

An **application architecture** is a blueprint you use when you build or buy application software for use in your business. Such an architecture defines the relationships between the various functions within the applications you use. It can also specify relationships between applications, and it can define how the applications software used will relate to specific business functions. Loggers have felled forests of trees to supply the paper for books that discuss various architectural techniques. Much of the existing literature applies to client/server and monolithic approaches to building applications. We will only make a few observations specific to client/server computing.

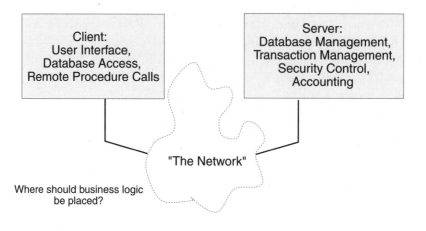

Figure 2.14. A sample two-tiered architecture.

Two-Tiered Client/Server Applications

A **two-tiered application architecture** is the easiest way to design a client/server application. Someone defines the processing to be done and then decides if each work item is best done on the server or the client. For example, a business application might include several services, such as user interface, data access, transaction management, security, or communications. A firm might buy or build services such as these to include in an application. Most often, companies would buy packages that provide these services. You would want the rules and policies that run your business to be different from other firms, however. That's where your business adds unique value for your customers.

It's simple to imagine allocating each needed service to the client system or the server system. Depending upon your staff's sophistication and the demands the software puts on the hardware and the network, you'd assign where components fit best. You can easily buy or build systems designed (some say "architected," a horrid word) in two tiers. This application architecture is shown in Figure 2.14.

Most client/server computing products today fit this application architecture. In a typical Resource Sharing Model workgroup, for example, members share hardware and data without regard to the way the business itself runs. The business rules usually reside in the client application, as if the software stood alone. Two-tiered approaches are good for problems that aren't complex and where the interaction doesn't change often. Some call the two-tiered approach **"first-generation client/server computing."**

However, if you were to build and use software that defines and automates your "methods of business," where would you put those rules? Let's say you decide to place them on the client and you want to change your accounts receivable practices: Instead of providing 15-day terms, you want to use 5-day terms with electronic payments. If you put the logic for this business rule on the client, you will have to change the software on all your clients when you want to change policy. This will be much more difficult than changing your business rules on a few server systems.

On the other hand, centralizing the data and logic that embody the rules can intertwine them with other services, such as transaction management and data access. This may make it harder for an organization to respond flexibly to local needs. If the business logic intertwines with other services, the application could become nearly monolithic, with all the rigidity this implies. Then, client/server computing would become a more complex version of existing programs on shared systems. Also, two-tiered designs use client hardware intensively and they use more network capacity. For LAN-based applications, two-tiered approaches might work, but for applications that use WAN lines, a three-tiered design can work better.

Three-Tiered Client/Server Applications

Unlike two-tiered designs, the three-tiered approach directly recognizes the importance of your rules of business. It defines these layers: the **user interface layer**, the **business logic layer**, sometimes called the **functional layer**, and the **data access layer**. In this view of building applications, all other services or components, such as a transaction manager or communications services, exist to make these three main components more effective. In building applications like this, you should keep the three main components separate, even if you might eventually run two of them on a single machine. Some refer to the three-tiered model as **second-generation client/server computing**. Figure 2.15 shows this approach.

Let's look again at Global Plumbing Supplies, Inc. Figure 2.16 shows the information flow through this example. All the logic resides on the client's machine. The servers read and write data for the client; they do no processing associated with GPSI's rules of business. Figure 2.17 shows this example using a three-tiered model. Here, the user interface layer resides on the client's computer. The business logic server provides the functional layer while the back end servers read and write data for it. The client software doesn't interact directly with the data access layer. Instead, it talks with the business

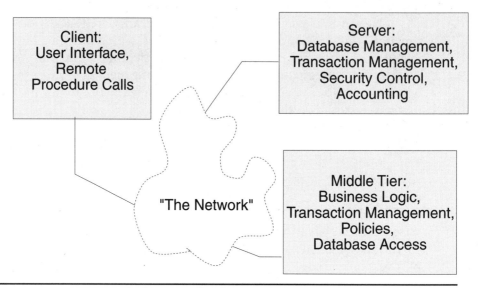

Figure 2.15. A sample three-tiered architecture.

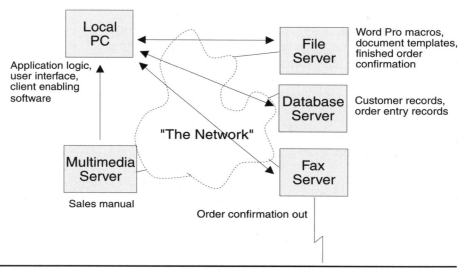

Figure 2.16. Resource sharing in two tiers.

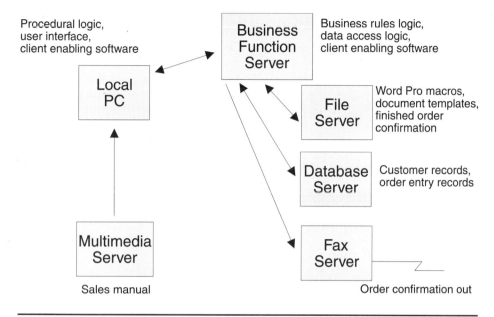

Procedural logic,
user interface,
client enabling software

Local
PC

Business
Function
Server

Business rules logic,
data access logic,
client enabling software

File
Server

Word Pro macros,
document templates,
finished order
confirmation

Database
Server

Customer records,
order entry records

Multimedia
Server

Sales manual

Fax
Server

Order confirmation out

Figure 2.17. Using three tiers.

logic server. Instead of using commands to read a table from a database, it might ask the business logic server to "get the payment history for customer ABC." Here, the client might talk with the business logic server using message passing, or it might use other techniques. Because they are isolated from many details specific to products, software clients don't care when you change from one database to another. Only the middle tier sees these details.

Occasionally, though, it may not make sense to use three tiers for all aspects of an application. Combining three tiers of control with two tiers of data access may sometimes be better. For example, sending multimedia images through the business logic server in our example may not prove economical. The business logic server might become far more expensive, and the delay caused by passing the images through it might be too great. It is reasonable to mix and match two- and three-tiered approaches in a complex design.

Finally, three-tiered application architectures fit "skinny" client systems better than their two-tiered counterparts. The reason is simple: More function resides on the servers. For some applications, the client could be as simple as a Web browser. These clients are less costly to acquire, and the software is less complex to manage, reducing ongoing support costs.

Why Client/Server Computing? Why Not Something Else?

Client/server computing, properly speaking, is a subset of what some call distributed computing. By definition, some work in a client/server computing system must be done on each part, some on the client and some on the server. Clearly, then, in a client/server computing system, the processing is distributed across more than one computer. However, you can use techniques besides client/server computing to build software systems that span multiple computers.

Using batch processors in a job entry network defines a way to build software that uses more than one computer. Alternatively, you could use several similar, networked shared systems to solve a common problem. Computer industry futurists say that object oriented computing using **distributed objects** is how software will be built into the next century. Given the many alternatives available, why is client/server computing the right technology for building today's software for multiple computers?

To answer this question, we must first discuss four trends in the computer industry. First, we'll look at advances in electronic hardware, particularly in how we'll work with this new hardware. Next, we'll discuss how businesses are reinventing themselves and using more small computers to help them increase revenues and profits. Then, we'll look at the economics of hardware and software. And finally, we'll talk briefly about object oriented computing and its promise for the future.

Advances in Microelectronics

The IBM ThinkPad 755CDV on which this book is being written calculates faster than most 10-year-old mainframes. The electronic circuits, or **chips**, within it are smaller, faster, less costly, and consume far less power than devices only two or three years old. The chip-making industry expects this trend to continue into the next millennium. As chips become smaller and less expensive, computers of equivalent capability become smaller and less expensive. As newer, faster chips become available, computers of equivalent cost become faster and more powerful. Faster computers enable new software ideas. Both cases are happening today.

One argument for building software that spans multiple computer systems is simple but compelling: there is no better way to use small, inexpensive computers. Today's small computers enable mobile personal productivity; tomorrow's microelectronics will change how we interact with our machines. Beyond keyboards and pointing devices, today's chips can learn to recognize our speech, turning it into electronic text. They can also display full-motion video and provide high-fidelity sound. As these chips become less expensive, they enable new kinds of software. The idea is to make computers work more the way people work, instead of the other way around.

Without new software on these small computers, your firm won't be able to exploit these new capabilities. If your computer can capture your voice or your expressions, you'll want to send them to others. You'll tie these machines into networks with your colleagues, suppliers, and customers. Client/server computing provides a simple, understandable way to harness hardware's new power for good purpose across your organization.

Reinventing Business Processes

Using small computers to collect, manipulate, and present information can change how you run your business. Many firms and government agencies are now reinventing, or "reengineering," the processes they use to conduct business. As we've seen in our examples, client/server software is an important part of many of these efforts.

With redesigned business processes, sales staff can use laptop computers as a "virtual office," in constant communication with corporate databases. Employees can work from home or at your customer's site, saving time and money while reducing air pollution. Point-of-sale kiosks based on small computers allow people with no training to buy concert tickets, apply for unemployment benefits, and buy travelers checks.

For example, a person selling insurance can use a laptop computer to build customized spreadsheets and graphs in a customer's home, showing the effects of buying an annuity. The customer can make a better choice, and the salesperson is more productive. If the customer chooses to buy a product, the salesperson finishes the "paperwork" before leaving.

Similarly, shipping companies now avoid clerical work by capturing signatures with small computers. These computers immediately transmit the delivery information and the signature to the firm's main shared systems, and a TP monitor changes shipment records immediately. Companies also use bar code readers to track a package as it moves through their distribution system. This lets them track a package's progress from shipper to recipient. Judging from its success, customers value this service.

Because they depend on up-to-date information, these processes would be far less effective without client/server computing. Without client/server software, a shipping company's couriers or clerks would need to enter or transfer the day's data at the end of a shift. The company might not know a package's location until several hours after delivery. When business processes such as these are redesigned using client/server computing, work flows more quickly and decisions become more timely and accurate. Customer satisfaction usually increases, and often revenue increases as well. Although client/server computing costs more than traditional software, a good application will increase revenue faster than these costs.

Manufacturing Hardware and Crafting Software

Today's hardware is incredibly complex, but manufacturers know how to mask this complexity. Their techniques are highly automated. So, computers help engineers to develop the next generation of computers. Still, the need to build ever-smaller, more complex circuitry causes significant costs: Building a chip fabrication plant can easily cost a billion dollars. Hardware's massive tooling and development costs must be amortized over huge volumes of chips, disks, and other common parts.

Software, by contrast, is still more crafted than manufactured. The barriers to enter the market are lower, so many firms enter and exit the software industry annually. Because these barriers are so low, firms in other industries, such as financial services or aerospace, build software components themselves instead of buying them. These same firms would never dream of producing their own hardware.

Good software is more easily customized than hardware, and can provide more substantial competitive advantages. Frankly, your competitors can buy the same hardware you can. If you build your own software, however, your idea for a new way of doing business could outflank your competitors. Of course, this idea must be very good. Otherwise, you won't recoup the lifetime costs to develop, support, and revise the software you've built.

Software changes more slowly than hardware, partly because it is produced in a less automated way and partly because software mirrors your business processes more closely. It isn't unusual for a successful business process to last for a decade or more. Similarly, parts of a software system might easily live for ten years or longer. Some batch programs from the 1960s, although reworked and patched, have worked faithfully for 25 years.

With client/server computing, you can choose whether to use prewritten software components or to build your own. If you build some of your own software components, you can decide which parts entail risk or advantage. Each such decision is smaller than it would be using older techniques. If one decision is wrong, you can change it more easily. Finally, as your hardware changes, it is easier to adapt a few components to the new hardware rather than reworking an entire software system.

Object Oriented Computing

In Chapter 1, we discussed how most software today is designed, using structured programming techniques. We also looked at how object oriented computing changes how teams of programmers attack problems. Instead of looking at each task, objects focus on what must be done and what communication must take place to solve the problem at hand.

Because objects focus on the "what" rather than the "how," vendors are considering offering prewritten collections of objects. Because an object's user doesn't know the "how", objects can function like black boxes. As long as the "what" remains the same, the "how" can change. The promise is beguiling: Prewritten objects might become inexpensive commodities, reducing software costs.

Today, standardized libraries of objects for systems that span multiple computers are rare. Instead, object oriented techniques are being used more often to build individual programs. These programs might be clients or servers in a larger system, and they might communicate using one of many techniques. The futurist's dream of common "intercommunicating distributed objects" isn't here today. Two slightly different ways for objects to interwork exist, so early adopters face the prospect that standards compliant objects from different vendors might not work together.

Even if the standards and vendors were ready for a world of distributed objects, your staff may not be. Little literature and fewer tools exist for operational issues, like capacity planning and problem diagnosis. So, while building applications with networks of objects appears beguiling, for many firms building large, mission critical applications using a purely object oriented approach may be risky today. As the technology matures, and as I/S professionals become more comfortable with objects and how they interact, we'll see greater use of this technology.

Isn't Client/Server Computing Just Downsizing?

The biggest mistake people make about client/server computing is to equate it with downsizing or rightsizing. So how is client/server computing unlike downsizing? After all, with client/server computing, you do reconsider how you use hardware. After reviewing your business processes and designing new software, your I/S team undoubtedly will reallocate where data processing work is performed. Sometimes, an appropriate client/server computing solution uses "bigger boxes," not just PCs.

The key to successful client/server computing is to renovate your software and your network to more closely match how you want to do business today. After that, you can buy the hardware that best fits your networked software's needs. Client/server computing isn't about cutting I/S costs. Instead, it's about investing to rework your software and your business processes to increase productivity and revenues.

So, Why Client/Server Computing?

To get back to our original question, why should you consider investing in client/server computing? It offers you a solid, well-understood way to build distributed software today, and it lets you use the computers you'll buy today and tomorrow more effectively than monolithic software can. You can change your client software to take advantage of new technologies such as speech recognition when you wish, while your servers stay the same. It gives you a way to reinvent your business processes today, increasing revenues and customer satisfaction. Client/server computing may be more expensive than using existing software technologies on shared systems, but it opens new opportunities for your business. And finally, an extensive industry infrastructure exists to support your client/server computing needs, from design and consulting services to prewritten software components.

IBM Client/Server Computing at the Olympic Games

To show a real example of how client/server computing enables innovative information processing, we'll describe some of the software IBM built and operated at the 1994 Winter Olympics. IBM is presently building and testing updated versions of this software for the 1996 Summer Games in Atlanta.

The first system is an information and communication package for all of the Games' participants and spectators. The second is a results management system, used by the press, volunteers, and broadcasters to see how athletes performed. Other applications, such as a comprehensive security system, payroll, and transportation coordination, used the same hardware and enabling tools. We'll focus mainly on the information and communication system and the results management system.

Info '94

For the information and communication system, IBM built and operated a system for over 50,000 untrained people to use. Anyone could walk up to a kiosk or booth in the competition venues, airports, broadcast center, or local hotels. This kiosk contained a PC, along with network connections. People could then use the system, called Info '94 to learn about venue details, event schedules, athletes' biographies, news, weather, and results. Users touched screens, moving through the menu system shown in Figure 2.18. When they

Figure 2.18. Info '94 menu system.

found the topic they wanted, they watched and listened as text, still images, video, and audio deepened their Olympic experience.

A commentator watching a cross country race, for example, could quickly find out the standings in ski jumping. Then, with a quick check of the schedule for the Nordic Combined, the broadcast team is armed with facts as they speculate about Norway's chances compared with another team. Spectators in their hotels could find out how their favorite athletes performed even if an event wasn't televised.

If people, such as athletes or press members, held credentials, they could also use the electronic mail system. A print photographer might use the system to set an appointment to visit Alberto Tomba. If a reporter needed information about an athlete's background after an upset victory, Info '94 stood ready to provide it. Because the mail system also used pagers, even if people were out in the snow, the system could relay messages to them.

The Results Management System

The results management system captured data from timing devices and scoring software located throughout the Olympic venues, feeding it into a server at each venue. That server, an IBM PC called a **Personal System/2 (PS/2)**, resided on a token-ring LAN. It passed a result or mark to a mainframe in Oslo after the event's judge validated it. The server then sent the results to its clients: other PS/2 computers on the LAN, broadcast network's computers, and scoreboards linked throughout the venue.

Timing and marking devices included several timing systems supplied by Seiko, along with marking systems for untimed events such as ice dancing. Timing devices included traditional methods such as photoelectric cells along with newer ideas, such as attaching timing devices to the athletes. The system posted results to scoreboards in less than half a second, and the commentator system posted results in under 300 milliseconds.

Overall System Requirements

These systems demanded fast, reliable computing that was easy to use. For any of these systems, IBM had less than an inch of space on a person's credentials to tell them how to use the information systems at Lillehammer. The credentials also sported a bar code to identify them, along with the bearer's birth date. Of course, the systems supported the two official Olympic languages, French and English, as well as Norwegian.

They ran continuously throughout the Games. The same hardware and enabling software provided strict security for the athletes and the Games' organizers and volunteers. It met the needs of impatient, untrained users. Finally, the network of systems spread across Norway, including the Olympic Village, the broadcasting booths, the scoring booths, the main press center, and airports, train stations, and hotels.

How IBM Built These Systems

IBM built these systems using a three-tiered client/server approach. The results management system's back end servers ran on an IBM **Enterprise System/9000 (ES/9000) Model 9121** mainframe computer. A second mainframe, an older but compatible IBM **3090 Model 300s**, controlled the network, and acted as a backup processor in case the first processor or its software failed. A third mainframe at a remote, secured site provided additional backup in case of disaster. All of these mainframes ran IBM's **MVS/ESA** operating system. These large computers could handle the required workload, and they stay up in the face of circumstances that stop lesser machines.

For critical, real-time functions, designers used the Distributed Logic Model, using IBM's **Customer Information Control System (CICS)** on several IBM operating systems. The electronic mail system used IBM's **OfficeVision/MVS** software along with a sophisticated front end to handle touch screen operations. Other IBM software on the mainframes included the MVS/ESA operating system, CICS and **Information Management System (IMS)** transaction processors, **DATABASE2 (DB2)** relational databases, and VTAM networking software, among other software packages.

The client systems ran on over 2500 PS/2 computers throughout Norway. IBM developed 40 different software configurations for different needs, but all the PS/2 systems ran OS/2 and most ran CICS. They also ran common software for personal productivity, such as **WordPerfect** for DOS word processing software and **Lotus 1-2-3** spreadsheet software. Across the 16 Olympic venues, IBM installed 250 token-ring LANs, running SNA software as part of the Olympic Network. IBM token-ring **bridges** and **3745 Communications Controllers** tied all the networks into a single Olympic Network.

Between middle-tier servers and back end servers, WAN lines ran SNA as well. IBM used its **Netview** network management and automation software, running on MVS/ESA, to monitor and manage the SNA network. Operations staff distributed and installed software changes to all of the systems using a mixture of custom software and IBM's **Netview Distribution Manager**. Whenever a client system restarted, it checked with the server to find out if it needed an update. If so, the server sent new files automatically to the client before any applications started.

Other servers included IBM **Application System/400 (AS/400)** computers and IBM RISC System/6000 computers. All the back end servers ran CICS transaction processing software, and used CICS' built in services to send messages and transactions over the SNA network.

The Lillehammer Olympic Organizing Committee used the AS/400 for such applications as ticket booking, accommodations management, transportation management, and facilities booking. It exchanged information with the ES/9000 mainframe systems, but it also acted as a server for some applications. Transport became a crucial application, because private transport was banned from the Olympic area during the day. Even residents applied for transportation tickets. The transport system allocated and reserved transportation according to accreditation: press, athlete, employee, resident, and so forth.

Why Client/Server Computing at the Olympics?

Without client/server computing, the Olympic system would have been much harder to use. As a result, fewer people would have the benefit of the information flowing throughout the Games. Broadcasters would need specially trained personnel to relay results, increasing their costs. Using client/server computing, the results management system grew more responsive. Once, it took two to three seconds to post a result; now it takes 300 milliseconds. Here is where client/server computing excels: processing information in new ways, taking advantage of smaller computers, and using innovative ways to interact with users.

As a result of this successful client/server project, IBM will provide technology, products, and services for the 1996 Summer Olympics in Atlanta, the 1998 Winter Games in Nagano, Japan, and the 2000 Summer Games in Sydney. IBM expects to use updated versions of the software proven in Lillehammer in these upcoming games.

An Update: IBM and the 1996 Olympic Games

In 1996, IBM's efforts will be larger and more far-reaching than in 1994. While many components are similar, now IBM will use the Internet to distribute information about the Games to people around the world. IBM's hardware contributions include 7,000 PCs, 80 advanced midrange servers, 18 scientific processors, 4 mainframe servers, 1,000 desktop laser printers, and 250 LANs.

Most of this technology will work in a three-tiered client/server environment. When the Games are over, IBM will generate three trillion bytes of data. If printed, the stream of paper containing this data would stretch from here to the moon.

IBM will rely on its operating systems, DB2 relational databases, CICS transaction processing manager, and MQSeries messaging technology for the real-time parts of the system. This includes the Results Management system. In 1996, the Results Management system uses wired and wireless LANs to post official scores in under a second. Results are stored in a relational database on a PC server at the venue, and then communicated to a mainframe server. Each LAN can function independently; if communication to the mainframe server is interrupted, the data is refreshed immediately when communication is restored.

The Results Management system updates the Commentator Information System (CIS). These PC-based notebooks will provide broadcasters with background information about athletes along with results from up to nine concurrent events. Biographical and background information is stored on the midrange servers. So, a commentator will see the athlete crossing the finish line, and literally be able to look down and see the results on their PC. The CIS uses a touch-screen interface, so little training is needed; the notebook looks like the Sports Information Book, the sports announcer's "bible". By touching a "tab" on the notebook, a broadcaster can find the winning athlete's biography, including comparative results from earlier competitions.

The Results Management sytem also updates the World Wide Web. When a result comes in, the mainframe servers transmit it to IBM's WWW servers. Within a second or two of the event's completion, the results, along with background information about the Games and the participants, is available on the WWW. If you're Internet literate, point your browser at http://www.atlanta.olympic.org for more details.

Info '96 kiosks will be placed throughout Olympic venues and at the Olympic Village. Wireless LAN technology simplifies their setup and operation. The electronic mail component of Info '96 includes message based requests for translations; if an Olympic participant receives a message that must be translated, the messaging software queues the request and forward the translated information appropriately. Info '96 will offer information about schedules, results, background information, Olympic history, cultural events, and weather. For Olympic participants, it provides an electronic mail system and an interactive electronic bulletin board.

Finally, IBM is providing a Games Management System. Running the Olympics is like operating the world's largest hotel chain while concurrently running 34 Super Bowls. Accreditation, security, crime prevention, medical emergency preparedness, and supply management are all part of this system's responsibilities. With IBM's Lotus Notes software, security and logistics personnel can collaborate to ensure the Games proceed as smoothly as possible.

Without client/server computing, this task would be impossible, not merely monumental. Harnessing the diverse strengths of the computers in these systems is the key to their success. Without the mainframe server's huge, fast storage, the reliable networks, and the PC's touch screen, the CIS wouldn't be nearly as effective. Without networks, the PC's friendliness, and the advanced midrange server's sophistication, Info '96 would fail. Taken together, client/server computing let IBM build a more effective system.

3

Networking: The Foundation of Client/Server Computing

A client/server system needs a reliable way for clients and servers to communicate. In this chapter, we'll investigate the many ways that computers and the software running on them can "talk" to one another. Building and supporting a network comprises much of the cost of installing and operating a client/server system. As a result, ensuring a solid, reliable network is a critical first step in building an effective client/server system.

Network design today is practiced by the skilled and the careful, the well meaning and the misinformed, and the incompetent. English majors with no I/S operational experience practice network design regularly in the trade press. Sometimes, technicians know one network or suite of products well and design everything around it. That approach may work at first, but it usually isn't cost-effective or easily changed.

A solid client/server network design considers capital costs, ongoing costs, added or changed performance needs, the costs of downtime, and the ability of your firm's staff to operate the network. When a new or changed application is considered, the network's design is reviewed and possibly changed. Many technological aspects are considered in this review. A smaller application, say, for a workgroup, needs much less engineering. Either way, you'll want to understand what your designers are asking you to approve and fund.

First, we'll give you a view of how designers look at data networks. We'll start our journey with the world's biggest network: the telephone system. Next, we'll consider the tools available to data network designers. Then, we'll look at concrete designs from IBM, relating them to the earlier discussion.

Network Design Basics and Trade-Offs

We defined the term "network" back in our first chapter as "a collection of compatible paths between points." Designers of networks, networking equipment, and networking software struggle to balance seven components: cost, distance, reliability, capacity, delay, fairness, and compatibility. The network that underpins your client/server systems will be no different.

The Fonhome Telephone Company

To illustrate these components, let's start a hypothetical firm, the FonHome Telephone Company, and build its network. Although FonHome runs a telephone network, the ideas discussed apply to data communications networks as well. First, FonHome must decide how to connect all the telephones. It need not worry if customers speak English, Spanish, or Swahili, or if they attach strange new machines that communicate using the network's wiring. All FonHome provides is a pathway over which electrical signals can flow.

How could FonHome connect the telephones inexpensively and reliably? Looking at costs, cabling is a large capital investment, so FonHome might want to avoid using too much cable. Figure 3.1 shows a simple solution, which strings wires between every possible pair of telephones.

Unfortunately, this network is costly. Also, the expense grows quickly with every telephone added. When FonHome adds telephone number 10,000, it needs 9999 new lines, one to each of the existing 9999 telephones. On the other hand, with every telephone directly connected to every other telephone, when one line broke, only one pair of telephones would fail. So, this impractically expensive telephone network design would be quite reliable.

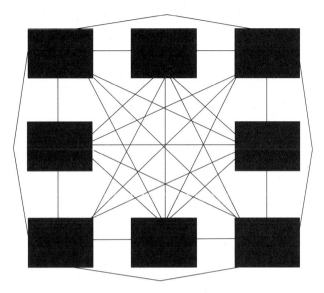

Figure 3.1. A fully connected network.

FonHome's Exchange

A more realistic approach uses a centralized **switch,** or an exchange, to restrict cabling costs. This exchange becomes FonHome's network hub. Now, FonHome only needs one "wire" from the switch to each telephone, and the exchange connects the telephones to each other as needed.

Early exchanges used many operators to connect calls. Then, mechanical exchanges let customers connect their own calls. This automatic switch revolutionized the telephone industry, and FonHome wants to use one. To use the automatic switch, each telephone needs a unique number, or **address,** making it known to the switch and to other telephone users. The telephone itself contains a device that communicates with the switch, say, a dial or a set of numbered buttons. When subscribers dial a telephone number, they tell FonHome's automated switch the address of the telephone they want to reach. However, if the telephone switch breaks, all of the attached telephones stop working until FonHome fixes the switch.

Shaping FonHome's Network

Next, FonHome must decide whether to use "party lines" or to run a cable to each telephone subscriber. Without party lines, FonHome's network **topology**, or shape, would resemble a star centered on the main switch. Networking technicians call this a star topology. If FonHome allowed party lines, it would run a single wire along poles to each affected subscriber, splicing a connection to the subscriber's home. In networking jargon, the main copper line is a **bus** and the splices are **drops**. Although the party line is shared, each telephone still has a separate address. Figure 3.2 shows how this might look.

Party lines are cheaper to build because they need less cable. People using the party line, though, need a social **protocol** to help them decide who can use the telephone at a given time. FonHome could help subscribers to use a party line correctly by teaching them the proper social protocol to use to ensure fair access to the shared line. Similarly, a social protocol could deter people from eavesdropping.

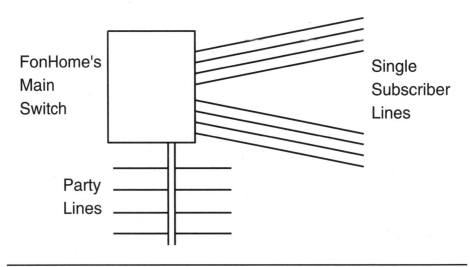

Figure 3.2. FonHome's network structure with one switch.

How FonHome's Telephones Work

FonHome's telephones work like this: First, a voice's vibrations move air toward a microphone in the telephone. The microphone converts these acoustic waves into electromagnetic pulses. As the electrical waves travel across lines, they change shape due to interference, or **noise**, from outside sources. They also decay the longer they travel, like waves in a pond. So, FonHome must rejuvenate, or **repeat**, the waves occasionally to send these waves a long distance. For this, FonHome uses electrically powered devices called **repeaters**. FonHome's telephone lines thus reside near reliable power sources. Eventually, the waveform reaches the target telephone, which changes it back into acoustic waves. In this way, an ordinary phone system transmits voices over copper wiring. This process is an **analog** process: A telephone simply converts one kind of waveform into another, analogous, waveform and back again.

Business Is Great—FonHome Plans Expansion

FonHome's business is doing well, and its switch is full; it can't add more telephones (or customers) to the network. FonHome could get a bigger switch, or it could develop a way for several switches to work together. The second idea holds two advantages: It can grow to serve far more subscribers than a single large switch, and the copper lines don't need to be as long if FonHome can distribute the switches among their subscribers.

However, lines between switches, called **trunks**, must carry more calls than the lines from the switch to the subscriber. You might think of trunk lines like the trunk of a tree; they are "bigger." From a telephone to a switch, FonHome carries one call at a time; between switches, it must handle many more calls simultaneously. FonHome will need several lines between the switches, one for each concurrent call. FonHome also might **route** the bundles of copper wiring along different paths, because a broken cable between switches disconnects more customers than a broken line to a single subscriber. FonHome would also want to arrange the switches into a more complex topology, such as a ring or a triangle, to provide for future growth and greater reliability.

Multiplexing Increases FonHome's Efficiency

Next, FonHome hired an electrical engineer to find a way to carry several calls on a single FonHome trunk line. The assumption here is this: The electrical equipment needed costs less than stringing more trunks. This person finds that FonHome can send multiple calls on a single line using **multiplexing** (muxing). Of course, FonHome must sort out the calls on the other side of the line; **demultiplexing** (demuxing) does this.

The engineer explains two muxing/demuxing techniques. One approach combines many analog signals into one, more complex waveform. A newer method converts analog waveforms into a series of electrical pulses in the switch. These pulses, called **digital signals** can have the value of "on" or "off" at any instant. Switches transmit these pulses very quickly and accurately to other switches. When the pulses reach the target switch, it changes them back into analog waveforms. This approach costs more at first, but it improves quality, so FonHome chooses it. Now, FonHome uses a different system for sending voice calls between switches than it uses between a subscriber and the first switch. The customers don't notice the difference because their telephones remain the same; their interface to the network doesn't change.

Avoiding Disruptions By Automatically Rerouting Calls

Multiplexed trunks increase capacity, and using digital transmission makes calls sound clearer. However, if the line or the electronics on either side breaks, FonHome disconnects several existing calls, and new calls may not complete. Here, FonHome may want to find a way to reroute calls around a network failure. It may need to design protocols that work between switches to help them track the network's current topology. FonHome will also want to monitor the network's state, perhaps using a centralized **network management system** to react to changes in the network.

FonHome Acquires the Behemoth Telephone Company

FonHome is busily and profitably connecting its switches, and its CEO notices a firm across the country in financial trouble. The Behemoth Telephone Company expanded too quickly and weathered a recent recession badly. FonHome's Board of Directors decides to go into the long distance business and acquires Behemoth.

Now, FonHome wants to connect the two firm's switches. So, it upgrades the old Behemoth switches to use the new digital technology. This works, but now customers notice a problem talking to people across the country. Sometimes it seems to take a long time for their voice to get through, and callers sometimes interrupt each other. The path these connections take is too long; the **latency**, or delay, to get through all of the switches and all of the lines is too long to allow a normal telephone conversation. To remedy the situation, FonHome now must add lines or remove switches from the path to reduce the delay.

FonHome Cooperates With Competitors to Ensure Compatibility

FonHome's competitors have expanded too. Now, one firm's customers want to talk to other companies' subscribers. So, FonHome must connect its switches to competitors' switches. This can only occur if FonHome's multiplexing and rerouting schemes are compatible with a competitor's methods. If FonHome develops, say, a more powerful multiplexing scheme, it might need to share it with competitors to profit from it. Otherwise, FonHome's customers would be isolated from other subscribers. Broad telephone connectivity is now more important to FonHome's customers than improvements in efficiency; an incompatible scheme doesn't give FonHome a competitive advantage. Figure 3.3 shows how part of FonHome's network now looks.

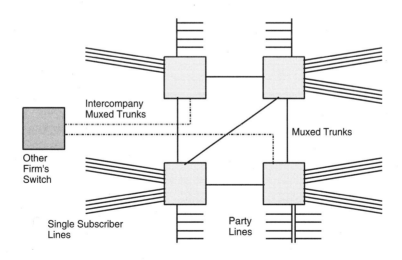

Figure 3.3. FonHome's network structure.

Building Blocks for Data Networks

Real telephone networks are more complex than FonHome's, but FonHome's concerns weren't trivial. It encountered networking's major issues: cost, distance, reliability, capacity, delay, fairness, and compatibility. Every time FonHome's business grew, it changed the network to adapt to that growth. As the business climate changed, the network adapted to those changes too. However, FonHome didn't worry about the compatibility of each telephone attached to its network. It simply provided a reliable electrical pathway between two addressable points: FonHome provided connectivity on demand.

In a voice network, this simplicity makes sense. If a voice waveform became slightly distorted along the way, the listening party might hear some distortion. Because the human ear and brain are highly trained and sophisticated, this distortion usually causes no problems. At worst, the listener might ask the speaker to say something again.

Networks of communicating computers, called **data networks**, care more about compatibility. Computers attach significance to sequences of digital pulses, so the network must take great care to transport these correctly. Otherwise, a $900 deposit might quickly become a $100 deposit. Sometimes, a data sequence may be split in the network. Some parts may take a different path through the network than others. They might arrive out of order. The receiving computer must somehow correctly reconstruct the original stream. Different computers may also use different techniques to communicate; no one way to build data networks exists.

Today's data networks can be best understood and evaluated by examining five key elements of data network design:

- Switching and multiplexing techniques

- Topologies

- Traffic management

- Standards and specifications

- The Open Systems Interconnect Model

Before we look more closely at each of these elements, let's first look at how computers represent information and discuss shorthand ways to define data networking speeds and capacities.

How Computers and Data Networks Represent Information

Because humans communicate by speaking, which creates sound waves, FonHome's fictitious telephone network transported electrical analog waves between humans. Almost all computers used today store and process information in digital formats. Because data networks are designed to move information between computers, they employ digital formats similar to those used in computers.

More specifically, computers encode each piece of information, like a character or a number, into a series of **binary digits** called **bits**. A bit must have a value of either 0 or 1, just as, for example, a switch must be either on or off. In fact, a switch can represent the value of the bit. You'll note the similarity between these bits and the digital pulses FonHome used between their telephone switches.

Many electrical devices including relays, vacuum tubes, transistors, and integrated circuits, act as switches, and can represent bits. Properly combined and coordinated, these switches can perform mathematical calculations or other operations on information represented by the switches. These switches turn off and on quickly, allowing computers and other devices built with them to process information encoded into bits quickly.

Most computers group bits into larger units. A group of eight bits taken together is called an octet or, more commonly, a **byte**. Some computers also have **words**, which can be comprised of 16, 32, 36, 64, or even more bits, but people who build data networks usually think about bytes.

Computer writers use a kind of shorthand when discussing many bits and bytes. A **KiloByte (KB)** equals 1024 bytes (2 to the 10th power), but most people use it as a synonym for 1000 bytes. Computers work easily with powers of two, like 256 or 1024, but people find powers of 10, like 100 or 1000, simpler. The abbreviation for a kilobit is Kb, and a million bits (properly, two to the 20th power) make up a **Megabit (Mb)**. (Note the lowercase b, referring to bits.) A billion bytes is called a **GigaByte (GB)**, and a million bytes is a **MegaByte (MB)**. (Note the uppercase B, referring to bytes.) Finally, if one of these abbreviations is followed by ps, this stands for per second. So, 100 MB means roughly 100 million bytes of data, and 56 Kbps means about 56,000 bits per second.

How Digital Networks Make Switching Decisions

Like FonHome's network, data networks make switching decisions. Two commonplace switching technologies exist: circuit switching and packet switching. A new technique, cell switching, is starting to see deployment. The kinds of switching a network, especially a WAN, uses is crucial. They affect the network's ongoing cost and reliability characteristics. They also define whether time sensitive data, such as digitized video or voice, will be delivered when an application needs it.

Circuit switching works like a telephone call. When you call someone, your carrier allocates part of its network's processing and memory capacity to you. When you hang up or when some event in the network causes a problem, the network releases the capacity for someone else. If the network cuts you off, you redial to get a new circuit. Circuit switching provides predictable, very short delays—a significant advantage for some applications, especially digitized voice and video. Most circuit switching devices, like traditional multiplexers (muxes), use **Synchronous Transfer Mode**. If a mux port has no data to send, then the time allotted to that port is filled with "idle" signals. The receiving mux knows to ignore any such signals, but they can waste expensive WAN capacity. This costly inefficiency is the main disadvantage of circuit switching.

Packet switching works differently. Here, the digital data stream is broken up into variably sized chunks called **packets**. Devices in the network switch each packet, one at a time. If a part of the network breaks, the rest of the network can often reroute packets around the failure. Packets may be lost, delayed, or retransmitted. Packet switching, however, incurs large, variable delays, especially when packets are lost or retransmitted. It is therefore not suitable for applications that require low or constant delays. Packet switched video, for example, can be jittery and tiring to watch.

Cell switching, a new technique, uses fixed-length cells to represent data, voice, and video. Cells arrive at a switch on different ports. The switch operates at very high speeds and forwards cells only for those ports that need to send information. This forwarding technique is called **Asynchronous Transfer Mode (ATM)**, in contrast to circuit switching's Synchronous Transfer Mode. ATM is more complex, but it works at higher speeds: Large ATM switches can transfer over 50 billion bits per second with very low delays per cell. ATM cell switching can provide the best of both worlds: It provides both low delays and nondisruptive rerouting around failures. Also, for the first time, ATM lets network designers use the same fast technology for WAN and LAN lines.

Multiplexing Conserves Capacity and Decreases Costs

Multiplexing is a major element in today's data networks. Broadly defined, multiplexing optimizes the use of an expensive object. A multiplexer (mux) is the heart of most circuit switched networks, because the mux switches information from many smaller lines into a few trunk lines. FonHome used multiplexing to economically increase capacity between switches. In a digital voice or data network, muxes combine many smaller lines into faster lines, resulting in less overall cost.

An Example: Multiplexing Trailers Onto Railroads

Multiplexing works with many kinds of networks. Consider a transportation network: A shipping firm might contract a railroad to carry many trailers "piggyback" between major cities, say, Chicago and Los Angeles. Trucks arrive in Chicago, and the railroad loads their trailers onto piggyback flatcars. Then, a train carrying many trailers travels to Los Angeles. Upon arrival, the railroad unloads the trailers and other trucks take them to their destinations. Using the railroad is cheaper, and possibly faster, than paying many drivers to take the trailers one by one.

How Multiplexed Voice and Data Networks Work

Multiplexed voice and data networks work similarly. Here, digital signals represent voice, video, and data. Muxes collect bits from many ports, combine them onto a few trunk lines, and reverse the process at the other end. Figure 3.4 shows a simple muxed configuration. If a trunk is much cheaper than stringing many lines, the mux and the labor pay for themselves easily. In the 1980s, this practice became common, with many large firms buying muxes and relying on carriers only for trunk lines. Carriers themselves also use muxes internally, combining signals from many customers into high-speed trunks.

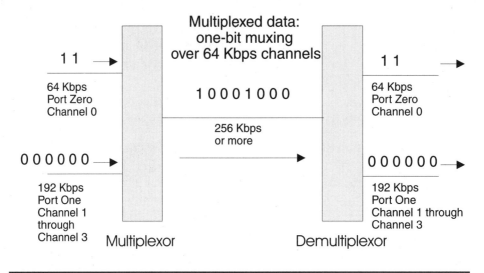

Figure 3.4. Multiplexing and demultiplexing data.

Shaping Networks with Topologies

The third important element of data networking is **topology**, the pattern in which the devices participating in the network are connected. A good topology places WAN lines, LANs, clients, servers, and network switching devices in a structure that is well understood, predictable, and easily supported. A network's topology affects a client/server application's predictability, performance, and reliability. Poor topology decisions can also increase capital and support costs.

Figure 3.5 shows several common topologies used alone or combined in data networks. Effective, large networks combine topologies in a hierarchy to form the overall network.

When we discussed FonHome, we first considered a **fully meshed topology**, since each telephone had a wire to every other telephone. This was highly reliable, but expensive. A **partially meshed topology**, created by removing lines from a fully meshed network, saves money and provides nearly equal reliability. FonHome used a partial mesh between switches. In data networks, partially meshed WAN links are common for the same reasons. A **star topology**, which looks like a hub with spokes, is inexpensive compared with meshes, but the hub creates a single point of failure. A **bus topology**, like FonHome's party lines, is cheaper still, but it exposes more stations to a connection failure than a star. FonHome didn't use a

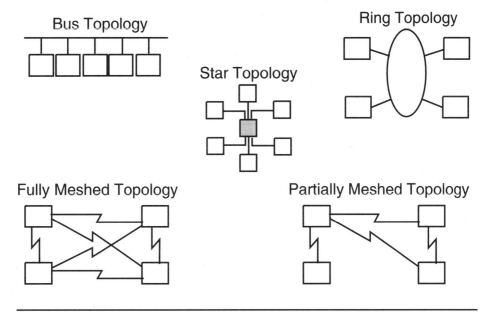

Figure 3.5. Typical networking topologies.

ring topology, although real telephone networks sometimes do. The star, ring, and bus all find use in data networks today.

Often, a topology decision also defines how a device accesses the network. For example, an Ethernet LAN uses a bus topology, and works very much like FonHome's party lines. Unlike FonHome's party lines, though, Ethernet includes no "high priority" way to use the line. A token-ring LAN, on the other hand, uses a ring topology, and it tries to ensure fair access to the ring: Permission to put data onto the ring rotates around the ring from one device to the next. It also has a priority scheme. So, fairness becomes a part of a topology decision.

A network's topology directly affects its reliability. If a client's link to a server traverses three devices, it will likely be less reliable than one that spans one or two devices. Usually, the fewer devices and links between a client and a server, the better.

If reliability is critical, a network can contain redundant components and links. A properly planned mesh topology will achieve redundancy, but it can become complex to understand, manage, diagnose, and fix. Most topologies can be **duplexed**, allowing two connections between a device and the network. Figure 3.6 depicts several possible duplexed topologies. Duplexing increases reliability, and it adds minimal complexity.

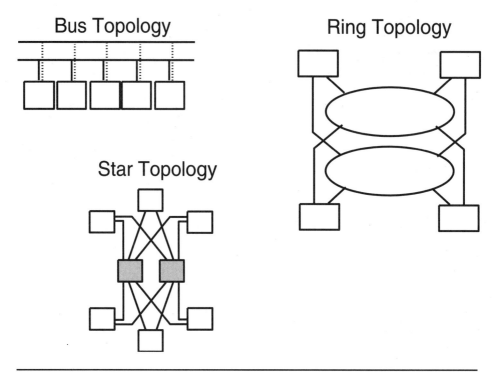

Figure 3.6. Common redundant topologies.

Designers sometimes divide a network's topology into sections or compartments, so a failure in one part of the network can't easily cascade. This improves the network's reliability much like a ship's watertight compartments. If one compartment of many springs a leak, the ship still shouldn't sink. If one part of the network breaks or becomes confused, the failure shouldn't spread and hurt the whole network. All of these decisions affect a network's topology.

Within and between topologies, a data network must send data to the correct destination. This is accomplished using **addressing** along with switching, **bridging**, and **routing**. Within a topology, it may be possible to simply address an end point with a local address. This is common in LANs. Using a local address is like dialing a colleague's extension rather than using the full number.

Figure 3.7 shows an example of addressing within and between topologies: A star topology connects the end stations to the switches; a ring connects the switches to each other. Within a switch, it one end station might address another by using only the last few digits. Perhaps station

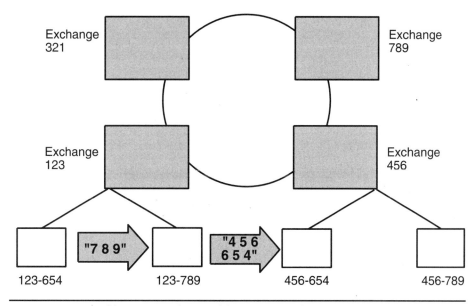

Figure 3.7. Addressing within and between topologies.

123-456 could address station 123-789 simply by connecting to address 789. However, for station 123-789 to address station 456-654, it must use all six digits. The first three define the target switch; the last three describe the target end station.

In a hierarchy of topologies, more complex schemes forward data correctly. Three major techniques exist to help get data to the correct place: switching, bridging, and routing. Switching is the simplest approach, routing is the most complex, and bridging is in between. As complexity increases, so does delay. Selecting appropriate topologies, along with finding the correct mix of switching, bridging, and routing forms part of the "art" in engineering data networks.

Automating Traffic Management

The fourth element in designing data networks is traffic management. In most data networks, especially packet switched data networks, a designer cannot predict exactly how the network will be used from minute to minute. A network's lines and devices usually won't keep up with demand during peak loads. When traffic fills lines, data awaiting transmission fills memory in **Data Communications Equipment (DCE)**. FonHome's switches and muxes might be considered DCE. In data networks, DCE includes devices such as bridges, switches, routers, and muxes.

When Networks Need a Decongestant

Congestion occurs when DCEs can no longer accept incoming data. Perhaps a DCE ran out of memory or processor capacity, or several bursts of traffic converged on it at once. When congestion occurs, the DCE may discard data or send it too late. This doesn't happen in voice telephony, so there's no analogy. You'd have to imagine your voice getting lost between switches.

Uncontrolled congestion is evil. In congested data networks, the sending **Data Terminal Equipment (DTE)** eventually sends the data again, asking the congested DCE or line to do more work. Congestion's effects snowball throughout the network, slowing or stopping all traffic. **Congestion avoidance** tries to avoid this condition; **congestion control** responds to it. For convenience, we'll call these techniques congestion management.

Some networks permit **priority** traffic. Priority is most meaningful when a line or a DCE is congested. Where priority exists, devices clear the way for time sensitive, higher priority traffic, perhaps by discarding or delaying less important traffic. For example, traffic to terminals usually receives a higher priority than traffic to printers. Some protocols have only high and low priority, but others use several priority levels. Usually, network management traffic gets the highest priority, since it can help to resolve congestion or other problems slowing traffic. This resembles the practice of pulling over to let emergency vehicles through to clear a wreck on a freeway.

A network's congestion management method and priority scheme decide a network's effectiveness under moderate and heavy traffic loads. Better congestion management smooths the peaks and valleys of traffic between devices. Lower priority traffic may suffer delay, but the most important traffic gets through predictably. Several congestion management and priority methods exist, some more effective than others. Good congestion management methods lower the cost to build and operate a predictable, reliable network.

Metering the Network's Entrance Ramps

While congestion management keeps data flowing through DCEs, **flow control** and **class of service** support keep both DCEs and DTEs working smoothly. When a receiving device cannot remove traffic quickly enough from the network, flow control tells the sender to put traffic into the network more slowly. Flow control works like the traffic signals on some freeway entrance ramps. At peak times, allowing cars onto the freeway at the rate drivers want to enter can cause congestion. So, these signals allow only a few cars onto the freeway at a time. Sometimes, they only allow one or two cars at time to proceed. At other times, they might let several cars on. Traffic engineers can sometimes change this behavior, adapting to current conditions.

Class of service support treats different kinds of traffic to the same end device differently. For example, terminal traffic to a personal computer from a TP monitor is usually more delay sensitive than printer output destined for the same PC. Class of service support lets you define how your network's devices behave under load.

Two ways exist to provide flow control and class of service support. One technique places these services in every DCE and DTE in the network. Then, as data is switched through the network, the next DCE in the path signals back to the current DCE that it can receive more data. This approach works best when the path a packet takes is known in advance. Traditional SNA uses this technique.

The second approach relies on DTEs only. One way is to have DTEs detect when they are placing too much information onto the network. Then, each DTE slows the data flow. A newer way has DTEs request speed and delay characteristics for each connection into the network. The network either grants or scales back these requests, depending on conditions. As it responds, the network might reserve the necessary processor, line, and memory resources for the connection. This idea is a bit like asking a freeway if you can go 140 kilometers per hour and being told the allowable speed.

Typically, most protocols, especially those designed for LAN use, provide only a rudimentary flow control. SNA, APPN, and OSI do better than most. Using flow control and class of service allows a designer to better predict how the network will react to heavy loads. The network can also use less expensive WAN links.

Without these control mechanisms, as a DTE becomes overloaded, it discards frames. Then, the originating station retransmits them. Senders thus inject useless, costly traffic into the network, because the receiver can't process it anyway. If slower links exist in the network, these extra frames can block or delay other, useful traffic. This cycle of sending frames again continues until the target system can process them quickly enough. With flow control and congestion management, specific data transfers might be slowed to ensure fair, reliable delivery for all the network's users.

Who Invents and Publishes Networking Standards?

Since standards are important to networking, let's pause and see where they come from. Several organizations create and publish standards. They take their guidance from academic researchers, computer companies, carriers, and engineers. In the data networking industry, several different spheres of influence exist. One set of groups influence specifications and standards for wide area networking; others consider topics such as local area networking and building wiring.

Standards Bodies for WANs

Several bodies influence standards in wide area networking for both voice and data networking. Wide Area Networks (WANs) typically use copper telephone lines or fiber optic lines provided by a long distance carrier or a government **Postal, Telephone, and Telegraph (PTT)** ministry. Telephone vendors and carriers therefore greatly influence WAN standards.

Foremost among bodies considering WAN recommendations is the **Comité Consultatif International Télégraphique et Téléphonique (CCITT)**. It is part of the **International Telecommunications Union (ITU)**, a body sponsored by the United Nations. In 1993, the UN reorganized the ITU, and so the CCITT is now called the **ITU Telecommunications Standardization Sector (ITSS or ITU-T)**. Despite the new name, many people still call it the CCITT, and, for now, so will we.

The CCITT makes recommendations for end-to-end services and interface services in public networks, but many organizations, including PTTs, consider these recommendations mandatory. CCITT recommendation **X.400** is a good example. It defines an electronic messaging service, while **X.500** defines how a message should be addressed. An X.500 address is valid anywhere in the world. The **International Standards Organization (ISO)**, the American National Standards Institute (ANSI), and other national standards bodies play key roles in defining WAN standards.

LAN Standards Bodies

In the 1980s, LANs became nearly a universal way to connect computers in an office or on a campus. Computer vendors influence LAN designs more than telephone companies or government agencies do. Because of this, groups of professionals in the computer industry take on important roles in defining standards.

The **International Institute of Electrical Engineers (IEEE)**, defines most LAN standards. Their recommendation 802, written in several sections, specifies various ways to wire and pass signals over LANs. **IEEE 802.3**, for example, defines how IEEE-compliant Ethernet LANs work, and **IEEE 802.5** defines how token-ring LANs work. Usually, the **ISO** adopts IEEE's LAN standards, as it adopts telephony standards defined by the CCITT and other organizations.

De Jure Standards, or Standards By Rule

Networking jargon calls standards defined by organizations such as the CCITT, ISO, and IEEE **de jure standards**. Translated somewhat loosely, this means "standards by rule." The process for defining and publishing a standard is long and hard, since companies and countries with competing interests must find acceptable compromises. This stability is desirable, but it slows adoption of technical advances between revisions of the standard.

Other Kinds of Recommendations and Specifications

Other kinds of recommendations and specifications exist besides de jure standards. Sometimes, a vendor wants to increase market share for a kind of product. With the idea that a rising tide lifts all boats, the vendor publishes a specification while retaining control over it. Most often, firms producing compatible products pay a royalty or a license fee to the inventing organization. We'll call this a **published specification**.

Sometimes a group of vendors or users forms a consortium, and that group defines and publishes its view of how to build networks. We'll call this a **consortium specification**. The Open Software Foundation (OSF) publishes specifications about distributed, multivendor computing, for example. Vendors pay royalties to the OSF if they use the OSF's technologies. Other published specifications, for example, most of those for the Internet, are in the public domain, freely available to anyone. A vendor can create compatible products without paying fees to the inventor.

Finally, some groups, such as the **ATM Forum** and the **Frame Relay Forum**, develop specifications for vendors to use. These groups are composed of ATM and frame relay vendors and users. Their specifications help vendors to choose between options in de jure standards. If vendors chose different, compliant, options, two products that comply with a standard still might not work together. Sometimes, consortia also extend the work of organizations like the CCITT.

800-Pound Gorillas Create "De Facto Standards"

Some pundits call unpublished specifications standards, particularly when discussing a market leading product. One reads regularly about products that are compatible with the "Microsoft Windows standard," the "Novell NetWare standard," or other "standards." Some call these **de facto** standards.

These are not standards; they are proprietary products with high market share. Nowhere does Microsoft or Novell openly publish a specification that lets other vendors produce products to compete with Windows or NetWare. No international organization monitors the balance of interest between Microsoft and Windows 95 users. When Microsoft wants to change its product, it simply changes it. This isn't evil, because businesses regularly use proprietary products to build useful systems. They're just not standards. We'll call them "unpublished specifications."

Summary of Specifications, Recommendations, and Standards

The characteristics of the most common specifications used in building networks are summarized in Figure 3.8. The table, though, omits "marketplace acceptance." Specifications not "ratified by the market" achieve slow or limited acceptance in the United States. For example, the **Integrated**

Services Digital Network (ISDN), is a set of de jure networking standards slowly being carried out in the United States. PTTs in Europe and Japan built and sold ISDN aggressively, with lower usage prices than in the United States. So, ISDN sees greater use to date in Europe and Japan than in the United States, even if it is a de jure standard.

Standard or Specification Type	Owner	Creation and Modification Process	Time Needed For Modification
"de jure"	National and international standards bodies	Members vote; uses formal, documented processes	Longest (years); up to 4 years between revisions
Forum or consortium specification	Vendor/user consortium like the ATM Forum or the Frame Relay Forum	Members vote; committee work	Moderate (months to years)
Proprietary, published	Vendor or consortium, but others can implement for a fee	Owners change in response to their customers' demands	Possibly some-what longer than unpublished specifications
"RFC"; Internet standard	User consortium, represented by IETF (Internet Engineering Task Force)	Multiple vendors implement; consensus emerges; IETF ratifies	Moderate
Proprietary, unpublished	Vendor	Vendors change in response to their customers' demands	Moderate (can't alienate large installed base)

Figure 3.8. Characteristics of common specifications used in building networks.

The OSI Model

Our sixth building block is a model used to describe, study, and understand data networks, namely, the OSI Model. The OSI Model is based on **layers**. Layers let network designers and developers build a network's functions more flexibly.

Designers must manage several technologies that combine to make a data network. In the 1970s, the ISO developed and approved a seven-layer model to describe data networks: the Open Systems Interconnect reference model, sometimes called the **OSI model**. The diagram used most often to depict the OSI reference model stacks these layers one over another; some people refer such a diagram as a "stack." Sometimes, you'll hear people referring to the "OSI stack" or the "seven-layer stack." Figure 3.9 shows the OSI stack. We'll explain later what each layer does, but first we'll discuss how they relate to each other.

How the Layers Work Together

The ISO believed each computer attaching to the network (a DTE) would contain hardware and software corresponding to all seven layers. It also tried to avoid dependencies between the layers. Layer 1 on the first computer would talk to the second device's first layer, and layer 6 would communicate with layer 6. A given layer is also not complete within itself. Instead, it relies on clearly specified services provided by the lower layers. Figure 3.10 shows how the layers in the OSI stack communicate. Each layer communicates with its peer using a common protocol; it is also common to speak of a "protocol stack" when discussing networks of various types.

DCEs often do not contain all seven layers, since they usually don't run applications or support users. Figure 3.11 shows the relationship between DTEs and DCEs in a network that corresponds to the OSI reference model. Different networks have different numbers of layers in the DCE, but a DCE usually lacks the top 2 to 4 layers of the OSI reference model. A network might have one, two, or many DCEs between DTEs. Finally, in the OSI Reference Model, DCEs may talk with each other using completely different protocols than those used to talk between a DCE and a DTE.

The OSI Reference Model is a framework for discussing how various network designs are similar or different. Many network designs, protocols, and products comply roughly with the model. OSI protocols also exist, giving rise to some confusion. Most protocol stacks correspond roughly

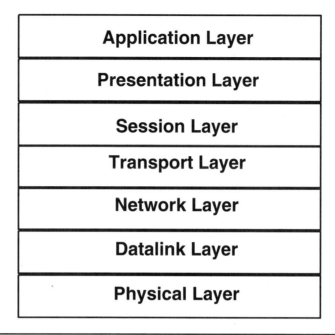

Figure 3.9. The OSI networking reference model.

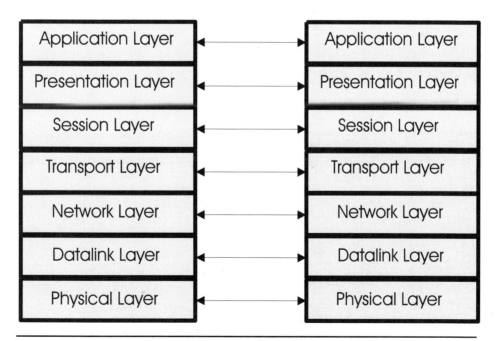

Figure 3.10. How OSI layers appear to communicate.

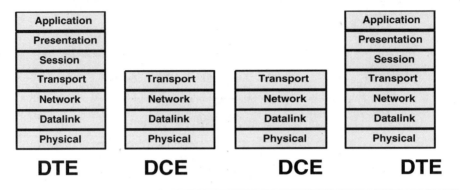

Figure 3.11.   DTEs and DCEs in an OSI Reference Model Network.

to the OSI Reference Model; most do not conform to ISO specified OSI protocols. When products do conform to these standards, their documentation normally includes the relevant ISO specification numbers; this reduces possible confusion in terminology.

To build a compatible network, each layer must talk with a layer in the network's other devices that uses the same specification. So, the OSI Reference Model can help you to visualize where incompatibilities can occur. Connecting one DTE's SNA transport layer to a DCE's TCP/IP transport layer will fail because the layers use different specifications.

A Closer Look at Each OSI Model Layer

The OSI stack contains seven layers:

1. Application Layer

2. Presentation Layer

3. Session Layer

4. Transport Layer

5. Network Layer

6. Datalink Layer

7. Physical Layer

The bottom four layers of the OSI stack, the Physical Layer through the Transport Layer, describe how information flows between devices in a network. The top three layers, the Session Layer through the Application Layer, describe how information flows between the programs and people that use the network.

The **Physical Layer** and the **Datalink Layer** control data transmission between two directly connected devices. Together, they provide a **subnetwork**. Subnetworks usually transmit data reliably between two directly connected devices.

The **Network Layer** transfers packets between any two devices in the network, whether they are directly connected or not. It may or may not be reliable; some Network Layer protocols discard packets when devices or lines become congested. The **Transport Layer**, the fourth layer, is somewhat like the Datalink Layer below it; it ensures reliable, sequenced packet delivery. Instead of delivering frames over a single line, though, the Transport Layer delivers data reliably across the whole network. Sometimes, people call the lowest four layers of the OSI model a **transport network**.

The fifth layer, the **Session Layer**, manages individual flows of data between the applications that use the network. For example, a single computer can maintain several sessions to another system using a single transport connection, managing each session separately. Each session presents the illusion of one reliable network connection to any applications or people who use the network.

The sixth layer, the **Presentation Layer**, encodes information to be passed over a session. Different computers encode text, integers, and other data differently. Sometimes even different lines of computers from the same vendor encode data differently. The Presentation Layer decides which encoding techniques to use for text, integers, and other data items. It also converts data between different schemes. When present and used by an application, the Presentation Layer thus allows computers with different internal encoding schemes to transfer information successfully.

The final layer, the **Application Layer**, is precisely what you'd expect: It's where useful work is done. Designers often use layers within applications, providing "sublayers" of the Application Layer. These are not standardized, however, but specific to each product or approach.

Finally, some of you may have noticed the absence of network management in our discussions so far. The ISO views management as a separate "plane" of the OSI stack. This plane covers all seven layers of the stack, so as a specific layer needs to report an event or receive direction, it can. Figure 3.12 shows the OSI stack along with the network management plane.

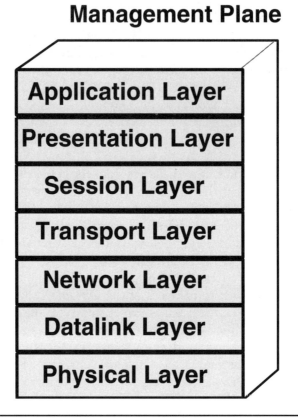

Figure 3.12. The OSI model, including network management.

The Physical Layer

The Physical Layer transmits bits over a physical medium, such as copper wire, optical fiber cable, or microwave carrier waves, accepts a stream of bits or bytes from the layer atop it, and then transmits these to the physical layer of the next device in the network. It only manages one **hop** in the network; if the signal is weak or must be changed, the physical layers of multiple devices cooperate to repeat the signal over the network. The Physical Layer decides such issues as what wiring can be used, how a chip should encode bits into an analog wave, and what frequency a radio link should use. The Physical Layer mediates between a computer's domain of zeros and ones and the world of noisy lines, rain storms, lightning strikes, and imperfect electrical waveforms. It sometimes makes mistakes, which a layer higher in the OSI stack must correct.

The Physical Layer uses three main transmission techniques, which are depicted in Figure 3.13. **Serial** transmission, the most common, is simple: only one bit crosses the link at a time. **Broadband** transmission works like a cable TV system; it can transmit multiple channels over a single cable. Each data channel exists within its own frequency range. All channels are sent together, but an attached device only chooses to see one of them at a time. Similarly, each channel is unaware of the other channels, and you can usually "tune in" to only one channel at a time. **Parallel** transmission isn't used often, but where speed is crucial, it can be faster than serial or broadband transmission.

Finally, two main techniques help electronic devices to interpret waves on a medium correctly. **Synchronous transmission** uses a fast clock in each device to define "slices" of time as waves progress over the medium. During each slice, an attached device measures a voltage and determines if a 0 or a 1 is present. **Asynchronous transmission** uses no clock, relying only on changes in voltages to communicate information. Most digital transmission methods for voice and data use synchronous communications; low-speed data links often use asynchronous methods.

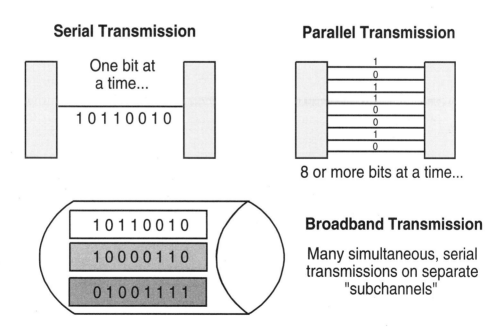

Serial Transmission

One bit at a time...

1 0 1 1 0 0 1 0

Parallel Transmission

1
0
1
1
0
0
1
0

8 or more bits at a time...

10110010
10000110
01001111

Broadband Transmission

Many simultaneous, serial transmissions on separate "subchannels"

Figure 3.13. Serial, parallel, and broadband transmission methods.

The Datalink Layer

Sometimes, the Physical Layer makes mistakes. Layer 2, the **Datalink Layer,** delivers bits reliably over the Physical Layer. It also decides how multiple DTEs can share a common Physical Layer. This becomes important when the Physical Layer is intrinsically shared. LANs, radio networks, and some kinds of WAN lines all need the Datalink Layer to decide which station can transmit at any given time. Many datalink protocols exist. Some fit best for WAN communications; others work best on LANs.

The Datalink Layer defines a **frame,** a unit of multiple bytes that the devices transmit and receive. Figure 3.14 diagrams a hypothetical datalink frame. Frames vary in size, although each datalink protocol defines a minimum and a maximum frame size. Frames contain the data to be sent, along with a **header.** Typical headers include a source address, a destination address, and control bits specified by the datalink protocol used. The frame also contains a **Cyclical Redundancy Check (CRC)** to help detect errors in transmission by the physical layer.

Together with the Physical Layer, the Datalink Layer forms a subnetwork. Subnetworks can contain two attachment points to the network, like a dedicated telephone line between two computers, or dozens, like a LAN. The datalink protocols used decide how higher layers of protocols use the subnetwork, and they decide how fairness is managed in a subnetwork.

Datalink protocols come in two main forms: connectionless and connection oriented. The Datalink Layer is not unique in this regard: The split between connectionless and connection oriented protocols exists also in the Network and Transport layers. In the higher layers, these differences become more pronounced, and I'll discuss them fully after I introduce the Network Layer to you.

| 8 bits Flag/Control | 16 bits Destination | 16 bits Source | 512 bytes Data | 32 bits Checksum |

Figure 3.14. A hypothetical datalink frame.

The Network Layer

The Network Layer decides which paths through the network are valid at any given time, and it manages memory and queues inside DCEs to smooth traffic flows. Unlike the Datalink or Physical layers, it monitors the topology of the entire network. If a route becomes overloaded or fails, the Network Layer finds an alternate path, if one exists. In some Network Layer designs one unit of data may be transferred over one path and the next may use a different path between the same two devices in the network (consider load sharing, for example). Some Network Layer protocols may even deliver data out of order.

Both DTEs and DCEs contain Network Layer software. The DCEs that implement a protocol stack's network layer can be called routers, bridges, or gateways. We will use the ISO term "router" to describe a Network Layer device. Typically, within a protocol stack, routers use one protocol to understand the network's current state and another to decide how to forward packets. We'll call the first kind of protocol a router-to-router protocol, and the second a packet routing protocol. A network's reliability depends on how well these protocols react to changes and use available capacity.

Connectionless Networking Protocols

In a **connectionless** protocol, a sender simply addresses and sends a frame. Sending a frame requires little preparation. The protocol includes a full target address along with a full return address and sends it into the network. If a frame is lost or garbled, higher-layer protocols send the frame again. Connectionless protocols rely on subnetworks with few errors to achieve predictable performance.

The connectionless approach corresponds closely to the techniques used by a postal service. When you send a letter, you don't know how or when your correspondent gets it. You simply address the letter, write your return address, and drop the letter into a mailbox. Theoretically, each time you send a letter, it could take a different path. The postal service routes it according to the conditions on their mail network at the time. Mostly, this approach works well. If your letter requested a response and you don't hear from the recipient soon, you might send the letter again. That is like an upper-layer protocol recovering from a lost frame over a layer using a connectionless protocol. On the other hand, if you received a "notice to disconnect" from your electrical utility before you received a bill, you might not care that lost data sometimes happens in an adaptive, connectionless network.

Adaptive, connectionless networks are robust, but they cause some operational problems. Because no fixed paths between two points exist, finding the cause of a performance problem or a failure becomes more difficult. The network also must adapt quickly if its topology changes or if it forwards packets incorrectly. Sometimes, due to topology changes or load balancing within the network, data arrives at the target DTE in the wrong order. Usually, application software prefers data received in order, so higher-layer protocols must sort received data before delivering it to applications.

Today, many products' Network Layers use connectionless techniques. The ability to reroute traffic around problem spots in the network automatically is highly desirable. Newer router-to-router protocols make large networks with connectionless protocols possible.

Connection-Oriented Networking Protocols

By contrast, **connection-oriented** protocols work like standard telephone service. If you place a telephone call, you first establish a connection, usually by dialing another telephone's number. As you speak, you know quickly if the other party heard you. You also expect the telephone network to deliver your voice in order. If the call goes dead, you also know this quickly, and you can then decide to restart the connection by calling again.

Connection-oriented protocols behave similarly: They use three phases for each communication. The first phase is the **setup phase**. It sets up a connection between the two devices that must communicate. Usually, this connection establishes an explicit path through the network. Also, the devices involved negotiate how the connection will work. This ensures that the sender does not overrun either the receiver or any DCEs along the connection's path.

During the **transfer phase**, information flows between the two DTEs, which monitor the connection. If the connection breaks, they inform higher protocol layers and formally end the connection. Traditionally, higher layers, application software, or users then try to restart the connection, just as if you unexpectedly lost a telephone conversation. Networking writers refer to this as **disruptive rerouting**. Users hate it because it interrupts work in progress. Only a few new connection-oriented protocols, such as IBM's APPN/HPR, provide **nondisruptive rerouting** today.

As the two sides establish a connection, they agree on how they will send and acknowledge frames. Some protocols send several frames before the recipient acknowledges receipt. This makes transmission faster and more efficient. One of a connection-oriented protocol's jobs is to decide how much data to send between these acknowledgments. Too much data may cause DCE congestion if several stations transmit at once. Too little data keeps the DTEs waiting as acknowledgments flow through the network. Because it is hard to choose an optimal amount, most connection-oriented protocols adapt to changes in the network's traffic. Better protocols react more quickly.

Because an analyst can infer a complete path for each connection, network diagnosis becomes simpler. Traffic management usually becomes easier because the network can regulate individual connections as well as aggregated traffic. A connection-oriented Transport Layer can avoid over-burdening the network during times of heavy use. This avoids retransmissions, which gives more predictable performance.

Connection-oriented protocols can reside at the Datalink, Network, and Transport layers of the OSI stack. Most often, the Transport Layer is connection oriented, even if the Network Layer is connectionless. This way, just as the Datalink Layer can fix any Physical Layer errors, the Transport Layer can resolve any errors that a connectionless Network Layer introduces.

Keeping the Topology Map Current: Router-to-Router Protocols

Two main types of router-to-router protocols exist. In the first, the **distance vector** method, each router sends a complete copy of its routing tables to its direct neighbors. These routers then either replace their tables or compare them with the newly received tables, looking for any differences. Most distance vector methods use the first approach. It has a simple disadvantage: If one router has a wrong view of the network, it may inflict this view on other routers as well.

Unfortunately, some common distance vector–based protocols sometimes cannot arrive at a correct, common view of the network. This **convergence** is crucial to the correct operation of the network. If a network isn't converged, data will be forwarded incorrectly or lost. This causes frequent service outages, unpredictable performance, wasted network capacity, and user frustration. In bad cases, the misconverged network may forward data incorrectly indefinitely. Or, a network failure can appear to shift as routers decide one or another is right. A simple typing error can cause problems such as these.

The second class of protocols, the **link state** method, transmits changes in state throughout the network as such changes occur. If a line attached to a router changes state, the router notes this and passes it on to the rest of the network. Routers also exchange periodic "hello" messages. If a router fails to answer, this is also passed on as a state change. When each router in the network receives such a state change, it recomputes its routing tables.

In a stable network, protocols based on the link state method produce less traffic, a useful trait. They do need bigger processors because computing the routing tables in a big network is a big job. In a changing network, routers using link state protocols converge more quickly. More importantly, they do converge. Link state protocols simply work better. Figure 3.15 shows several common protocol stacks, the protocol's predominant vendors, and frequently used router-to-router protocols.

Kind of Network/Vendor	Link State	Distance Vector
TCP/IP networks/various, including IBM	Open Shortest Path First (OSPF)	Routing Information Protocol (RIP), and various unpublished
IPX/SPX networks/Novell and various, including IBM	NetWare Link State Protocol (NLSP)	Routing Information Protocol (RIP)
OSI networks/various, including IBM	IS–IS	None
APPN networks/IBM and various	APPN (built in)	None
APPN/HPR networks/ IBM and various	Built in	None
DECnet/Digital Equipment Corporation	DECnet Phase V (built in)	DECnet Phase IV (built in)

Figure 3.15.   Common protocol stacks.

Packet Routing Protocols

Once the Network Layer knows the network's topology, it can forward packets accurately through it. Like the Datalink Layer, packet routing protocols store information in a header in each frame. The Network Layer header contains either addresses or connection numbers, depending on the protocol. Connectionless protocols use longer, complete addresses. Connection numbers are shorter, using less WAN bandwidth.

Sometimes, network layer headers contain an explicit route through the network, called a **source route**. Source routing is commonly used with connection-oriented protocols. A second possibility, used mostly with connectionless protocols, is called **destination routing**, or **adaptive routing**. It makes a routing decision based only on the destination address in the packet. A third approach, called **label swapping**, works in connection-oriented networks. It alters the packet's header at each hop and inserts the information needed for the next hop. Figure 3.16 shows how source routing, destination routing, and label swapping work. Operational problems are easier to resolve if the protocol uses source routing or label swapping.

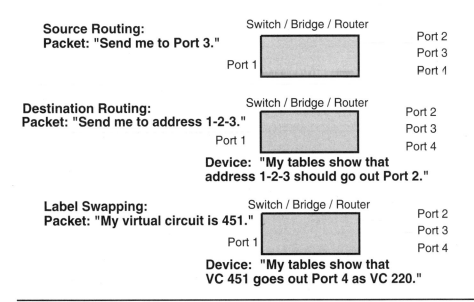

Figure 3.16. Source routing, label swapping, and destination routing.

The Transport Layer

The Transport Layer ensures sequenced, reliable delivery across arbitrary networks of devices. Unlike the Network Layer, found in both DCEs and DTEs, the Transport Layer usually resides only in DTEs. If both connectionless and connection-oriented Network Layers are allowed, the Transport Layer usually assumes all network connections are unreliable and compensate, even if this means doing extra work.

In protocol stacks with reliable, connection-oriented network layers, the Transport Layer has little work to do. Minimally, it sets up and tears down connections, and fragments or coalesces requests for greater efficiency. It multiplexes data from several sources within a computer onto the network and demuxes packets to their proper sessions. It may also manage the flow of information into and out of DTEs, using flow control or quality of service.

In other protocol stacks, a connectionless Network Layer can drop packets or deliver them out of order. The Transport Layer should then retransmit and reorder packets. Without the Transport Layer delivering data reliably and sequentially, each application would need to incorporate the same logic, making software larger, more complex, more expensive, and less reliable. The Transport Layer also plays a key role in congestion detection or avoidance when the stack uses a connectionless Network Layer. With TCP/IP, for example, TCP (the Transport Control Protocol) detects and reacts to congestion.

The Session Layer

The fifth layer is the Session Layer. The lower four layers deliver information across the network between devices; the Session Layer sets up, disconnects, and transfers data between specific sets of programs or users. If the Transport Layer provides a simplex service, where only one side of a transport connection can send at a time, the Session Layer manages when each side can talk. Some protocol stacks, such as TCP/IP, have no Session Layer; some have a "skinny" Session Layer; others have a more comprehensive layer, which can regulate the flow of data into the network more carefully.

In some protocols, such as APPC and APPN, the Session Layer also can **synchronize** transactions across the network. If a transaction requires several network transmissions, the Session Layer can ensure that they are received and acknowledged correctly before continuing into a new transaction. Usually, an application sends data back and forth, and when everything is complete, the controlling system acknowledges that everything is complete and waits for synchronization. For applications like distributed TP monitors or distributed databases, Session Layer synchronization simplifies software while improving its reliability.

The Presentation Layer

The sixth layer, the Presentation Layer, defines how data is presented for transmission over the network. Over the years, vendors developed machines with incompatible ways of encoding numbers, text, and other data items. For example, large IBM systems use a text encoding technique called EBCDIC, whereas personal computers use a technique called ASCII. ASCII and EBCDIC each use one byte to encode a character, but they encode characters differently. Although one byte can encode up to 256 different characters, ASCII started using 128 characters, mostly those useful in the United States. EBCDIC began with 256 characters, including characters suitable for most European languages.

Computers in some Asian countries, which use more characters than their Western cousins, encode their symbols using two bytes instead of one. If a Japanese computer wants to communicate in English with a United States computer that uses ASCII, the Presentation Layer handles this translation. Eventually, perhaps we'll agree on a worldwide, 2-byte standard, such as **Unicode**, but until then translation is needed.

Even if we eventually agree on how to represent text, computers represent binary numbers differently. The chip in the IBM PC, for example, uses up to 32 bits to represent whole numbers. The IBM Application System/400 uses up to 64 bits. Some computers number their bits from "left to right," while others number from "right to left." Assuming eight bits, one type of machine might represent the number 9 as 00001001, whereas the other might encode it as 10010000. Again, the Presentation Layer masks these differences from applications.

Finally, in the ISO view, the Presentation Layer handles such details as data encryption or compression. Some vendors provide encryption and compression devices that work at the Datalink Layer, but the "classical" view encrypts or compresses data before it enters the transport network. So, the Presentation Layer performs this work as well.

The Application Layer

Chapter 5 discusses specific Application Layer issues. Here, we'll examine how the Application Layer differs from the other layers of the OSI model.

The Application Layer decides the semantics of most data transfers. The Session Layer provides a pipe over which data may flow, but the Application Layer determines how that data flows. It decides if the data flows in one direction or two. If the target application or system is not available for some reason, software within the Application Layer might try to get the data to a system "closer" to the target. IBM's Network Job Entry (NJE) software uses such an approach.

Three main models exist for Application Layer communications. The first behaves like a conversation. The second uses messages, like those discussed in the Process-Driven Model in Chapter 2. The third model is the **Remote Procedure Call (RPC)**. It executes a small program on another system and passes the results back to the originating system. Most applications today use one of these three models.

Now that we've covered basic data networking concepts, we can consider specific networking designs. The following section begins by discussing how subnetworks work, covering traditional WAN designs and then LANs, then introduces specific Transport Network schemes, such as the Internet's TCP/IP and IBM's APPN. Finally, we discuss asynchronous transfer mode networks and how ATM will begin to blur the distinction between LAN and WAN.

How Wide Area Subnetworks Work

WAN lines can use almost any physical medium you can imagine. Carriers, including telephone companies and bypass carriers, commonly use optical fiber cables, twisted pair copper cables, microwaves, and satellites. Cable television companies usually use optical fiber cables or broadband transmission over coaxial copper cables. The government, cellular carriers, and specialized companies such as ARDIS use radio frequencies. Private networks can use microwaves, radio waves, optical fiber cables, copper cables, laser light, or any other legal, vendor supported medium.

Two big differences exist between most firms and a carrier. First, government agencies regulate common carriers. Second, most firms have no legal right to place permanent structures, such as cables, over or under a public right of way. This is why methods like microwave and laser transmission sometimes hold appeal; if you must only cross the street, you may not want to pay a carrier for the link. Exceptions to this broad statement exist. For example, a hospital might have an understreet tunnel between two buildings for staff to use. If it wanted to place cabling inside that tunnel, most local authorities wouldn't object.

Each physical medium possesses advantages and disadvantages. The correct mix for your WAN lines often depends on a mixture of politics, carrier capacity, weather, and many other considerations.

Most WAN links today use copper lines provided by a carrier. Those firms that need high capacity maintain a private fiber plant or lease fiber capacity from a carrier. Lately, carriers in the United States have aggressively courted businesses, using customized pricing plans. These plans usually cover both voice and data networking. They can lower lease costs dramatically for volume buyers, especially those that purchase several years of service. Because of these pricing changes, firms that once maintained private WAN lines now lease capacity from a carrier or a **Value Added Network (VAN)** such as the IBM Global Network.

Putting Bits onto WAN Media

Today, you can buy WAN equipment and lines that work digitally, and you can purchase equipment and lines that use analog techniques. Most high-speed hardware and networking links present a digital appearance, or interface, to the computers that attach to them. Analog equipment uses waves that look smooth, called **sine waves**. Digital equipment uses a different kind of wave, called a **square wave**. Figure 3.17 shows the difference between analog waves and square waves.

In most countries, slow lines provide analog service. When using an analog line, standardized devices called **modulator/demodulators (modems)**, turn a computer's digital bits into analog waveforms and back again. Modems vary from country to country, and each carrier maintains its own rules about what types of modems you may attach to its network. Some modems let you plug directly into an ordinary **RJ11** modular voice jack. Others require a leased, conditioned line. Modems also exist for cellular or radio links.

Digital WAN interfaces use a different approach. Here, a **Data Service Unit (DSU)** attaches to a computer or a router while a **Channel Service Unit (CSU)** attaches the DSU to the line itself. Usually, vendors combine these devices into a single **DSU/CSU**, which often supplies the clock for a synchronous service. Digital WAN interfaces work faster (up to 45 Mbps)

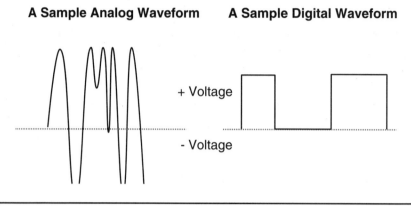

Figure 3.17. Analog and digital waveforms.

than their analog cousins. Using digital WAN approaches, you can also mux several streams of bits at low speeds into higher-speed trunk lines.

How Digital Muxes Bundle Traffic Together

Despite appearances, today's telephone network isn't the same globally. If your firm is international, these differences cause irritating incompatibilities. Regions decided on different schemes to define a digital line and used different schemes to combine lines into fast trunks, so no worldwide standard emerged. In North America, AT&T defined a scheme combining twenty-four 64 Kbps digital lines plus one signal bit into a single digital trunk at 1.544 Mbps, a **T1** line. Every 125 microseconds, the mux sends 193 bits down the trunk. Similarly, six hundred seventy-two 64-Kbps lines plus signaling bits form a **T3** line at 44.736 Mbps. Japan, Taiwan, and South Korea use a subset of this hierarchy.

In Europe, the **Conference of European Postal and Telecommunications (CEPT)** administrations use a different standard. There, thirty-two 64-Kbps channels form a trunk at 2.048 Mbps, called an **E1** line. Thirty of these channels carry data, one channel ensures frame alignment, and the last channel carries signaling data. This framing scheme cannot work with the AT&T approach without muxes that convert one to the other. The E1 scheme sends 256 bits every 125 microseconds. Figure 3.18 compares the layout of T1 and E1 frames. An **E3** trunk takes 480 voice lines plus signaling channels and forms a 34.368-Mbps line.

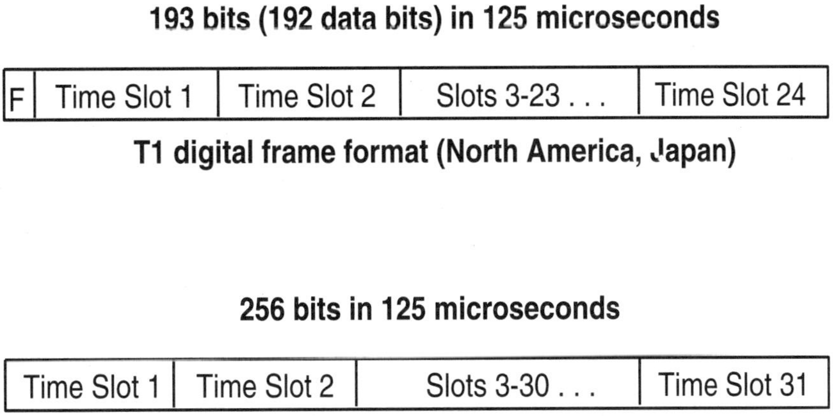

193 bits (192 data bits) in 125 microseconds

F	Time Slot 1	Time Slot 2	Slots 3-23 . . .	Time Slot 24

T1 digital frame format (North America, Japan)

256 bits in 125 microseconds

Time Slot 1	Time Slot 2	Slots 3-30 . . .	Time Slot 31

Figure 3.18. T1 and E1 frame formats compared.

These speeds, 64 Kbps, T1, E1, T3, and E3, form the fundamental building blocks of digital telephone networks over copper wiring worldwide. In the United States, you can also lease lines at other multiples of 64 Kbps, such as 384 Kbps, as part of a **fractional T1** service. Here, a T1-capable line comes into your facility but the carrier uses a mux to restrict the bit rate to, say, 384 Kbps, or six 64-Kbps channels.

An Evaluation of Muxing over WAN LSinks

Because muxing works well for digitized voice and acceptably for data, muxes are popular. Carriers can employ muxes to consolidate traffic, just as FonHome did. Muxes form the heart of many data services from carriers today, including leased line services and fractional T1 service.

Using muxes for a medium-speed private or public voice network makes sense. Most muxes support voice, data, and low-speed video traffic, such as video conferences. Muxes can detect broken lines, and some can nondisruptively reroute traffic around them. Some muxes can balance available capacity, directing traffic to lines with lower delay. Most important, compared to other networking devices, muxes add only a few hundred microseconds of delay to the traffic going through them. This is why they fit voice traffic: Humans cannot tolerate long or unpredictable delays in conversations.

For some data networks, though, muxes can waste WAN line capacity. Voice traffic, mainframe-to-mainframe traffic, and terminal-to-mainframe traffic is quite "smooth." In comparison, LAN traffic usually comes in large, fast bursts. At any given instant, one data channel may need 500 Kbps of capacity, whereas another may need only 2 Kbps. Since muxes allocate WAN line capacity in fixed "chunks," a designer must decide in advance what speed fits the line's needs. Giving both channels 512 Kbps wastes expensive WAN capacity, but using less causes queuing delay during bursts.

In the future, circuit switching and muxing will become less important as a data networking technique for large firms and carriers. Already, some companies use the public switched telephone networks to carry voice and data because some carriers have introduced aggressive pricing structures. As WAN speeds increase to 45 Mbps and more, and as networks carry voice, data, and digital video, cell switching techniques will displace muxing. For lines that don't use video or don't need these speeds, muxing remains a useful choice.

A Look at Traditional Datalinks for WAN Lines

Several datalink protocols provide access to WAN lines. Some exist for a single purpose, tightly bound to higher-layer protocols. Others can support many higher-layer protocols. We'll discuss three common datalink protocols first and then quickly cover several other protocols you may encounter.

The Bisynchronous and SDLC Datalink Protocols

IBM defined two of the most common datalink protocols for WAN use, the **BiSynChronous (BSC)** protocol and the **Synchronous Data Link Control (SDLC)**. BSC is a character-oriented protocol; a BSC frame consists of many 8-bit characters. For computers that represent data in 8-bit bytes, this works fine. Some devices, though, use 36-bit words to represent a location in memory; they might use 6 to 9 bits to represent a single character. BSC is not well suited for them.

SDLC is a bit-oriented protocol. It works for arbitrary bit streams and works well with machines from several vendors. Figure 3.19 shows an outline of an SDLC frame. The **flag bits** are important; they tell the receiving station where a frame starts and stops. Because you can transfer any

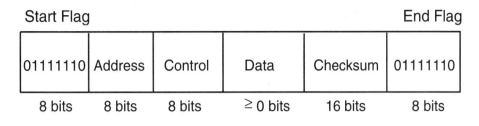

Figure 3.19. SDLC/HDLC/LAPB frame format.

bit stream using SDLC, the flag bit pattern might occur in the data itself. This could confuse the networking hardware and software for the link. SDLC defines a way to "stuff" extra bits into the data stream as it goes over the wire to make sure that the flag bit pattern doesn't occur.

SDLC is a connection-oriented protocol: It delivers frames reliably, in sequence. So, data bearing frames all have numbers to ensure correct sequencing. SDLC allows up to either 7 or 127 frames outstanding before it needs an acknowledgement (ACK). Using the higher number of outstanding frames makes better use of reliable lines with high delays, such as satellite links. SDLC also defines supervisory frames that concern the well-being of the network itself and have higher priority than ordinary frames.

SDLC provides a master/slave relationship, typical for hierarchical networks. SDLC can still work in peer-to-peer networks, if the devices negotiate which will be master when the link starts. This lets IBM maintain compatibility with older devices that couldn't be a master while giving peers a change to negotiate which machine manages the link.

ISO- and CCITT-Approved Datalink Protocols

Shortly after IBM invented SDLC, it submitted the protocol to ANSI and ISO for acceptance as an international standard. ANSI modified it to become ADCCP, which we rarely see today. The ISO changed ADCCP, calling the results the **High-level Data Link Control (HDLC)**. HDLC is the basic leased line WAN technology for OSI-compliant networking products. CCITT then used HDLC several times as the basis for LAP, LAPB, LAPD, LAPF, and LAPM, de jure standards for slightly different uses. They are incompatible with each other, so both ends of a given must use the same variant. These protocols all provide a **balanced mode** that views both sides of the datalink as equals. Otherwise, they are similar to SDLC in concept, with minor modifications. As is usual in networking, these ideas will continue to be modified and extended until something revolutionary arrives, such as ATM.

How WAN Datalinks Are Used Today

Today, most leased line networks use SDLC, HDLC, or their descendants. Very few networks use BSC today, but those that do are important: Some of global financial networks still use BSC. Digital, Unisys, and other equipment vendors also have their proprietary datalink protocols. Mostly, these support terminal access to their processors.

TCP/IP networks can use the **Serial Line Interface Protocol (SLIP)**, mostly to provide dialup access for TCP/IP software. They also use the **Point-to-Point Protocol (PPP)**, a more robust protocol often used between multiprotocol routers in a TCP/IP based internet. SLIP and PPP are both character-oriented protocols, like BSC. They also both run over inexpensive asynchronous modems like those commonly found in PCs or laptop computers, and therefore they are finding more use as Internet use expands.

Integrated Networking with Narrowband ISDN

In the 1980s, CCITT and others defined an **Integrated Services Digital Network (ISDN)**. ISDN brings a "digital pipe" to a subscriber, carrying anything that can be represented by bits. A single ISDN connection can carry data, voice, video, audio, facsimile, and other traffic. ISDN allows services such as call waiting, call blocking, caller ID, and others you can find in some parts of the United States today. ISDN also specifies a common, global way to provide services, such as multipoint videoconferencing, that you can't find easily today.

ISDN comes in two kinds: narrowband and broadband. Heavily hyped during the mid to late 1980s, narrowband ISDN is slowly catching on in the United States. N-ISDN is one abbreviation for narrowband ISDN; however, N-ISDN also an abbreviation for Bellcore's specification for National ISDN. We'll use N-ISDN to refer to narrowband ISDN, compared with B-ISDN for broadband ISDN.

You can best think of N-ISDN as an enhancement to your local telephone (or cable TV) service that gives a small business or a home a digital link into the world. N-ISDN is best suited for homes, branch offices, and small businesses, because the greatest speed it supports is T1 or E1. Most large businesses or campuses probably will continue to use high-speed leased lines or the **Broadband ISDN (B-ISDN)** services discussed later. Since N-ISDN service is entirely digital, it provides good sound quality for voice calls and it transfers data faster and more reliably than analog lines with modems.

N-ISDN runs at two main speeds: The **Basic Rate Interface (BRI)** provides up to 144 Kbps for user data, and the **Primary Rate Interface (PRI)** runs at either T1 or E1 speeds. Most carriers expect PRI lines to end at a digital PBX, probably at a small business. A typical home user will have up to 144 Kbps of digital capacity, and a small business would have 1.5 to 2 Mbps available. Unfortunately, existing analog telephone equipment won't work directly with a digital line. A PBX could encode the analog transmissions into the appropriate digital signals, or an ISDN **Terminal Adaptor (TA)** could convert the signals and mux various analog devices into the faster ISDN data stream.

Many applications for N-ISDN exist. IBM uses N-ISDN to let developers work from home; these users previously used high-speed analog modems, and they report that data transfers are two to three times faster with N-ISDN. N-ISDN also is suited to low-speed videoconferences, home and business security services, remote energy management, and electronic mail, including audio and still images, fax, and other services. N-ISDN is not suited to broadcast video distribution, full-motion videoconferencing, and other high-bandwidth services. These require B-ISDN's higher speeds.

Switching Datalink Frames with Frame Relay

N-ISDN is slowly catching on as an integrated service, but parts of N-ISDN, such as **frame relay** data networking services, exist throughout most of the United States today. Frame relay is a data-oriented Datalink Layer technology for WANs. It is what networking technologists call an "unreliable" service; if the network discards a frame, it doesn't tell anyone. A DTE's higher layers must detect this condition and decide how to proceed. It is therefore not easily adapted to voice, audio, or video transmissions. Frame relay uses "virtual circuits" between two end points. These can be **Permanent Virtual Circuits (PVCs)**, or **Switched Virtual Circuits (SVCs)**.

The CCITT defined frame relay, and a consortium of firms is further recommending how best to use frame relay hardware and software. Unfortunately, two different products might comply with CCITT standards and not work together. The **Frame Relay Forum** provides guidance on how best to use frame relay technologies. Most products today adhere to Frame Relay Forum recommendations.

Figure 3.20 shows frame relay's topological characteristics. In it, subscriber A has three PVCs, two to subscriber B and a third to C. The carrier brings one T1 line into A's facility. It may place a CSU/DSU onsite, or it may use A's muxes. B gets a T1 line and a CSU/DSU, and C gets a slower, 56 Kbps line with a CSU/DSU. For PVC 100, B has paid for 128 Kbps minimum; this is the **Committed Information Rate (CIR)** for this PVC. PVC 101 has a CIR of 0 Kbps. Here, the carrier fulfills its obligation to B if it transfers no data. In practice, this is unlikely, but B accepts a risk by buying a CIR of 0 Kbps. B's maximum rate is 256 Kbps for PVC 100 and 56 Kbps for PVC 101. C has bought a CIR of 19.2 Kbps with a maximum rate of 56 Kbps. This means both the network and A's DTE must be able to accept a maximum of 368 Kbps (256|+|56|+|56).

For PVC 100, B can put more than 128 Kbps of traffic into the network, but the carrier has only committed to transmit 128 Kbps. If the carrier can transmit more, it may, up to a previously agreed maximum limit. After that limit, the network may discard frames immediately. Between the CIR and the maximum limit, any switch in the network can set a **Discard Eligible (DE)** bit in each frame above the CIR. If the carrier's equipment decides that the network is congested, frames with the DE bit set die first.

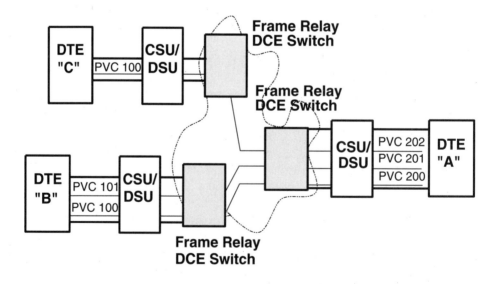

Figure 3.20. A sample three-site frame relay network.

The wire going into A's building sends bits at T1 speeds, but the DTE doesn't necessarily put frames onto the wire that quickly. If the network detects congestion, it may tell the sending and receiving DTEs to slow down. Three means exist to tell other parts of the network about congestion, but none of these is mandatory. It is therefore up to your firm to determine how well a vendor's frame relay hardware and software works together under stressful conditions. Be sure to ask your vendors and carriers how they handle congestion management.

Frame relay uses variable length frames in the network. Most carriers in the United States use frame sizes of less than 4000 bytes, but many devices use a frame size of 1600 bytes. Private frame relay networks also exist: IBM's larger communications controllers can act as a frame relay DCE, among other things. For data traffic, frame relay offers a cost-effective alternative if your traffic meets several conditions. First, higher layers of your networking software must be able to adapt to an unreliable datalink. Next, your traffic must tolerate unpredictable delays. Third, although frame relay can accommodate short bursts of traffic, it cannot handle sustained bursts. If you need sustained bursts of more than a half a second or so, you should negotiate a higher CIR with your carrier.

Frame relay lets subscribers share capacity in a carrier's network better than they can by using muxes. So, carriers can use their capacity better, which sometimes results in savings to their customers. Also, in our example, you'll note that A's DTE only had one WAN interface. Using traditional leased lines, A would need three WAN interfaces. By using frame relay, A reduced hardware acquisition and maintenance costs.

How Local Area Networks Work

This section covers how major LAN types work. First, we investigate the common characteristics of major LAN types. Following this, we discuss Ethernet, token-ring, and FDDI LANs, the most common LAN types. Finally, we consider ways to extend LAN capacity using switches.

Wiring Buildings for LANs

Older campus or building cabling plants consisted mostly of single-purpose cables that supported specific hardware. Each computer type used different cabling schemes, causing needless cost and aggravation. Moving and adding users and departments was an expensive nightmare. Unfortunately, early LANs weren't much better.

Building Reliable Cabling with Star Wiring

Again, the telephone system became a model for computer networks. Using the same cables for all telephones makes moves and changes simpler. Also, telephones use star wiring within a building or campus, permitting simpler problem diagnosis. During the 1980s, IBM, AT&T, and others defined LAN cabling systems using interconnected star topologies. Later, the **Electrical Industry of America (EIA)** and the **Telecommunications Industry of America (TIA)**, issued recommendation **EIA/TIA 568**, covering campus or building wiring plants. EIA/TIA **structured wiring** provides greater flexibility because it uses standard cables over specified distances. Now, if a person moves from one part of a building to another, the same kind of wall jack awaits. Computers, terminals, and telephones from hundreds of vendors plug into one of five or six standardized wall jacks.

Structured wiring divides a wiring plant into two major sections, **horizontal distribution** and **vertical distribution**. These terms refer mostly to skyscrapers, where the unit of horizontal distribution is often a floor of a building. The principles can as easily apply to sprawling campuses, stretching between buildings, as Figure 3.21 shows.

Each horizontal distribution area uses a star topology, and is served by a **wiring room**, sometimes called a **wiring closet**. A floor of a building may have one or more wiring rooms, or a single wiring room might service devices on multiple floors. EIA/TIA 568 cabling plants keep the distance between the farthest user and the nearest wiring room under 100 meters. This affects a building's floor plan, since wiring rooms must be dispersed properly throughout a building.

Serving Your Horizontal Distribution Needs

The EIA/TIA's horizontal distribution uses a single "wire" for each device. No "daisy chaining" or "party lines" are allowed. These cables usually contain twisted pairs of copper wire. Some copper cables incorporate shielding to protect data signals from stray electromagnetic radiation; these **Shielded Twisted Pair (STP)** cables support high-speed data transmissions easily. Others remain unshielded, and these **Unshielded Twisted Pair (UTP)**

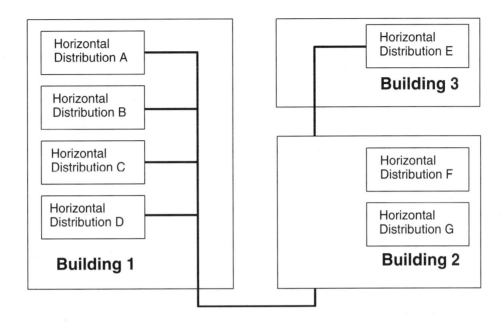

Figure 3.21. EIA/TIA 568 cabling in a campus.

cables work well for voice or lower-speed data transmissions. UTP is smaller than STP, which may be too bulky for some applications. For high performance or clean transmission in environments with radio or electrical noise, EIA/TIA also allows optical fiber cabling.

The **IBM Cabling System (ICS)** specifies several cables, mostly STP. IBM does not manufacture cables; it specifies, installs, and certifies them. STP cables usually use large connectors (about 1 inch square). Others have adapted smaller connectors called **RJ45** connectors for use with shielded wiring. RJ45 connectors look like larger versions of standard U.S. modular telephone jacks; they contain eight wires, whereas a typical RJ11 jack contains four. IBM has submitted a proposal to standards bodies, describing how to use STP cables for speeds up to 155 Mbps.

Several UTP cables, along with supporting equipment like patch panels, also exist. The EIA/TIA, along with cabling and telephony vendors, specifies several categories of cable quality for UTP. Most UTP cables use RJ45 connectors. Figure 3.22 shows their characteristics.

UTP cabling's chief problem is ambient electrical noise. Noise can come from sources such as copy machines, printers, fluorescent lights, and factory machinery. Noise creates intermittent problems that are difficult to diagnose. A technician should certify that each line meets EIA/TIA specifications and inform you if any noise problems exist.

Most businesses today use Category 5 UTP or STP for horizontal distribution. Although it is expensive initially, optical fiber cabling gives the highest speed, greatest flexibility, and longest life.

Going Up: Vertical Distribution

Vertical distribution cables can be optical fiber, UTP, or STP cables. Most data networks use optical fiber cables because they support much higher speeds at lower error rates and because they electrically isolate wiring closets. Within a campus, underground optical fiber cabling also minimizes the effects of nearby lightning strikes.

Optical fiber cables come in two main varieties, **single mode** and **multimode**. Single-mode cables, powered by lasers, provide much higher capacity, over 1 billion bits per second, for up to 60 kilometers between repeaters. Single-mode cables are often used in long distance telephone

UTP Category	When Installed	Maximum Speed	Fastest Application
Category 1, 2	Before 1985	2 Mbps	Voice, terminals, low-speed modems
Category 3	1985–present	10 Mbps	10 Mbps Ethernet LANs, 25 Mbps ATM switched networks
Category 4	1990–present	16 Mbps	16 Mbps token-ring LANs
Category 5	1993–present	155 Mbps	100 Mbps LANs, up to 155 Mbps ATM switched networks

Figure 3.22.   Characteristics of UTP cables.

systems, although some private networks use them for data rates exceeding 155 Mbps. Most private data networks use multimode fiber, driven by Light Emitting Diodes (LEDs). LEDs cost less than lasers, but they produce a less coherent light, which doesn't cover as great a distance. Multimode fibers can drive over 155 Mbps of data a distance of 2 km or so between repeaters.

Multimode optical fibers contain two types of glass, the core and the cladding. Vendors classify these cables by the diameters of each type of glass. For example, the most common type of multimode fiber in North America is 62.5-micron/125-micron fiber, sometimes called 62.5/125 fiber cabling. In this fiber, the core is 62.5 microns and the complete fiber diameter is 125 microns. For most data networking applications, multimode fibers suffice.

Wiring Room Considerations

Data networks usually require powered, active equipment in the wiring room. These **hubs** provide a place where a data network's managers can control the network. Early hubs were little more than repeaters packaged together. Now, active, **intelligent hubs,** dominate the market. These hubs can repeat signals, maintain moderate security, and report simple outages. Some hubs provide backup paths from the user to the hub and between hubs, allowing designers flexibility in building reliable subnetworks.

Because wiring rooms usually contain active electronics, a network's uptime depends on them. Hundreds of data connections can come into a wiring room. If these connections support mission critical applications, the integrity of the electronics in the wiring room becomes as important to them as the uptime of any mainframe, server, or other shared system. Conditioned power, battery backup, air conditioning, and, sometimes, two independent power sources support these rooms. In short, they are distributed computer rooms.

The Rise of the Large Intelligent Hub

Early LAN hubs supported one LAN type and usually one physical medium. If some of devices used optical fiber cabling and others used STP, one hub didn't suffice. Also, a single device couldn't service both Ethernet and token-ring users.

Many large firms use both Ethernet and token-ring. Because people and departments move regularly, network planners need both LAN types in each wiring room. To simplify network planning and operation, vendors made more modular products. Now, hubs could support several LAN types and several physical media. With these more complex hubs, though, came the need to manage them easily. Complex hubs include a way for a network's technicians to change them "on the fly."

Reliable, inexpensively operated LANs use intelligent hubs. Intelligent hubs allow subnetworks to grow and change easily. If a firm needs token-ring and Ethernet today and wants token-ring and FDDI tomorrow, a simple card swap will meet these requirements. Some hubs will even allow nondisruptive changes. Certain hubs also provide proprietary, redundant links between hubs and a segment's devices. If a card fails or if a hub fails, a redundant device can take over almost immediately. Intelligent hubs cost more at first, but their operational costs are much lower.

Common LAN Characteristics

Most LANs are "shared medium networks." The attached devices share the physical medium's capacity, and a **Media Access Control (MAC)** protocol defines how they use it to send and receive data. A LAN's stated speed, such as 10 Mbps or 16 Mbps, approximates its maximum capacity under nearly ideal conditions. Similarly, each computer attached to a fast LAN may not be able to send data quickly enough to "fill the pipe." Buying a "100 Mbps" card rarely means a computer will send or receive 100 Mbps of data.

A LAN depends on a consistent addressing scheme. IEEE's 802.1 committee defined a 48-bit address for each station on a compliant LAN. Some people refer to these 48-bit addresses as **MAC addresses**. Most non-IEEE LANs also follow this general convention. Each device attached to a LAN should thus have a unique MAC address. Some LAN software allows a **Locally Administered Address (LAA)**. A firm using LAAs accepts the responsibility to ensure the addresses they use are unique.

IEEE 802.1 also standardized devices called **LAN bridges**. Bridges connect LAN segments into a larger, extended LAN. Technically, MAC addresses must be unique within a bridged subnetwork. In certain unique situations, bridged token-ring LANs can tolerate duplicate addresses. Some firms use this to their advantage to build highly available subnetworks more easily.

MAC addresses can refer to one device or to several devices with common interests. For example, on a single IEEE LAN segment, several devices might use protocol A, others might use B, and some may use both. Those using only A shouldn't receive the frames on the LAN related to B and vice versa. If protocol A uses a **multicast address** or a **group address** to communicate, then devices interested in A listen for that address as well as their unique address. This saves bandwidth and time, because a device doesn't need to send the frame to every device on the LAN, one device at a time. B can then use different multicast addresses.

An address called a **broadcast address** is special case of a multicast address. A broadcast address contains forty-eight 1 bits. In token-ring circles, some may call this an **all stations copy address**. Broadcast addresses should only be used for frames of interest to all devices on a LAN. Unfortunately, some lazy, ignorant, or evil designers of higher-layer protocols use broadcast addresses for many purposes. Too many broadcast frames on a LAN wastes bandwidth and causes the devices on the LAN to waste time processing frames they don't care about.

Multicast and broadcast frames cause so-called **broadcast storms**. Broadcast storms result from improperly configured devices, broken software, babbling LAN hardware, and other sources. They are difficult to diagnose and can freeze a bridged LAN in its tracks. Thus, although broadcast and multicast traffic is useful, it can hurt a network when improperly used.

How the IEEE Defined LANs

Datapoint Corporation developed the first LAN, called **ARCnet**. When the IEEE began to standardize LANs, four main kinds of LANs already existed: ARCnet, token-ring, Ethernet Version 1, and Ethernet Version 2. Another group, consisting mostly of manufacturers, found existing LANs unsuitable and defined a token-passing bus LAN. The IEEE chose not to standardize ARCnet, and concentrated on Ethernet, Token-Ring, and token bus. It issued five series of LAN recommendations under its 802 committee. The IEEE called the first group 802.1, the second 802.2, and so forth. Subcommittees 1 and 2 discussed issues appropriate to all LAN types, such as bridging; subcommittees 3 through 5 looked at MAC and Physical Layer issues. Today, several more groups exist, discussing everything from wireless LANs to LAN security.

The IEEE broke the Datalink Layer into two sublayers. They called the lower sublayer **Media Access Control** (**MAC**) and the higher sublayer **Logical Link Control** (**LLC**). Two main LLC protocols exist, one connectionless (**LLC 1**), and the other connection oriented (**LLC 2**). A third,

LLC3, provides acknowledged connectionless services, but it finds rare use. IEEE 802.2 defined LLC protocols for all IEEE LAN types. The idea was to allow a consistent way to transfer data. Unfortunately, reality intruded.

By the time the IEEE started their discussions, Ethernet and token-ring LANs had many users. Their committees wanted to avoid significant incompatibilities, avoiding disruptions for these users. The problem is, these major LANs order bits in addresses differently. Each uses a 48-bit address, but an Ethernet or 802.3 address is useless on a 802.5 token-ring LAN without translation. This wasn't planned, but by the time everyone noticed the problem, it would have been expensive and disruptive to change one or the other. So, the problem continues to this day.

Ethernet's Party Line Approach to LANs

Xerox developed **Ethernet**, the most successful LAN type. Ethernet uses a bus topology to connect computers. The first Ethernets ran at 1 or 2 Mbps, but the IEEE standardized version usually runs at a nominal 10 Mbps rate. Ethernet is a party line for computers. If you'll recall FonHome, their party lines had a main telephone line with spliced lines going to each subscriber. We called the main line a "bus," and we called the spliced lines "drops." In Ethernet terms, the main line is a bus, and the spliced lines are **Attachment Unit Interface (AUI)** cables. The bus transmits serially, one bit at a time. A transceiver attaches AUI cables (and therefore computers) to the bus. Figure 3.23 shows how to build a trivial Ethernet.

Like a party line, the computers use a protocol to tell when they can place data onto the bus. If a sender senses that the bus is busy, it waits a random time before trying again. This **deferral** slows the computer trying to transmit but doesn't interrupt the transmission in progress. If the bus is quiet, the computer sends its data, and then tests to see if another device sent data at the same time. Collisions occur when two devices send data simultaneously. If a collision occurs, then each computer waits a random time and tries to send the data again.

To receive information, a computer pulls all of the signals off the bus. It then throws away frames that don't have one of its addresses as a destination address. However, like real party lines, 802.3 devices allow eavesdropping. This **promiscuous mode** is the basis for 802.3 LAN analyzers, which are important diagnostic tools. Promiscuous mode also lets a competent PC programmer steal data, even passwords, from the LAN. Some intelligent hubs provide ways to filter the data going to individual devices on the

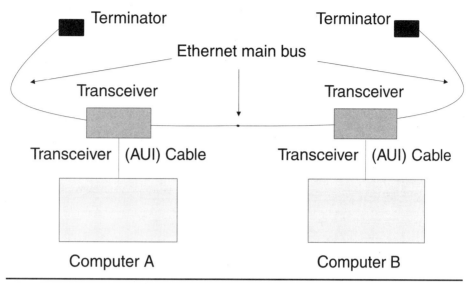

Figure 3.23. A trivial Ethernet.

LAN, but many 802.3 and Ethernet LANs today provide no security.

This broadly describes Ethernet and IEEE's recommendation 802.3. Although similar, the two protocols are incompatible; 802.3 changed some electrical characteristics and altered the frame's format significantly. Both Ethernet and 802.3 frames can coexist on the same physical medium, and most computers can send and receive both types of frames. Unfortunately, a computer expecting an 802.3 frame will ignore an Ethernet frame sent to its address. Improper Ethernet/802.3 LAN design can thus lead to problems that defy simple diagnosis. Figure 3.24 shows the two frame formats, with Ethernet at the top and 802.3 at the bottom.

Cabling Ethernet/802.3 LANs

IEEE 802.3 initially defined only one physical medium, a thick coaxial cable. It proved difficult to manage, and it had only one use. Over the years, 802.3 added newer cabling options to Ethernet. The most recent changes to 802.3 definitions allow Ethernet-style LANs using structured wiring. These are contained in the **10 Base T** and **10 Base F** recommendations. The T stands for twisted pair, and the F for fiber cabling. 10 Base T and 10 Base F emulate Ethernet's bus in one or more active wiring hubs, allowing star wiring and simpler problem diagnosis.

Ethernet Version 2 (Digital Intel Xerox Specification)

48 Bits Destination	48 Bits Source	16 Bits EtherType	46+ Bytes Data	32 Bits Checksum

IEEE 802.3 / ISO 8802.3 Specification

48 Bits Destination	48 Bits Source	16 Bits Length	46+ Bytes LLC + Data	32 Bits Checksum

Figure 3.24. Ethernet and IEEE 802.3 frame formats.

10 Base T defines an Ethernet LAN over UTP, but some vendors extend 10 Base T to run over STP cabling as well. Existing devices can use the newer wiring structures by using 10 Base T transceivers attached to AUI cables. Newer LAN cards often contain a 10 Base T transceiver on board to simplify wiring and increase reliability. Optical fiber cable plants almost always need separate, external transceivers, connected to computers with AUI cables.

Some firms with existing coaxial Ethernet cabling plants want to use structured wiring for new or renovated facilities. IEEE 802.3 allows this if a repeater exists between the two media types. So, if one group uses coaxial wiring and another uses 10 Base T, they can communicate easily. Figure 3.25 shows several different kinds of physical media that build a single, repeated, 802.3-compliant LAN segment.

The Pros and Cons of Ethernet/802.3 LANs

Large IEEE 802.3 LANs possess several disadvantages. Because an Ethernet is a party line, as more parties talk, more collisions occur. In rare cases, I have observed badly designed, heavily loaded 802.3 LANs transmit as little as 3 Mbps. The rest of the nominal 10 Mbps evaporated as collisions and deferrals took their toll. On the other hand, I have also observed well-designed 802.3 LANs transmitting over 9 Mbps. So, although a good network designer can avoid performance problems, an 802.3 LAN's predictability depends heavily on low collision and deferral rates. In addition, the MAC

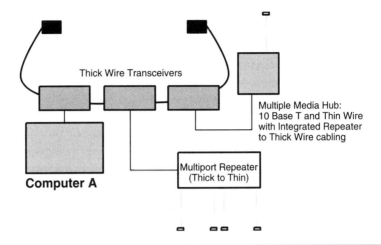

Figure 3.25. Ethernet with multiple physical media.

protocol includes no priority or fairness scheme, and network management and security isn't built into the LAN's structure.

The advantages of IEEE 802.3 LANs are simple. Today, you can buy an 802.3-compliant LAN inexpensively. Some computers come with 802.3 LAN chips built in. When lightly loaded, 802.3 LANs add minimal delays to traffic being sent over them. Networking professionals understand these LANs, and many products exist to help them diagnose problems. Ethernet/802.3 LANs, using 10 Base T or 10 Base F, are a good choice for workgroups or businesses running applications that are not performance critical.

Pass the Token, Please: The IBM Token-Ring LAN

IBM didn't develop the first token-passing ring LAN, but it advanced the technology and made it commercially successful. IBM mapped a logical ring topology over a structured cable plant's star, as shown in Figure 3.26. This provides simple diagnosis and a backup path if a cable or a station fails. The ring also heals itself in most cases. IBM gave their specifications to the IEEE for modification and approval. IEEE 802.5's first recommendation defined a 4-Mbps token-ring; later changes defined a 16-Mbps token-ring LAN.

On token-ring LANs, a frame, called a **token**, circulates on the ring until a device has data to transmit. No device can send data until it holds the token. Once a device gains the token, it sends one frame. The sending station generates a new token when the frame it sent completely traverses the ring. The token then passes to the next device on the ring. This way, no device can monopolize the ring. Later, IEEE 802.5 modified this approach, allowing a station to generate a new token more quickly. This **early token release** uses long rings more efficiently. Unlike Ethernet/802.3 LANs, token-rings allow eight priority levels. Most often, only two or three find use in higher layer protocols.

A token-passing LAN is never completely idle because a token normally exists. Tokens can be lost or destroyed, but after a short wait, the LAN's **active monitor** recovers and issues a new token. While a token is lost or destroyed, no devices on the LAN can send or receive data.

Receiving information on a token-passing LAN is simple. All transmissions pass by all devices on the LAN, so each device examines each frame. If the frame is addressed to another computer, the device repeats the frame to the next station on the LAN. If not, it copies the frame into memory, sets the "frame copied" bit in the frame, and repeats it down the ring. When the frame goes past, the sending station watches the frame copied bit to see that the receiving station copied the frame into memory.

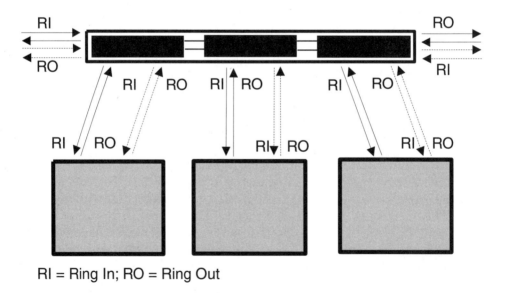

RI = Ring In; RO = Ring Out

Figure 3.26. The IBM token-ring: ring over star with a backup path.

Token-Ring LAN Network Management

Token-ring LANs include LAN management hardware and microcode on every station. For example, each station monitors the ring for noise and other **soft errors**. When devices notice problems, they forward periodic error reports to a group address. This address should belong to a device running LAN management software. IBM's token-ring LAN cards also include a security mechanism built on top of this LAN management capability. Many installations, however, do not take advantage of this built-in circuitry because they don't use LAN management software on their token-ring LANs.

Each token-ring station must be able to take on the role of the ring's active monitor. The active monitor watches for problems such as missing or invalid tokens. Every few seconds, it also starts a **ring poll** to see which stations are attached to the ring. Software can watch the ring poll or ask the active monitor to discover who's on the network. 802.5 further specifies management frames that software can use to depict the state of a LAN segment. This openly published, multivendor approach works no matter which higher-layer protocols use the LAN's services.

Token-ring LANs are self-healing. If someone accidentally cuts a correctly configured token-ring LAN in two, the ring wraps to the backup path. With a network management station, or with intelligent hubs, networking staff can tell if a ring is in a wrapped or a normal condition. With a second cut, the ring reconfigures itself into two disjunct rings. Here, a management station can only see the state of the ring to which it is attached. Figure 3.27 shows how this process works.

Token-Ring LAN Evaluation

Token-ring LANs run at 4 Mbps and 16 Mbps, and they run effectively under heavy loads. Under moderate loads, token-ring networks perform well, but not significantly better than 802.3 LANs. Typical 16 Mbps token-ring LAN segments can run comfortably with 50 to 200 stations, and these stations can use up to 90% of the available capacity without causing undue delays. Token-ring LANs are more predictable than their 802.3 cousins.

Today, token-ring provides a robust, baseband LAN over structured UTP, STP, and optical fiber cabling. It avoids many of the physical problems that plagued early Ethernets. Token-ring LANs can span up to 2 kilometers, using optical fiber repeaters. Rings can also span hubs and wiring rooms. Large token-ring LANs can have problems called **jitter** if the hardware that makes up the network doesn't behave correctly. When 16 Mbps LAN hardware first became available, jitter became a well-publicized problem when LANs included certain non-IBM hardware. Fortunately, it has been tamed since then, except in LANs that are too long or have too many attached devices.

The 16 Mbps token-ring LANs allow data frames as large as 17,997 bytes. This transmits large files efficiently. The 4 Mbps rings can only move up to 4501-byte frames. A bridged token-ring LAN must understand these differences or some transmissions will fail. Note that Ethernet and 802.3 LANs only allow frame sizes of up to 1500 bytes. In sites that have both Ethernet and token-ring, this difference, along with the different bit ordering of addresses, becomes challenging, affecting network performance and making bridging more difficult.

16 Mbps token-ring adapters cost more at first than their Ethernet/802.3 counterparts. Operationally, token-ring is quite stable when configured correctly. The most common cause of a token-ring problem is an adapter entering the ring at the wrong speed. Today, the newest adapters and hubs sense a ring's speed and either enter at the correct speed or keep a rogue adapter off the ring.

Primary path shown on outside, backup path depicted on inside

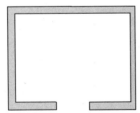

Token-Ring "wrapped" after being cut once

Token circulates using all four wires, primary RI/RO and backup RI/RO.

Primary path shown on outside, backup path depicted on inside

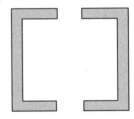

Token-Ring "split" after being cut twice

Stations on left side cannot talk to stations on right side; two tokens circulate.

Figure 3.27. Token-ring LAN behavior when cut.

ANSI's Fiber Distributed Data Interface

Somehow, IEEE standardized LANs with speeds under 100 Mbps and ANSI took speeds of 100 Mbps and higher. Fortunately, the two groups worked together closely, and ANSI's **Fiber Distributed Data Interface (FDDI)** uses the common 802.2 LLC protocols. (It also used 802.5 token-ring as the start of its efforts.)

FDDI transmits up to 100 Mbps on one of two counter-rotating, token-passing rings. The second ring normally remains idle in case a link or a station fails, although some products use the second ring continuously in special configurations. Stations attach to an FDDI LAN in one of two main ways. A **Single Attached Station (SAS)** attaches to only one of the two rings. A SAS can't use the backup ring, but if its hardware goes "south," it can't damage the integrity of the FDDI LAN. The other way to attach is as a **Dual Attached Station (DAS)**, which attaches to both rings. Figure 3.28 shows how dual and single attached stations work. Usually, hubs and large, shared systems use DAS techniques, whereas smaller computers usually use SAS methods. ANSI also defined a way to manage the FDDI LAN called **Station ManagemenT (SMT)**. Like token-ring, where all adapters support 802.5 network management commands and responses, all FDDI adapters and concentrators should support SMT.

FDDI rings can use either multimode optical fiber cables and LED light sources or single-mode cables and lasers. FDDI allows frames up to 4500 bytes long, up to 500 stations, and a total ring length of 100 kilometers. Unlike token-ring, however, no active monitor exists and clocking is specified differently in FDDI to control jitter more carefully.

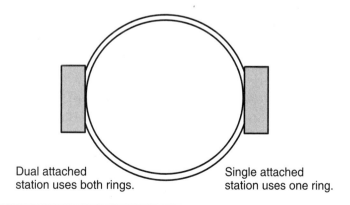

Dual attached
station uses both rings.

Single attached
station uses one ring.

Figure 3.28. FDDI single and dual attached stations.

FDDI was supposed to "catch on" on the late 1980s and early 1990s. Unfortunately, concerns about the costs of building and maintaining a optical fiber cable plant kept many from considering FDDI seriously. Recently, ANSI specified a new physical medium dependent sublayer for FDDI, called **TP-PMD/306**. It defines FDDI over UTP Category 5 and STP copper wiring. TP-PMD/306 has made it easier and less expensive to build an FDDI LAN segment.

Extending LAN Subnetworks Using Bridges

Devices called **bridges** can extend LAN subnetworks throughout a campus and between sites. Bridges come in four kinds:

- Transparent bridges

- Source routing bridges

- Source route transparent bridges

- Translational bridges

Of these, the IEEE has issued recommendations for the first three types, and the first two dominate today's market. Transparent bridges find use mostly in Ethernet or FDDI LANs; source routing bridges most often appear in token-ring and FDDI LANs. The other two types are attempts by vendors and the IEEE to bridge between token-ring and Ethernet LAN segments. Most bridged LANs, though, link one LAN type; Ethernet LAN segments usually bridge to other Ethernet segments. Bridges can be local, or they can be "split" by a telephone line. Split bridges, sometimes called remote bridges, provide a simple way for different sites to talk as if they were on the same LAN segment.

Most bridges provide a filtering capability. **Filters** allow a bridge to selectively forward or discard frames based on values embedded in the frame. If a designer wanted to make sure some traffic never left a particular segment, bridges could filter it out.

How Transparent Bridges Work

Transparent bridges, as defined by IEEE 802.1d, require no changes in DTE hardware or software to use a bridge. They work especially well for Ethernet LANs. The IEEE decided the bridges had to work with existing equipment and software; it had to be transparent to DTEs. Although less common, transparent bridges for token-ring and FDDI LANs also exist.

Transparent bridges maintain internal tables that reflect the bridge's view of the network. Figure 3.29 shows a simplified overview of a two-port transparent bridge. If the bridge sees a frame from A on port 1, it puts an entry into its table. Then, if it sees frames destined for machine A on port 1, it knows not to forward the frame onto port 2. If it sees a frame for machine X, it doesn't know yet where X resides, so it must forward the frame. If it sees a frame on port 1 for machine B, it knows it must forward the frame to port 2, but if the frame for machine B originates on port 2, say from machine C, then the bridge knows that B has already has seen the frame on the segment, and it doesn't forward the frame. Multicast and broadcast frames must be forwarded to all segments. Transparent bridges with more than two ports operate using the same general principles.

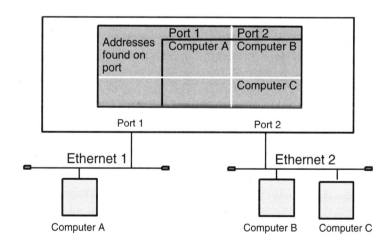

Figure 3.29. A simplified transparent bridge.

Transparent bridges also talk among themselves, using a method called a **spanning tree algorithm**, to avoid loops in the network's topology. Loops cause more than one copy of a frame to be forwarded to the target LAN segment, wasting capacity, and possibly confusing DTEs.

How Source Routing Bridges Work

IBM and IEEE 802.5 defined source routing bridges for use with token-ring networks. Figure 3.30 shows several token-ring LAN segments connected with source routing bridges. Unlike transparent bridges, source routing bridges allow several concurrently active paths between any two segments. First, a network's manager sets up a source routed LAN by numbering every bridge and segment in the network. As a station generates a frame for another segment, it inserts a **Routing Information Field (RIF)** into that frame. Each bridge examines the frame's RIF for a "ring bridge ring" sequence that matches the numbers of the segments it connects and its own bridge number. If the bridge finds a match, it forwards the frame; otherwise, it ignores the frame. When a frame crosses a bridge, this is called a hop. The IEEE fixed the size of the RIF at 13 hops, but many existing token-ring cards and software only allow 7 hops. Seven hops may seem like a lot, but in a large network, it sometimes isn't enough.

In Figure 3.30 two possible routes exist from computer A to computer B. The first route uses bridge 0 between rings 005 and 002; the second uses bridge 1. The figure also shows how the RIF might appear for an explicitly routed frame using either route. In a source routing bridged LAN, the combination of a computer's address and the route to the computer must be unique; under certain conditions a computer can have the same address on two different rings. If computer B in the figure had a second adapter attached to ring 002, that adapter could have the same MAC address as the adapter attached to ring 003. This seems to violate IEEE addressing rules, but it works correctly and finds common use. A LAN like this can be tricky to configure, but it provides high availability.

Source routing bridges forward three kinds of frames. An **explicitly routed** frame contains a RIF. These are the least disruptive kinds of frames. Other frames are **Single Route Broadcast (SRB)** and **All Routes Broadcast (ARB)** frames. They have their uses, but like Ethernet broadcasts, some software designers abuse them. The most common problem we see in bridged token-ring LANs involves a vendor making poor choices between SRB, ARB, and explicitly routed frames. In a poorly designed LAN, with poor software, ARB frames can multiply and congest the LAN. This problem has been heavily hyped; the cure is to find the offending software, and remove it until the vendor fixes it. Another cure might be to redesign the network to mask the effects of poorly written software.

Most often, you'll see transparent bridges used with Ethernets and source routing bridges used with token-ring LANs. The other two types of bridges are less common, and with good reason. Their use requires careful planning. It takes care to design and build a reliable, fast, large bridged LAN subnetwork. Smaller bridged LAN subnetworks, though, are simple to design, build, and operate. Bridges are also relatively inexpensive and fast, and so they will continue to see use over the next few years.

Making the Remotest Connections

Today, many users find themselves outside the office, trying to use the information they would have if they were in the office. Two main ways exist to provide this connectivity. The first uses a PC to emulate a terminal, using a dialed connection to the larger computer. The second makes a LAN appear to extend out to the user. This approach, called **remote LAN node** is more

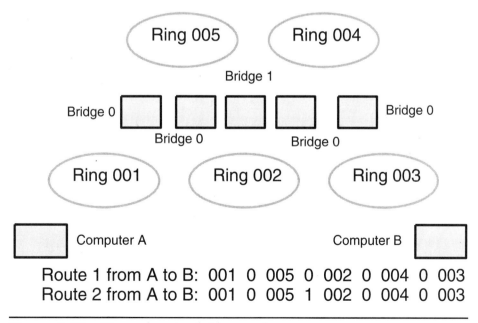

Figure 3.30. How token-ring bridges work.

costly, but it lets the remote person use any system on the LAN. The only difference should be performance: Some operations will be awfully slow on a remote link.

The remote LAN node technique provides a client/server approach to networking mobile PCs. It lets you use any LAN protocol you like. The caveat is this: The software used must support either the **NDIS** or the **ODI** interface to the PC's LAN card. Microsoft, 3-Com, IBM, and others have specified and use NDIS. Novell designed and uses ODI; it works similarly.

NDIS takes the job of building a program to manage the PC's adapter, called a **device driver**, and splits it into three main pieces. The first piece defines a clean interface to higher-layer protocols; the second physically runs the card. The third, called the **protocol manager**, acts like a traffic cop, directing requests for service to the right place. Figure 3.31 shows how you can use NDIS to run two higher-layer protocols over a single LAN adapter. Several software and adapter suppliers support NDIS, including IBM, Digital, Microsoft, 3-Com, and others. With "shim" software, you can convert ODI information to NDIS (or vice versa). Normally, the hardware-oriented NDIS device drivers come from your network adapter vendor, typically packaged with the card. The higher-layer drivers usually come from your LAN software vendor. Either firm can supply the protocol manager.

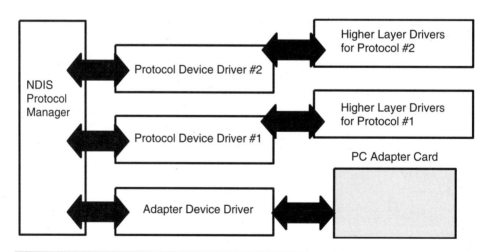

Figure 3.31. Using NDIS to share a PC's adapter.

To build client software for a remote LAN node, vendors modify the client's NDIS device drivers. The modified lower layers run over an ISDN link or an RS-232 asynchronous serial link instead of over the LAN. The server software runs on special hardware or on a PC. This approach offers flexibility because it supports many different protocols, perhaps simultaneously.

Moving from Shared Medium Lans to Switched Lans

New LAN equipment combines switches and intelligent hubs. With hubs, hardware designers can change how the inside of the LAN works without affecting any existing DTEs. LAN designers use switching hubs to extend the capacity of their LANs at low cost.

Speeding Up Existing LANs with Switching Hubs

Looking at inexpensive ways to make LANs work faster, vendors noted two things. First, the biggest investment in a LAN resides in the cables, software and cards that attach devices to the LAN itself. Second, the capacity of the shared medium hasn't increased as the capabilities of the attaching devices. If a device looked like an Ethernet or token-ring network to a DTE, but provided much higher capacity, it would probably sell like hotcakes.

That's how a firm called Kalpana developed the first successful Ethernet switching hub. The switching hub can reduce collisions and make an Ethernet appear as if it has several times 10 Mbps of capacity. Later, IBM worked with Kalpana and others to develop a specification for **full duplex Ethernet**. This approach uses a 10 Mbps "send" channel and a 10-Mbps "receive" channel between a DTE and the switching hub. A likely candidate for a full duplex attachment might be a file server or an image server. A switching hub might have an internal capacity between 30 and 70 Mbps; this depends on the number of ports and the traffic patterns among the attached devices. In all cases, devices attach to the switch using 10 Base T or full duplex Ethernet hardware. Each device attaches at 10 Mbps for 10 Base T compatibility or at 20 Mbps to use full duplex Ethernet.

The basic LAN switching idea applies to all common LANs, including token-ring, Ethernet, and FDDI. DTEs don't change, but the way the inside of the LAN works improves. This is similar to the way FonHome changed how their trunks worked while keeping the same interface to subscribers. The full duplex idea can also work for each of these shared medium LAN types.

Eventually, shared medium LANs will fade away as ATM and other switching technologies provide higher aggregate capacity than shared medium methods can provide. Until then, switching hubs will extend the lives of countless Ethernet, token-ring, and FDDI LANs.

Hundred-Megabit Switching Data Hubs

Other ideas for switching hubs abandon the traditional Ethernet and token-ring interfaces in favor of other techniques. The trade press refers to these approaches as **fast Ethernet.** They provide data-only networking at 100 Mbps.

One approach, currently working its way through a subcommittee of 802.3, preserves 802.3's MAC layer framing. It specifies a maximum distance of 100 meters and a signaling rate of 100 Mbps over two pairs of Category 5 UTP. Many writers refer to this approach as **100 Base X.** It can only support smaller subnetworks, though, because it specifies a maximum of two switching hubs per subnetwork.

Hewlett-Packard and AT&T originally advanced the second approach. They called it **100 Base VG.** The idea was to use four pairs of Category 3 UTP wiring, with a signaling rate of 25 Mbps on each pair. In a way, this approach sidesteps the noise emissions issue by keeping the transmission rates lower. This also lets 100 Base VG run reliably over older cabling.

IBM endorsed this technology and adapted it for token-ring semantics as well. The name then changed to **100 Base AnyNet.** A 100 Base AnyNet hub runs at 100 Mbps with either Ethernet or token-ring semantics. The IEEE 802.12 committee has responsibility for this technology.

Both of these approaches require all new LAN hardware, although existing cabling may work. Both alternatives are less expensive than FDDI, but they lack FDDI's ability to drive a signal several kilometers. They also cost less than ATM, but they support data only, and provide no WAN capabilities.

Although they are finding use in important niches such as computer assisted engineering, products based on these ideas aren't enjoying the explosive growth of switching hubs that preserve existing Ethernet and token ring LAN cards. Finally, the industry doesn't yet have much experience integrating these technologies into large networks.

Building the Infobahn with Broadband ISDN

Broadband ISDN (B-ISDN), sometimes called Broadband Networking Services, is the Information Superhighway. Without B-ISDN, all the politicians' claims are mere election-year puffery. Fortunately for our elected officials, networking professionals worldwide are considering how to build a digital network to support nontraditional data types such as full motion video and audio.

Telephone and cable television companies in the United States are betting heavily on the eventual success of this technology. Other industrialized and newly developing countries also expect to install similar networks. For example, BellSouth, a regional Bell operating company, says that each week they install enough optical fiber to equal their total prefiber capacity. Broadband networks today supply services that roughly correspond to layers 1 through 4 of the OSI stack, although more services will likely become available from carriers and vendors over time. For now, most firms use B-ISDN techniques, especially ATM, as a subnetwork technology.

Cell switching resides at the heart of B-ISDN networks. It is like a streamlined version of frame relay, and it is one **fast packet switching** technique. Unlike frame relay, which uses variable length frames, cell switching uses short, fixed-length cells. This causes minimal queuing and switching delays in the network, and makes cell switching suitable for voice, video, and other delay sensitive traffic.

The telephony and computer industries have standardized Asynchronous Transfer Mode (ATM) as the foundation for tomorrow's LAN and WAN networks. ATM is a specific cell switching technology that uses a 53-byte cell; a 5-byte header precedes 48 bytes of data. As the use of optical fiber cabling increases, capacity increases and error rates decrease, so less checking and control is needed at each hop. As speeds increase, all traffic, even voice traffic, becomes "bursty," the delay an end point can tolerate decreases, and the number of bytes "in flight" across the network increases dramatically. ATM and other fast packet switching technologies were designed to meet to these needs.

Fast Packet Switching: Taking Your Network to Warp Speeds

Fast packet switching technologies adapt networking links to the unique advantages and concerns optical fiber brings. They provide four main advantages that other LAN datalink or WAN technologies can't match. First, a simple packet or cell structure lets vendors optimize processor and memory sizes in switches and adapters, minimizing queuing delays. This reduces delays at high speeds and reduces the amount of data "in flight" at a given time. It also lets high-protocol layers predict how the network will respond to more or less traffic; flow control can become more accurate. In short, the network becomes more predictable.

Next, connection-oriented datalink protocols let ATM and other fast packet switching approaches emulate leased lines and voice circuits while transferring other types of data simultaneously. Fast packet switching also allows two kinds of connections: **point to point** and **point to multipoint**. Point-to-multipoint connections allow services like multiparty video or audio conferencing and broadcast television. Current WAN and campus networking technologies don't allow point-to-multipoint connections easily, if at all.

Third, a fast packet network gives each virtual circuit a **Quality Of Service (QOS)** guarantee. Often, some data transmissions can tolerate some delay, whereas others cannot. Most data transmissions also require every bit to be sent correctly. Video transmissions, though, can often tolerate a small loss of content—you may not care if a pixel is the wrong color for 1/30 second—but they can't tolerate delay well. ATM and other fast packet technologies provide for the needs of each kind of traffic.

Finally, fast packet switching technologies, including ATM, are scalable, offering speeds between 25 Mbps and gigabits per second with the same switching technology. This differs from most LAN or WAN technologies, which specify one particular speed, such as 10 Mbps or T1. Upgrading an existing Ethernet segment to FDDI means replacing every adapter and hub on the segment, even if only one or two devices are constrained. Fast packet switches can contain links operating at different speeds. Users might connect to the network at 25 Mbps or 100 Mbps, and a server might run over a 155 Mbps or a 622 Mbps ATM link. Capacity planning becomes simpler, and adding capacity becomes less expensive.

A Cellular View of How ATM Switches Work

An ATM network carries cells over transmission paths composed of **Virtual Channels (VCs)** and **Virtual Paths (VPs)**. Some people call virtual channels "virtual circuits." A virtual path contains several virtual channels that have the same end points. An ATM switch switches cells based on either virtual channels or virtual paths. ATM cells contain connection identifiers instead of full addresses; connection identifiers are smaller, which is critical when the whole cell contains only 53 bytes.

An ATM switch forwards cells using a simple technique. If a cell arrives on one virtual channel, the switch examines a table to see where it should go. That table, built when connections start, contains the information for the next "hop." The switch then puts that information into the ATM cell's header and puts it out onto the appropriate virtual channel or virtual path. ATM switches use label swapping, and the header changes at each hop in the ATM network.

ATM Standards and Specifications

As it did for frame relay, the CCITT defined the basics of ATM. Also, as it does for frame relay, a consortium of ATM vendors and users exists, the ATM Forum. The ATM Forum takes CCITT's work, extends it, clarifies it, and helps vendors and users develop both compatible and conforming ATM products.

Currently, the ATM Forum, comprised of over 500 vendors and prospective users of ATM technology, endorses several speeds for ATM. Some of these speeds, 155 Mbps, 622 Mbps, 1.2 Gbps, and above, are based on the North American **Synchronous Optical NETwork (SONET)** hierarchy. Most SONET speeds are the same as the international **Synchronous Digital Hierarchy (SDH)**. The ATM Forum has endorsed a 100 Mbps speed and a 25 Mbps speed as well. Currently, most ATM links use STP, Category 5 UTP, or optical fiber cabling.

ATM specifications divide into several parts. The first part concerns the interface between the user and the network, called the **User-to-Network Interface (UNI)**. The **Network-to-Network Interface (NNI)** covers the interfaces between the devices in an ATM network. The UNI and NNI specifications are complete for both Permanent Virtual Circuits (PVCs) and Switched Virtual Circuits (SVCs). The ATM Forum also publishes many other specifications regarding how to design and build ATM networks.

The most complex ATM interface, the interface between carriers, isn't yet complete, so building a global, multivendor, multicarrier ATM network is difficult. The ATM Forum has defined some preliminary specifications to allow interim networks while it finishes. Within two or three years, the ATM Forum is likely to complete these specifications, and compliant products should be available from several vendors.

Although the ATM Forum and CCITT make recommendations on interfaces and formats, they do not comment much on the internal control structure of the ATM network. This leaves much room for vendors to offer distinguishing functions and features.

AAL Aboard!

Within an ATM network, each kind of data has a corresponding transmission service, which has one or more **ATM Adaptation Layers (AALs)**. Figure 3.32 shows how different kinds of AAL services relate to each other.

When sending information, these AALs take the raw traffic flows and adapt them to the ATM cell switching layers below. When receiving, they reconstitute the original traffic correctly. Each AAL understands the needs of its particular kind of data, adapting it accordingly. Class A traffic, with AAL type 1, emulates lines at a constant bit rate, such as leased lines or voice circuits. Class B and AAL type 2 are for synchronized, time

	Class A	Class B	Class C	Class D
Timing sensitive?	Yes	Yes	No	No
Bit rate	Constant	Variable	Variable	Variable
Connection oriented?	Yes	Yes	Yes	No
AAL type	1	2	3/4, 5	4

Figure 3.32. How AAL services relate to each other.

sensitive applications that don't need a constant bit rate, such as compressed audio and video traffic. Class C traffic is best for connection-oriented data traffic, such as frame relay, whereas Class D is for connectionless data traffic. Most existing switches and adapters for local use support only two or three AALs, not all of them.

By "slicing" information into 53-byte cells at high speed, ATM adapters can transfer voice, audio, video, and data. For some data switching applications, though, such as carrying large file transfers or LAN traffic over ATM connections, a 48-byte data payload may introduce too much overhead. So, some vendors, including IBM, build switches that understand both ATM fixed-length cells and variable-length data packets at the same hardware speeds.

Why Is ATM Important?

ATM is the first global datalink standard for both WAN and LAN links. Carriers, PTTs, computer vendors, and LAN vendors all expect to produce ATM-compatible products within the next few years. So, it seems likely that ATM will achieve wide penetration early in the next century as telephone carriers and computer vendors build it into their products. This should also drive down silicon costs, making ATM more cost-effective than high-speed, data-only technologies. With ATM, businesses can build fast, global networks.

ATM especially applies to applications such as peer-to-peer video and image processing. Even 100 Mbps LANs are too slow when several people manipulate digital video and images if other software uses the LAN at the same time. Generally, LANs treat all kinds of traffic in the same way, so a video frame might wait behind a printer's traffic before it traverses the LAN. In applications such as video, audio, and scientific visualization, these delays become intolerable. ATM, though, provides a QOS negotiation when connections start. A switch can forward delay sensitive traffic before other traffic. It can also try to keep the variations in frame delay small, something LAN technologies cannot provide. Because of this, even "slow" (25 Mbps) ATM cards can provide better performance in some time sensitive applications than nominally "faster" 100 Mbps LAN technologies.

ATM networks change more easily than traditional LANs. Consider a typical client/server scenario. The system running the server software needs a faster network adapter card than the clients because it services several clients at the same time. Traditional LANs, though, can't run the network into the server at a different speed than the clients. Upgrading a traditional LAN means buying new cards and new hubs at the same time.

With ATM, the user puts a 25 Mbps ATM adapter card into the client computer. It communicates with an ATM switch. The switch muxes several cell streams onto a single, faster output port, say, running at 155 Mbps. So, the server system communicates with the ATM network at 155 Mbps and the clients use 25 Mbps. ATM puts capacity only where it is needed, saving money over traditional alternatives. Using ATM also minimizes disruptions, because a technician can change one machine at a time.

ATM LAN Emulation

No networking technology today would succeed if it didn't work with existing software. Since most software designed for faster networks today works with LANs, most ATM vendors provide LAN emulation hardware and software for their customers. The ATM Forum recently offered recommendations to vendors about how to supply this compatibility. Now, it is possible to build LANs using only ATM technology, or using a combination of ATM and traditional LAN datalinks.

The ATM Forum decided in early 1995 to define a scheme that emulates a LAN on an ATM network. It also defined how existing LAN devices work with devices on ATM networks with LAN emulation. So, vendors can now build bridges between token-ring LANs and ATM subnetworks and between Ethernet LANs and ATM subnetworks. The ATM Forum didn't resolve existing issues about bit ordering that make token-ring–to–Ethernet bridges a challenge. So, Ethernet devices can only talk to emulated Ethernet stations, and token-ring stations talk with emulated token-ring devices.

The first problem in emulating a LAN over ATM is how to send multicast frames over the ATM network. The second challenge is mapping 48-bit LAN addresses to 20-byte ATM addresses. The third question is how to allocate virtual channels and virtual paths for LAN emulation use. Without answers to these three issues, LAN emulation couldn't happen.

To meet these challenges, the ATM Forum defined several components to emulate LANs. First, the Forum defined a **LAN Emulation Client**, software that might reside in a computer or in a bridge. The LEC talks to ATM hardware, but it presents the appearance of a LAN card to software above it. Next, a **LAN Emulation Server (LES)** helps LECs to resolve Ethernet or token-ring addresses into ATM addresses as needed. The **Broadcast and Unknown Server (BUS)** forwards multicast and broadcast addresses.

Finally, the **LAN Emulation Configuration Server (LECS)** tracks how the emulated LAN is configured and gives it to a LEC when needed. The LECS contains the address of the LES. When a LEC comes up for the first time, it asks the LECS for the address of the LES. The LECS provides it and also tells the LEC whether the emulated LAN is Ethernet or token-ring. The LECS also could be used to track several **virtual LANs** in an ATM network; one physical subnetwork can thus support many emulated LANs. Indeed, with the right software, one computer might use both an emulated Ethernet LAN and an emulated token-ring LAN.

The ATM Forum does not specify whether all of these LAN emulation components reside in a single device or in multiple devices. In practice, vendors will likely combine the LES, the BUS, and possibly the LECS into a single device for simplicity and lower cost.

How Transport Networks Work: Comparing TCP/IP and APPN

So far, we've discussed ways to build subnetworks, but not how to connect subnetworks into larger transport networks. The easiest way to see how real transport networks are built is to examine several different protocol stacks. We'll discuss TCP/IP, the popular protocol stack that makes up the Internet, first. Then, we'll look at IBM's SNA and APPN, using **Intermediate Session Routing (ISR)**. SNA and APPN/ISR are reliable, predictable networks, and they show how connection oriented networks work with low speed, noisy lines. Finally, we'll consider IBM's new APPN, which uses **High-Performance Routing (HPR)**. APPN/HPR is designed to last into the next century, to work with high-quality optical fiber lines, and to minimize congestion in the network.

The Internet's Network Layer

The TCP/IP protocols used today are actually the protocol's fourth version, but the Internet (formerly the ARPANET), has always assumed a relationship between peer computers. This makes it different from, say, SNA, where some networked devices aren't as intelligent as others. TCP/IP began life in the Department of Defense, so its designers wanted the network to survive disruptions and adapt to new conditions. These needs led to a connectionless Network Layer and a robust Transport Layer with both connectionless and connection-oriented protocols. Figure 3.33 shows how a TCP/IP network's protocols and layers interact.

The Internet Engineering Task Force is now developing a new version, called **IP new generation (IPng)**, because the worldwide TCP/IP network, called the **Internet**, is running out of addresses. Sometime shortly after the year 2000, all possible IP addresses will be allocated for use. IPng also better supports newer applications such as video distribution. However, the basic philosophies of the Internet, like the connectionless network layer, remain.

The current IP protocol uses a 32-bit address but divides it into two parts, a **network part** and a **host part**. The network part of the packet's destination address is used for routing; each router in the network examines the network part of an incoming packet's destination address and forwards the packet based on its routing tables. The host part determines which computer on the target network gets the packet. Every "wire" is a different network; if a packet traverses a token-ring and an Ethernet network, a leased line, and an FDDI ring between two computers, it is routed over four different network numbers, one for each subnetwork. By implication, three routers assist the packet on its way, one between each pair of "wires." Figure 3.34 illustrates how IP addresses networks and computers.

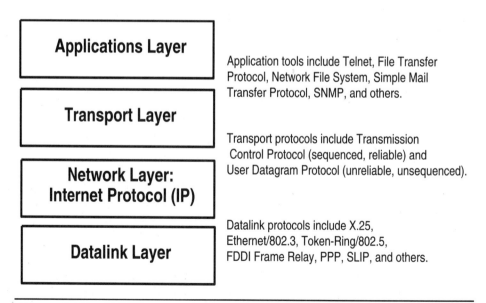

Figure 3.33. TCP/IP protocol stack.

When IP's Network Layer has problems, every user and session should share the pain equally. For example, if a router becomes congested, it simply drops arriving packets. Higher-layer software eventually detects the missing packets and retransmits them. Usually, these retransmissions increase congestion briefly, then the Transport Layer reacts and slows transmissions from DTEs. So, in IP networks, congestion management occurs not at the network layer, but at the transport layer; IP itself places few restrictions on the traffic coming into the network. Because IP products usually provide no class of service support, discarded frames might be data, network management commands, or network status information.

Router-to-Router Protocols in the Internet

To track an IP network's topology, DCEs and DTEs can use several methods. A network's administrator can program **static routes** into a DTE or DCE's routing tables directly. For most PCs, for example, a single **default route** to a DCE suffices. Within an **Autonomous System (AS)**, a part of the Internet under a single administration, several protocols can dynamically update routing tables. The **Routing Information Protocol (RIP)** is most heavily used today, particularly on DTEs. It is an older, distance vector pro-

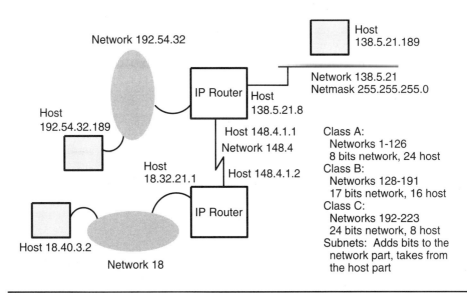

Figure 3.34. Addressing in a TCP/IP network.

tocol, and suffers accordingly. The **Open Shortest Path First (OSPF)** protocol is the best standardized approach for routing within an autonomous system; it is a link state protocol. Most routers support OSPF today, although it is not often available on DTEs. Between autonomous systems, the **Exterior Gateway Protocol (EGP)** is used between the Internet's core systems.

The Internet's Transport Layer Protocols

TCP/IP networks have two possible Transport Layer services, the **User Datagram Protocol (UDP)** and the **Transmission Control Protocol (TCP)**. UDP is a simple interface to IP that adds a source port, a destination port, a message length, and an optional checksum to the IP packet. Port numbers are specified because several different programs and services might use UDP in the same DTE; port numbers help the network to decide where to direct an incoming packet. For example, on most UNIX systems that run TCP/IP, UDP port 7 is reserved for the "ECHO" protocol, while ports 161 and 162 are for **Simple Network Management Protocol (SNMP)** monitoring software.

TCP provides a reliable, sequenced transport service. It presents an data stream to a program; bytes are ordered correctly, errors are corrected, duplicated packets repressed, and lost packets retransmitted. TCP allows bidirectional transfers, and it provides a rudimentary flow control. TCP, like UDP, muxes transmissions onto the network using port numbers. Unlike UDP, however, TCP muxes connections and gives each connection a number. UDP cannot allow multiple programs to use the same port at the same time, whereas TCP can.

TCP is complex, but it provides good performance when the underlying lines are free from noise and errors. It suffers when the network becomes congested, whether due to line problems or DCE congestion. When congestion occurs, TCP tends to cause an oscillating behavior. Although it performs under heavy load better than earlier versions, TCP's congestion management is not as effective as newer techniques.

SNA and APPN

The first SNA networks, in the mid-1970s, contained a mainframe, with communications controllers, terminals, RJE workstations, and other devices attached to it. The mainframe controlled the network in those days; nothing else could run the sophisticated software needed. Most communication used a master/slave model: The mainframe was the master, and less capable, less expensive communications controllers were slaves. Lines were slow, unreliable, and noisy. Early SNA networks mostly used WAN links running the SDLC datalink. An SNA network's **Path Control** Layer, analogous to the OSI reference model's Network Layer, provided an error-free, sequenced, connection-oriented path between SNA devices. Because the lines were slow, SNA optimized their use wherever possible.

When customers wanted SNA networks to connect multiple mainframes, IBM extended SNA by defining a domain, or subarea, as a part of an SNA network. A mainframe controls each subarea, but mainframes and large communications controllers, called **subarea nodes**, also route data between and within domains. Smaller, less capable devices lacked this sophistication; IBM calls them **peripheral nodes**. They use slightly different protocols to communicate with subarea nodes than subarea nodes use between themselves. A **boundary function**, contained in subarea nodes, translates from one protocol to another.

SNA networks contain several types of devices, or **Physical Units** (**PUs**). An SNA **PU Type 5** runs VTAM software and controls the network. A **PU Type 4** is usually a large communications controller running IBM's **Network Control Program** (**NCP**) software. Subarea nodes are PU Type 5 or PU Type 4 devices; they can route information between subareas. An SNA **PU Type 2** is usually a terminal controller or a minicomputer. Figure 3.35 shows a typical, older, SNA subarea network, oriented toward WAN communications.

Within a PU, SNA defines several Logical Units (LUs). LUs communicate in pairs. Several kinds of LUs exist; an **LU Type 2** is a 3270 display, an **LU Type 1** is an RJE workstation, an **LU Type 3** is a 3270-style printer, and **LU Type 0** is for unstructured communications between programs. Later, IBM developed **LU Type 6.1** and **LU Type 6.2** for structured, synchronized communications between programs. LU Type 6.1 mostly works with IBM's **Information Management System** (**IMS**) on a mainframe; LU 6.2 exists throughout IBM's product line. LU 6.2 is the newest and best form of LU today, and it is the LU that will last into tomorrow, with APPN/ISR and APPN/HPR.

How SNA Transports Information Between PUs and LUs

Between nodes in an SNA network, several lines may exist. A network's administrator usually divides these lines into **transmission groups**. For ex-

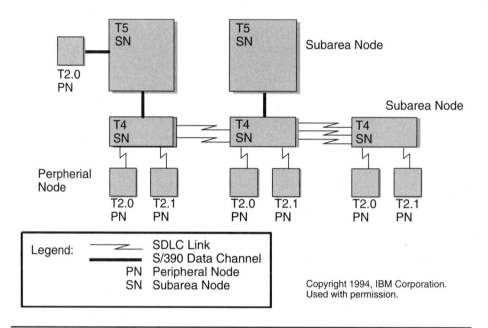

Figure 3.35. A sample SNA subarea WAN.

ample, the lines in one transmission group might use satellite links for large file transfers, whereas another transmission group might use land lines for transaction processing. Alternately, a transmission group might include two lines, one fast and one slow. Each would be used in normal operation, but one provides backup for the other. Transmission groups can increase reliability or offer differing classes of service.

An **explicit route** is a series of transmission groups concatenated together. This is like a token-ring LAN's source routing, but lines in a transmission group can deliver packets out of order. Since SNA offers an error-free service, SNA's Path Control Layer resequences packets at each hop. Because several explicit routes may exist between two SNA devices, a session uses a **virtual route** through the network. Virtual routes then pick appropriate explicit routes. Like explicit routes and transmission groups, several virtual routes may exist between subareas.

Virtual routes are important for two reasons. First, when a session starts, SNA chooses the best available virtual route for it based on the network's current load and the class of service the session requires. SNA then maps the virtual route onto an explicit route, which in turn maps packets onto transmission groups. Second, the Path Control Layer manages congestion in the SNA network across virtual routes, not explicit routes or transmission groups. When congestion occurs and data must be sent into the network more slowly, it affects only the sessions using some virtual routes, not all. Also, sessions using the same virtual route are likely to have the same characteristics, so, for example, a large file transfer probably won't cause congestion in the SNA network for terminal users.

Starting up, or **binding** a session, is crucial in an SNA network because SNA offers different classes of service. The information contained within the bind request and responses determine a session's class of service. The binding process can use as many as a dozen frames in a large SNA network, as the network decides how to provision resources for the new session.

Once a session binds, it uses the same virtual routes, explicit routes, and transmission groups until the network's topology changes. For example, if all of the lines in a transmission group fail, SNA chooses new explicit routes for all of the sessions using the affected explicit routes. If none are available, then it chooses new virtual routes for these sessions. If no new virtual route is available, then SNA aborts the sessions. Such failures occur infrequently, and network designers choose backup paths carefully, so SNA in practice is predictable and reliable. When failures do occur, though, sessions are disrupted.

SNA's Path Control Layer is analogous to the OSI model's Network Layer, but it also provides some Transport Layer services. The remaining functions of the OSI model's Transport Layer fall into SNA's **Transmission Control** Layer. This binds and tears down sessions, manages flow control, and further ensures that information is delivered in the correct order.

Keeping an Appropriate Pace in SNA Networks

In an SNA network, **pacing** manages congestion in virtual routes, and flow control manages congestion within individual sessions. Both use the same general approach. As a packet goes through the SNA network, congested DCEs on the virtual route set one of two bits in the packet. The first bit indicates moderate congestion, the second serious trouble. The receiver notes the bits' state, and modifies how much data it will allow a sender to transmit accordingly. For flow control, the sender sets a bit in the Transmission Control Layer header requesting to send n packets; when the sender receives a packet, usually an acknowledgement, from the receiver with the same bit set, it knows the receiver is ready. In both cases, the receiver decides how much data the sender can send.

Because SNA uses connections, class of service, pacing, and flow control, when congestion occurs, sessions with a lower class of service suffer more. This is both intuitive and desirable. Generally, network management traffic gets the highest class of service; interactive terminal traffic and program-to-program sessions get the next highest. Batched file transfers usually get the lowest class of service, unless jobs need to finish in a tight schedule. SNA's congestion management approach also uses costly links effectively; it isn't unusual to see links utilized above 90%.

The "Static" Nature of Subarea SNA

Subarea SNA relies heavily on static information set up by a network programmer. Unlike, say, a TCP/IP network using OSPF, a human or a program puts information about every transmission group, explicit route, and virtual route (and more) into tables on each subarea node. If a path exists between two systems that hasn't been explicitly defined to the networking software, subarea SNA won't consider using it. This can be frustrating, but it also makes subarea SNA traffic highly predictable. Over time, IBM has added products to ease these definitions and made it possible to define network elements more dynamically.

Nevertheless, maintaining the tables needed for SNA grew tedious in large networks, even though many sites have automated the necessary support processes. In networks based on many small computers, it becomes impossible for each computer's user to maintain routing tables by hand. So, IBM developed APPN to manage the network's routing tables automatically.

How APPN/ISR Helps

Even with LU Type 6.2, where programs could talk with other programs and look like peers, early software really used a master/slave relationship. The networking software negotiated, and one of the programs was anointed the master of the conversation over the two LUs. Further, moving one of the LUs, say, from one mainframe to another, broke the programs. Clearly, in large networks of smaller computers, this wouldn't work.

IBM took several steps to confront this problem. First, it added to the PU Type 2, making it independent. IBM called this a **PU Type 2.1**, because it still was a peripheral node, not a subarea node. Several PU Type 2.1 nodes on the same LAN, for example, can communicate without help from VTAM or another subarea node. This solved the master/slave problem for the PU. Next, the LU Type 6.2 became an independent LU: It could be a true peer in a conversation. This solved the master/slave problem for the LU. Now, programmers build LU 6.2 programs on PU 2.1 nodes without regard to which program initiated a conversation. Further enhancements allowed a single LU to support several sessions, or **parallel sessions,** simplifying programming. The only remaining problems were related to finding the required LU: These definitions still remained static.

APPN/ISR adds several capabilities to a peer SNA network. First, **APPN Network Nodes (NNs)** maintain a directory of **Control Points (CPs),** PUs, and LUs in the networks attached to them. Next, these NNs exchange directory and topology information periodically. When PU Type 2.1 nodes or **APPN End Nodes (ENs)** bind sessions, the NNs find the best path through the APPN network to the target LU Type 6.2 LU. When this path crosses APPN networks, the NNs also forward the traffic along, using software called the **session connector.** APPN networks use a label swapping technique to forward frames; the topology exchange uses a link state algorithm to reduce traffic on WAN links. Figure 3.36 shows how an APPN/ISR network works.

APPN first became available on IBM's System/36 line of minicomputers. It maintained subarea SNA's stability, ruthless efficiency, and class of service support, but it simplified the network administrator's life dramatically. Also, using an APPN/ISR network, network administrators could move LUs around the network, as long as the programs using these LUs were down at the time. Like subarea SNA, when a virtual route goes down, if no other compatible virtual routes are available, the session aborts. Users don't like this behavior better now than they did when using subarea SNA, but at least APPN will try to find any existing compatible path before it aborts sessions.

At first, APPN networks couldn't talk to mainframes without using subarea SNA, but IBM later amended subarea SNA to understand APPN nodes better. Now, a mainframe complex can be part of both an APPN network and a subarea network. A **composite node** like this is crucial to easing the transition to APPN because APPN doesn't support dependent LU types, like LU 0, LU 1, LU 2, and LU 3.

Another concern in the transition from subarea SNA to APPN occurs with existing hardware devices, such as 3270 displays, that don't understand LU Type 6.2. Here, IBM defined an approach, called **Dependent LU Requester/Server (DLU/R** and **DLU/S),** that takes an ordinary 3270 data stream and places it inside an APPN-based LU 6.2 session. At the host VTAM, the data stream is removed and passed to the target application as

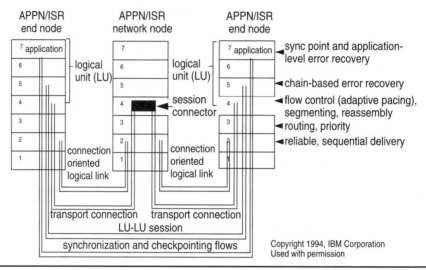

Figure 3.36. APPN intermediate session rerouting.

if it were an ordinary LU Type 2 session. Note that DLU/R and DLU/S doesn't encapsulate the LU Type 2 session; it provides a native APPN, LU 6.2 session through the network. This is more efficient, both in line use and in CPU use. Some devices need new software or microcode to take advantage of DLU/R and DLU/S.

APPN/HPR: IBM's SNA for the Next Century

Although APPN/ISR improves SNA, it still aborts sessions if the session's path through the network is disrupted unduly. Also, because it is connection oriented at the Datalink, Network, and Transport layers, it is computationally expensive to forward many frames through a NN. So, as line speeds increase dramatically with the advent of optical fiber cabling in both WANs and LANs, another approach is needed. The challenge is to keep the predictability of SNA and APPN while making the network faster and more robust.

APPN/HPR, depicted in Figure 3.37, is IBM's answer to this question. APPN/HPR uses a different series of protocols than do subarea SNA and APPN/ISR. Instead of a fully connection-oriented stack, the lowest layer of APPN/HPR, in the Datalink Layer, is connectionless. This allows APPN/HPR to adapt, like TCP/IP, to the changing condition of the network. It also gives APPN/HPR networks high frame forwarding rates. Then, the Datalink Layer finishes with a connection oriented, "transport-oriented" LLC layer. This is similar to running TCP over IP, but instead of occurring at the Transport Layer, the pairing occurs at the Datalink Layer.

Instead of traditional SNA routing, pacing, and flow control, APPN/HPR uses new techniques. IBM calls its new routing method **Automatic Network Routing (ANR)**. ANR lives in switching hardware and performs routing and switching at high speeds. It is suited to WAN or LAN links running at speeds up to hundreds of Mbps, including ATM links.

Adaptive Rate Based (ARB) flow control is an IBM innovation that uses sampling to measure the end-to-end delay in the network. Periodically, on each connection, an APPN/HPR device sends out a time-stamped sample cell that its counterpart picks up and returns. Based on the round trip delay and the connection's quality of service needs, the devices in an APPN/HPR network adjust the amount of bandwidth they make available to that connection. Here, no congestion management is assumed below ARB's level. Also, note that ARB works on a connection by connection basis, so quality of service for each session can be maintained.

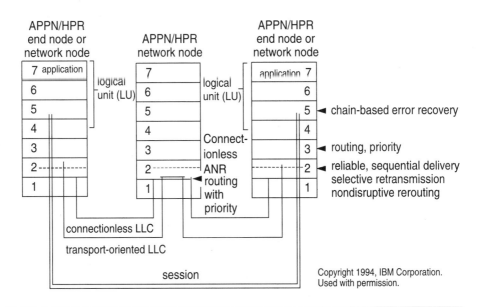

Copyright 1994, IBM Corporation. Used with permission.

Figure 3.37. Relationships between SNA functions within APPN/HPR.

How IP and APPN Relate to Other Transport Network Protocols

Although IP is more complex than most connectionless network layer protocols, it works like many other such protocols. A list of these network layer protocols would include at least

- Digital's DECnet Phase IV

- Apple Computer's AppleTalk

- Novell's IPX

- Xerox's XNS

- The OSI ConnectionLess Network Protocol (CLNP)

Most devices designed for IP routing route the datagrams from these connectionless protocols efficiently because they are like IP.

Subarea SNA is similar to other connection-oriented protocols, such as **OSI** and **NetBEUI**, in some ways, but not in others. Because of its hardware-oriented, hierarchical networking heritage, subarea SNA maintains backward compatibility with devices other protocols need not understand. As a result, IBM has added to SNA slowly. APPN/ISR can be viewed as an important extension to subarea SNA. APPN/HPR, on the other hand, is quite different, being suited to high-speed, hardware switched links for applications such as voice, data, video, and scientific visualization. Existing SNA applications will work over APPN/HPR, but the network itself is completely different from subarea SNA because of the demands of higher speeds.

An Evaluation of TCP/IP and SNA/APPN

I chose to discuss TCP/IP and SNA/APPN because they are so different. Today, TCP/IP enjoys increasing popularity, due to the Internet. Hundreds of applications support it, and new applications will likely support TCP/IP before other protocols. TCP/IP software also comes with a suite of applications, such as file transfer and terminal emulation, that make it immediately useful. Many vendors support TCP/IP, enabling multiple sources of supply.

Strangely enough, independent tests conducted by the Tolly Group found several TCP/IP implementations less compatible than products based upon SNA. This is especially odd because many writers and consultants view TCP/IP as "open," whereas SNA is viewed as "proprietary." In fact, TCP/IP, SNA, and APPN all use published specifications. IBM, though, influences TCP/IP's development less than SNA and APPN.

SNA, APPN/ISR, and APPN/HPR use WAN links more effectively than TCP/IP. This reduces costs in large networks. SNA and its successors also provide more predictable delays for transaction processing users. Although SNA and APPN/ISR suffer from disconnected sessions at times, APPN/HPR remedies this defect while retaining SNA's performance characteristics. Given a choice, I would choose APPN or APPN/HPR where possible, because I value predictability and lower line costs. Because of differing applications needs, though, the correct choice isn't "one or the other," but "both." Indeed, I use both regularly on my ThinkPad. Most large firms will thus have all of these protocols, plus others, in an effective, multivendor corporate network.

Conclusions: Networking

As you can see, planning, designing, building, and operating predictable and reliable data networks is a complex endeavor that demands informed choices. On the other hand, your network is an integral cost of your client/server system and most tend to give it less importance than it deserves. We hope you'll feel better informed and more confident as a result of our explanations.

What networking choices are right for you? The correct answer is, "It depends." Only you can say, although we'll help you work through several important issues in Chapter 6. We'll also detail IBM's offerings in Chapter 4. Given financial guidelines, your staff or a good consultant can help you navigate your way through the hype to find what's useful for your organization's needs.

4

IBM Hardware for Client/Server Computing

At the rarified levels of physics and mathematics, all digital computers are similar. They all contain tiny electrical switches that manipulate zeros and ones. So why all the fuss about this kind of hardware versus that kind?

Imagine designing an inexpensive computer that stores enormous amounts of characters, calculates quickly enough to meet the needs of a thousand engineers simultaneously, and says "hello" to you in the morning. I can't imagine a single computer that can do all that. But combinations of different computers can.

Some computers, such as the IBM System/390, are designed to store, retrieve, and search vast amounts of data. Other computers, such as IBM's Application System/400, can run businesses of nearly any size. Still others, such as the IBM RISC System/6000, excel at complex calculations and graphics, and, with the right optional hardware and software, the IBM Personal Computer (IBM PC) can even recognize your voice and say "Hello." A computer's hardware design dominates how it operates and determines the nature of the software it runs best. Knowing how different approaches work and matching the right computer to the job will make your client/server system more productive.

In this chapter, we'll tell you about computer hardware. We'll first cover how chips and computers work, because this heavily influences the performance and costs of computers. Then we'll describe IBM's simplest computer architecture, the IBM Personal Computer. Next, we'll consider the IBM RISC System/6000. After that, the Application System/400 and System/390 gain our attention, as we look at how computers optimized for commercial workloads differ from scientific and personal computers. As we look at each kind of computer, we'll discuss how each might fit into a client/server system.

As we examine each of IBM's computer families, we'll look at some optional equipment used to attach them to networks. Finally, we'll cover some hardware (and supporting software) for building a networking infrastructure. Then, we'll have the stage set for Chapter 5, which covers client/server software.

Chip Technology—The Key to Today's Computers

Building silicon chips is one of this century's biggest accomplishments. In some chips, manufacturers reliably deposit chemicals in controlled patterns as small as a third of a micron. Chipmaking plants stress the state of the art in air filtration, optics, conveyance, and chemistry. Sometimes, it feels like magic that it works at all, but silicon chips remain one of the most reliable devices ever invented. Once fabricated, almost all chips work as designed unless they overheat.

Manufacturers design and build chips using many different processes. Today, three fundamental techniques dominate. The technique used for a particular chip determines the chip's speed, power consumption, and cooling requirements. For a computer manufacturer, choosing chips that use one technique or another can change a computer's performance, purchase price, and operational costs.

Bipolar. The first technique, called **bipolar**, is in decline today. Bipolar transistors switch very quickly both within or between chips. Unfortunately, they generate lots of heat. Fast computers must pack chips tightly together, thereby concentrating the heat. So, the biggest, fastest computers are liquid cooled; the liquid carries the heat away, just as your car's cooling system carries heat to the radiator. Bipolar computers also use lots of electricity. Their operating costs are therefore very high.

Bipolar chips are at the heart of today's fastest computers. When analysts say "mainframes are dead," what they really mean is that "liquid cooled bipolar computers are expensive to design, build, and operate." When the first bipolar computers were designed, nobody knew how to automatically break a program into different parts that execute at the same time. Big batch jobs needed big, fast processors to finish on schedule. Since then, the industry has discovered how to use many processors more effectively. Because of this, it will be hard to find a new bipolar computer after the year 2000.

CMOS. The second, and most commonly used, process is called **Complementary Metal Oxide Semiconductor (CMOS).** CMOS chips use comparatively little power and run "cool." CMOS chips perform poorly when signals must travel from one chip to another. They also do not switch as quickly. Because they generate less heat, a CMOS chip's designers can pack more circuits into a square millimeter. So, a single CMOS chip can perform the functions that might require two chips using another process. This single chip might perform as well as a two-chip approach, and it lowers costs. Deciding how to disperse circuitry among chips is a delicate decision that changes from year to year. Finally, without CMOS, battery powered computers would be a dream.

BiCMOS. A hybrid approach, called **BiCMOS,** builds chips with CMOS circuits for use "inside" the chip and bipolar circuits for "chip-to-chip" communications. This is the approach that is putting pure bipolar computers out of business; the resulting chips run nearly as fast, use much less power, and generate much less heat than bipolar chips.

Chip designers and manufacturers rely upon two main ways to drive down prices. They pack more circuits onto a single chip, and they sell more chips using the same process. Packing more circuits onto a chip saves circuitry, but it also improves quality and reduces the price of finished goods. A computer made up of 50 chips is less expensive and more reliable than one made from 100. Using the same process to make different kinds of chips uses chipmaking factories more efficiently.

The most common chip in the world today is a CMOS memory chip. Memory chips have a very regular, repetitive layout, suitable for high transistor counts. CMOS circuits can be packed tightly together, so the technology is well suited for memory chips. CMOS is also required for laptop computers and useful for PCs. So, CMOS is the favored chipmaking process today, unless a chip needs higher performance than CMOS can provide.

How Computers Work

Every digital computer today consists of five main components: **input, memory, control, datapath,** and **output.** Most often, the control and datapath components are combined into a unit called a **processor.** Usually, one or more chips combine to make each component. Sometimes, older, smaller computer designs can be reduced to one chip. These single-chip computers find use mostly in real-time control applications such as traffic lights and automobile engine control.

Computers can have many inputs, memories, processors, and outputs. If a computer contains several processors, then it can also act upon multiple instructions at the same time. We'll examine memory first, then processors, and finally input and output.

The Stored Program Model of Computing

Almost all computers today operate using "stored programs." Each memory within a computer is organized like a long line of postal boxes. Each location has a number, called an **address**, and each location is a fixed size, typically one byte. Like a postal box, the contents of a memory location can change with time. Unlike a postal box, without power, most memories lose their contents. Only certain, more expensive kinds of memory retain their contents when power is absent. **Memory controllers** determine when the processor and other parts of the computer read and write values to and from memory. Computers store instructions for the processors in memory, and the data on which the instructions operate also resides in memory.

How Does a Computer Use Memory?

When the computer begins running, or **boots**, the main processor loads instructions from a ROM at a predetermined address and executes them, one after another. Usually, this program verifies the state of the machine and loads another program. Then, it passes control to this new program. This sequence of run, load, and pass control repeats, with each new program being more sophisticated. The last such program executed is the computer's operating system. The operating system, perhaps with input from users, decides which applications to run, and the computer can begin to do useful work.

When a computer performs many input or output operations, the data input or output must come into or go out from memory. Most computers today include hardware that allows input and output to occur without the continuous involvement of the main processors. If the processors can't get instructions and data to or from memory in a timely and coordinated way, a fast computer gets slower. If input and output devices can't use memory, again, a fast computer slows. So, a fast computer needs one or more fast memory controllers.

A computer program doesn't just run from beginning to end. Instead, control moves from one part of the program to another based upon the data's state. For example, a hypothetical statement such as "IF x=3 THEN add 2 to x" causes control to **branch** to one of two places. The first location adds 2 to the value in location x. The second simply continues. This branching becomes important when a computer performs repeating tasks, or "loops."

Because of loops, a computer might spend 80 percent or more of its execution time running less than 20 percent of the stored program. Computer people refer to this as the "Principle of Locality" or the "80/20 rule." Some programs, especially scientific calculations, are more local than others. Similarly, a program might only read or write some of the data it might use.

How Do Computer Designers Set Up Memory?

Usually, computer designers arrange a computer's memories in a hierarchy. The memories at the top of the hierarchy are the fastest and most expensive; those at the bottom are slower and cheaper. This takes advantage of the principle of locality: The faster memories should contain the most frequently executed instruction sequences and the most frequently used data.

Registers. The fastest memory locations reside inside a computer's processors. Programmers and compilers explicitly say how to use registers, mostly for temporary storage and for calculations. Newer processors, in particular, depend upon compilers using registers effectively for increased performance.

Cache. The word cache comes from the French "cacher." Translated roughly, it means to hide. A cache is invisible to programmers and compilers, hence its name. Caches exploit locality, keeping the contents of frequently referenced locations in faster memory. Mainframe caches can store or recall data in 2.5 billionths of a second (nanoseconds). PC caches are slower, taking 15 nanoseconds. Both are faster than main memory, which typically takes 50 to 85 nanoseconds.

One common kind of cache stores information read from memory. If the processor asks for data from the same location, then it gets the copy from the cache. This kind of cache is especially useful for keeping looping instructions close at hand to the processor. Another type of cache receives data written from the processor to memory. If the program's instruction stream refers to the target memory location, then it gets the copy from the cache. This kind of cache is useful, for example, when performing calculations.

Caches have a fixed size: They can't just grow indefinitely. So, over time, some values must be removed from the cache. Especially in multiple processor systems, caches must also have a method to ensure the values held are correct. Other kinds of caches exist as well as the two examples we've cited; however, because they are transparent, most people don't care exactly how they work.

Caches use more expensive memory chips than main memory. Typically, they are small. On a PC, a typical cache might hold between 256 and 512 KB; on a large, shared system it might be a few MB. Cache bandwidth also affects the price of cache; the higher the cache's bandwidth, the more expensive the cache. Finally, if a computer system contains several processors sharing a common main memory, caches become more complex and expensive.

Main Memory. This is what most people mean when they discuss memory. Main memory is typically arranged in arrays of 8 or more chips. A common arrangement has 8 or more 4- or 16-Megabit (Mb) chips to make up 4 or 16 MegaBytes (MB) of main memory. Each chip stores one bit of a byte. Main memory typically takes between 50 and 85 nanoseconds to store or retrieve data.

Values in main memory can unintentionally change, due to rare, random electrical events. If an array like this uses 8 chips, it has no way to detect these errors. If an array uses 9 chips, it uses the extra chip as a **parity bit.** In this scheme, the memory array can detect a single bit error, but it cannot tell which bit is wrong. It simply signals that an error has occurred.

If the array uses more than 9 chips, the "extra" chips beyond the 8 used for data contain an **Error Correcting Code (ECC).** This multiple bit code detects and corrects bit errors in the array. One-bit errors are the most common, although multiple-bit errors do occur. Some memories go even further, and can detect or correct multiple-bit errors.

When an uncorrectable memory error occurs, the hardware usually signals that an error has occurred. The operating system then decides what to do about it. Many PC operating systems freeze for no apparent reason. Some are polite enough to tell the user where the memory error occurred before they crash. Better computers and operating systems take the offending area of memory out of service and continue to work without it. IBM's large systems will even call IBM service automatically.

Main memories come in many sizes. My ThinkPad 755CDV has about 40 MB of main memory, with parity. Most PCs sold today (early 1996) come standard with 8 or 16 MB of nonparity memory. Large, shared systems might contain up to 10 GigaBytes (GB, one billion bytes) of ECC main memory each, and it isn't uncommon to see 4 GB systems.

Fast main memories use complex, expensive memory controllers. IBM's largest systems, for example, allow hundreds of I/O operations to progress at once. Each of these I/O operations must access memory, transferring data with little processor involvement. The main memory controller is thus crucial to the system's performance. On the other hand, a PC can allow only a few simultaneous I/O operations. There, a simpler, less expensive main memory controller makes sense.

Using parity or ECC memory distinguishes one computer vendor from another. In a price sensitive market, especially personal computers, it is tempting to forgo safety for price. Many PCs today come with memory that provides no error detection. I have seen firms take such PCs and use them as servers. This is the computational equivalent of wearing a "Kick Me" sign. Your business data deserves good, error correcting memory.

Virtual Memory. In early computers, all memory was "real." A technician could touch it, and point to each address. Memory was expensive, and programs that didn't fit into real memory weren't very useful. In 1962, in a computer called Atlas, virtual memory was born. Virtual memory exists only in the computer's processor "mind." Virtual memory enabled more complex software, and it also eliminated some tedious programming and some nasty software bugs. IBM's first virtual memory machines appeared in 1972.

Virtual memory uses a computer's long-term storage devices, usually one or more disks. It stores onto disk the contents of virtual memory locations that the processor can address but that can't fit into real memory. Real memory thus serves as a sort of large cache for virtual memory.

Virtual memory is nearly free, but it can be slow because it isn't based solely upon chips. When main memory fills, parts of memory not recently used get written out to disk. When a program refers to memory currently on disk, the operating system schedules another program to run temporarily and gets the data from the disk. This could take several milliseconds. If a disk access takes 5 milliseconds and main memory takes 65 nanoseconds the processor could store or recall 3.25 million pieces of data in main memory before the disk access completes.

Protecting Memory

Because memory is available to all a computer system's users, main and virtual memory protection becomes important. Otherwise, memory allocated for one program's use might be inadvertently used by another. Most systems define each area of memory as either "read only" or "read write." Designating an area of memory as read only means that after the operating system loads something into it, an errant program can't write over it. Such an area might contain a program's instructions or data that must remain constant. Read write memory contains data that may be changed. These simple precautions catch many programming errors.

A computer system's hardware and operating system work together to protect memory. Most operating systems use an approach that allocates memory on a task by task basis. Under normal circumstances, only the task's owner can "see" virtual memory allocated to that task. The IBM AS/400 system uses a different approach, based upon an integrated, object based security system, that we'll describe later. PC-DOS and MS-DOS provide no protection; one ill-behaved program can overwrite other programs or data in memory, causing random behavior later.

How Does Memory Affect Computer Designs?

By now, you probably have some idea of the ways computer designers can use memory technologies. To lower costs, use small caches, and small amounts of nonparity main memory. If the computer's operating system uses virtual memory, programs will still run, albeit slowly. To provide the appearance of high performance, use optimal caches and a large main memory. This is especially important in computers submitted to the trade press for "performance evaluation." To ensure your data's integrity, use ECC memory designs.

A good memory design balances the processor's needs, the I/O path's needs, the value of correct data, and cost. This balance changes from computer to computer and from application to application. It depends chiefly upon the number of I/O operations and processors that must be able to access memory concurrently. Using ECC memory, for example, would be appropriate for a server system. A CEO's system probably gets lots of ECC main memory, but it's overkill for my ThinkPad. A server that performs many I/O operations concurrently will need a faster, more complex memory controller than an ordinary PC can give. Using an operating system on your servers that protects virtual and real memory from errant programs is also sensible.

How Does a Computer Use Processors?

A computer's processors take instructions from memory, decode them, and execute them. For most computers, the processor's design forms an immutable part of the computer's architecture. If the processor's **instruction set** changes, software breaks. Designers usually avoid this problem by extending existing processor designs. That's how System/360 programs can still run on System/390 computers; the System/390 architecture is compatible with earlier System/360 and System/370 computers. Similarly, new PCs continue to run older PC software.

This issue of compatibility over time is crucial; your investments in software, tools, training, and staff time dwarf your hardware budget. For you, compatibility avoids a writeoff of this accumulated I/S "goodwill." For I/S staff, compatibility affords a little breathing room between major changes. Software changes to exploit new processor capabilities can occur one at a time, instead of all at once. For vendors, compatibility helps insure against the failure of a billion dollar investment. These interlocked economic interests cause improvements in processor technology to occur gradually, keeping disruption to a minimum.

Another approach to processor design considers the processor interface interesting but irrelevant. This is the approach taken by some enthusiasts, who buy the box that runs UNIX the fastest at a particular instant. Sometimes, using computers that are a few percent faster than your competitor's machines can give your firm a short-lived advantage. Over time, though, this approach can be expensive because of duplicated facilities, skills, staffing, and processes. Also, although portable software and purchased software reduce the effort of changing computer systems, they don't eliminate it entirely.

IBM's AS/400 processor interface to software is seriously cool; it is head and shoulders above the rest of the industry. It doesn't have an assembler language, so it inherently avoids this compatibility problem. Instead, it uses an approach called the **Technology-Independent Machine Interface**, usually called the **MI**. We'll treat it separately, when we describe the AS/400 family.

Microprocessor Wars: CISC Defenders vs. RISC Rebels

When a technological war reaches the *Main Street Gazette*, it's a big deal. That's what happened with computer main processor designs in the last few years. **Reduced Instruction Set Computing (RISC)** processors have invaded.

IBM's mainframe processors are **Complex Instruction Set Computing (CISC)** processors. CISC processors simplify programming and compiler design by putting complexity into the processor. The processor executes fewer instructions, saving memory space and increasing performance. When memory was expensive, this made sense. Intel Corporation's processors, the heart of most PCs, also use CISC principles. CISC ideas continue to work well for many applications.

Designers making faster CISC processors run into a problem: Instructions get too complex. CISC hardware can't execute most instructions directly, and this slows the processor. To add improvements without causing chaos and strife, CISC processors can only get more complicated, not simpler. Also, main memory continues to get cheaper, reducing some of CISC's advantages. In contrast, during the 1960s and 1970s, scientific computer designers such as Seymour Cray investigated ways to shorten how long it took for each instruction to execute. IBM researcher John Cocke then took these ideas and developed RISC principles.

RISC's ideas are simple. First, instructions must be simple and of a consistent size. This speeds decoding and execution. Next, memory-to-memory operations aren't allowed. Again, this simplifies the instructions and speeds execution. Third, a technique called **pipelining** lets the processor actually begin decoding and executing a new instruction before the current instruction is done. Compilers thus work hard to keep the pipelines full. Indeed, some wags suggest that RISC really stands for "Relegate Interesting Stuff to Compilers."

Simple, consistent, pipelined instructions that execute quickly let a RISC processor outperform a CISC processor, given the same chipmaking process. Or, put another way, a RISC processor of equal speed should cost less and dissipate less heat. RISC processors require larger memories, but if main memories are inexpensive, the performance boost is worth the cost.

Bit Counts: A Processor's Width

One way to distinguish processors from each other is to describe the size of the units of data they process. A 16-bit processor acts upon 16 bits of data at a time. Today, 8-bit, 16-bit, 32-bit, 48-bit, and 64-bit processors exist.

Processors with higher "bit numbers" calculate large numbers faster. They also support more main and virtual memory, so they can more easily handle large, complex programs and large volumes of data.

Going from, say, a 16-bit processor to a 32-bit processor isn't trivial. Only new operating system versions and new application software can exploit the processor. If the new processor extends the old design, then older applications will still work, albeit less optimally. Intel delivered its first 32-bit processor six years ago, and the PC software industry is still struggling to exploit it. IBM has seen two similar transitions in its mainframe products. Because Intel, IBM, and others make most processors compatible with earlier processors, existing software doesn't break.

Clock Rates, MIPS, and Processor Performance

A computer's clock decides the basic rate at which a processor operates. The clock creates millions of electrical pulses per second. One million clock pulses per second is called 1 megahertz, abbreviated 1 MHz. Particularly in the PC trade press, clock speed is considered a relative measure of processor speed.

If two processors use identical architectures and chipmaking processes, clock speed can measure relative processor performance. A 33 MHz Intel 80486 will execute a program faster than a 25 MHz model. However, the Intel Pentium processor uses a slightly different, although still compatible, architecture. Due to a more effective internal design, a 60 MHz Intel Pentium processor will usually execute a program slightly faster than a 66 MHz 80486. Today's processors execute at speeds between 25 and 300 MHz.

The performance difference at the same clock speed becomes more apparent when comparing RISC and CISC processors. Some RISC processors can execute several instructions per clock pulse, whereas CISC processors execute one more complex instruction in one, two, or a few pulses. Comparing these vastly differing approaches with a single number is very difficult. A 66 MHz RISC processor can sometimes outperform a 100 MHz Intel Pentium processor.

Another common way to compare processor speeds is Millions of Instructions Per Second (MIPS). Again, like clock speeds, it is only meaningful when comparing processors with identical architectures. Otherwise, MIPS becomes a "Meaningless Indicator of Processor Speed."

Specialized Processors

Some processors aren't intended for general use. For example, a PC's sound processor usually isn't available for most programmers to use. Instead, vendors of such special-purpose processors supply a library, with software APIs, along with the processor. That way, software developers can write software that doesn't change when the processor changes.

Other types of processors exist as well. For example, mainframe computers use specialized processors to perform input and output. PCs, printers, and other devices use special processors to render graphical images. These **coprocessors** improve overall system performance by removing tasks from the main processor.

How Do Computers Use All These Different Processors?

To compete in today's fragmented computer market, vendors optimize computers to their markets. So, scientific computers use processors optimized to numeric intensive computing. Commercial computers use processors that calculate less well but move data more efficiently. Low-cost computers use inexpensive, high-volume components, including processors. Computers that interact heavily with people may use video, sound, and other processors.

Client/server computing, viewed one way, harnesses these diverse, specialized processors to their best effect. Instead of forcing unity, client/server computing embraces diversity.

So, how do computers use these differing processors? Desktop and laptop PCs today have between two and four processors; most have a main processor and a graphics processor. Some might have a sound processor or a disk processor as well. However, the main microprocessor runs the show.

PC based server hardware uses newer Intel chips along with a large cache and a quicker memory controller. These systems sometimes also support **Symmetric MultiProcessing (SMP)**. SMP systems use more than one main processor, sharing memory between them. PC mavens think this is a new idea, but it has been around for nearly 30 years. IBM sold its first SMP system in 1972. All of IBM's server systems and shared systems today can use SMP.

SMP systems usually contain between 2 and 8 main processors; processing capacity does not increase linearly with more processors because memory becomes a bottleneck. So, after a while, adding main processors with shared memory isn't effective. A typical PC-based SMP system might contain between 5 and 10 processors, including main processors, video processors, and disk processors.

Highly parallel computers (sometimes called Massively Parallel Processors, or MPPs) use many processors together to solve complex tasks. Some parallel computers can contain over a thousand processor complexes. Each processor complex has its own memory, and it might use SMP with multiple processors. These highly parallel computers forecast the weather, detect stock market patterns, and sift through sales data for buying habits. Such tasks can be broken into many parts, so a highly parallel computer works well here. IBM produces highly parallel computers based upon System/390 and RISC System/6000 processors.

Large computers also use many I/O processors. We'll discuss these in greater detail in our I/O section later, but these specialized processors act like coprocessors. They reduce the amount of work the main processors must do. This is particularly important in computers for commercial applications. Today's AS/400 computers can use up to 238 I/O processors. IBM's mainframes can use up to 256 specialized I/O processors, called channel processors.

IBM's General-Purpose Processor Designs

IBM uses three main processor designs in its computers. Ideally, financial analysts might like IBM might to use one design, but this is foolish. Building only a computer that renders either a trillion dollars of mainframe software or all the PC software in the world useless is a lousy idea.

IBM uses Intel's single-chip, CISC processors for its PCs. Today's Intel processors descend from the original IBM PC, which used a 16-bit chip called the Intel 8088. The Intel 80386 jumped to 32 bits. Intel's newer designs extend the 80386 approach. They also support virtual memory, caches, coprocessors, SMP, and other performance enhancements. IBM's PCs today use the Intel 80486 and the Intel Pentium processors. Intel produces these 32-bit processors using a CMOS process.

IBM's System/390 processors are a sophisticated, fast 48-bit CISC design. They extend the earlier System/360 and System/370 commercial processor architectures. Some System/390 computers are optimized for fast, single-stream execution. This is useful for some long batch jobs, and it improves individual user response times. These computers use Bipolar proces sors, with liquid cooling. Figure 4.1 shows a System/390 processor like this, with part of it cut away to show the cooling. Other System/390 computers use SMP CMOS processors for greater multithreaded throughput. Some server models are highly parallel, too. These CMOS models are air cooled and are less expensive to produce and operate than their bipolar ancestors.

IBM's RISC System/6000 systems, POWERparallel systems, and some IBM PC models use RISC processors. The smaller systems use **PowerPC** RISC processors, developed by IBM, Motorola and Apple, and shown in Figure 4.2. The PowerPC is usually produced as a 32-bit chip, via a CMOS process, although the architecture allows a 64-bit version. The faster RISC System/6000 and POWERparallel systems use a processor called **Performance Optimized With Enhanced RISC 2 (POWER2)**. These multiple-chip proces sors extend RISC techniques by decoding and executing several instructions in parallel. These **superscalar** POWER2 processors are optimized for scien tific computing needs, although highly parallel machines are also good for scanning huge databases.

Figure 4.1. IBM System/390 processor.

Figure 4.2. PowerPC 601 RISC microprocessor circuitry.

The AS/400 uses two kinds of processors. The older models use a 48-bit CISC approach. The AS/400 Advanced Series computers use an extended PowerPC approach called PowerPC AS. These extensions are not compatible with POWER2, as they are intended to address commercial, not scientific, computing needs. IBM makes PowerPC AS processors using two technologies today. One uses a two-chip CMOS process; the other uses seven chips and a BiCMOS process.

I/O, I/O, It's off to Work We Go

The most underappreciated part of a computer is the input/output or I/O system. Perhaps articles about comparative I/O subsystem design doesn't sell newspapers and magazines because it is more complex than the "processor wars" pervasive in the media. For commercial applications and for server software, though, I/O can be a computer system's most important attribute.

For example, the main processor in older IBM AS/400 models was slower than many competing main processors. But, the AS/400 routinely leaves other computers behind in real-world performance comparisons. This is because the AS/400's I/O system is superior to many in the industry. As another point of comparison, a single IBM Parallel Enterprise Server during testing handled over a quarter of a billion messages a day for the SABRE computerized reservation system. That's 4100 messages a second during peak times. Each message generates several I/O operations.

Without I/O, a computer would have little to do, because it couldn't read any stored programs into memory. It couldn't load data or store output. It certainly couldn't say "Hi" to you in the morning or run in a networked client/server system.

I/O Buses

The simplest I/O hardware uses a single set of electrical wires, called a **bus**, to connect the main processor, memory, and any I/O controllers. If an I/O controller needs to transfer data to or from memory, it asks to gain control of the bus, waits for permission, and then transfers the data. While the transfer is in progress, the processor cannot send data to or from memory.

Transfer rates for a copper bus range from 80 Mbps to 1000 Mbps or so. This may seem like a huge amount, but it isn't. A 50 MHz RISC processor, with no cache, executing one 32-bit instruction per clock cycle, uses 1.6 Gbps (50 million x 32) of bus bandwidth just for instructions. That doesn't include data. Even assuming a cache with 90% effectiveness, that's still 160 Mbps just to get instructions from memory to the processor.

If a bus uses more electrical wires, then it can transfer more data, assuming a constant clock speed. Matching bus width to processor bit sizes and total system costs forms part of the art of designing a computer system. For example, most PCs today use a 32- or 64-bit bus along with a 32-bit processor. Most system to memory buses on PCs run at clock speeds between 25 and 75 MHz. So, a fast Pentium processor with a 50 MHz bus interface can transfer at most 3.2 Gbps to and from memory. Most PCs have bus transfer rates of about 1 or 2 Gbps.

Larger, faster computers usually need more than one bus to keep the processors from starving. One kind of bus might connect the processor to memory; another bus type might connect memory to I/O controllers. Some designs use a memory read bus that is separate from the write bus. Another design uses one bus for instructions and another for data. Many variations exist.

To cite a specific example, IBM's fastest AS/400 RISC processor, the A30 Micro-Processor runs at 154 MHz. The A30 is a 64-bit processor, and it uses a 128-bit cache to main memory bus. From the cache to the processor, the A30 uses a 256-bit bus for reads and a separate 128-bit bus for writes. The systems that use the A30 have a maximum system bus capacity of 17.6 Gbps, and the A30's processor to cache bus transfers up to 39.2 Gbps.

Memory and System Controllers, Revisited

While bus designs are decided, a computer's designers must also decide how to keep I/Os from these buses from interfering with each other. This is where memory and system controller designs become more complex.

Why all the complexity? These controllers define a system's balance between processor speed and I/O capacity. In many business computing and server applications, a fast processor starves without I/O. So, to increase processing speed, I/O throughput must also increase. Since transistor switching speeds are fixed by the chipmaking processes used, improving I/O throughput usually means adding more buses. However, the memory and system controllers physically cannot increase their speeds linearly for each bus added. So, they become more complex, performing more operations in parallel. As they become more complex, they also become more expensive to produce.

I/O Channels

One approach to improving I/O throughput uses **channel processors**. These processors have an instruction set optimized for I/O operations and bus control. One channel processor controls one bus, which may have one or more I/O controllers on it. The main processor tells the channel processor where in memory a **channel program** begins. The channel processor then executes this channel program without bothering the main processor any more. Then, when the channel program is complete, the channel processor interrupts the main processor, signaling I/O completion. This allows many I/O operations to happen simultaneously, while the main processor performs other tasks.

Channel processors and their buses, called **channels**, can typically transfer between 32 and 1000 Mbps each. IBM's largest mainframes allow up to 256 channels running at about 17 MBps each. This provides a theoretical aggregate I/O throughput of just under 35 Gbps. That doesn't include any memory to processor transfers.

Some channels can span long distances; IBM's optical fiber channels reach up to 20 kilometers between devices. This is useful if your firm needs a disaster recovery site a few miles away from the main data center. It's also useful if a data center houses several trillions of bytes (TeraBytes, or TB) of data, as more and more do today. Traditional buses couldn't physically reach all the disk and tape devices required. Channels can.

Unlike buses, which reside within a computer, channels link computers together. A large mainframe computer system actually is comprised of dozens of independent computers. Because channels link computers together, systems programmers can also configure channels to provide redundant pathways. If one channel controller fails, data can take a second path. Some devices use this multiple path technique to increase I/O throughput beyond what a single channel might allow. This is impossible with traditional buses.

Many IOPs, Many Buses

Another approach to I/O is a hybrid of the bus and the channel approach. This idea uses many buses, along with intelligent **I/O Processors (IOPs)**. These IOPs are typically complete microcomputers within themselves. They run a specialized real-time operating system, with a few exceptions. Again, the idea is to relieve the main processor of I/O control responsibilities. Once the main processor initiates data transfer to or from an IOP, it can go on to other tasks. However, the IOPs communicate with main memory via a bus.

In IBM's product line, the AS/400 most commonly uses IOPs. Most AS/400 IOPs use Motorola microprocessors, although sharp-eyed observers noted that some new IOPs use PowerPC processors. One AS/400 IOP, the **File Server I/O Processor (FSIOP)**, contains a complete PC, running OS/2.

Storing Data for the Long Term

The final area of computer hardware is storage. Storage devices, such as disks and tapes, keep data safe over long periods of time. Since the data stored on these devices is often a valuable corporate asset, long-term reliability is crucial.

Tape storage uses several formats, but the principles are the same. Disk storage has undergone a significant change recently. Before, disk storage was matched to processors. IBM mainframes used one kind of storage; PCs used another. Recently, however, **Redundant Arrays of Inexpensive Disks (RAIDs)** have become IBM's disk storage approach.

Magnetic Disk Storage

Early disk storage devices were large, often 12 to 14 inches across. However, as we discussed briefly in Chapter 1, storing information on disks is a physical process. The disk's read/write heads move across the platters, and the platters spin to position the data correctly on the disk. This pushes disk designers to increase disk recording densities, decrease disk sizes, and increase disk rotation speeds. Higher recording densities mean the disk can transfer more data without having to move the heads and the heads must travel less distance to seek from one part of the disk to another. Smaller disk sizes mean the heads and the comb that holds them can be lighter and move more quickly. Faster spin rates decrease access times.

The problem was that smaller disks weren't as reliable as larger ones at first. Where data integrity was important, the smaller disks didn't get used as often, although they were less expensive. RAID disk controller technology has changed this. It allows one small disk to fail without necessarily causing lost data.

RAID technology has several variations. RAID level 5 is the most common variety today. RAID 5 uses extra disks to store error correcting information, much like the memory arrays described earlier. This information can reconstruct the original data even if one drive is damaged, taken out of service, and replaced. Of course, the reconstruction process isn't trivial, so the RAID controller must be a sophisticated device.

If desired, a storage administrator can mirror data from one RAID disk to another, automatically keeping two copies. This provides even better protection. Some RAID implementations also allow redundant RAID controllers, providing high uptime. Others can "stripe" long data transfers across several disks, improving I/O system responsiveness. Between mirroring, striping, and storing parity information, RAID improves storage uptime, increases performance and maintains data integrity.

RAID reduces costs because it lets computer storage designers use small, common components. Like chips, disks have economics: Higher volumes drive prices down. It is cheaper to build millions of smaller drives than to build thousands of larger ones. Today, most IBM storage devices use common 3.5-inch or 5.25-inch disks. These devices store up to 8 GB each, although the most common disks store 2 to 4.5 GB each.

RAID devices are most applicable for shared systems and servers. For single-user systems, simple disk storage devices suffice. For example, I have two 810 MB removable fixed disks for my ThinkPad. The drives fit into the palm of my hand. Another available disk has the same form factor, but it holds 1.2 GB. For a ThinkPad user, this is sufficient for now.

Today, mainframe users have "disk farms" that store huge amounts of data. Up to 10 TB (TeraBytes, or trillion bytes) isn't uncommon today. Disk capacities seem to double about every 2 years or so; prices per GB of storage have dropped even more quickly.

Disk Storage Controllers

The fastest I/O is an avoided I/O. Earlier, we discussed how computer system designers use caches to increase apparent memory access speed. Storage system designers do similar things to avoid repeatedly accessing the same data on disks. Here, though, the payoff from successful caching is even greater: While a memory cache avoids nanoseconds, a storage cache avoids milliseconds.

So, large commercial systems use storage controllers to avoid and manage disk I/Os. Some IBM storage controller models even take pending disk writes, write them to **nonvolatile memory**, and signal that the I/O has completed. Then, at the controller's leisure, it actually writes the data to the disk. This can only work if the controller uses nonvolatile memory, which retains data values correctly even if power is lost. Otherwise, a power failure could cause lost data.

Some controllers also allow a "dual copy" feature. With dual copy, a single I/O from the main processor turns into two copies of the data on disk. The storage controller performs the dual copy on behalf of the main computer, so the computer can do other processing. This is useful, particularly in mainframe installations with optical fiber channels, for providing online backups in case of device failure or a disaster, such as a fire. An IBM mainframe user could keep a second copy of data online up to 20 kilometers away.

Finally, as shared systems and servers operate around the clock, some firms have discovered that their traditional "backup window" has disappeared. That is, they no longer have time to make backup copies of data to tape. Some storage controllers can create a backup copy of a disk or a database's information while production continues. Again, the more sophisticated storage controllers offer such capabilities.

Some sophisticated storage controllers support RAID devices. Others support older but still useful and reliable disk technologies. Generally, the most sophisticated storage controllers work with mainframe systems that perform high-volume transaction processing. There, the high-uptime, caching, expensive controller makes the most sense. A departmental code server doesn't need these high-end features, especially if it uses RAID technologies.

There, an onsite spare controller and disk might be all the features you'd need.

Tape Storage Technologies

In early computers, tapes were the magnetic alternative to decks of punched cards. Tape processing was therefore as common as running a program. Magnetic tape was wound onto large reels, typically a foot or so in diameter. Now, much smaller, self-threading tape cartridges hold much more data. The old reel-to-reel tapes still exist, but they aren't often in production use today. They are still useful for exchanging data between sites or for reading old business records.

Today, IBM uses three major tape technologies. The first is an 8-mm tape cartridge. The drive for this rectangular tape cartridge works like a videocassette player; the read/write head spins at a high speed while it records and retrieves data. This design causes wear, but it increases recording density—8-mm tape cartridges, with compression, can hold up to 10 GB of data.

The second kind of tape technology is Digital Audio Tape (DAT). It uses a 4-mm tape, with videocassette-like **helical scan** read/write heads, and, like 8-mm tape cartridges, it is rectangular. The 4-mm cartridges are becoming more common, and they hold more data in a smaller space than 8-mm tapes. At first, DAT cartridges were expensive, due to concerns that they would be used to pirate audio works sold on compact discs. Lately, this concern has eased, and prices have dropped.

IBM invented the third tape technology for use with its shared systems, especially mainframe systems. The cartridge is square, and the read/write head is stationary. The tape contains either 18 or 36 tracks of data. This IBM 3490 cartridge tape doesn't hold as much data, but it is faster and more reliable; the IBM 3590 tape drive can transfer 9 MBps when attached to an optical fiber channel.

IBM and others offer tape drives for any of these three tape technologies. Some vendors include stacking tape loaders, which automates the transition from one tape to another. This is particularly useful for automating server or shared system backups. Instead of needing intervention after each tape is written or read, an operator only attends to the tape drive when a stack is done. This reduces staffing costs. Of course, to back up a small server, two or three tapes may suffice. In that case, the backup could proceed completely unattended.

Sometimes, to store huge amounts of data, it is best to use larger, automated tape libraries. The IBM **3495 Tape Library Dataserver** manages and automates tape handling of 3490 cartridges. This is a large device, up to 92 feet long, featuring two walls of tapes. Figure 4.3 shows a 3495. It can store nearly 19,000 tapes, for a maximum capacity of about 35 to 45 TB. The exact capacity depends upon the effectiveness of the device's automatic data compression, which depends upon the data being stored. Between these two walls of tapes, a yellow robot, named "Big Bird" in at least one installation, finds the correct tape, picks it out of the wall, and loads it into a drive for reading or writing. When finished, it returns the tape to its correct location. This is a fascinating device to watch, but don't get into Big Bird's way.

Optical Disk Storage

Three main kinds of optical disk storage exist. The first, **Compact Disc Read Only Memory (CD-ROM)** is probably the most familiar. It uses the same medium as audio CDs, only instead of audio signals, the bits on the disk are interpreted as data. As the name suggests, a computer can only read bits off a CD-ROM. This, along with CD-ROM's large capacity, makes it useful for publishing information, such as software or encyclopedias. Because CD-ROM has a large capacity, firms publish digitized audio and video information on them as well. So, CD-ROM technology is becoming a standard device on many PCs. Besides, CD-ROM based computer games are just more fun.

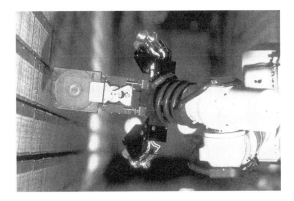

Figure 4.3. IBM 3495 Tape Library Dataserver.

The second kind of optical disk is a **Magneto-Optical (MO)** disk. This disk is rather a hybrid, having both a magnetic and an optical component to the read/write head. It finds use as an archival medium, and as a lower-cost magnetic disk.

Write Once Read Many (WORM) optical disks can only be written once. WORM drives have the advantage of being permanent; this is useful in certain situations where the law or prudence requires a permanent record. They are also useful in image processing environments, where, say, an automobile insurance company might use them to archive photographs of a damaged vehicle. Finally, all of today's optical storage devices are slower than magnetic disks.

Storage Hierarchies

Like memory, storage has a hierarchy. Magnetic disks are the fastest but most expensive storage medium. Next come the optical disks. Finally, slower, inexpensive magnetic tapes reside at the bottom of the storage hierarchy.

System managed storage software automatically manages all of a system's attached storage devices and associated media. It optimizes how disk space is used; it migrates less frequently used files to less expensive storage; and it moves more frequently used data to faster media. We'll discuss IBM's software in the next chapter, but you should be aware that system managed storage exists on IBM's shared systems. It provides a significant operational cost advantage. First, less expensive devices are used properly, and second, very little staff time is required to perform this optimization.

SCSI Buses Speed Storage

When the personal computer was young, storage designers defined a standard way to attach storage devices to computers. The **Small Computer System Interface (SCSI**, pronounced "scuzzy"), found use with many computer systems, including PCs, Apple Macintoshes, and many UNIX-based systems. SCSI assumes that each device attached to it is intelligent, and it allows up to seven attaching devices per bus. Each attaching device has a unique SCSI ID; usually, a technician sets this ID before placing a new device into service. The original SCSI bus used an 8-bit data path and ran at a relatively quick 4 MBps; of course, this is sedate today.

Today, two SCSI versions exist: SCSI and SCSI-2. Within SCSI-2, two variants exist, "fast" and "wide." Some devices can be SCSI-2 compliant, and only support one of these two. A wide SCSI-2 device supports a 16-bit data path; a fast SCSI-2 device transfers data at 10 MBps. So, a fast and wide SCSI-2 device can transfer data at up to 20 MBps. The new definition allows for some compatibility with existing SCSI devices as well. Today, SCSI and SCSI-2 devices find use mostly in PCs and smaller multiuser systems. Many optical storage devices also use SCSI or SCSI-2 I/O interfaces.

IBM's Four Computer Families

From here, we'll take a look at IBM's four basic product lines and explore the strengths and limitations of each from a client/server standpoint. Complete coverage of IBM's computer families is beyond the scope of this book, but the following books (see the order form in back of this book) provide further reading for those interested more comprehensive coverage:

- *IBM Personal Computers: A Business Perspective,* Hoskins

- *Exploring the IBM PC Power Series,* Hoskins and Bradley

- *IBM AS/400: A Business Perspective,* Hoskins

- *IBM RS/6000: A Business Perspective,* Hoskins

- *Exploring IBM's New System/390,* Hoskins and Young

In this section, we'll look at each family's architecture, stressing any unique features, and then we'll describe two or three typical models. Then, we'll discuss in detail ways to attach each family to networks used in client/server computing. Finally, we will cover how each family works as a platform for client or server software.

The IBM Personal Computer Family

Fundamentally, today's Personal Computer (PC) is a single-board computer, built around an Intel CISC processor. Today's models use the Intel 80486 and Pentium processors, clocked at between 50 and 150 MHz. Models designed for individual use might include between 8 and 32 MB of main memory and hard disk storage of between 1 and 2 GB. Models designed for use as server platforms sometimes provide SMP, and they always come with more memory and disk storage. New PC models use at least two buses, one for processor to memory access, and the second for I/O. Some models, particularly IBM's **Aptiva** brand, come with coprocessors for sound and high-quality video playback. IBM usually sells the Aptiva through outlets, such as Radio Shack in the United States, associated with the home market.

A PC typically uses a graphical display with at least 640 dots across and 480 dots up and down (640|x|480 resolution). High-end models can display graphics, images, and video streams with resolutions of 1024|x|1280 and above. PC displays usually provide between 256 and 16 million possible colors per dot. A user inputs data into the PC using a keyboard or a pointing device, such as a mouse or a TrackPoint. We'll describe the TrackPoint below. The PC's video, graphical, and sound capabilities make it a great platform for client software.

Mechanically, PCs come in many shapes and sizes. Most models are designed to sit on a desk or astride one. Displays typically range between 14 and 17 diagonal inches of viewing area. Usually, the greater the display's resolution, the more expensive it is, and the larger it should be. Plugging cards directly into slots located on the PC's I/O bus expands a PC's capabilities.

Currently, IBM sells more than 40 different PC models. Various designs have different processors, different processor and bus speeds, more or less memory and disk storage, or different kinds of buses. Of course, they also vary in price. The most visible electronic difference between models, though, is the kind of I/O bus they use. We'll discuss common PC buses next.

Personal Computer Bus Architectures

The most common I/O bus design IBM uses is an old bus, descended from the IBM Personal Computer AT. Some writers call this the "Industry Standard Architecture," although no standards body exists for this bus. We'll call this 16-bit bus the **AT bus**.

The AT bus is suited mostly for individual PCs or for clients in a client/server system. It is an 8-bit or a 16-bit bus that operates at 8 MHz and can sustain maximum transfer rates of about 30 Mbps. In today's world, that's not much, but the existing inventory of AT bus devices continues to encourage vendors and users to use this bus. The bus also lacks some data integrity features of newer buses.

In 1987, IBM announced the **Micro Channel Architecture (MCA)** bus. Then, it was the system bus, running at a maximum rate of 320 Mbps. MCA is faster, more reliable, and more flexible than the AT bus. It defined a way for personal computers to use more than one bus and multiple processors, a sign of times to come. Today's MCA bus is a 640 Mbps I/O-only bus; memory access uses another bus. IBM used the Micro Channel in many of their **Personal System/2** models of PCs. Again, the existing inventory of MCA bus cards makes the design useful as an I/O bus.

Newer personal computer models and RISC System/6000 computers use it as an I/O bus. The Micro Channel Architecture allows a 16-bit, a 32-bit, and a 64-bit bus. PCs use the 16-bit and 32-bit versions; RISC System/6000 computers use 16-, 32-, or 64-bit devices. So, if a device driver exists for the RISC System/6000's operating system, AIX, Micro Channel cards will work both in PCs and in RISC System/6000 computers.

The **Extended Industry Standard Architecture (EISA)** bus is a design that IBM didn't invent. As the name implies, it extends the AT bus to 32 bits, and it runs faster as well. It is not as reliable as the MCA, but that fact got lost in the hype surrounding the "bus wars" in the late 1980s. It does, however, share MCA's flexibility.

The newest personal computer bus designs, the **Video Equipment Standards Association (VESA VL)** bus and Intel's **Peripheral Component Interconnect (PCI)** are limited distance and limited slot designs. They are designed to achieve higher speeds than other PC buses, and they are tightly bound to the Intel processor. The VL bus got its start when several graphics coprocessor designers wanted to achieve higher processor to coprocessor speeds than was previously possible. Although a PC might have 3 to 8 ISA, MCA, or EISA expansion slots, it would only have one or two VL bus slots. Over time, other device vendors used the VL bus design as well.

Intel's design is a more recent and more general-purpose approach. It assumes a separate processor to memory bus and directs all I/O to the PCI bus. In a VL bus design, by contrast, the processor must decide whether to direct the I/O to the VL bus or to the ISA bus. PC providers can attach

I/O controllers directly to the PCI bus, or they can attach devices that convert PCI signals to older bus technologies, such as AT, EISA, or MCA. PCI bus designs are the future for personal computers with Intel processors.

Personal Computer Operating Systems

The first PC operating system was PC-DOS. It is a simple, text-oriented operating environment. It includes no virtual memory and no memory protection. It only supports one user, and it provides no direct support for multitasking. However, it has a large software portfolio.

Microsoft extended PC-DOS and its version, MS-DOS, with its Windows software. Microsoft Windows adds a GUI to PC-DOS. It also provides rudimentary support for **multitasking,** so the computer can appear to do two things at once. However, it does not protect memory well. Because Windows sits on top of PC-DOS, it does not overcome PC-DOS's limitations. In particular, memory management is challenging. Like PC-DOS, Windows has a large applications portfolio. Like PC-DOS, Windows is only suitable as a client environment.

Recently, Microsoft extended Windows with its Windows 95 product. It removes some of the earlier restrictions of Windows, but it still doesn't protect memory or multitask as well as it should. Unlike other new operating systems, it is not object oriented at its core. It does, however, have a nifty looking GUI and a huge advertising budget. Microsoft also provides another form of Windows, called **Windows NT**. Windows NT is good for either a client or a server system. It runs on most IBM PCs, assuming a fast processor and at least 16 MB of memory.

IBM's premier PC operating system is Operating System/2. OS/2 provides a consistent, object oriented GUI, virtual memory, memory protection, and multitasking. It can run OS/2, Windows, and DOS programs at the same time. It requires less memory than Windows NT, and it provides more function and stability than Windows 95. Writing this book, I regularly use OS/2 Warp Connect, IBM's Internet software, Freelance Graphics for Windows, and WordPerfect for DOS on my ThinkPad. OS/2 is suitable for both client and server systems.

OS/2 comes in various forms. The latest versions are known by the moniker "Warp." The original version of Warp extended Microsoft's Windows versions 3.1 and 3.11 with OS/2 operating characteristics. First a user installed Microsoft's Windows software, then Warp. In a "Warped" machine, OS/2 took over the computer's basic operation, but when a user ran Windows applications, the computer essentially ran Microsoft's software.

This protected and enhanced your existing software investments, especially if your computer came preloaded with Microsoft's operating system products. Note that Warp doesn't yet work with Windows NT or Windows 95. It does, however, work with Microsoft's Windows for Workgroups.

The other two versions of Warp are "fullpack" versions. Here, IBM's **WIN-OS2** software replaces, or lives separately from, Microsoft's Windows software. If Windows is already installed, this uses more disk storage space. However, if only PC-DOS is installed, then Warp Fullpack provides the ability to run Windows applications along with DOS and OS/2 software. The latest version of Warp is **OS/2 Warp Connect**, which includes integrated networking software. Warp Connect includes peer to peer disk, file, and printer serving software, along with a full functioned TCP/IP suite, **LAN Distance**, and LAN Server Requestor software. We'll cover LAN Distance later, and LAN Server in the next chapter.

Other operating environments, such as Novell's NetWare and various flavors of UNIX, run on IBM's PC hardware. However, these are less common, except on systems used as servers. There, NetWare is king; OS/2 and Windows NT combined have less market share than NetWare, although this is slowly changing.

Typical IBM Personal Computer Models

Next, we'll consider three IBM Personal Computer models. The first is the latest in a successful series of laptop and notebook computer products, the IBM ThinkPad brand. Most ThinkPad models use a traditional keyboard and pointing device for input, but some use only a penlike stylus. The pen computers are useful, but they are not as common, so we'll consider the IBM ThinkPad 760 CD, a more traditional model.

The IBM ThinkPad 760 CD

Figure 4.4 shows the IBM ThinkPad 760 CD. It uses an Intel Pentium processor running at either 90 or 120 MHz, along with a 256 KB cache. It also includes a built-in video processor. For memory, it comes with 8 MB of 70-nanosecond main memory, expandable up to 40 MB with an optional memory card. It provides a Thin Film Transistor (TFT) flat panel display with 1024|×|768 resolution, and can display over 65,000 colors. TFT is the best laptop display; it uses three individual transistors for each dot of resolution, one blue, one red, and one green. The ThinkPad series uses local bus

Figure 4.4. IBM ThinkPad 760 CD.

technology to speed graphical displays. IBM offers two choices of display; the smaller is 10.4 inches measured diagonally, and the larger is 12.1 inches.

The ThinkPad has a unique pointing device, called the TrackPoint III. It looks like a little pencil eraser between the keys on the keyboard. It works rather like a joystick. When a user applies pressure to the TrackPoint III, it moves the cursor across the screen. The TrackPoint III also has two buttons, so it can replace a traditional PC's mouse.

With or without an optional **docking station**, the ThinkPad CD is a competent mobile or desktop computer, removing any need for multiple PCs. It attaches easily to a full sized keyboard, a different pointing device, or a standard, CRT-based display. Using a standard display, the ThinkPad 760 CD provides even better resolution, up to 1280|×|1024 dots. The ThinkPad's I/O capabilities expand via its two **Personal Computer Card (PC Card)** slots. Although the ThinkPad uses an AT bus as an I/O bus, until it is docked, a user never sees the bus itself. The docking station includes a standard SCSI disk controller and one AT bus slot.

A user can remove the ThinkPad's hard disk drives, which range in capacity from 540 MB to 1.2 GB. The ThinkPad's keyboard is hinged, and when it is lifted up, a user can swap the disk drive or the battery. The diskette drive also swaps with a CD-ROM drive. An **IBM SCSI Credit Card Adapter** provides a path to additional disk storage. It connects to either

SCSI or SCSI-2 disk drives, at speeds up to 10 MBps. It does not, however, support the wide mode of SCSI-2, only the fast mode.

Included with the ThinkPad 760 CD is IBM's **Mwave** digital signal processor. It functions as a CD quality sound processor, or as a data/fax modem. The ThinkPad packages a microphone and speakers into the computer. The ThinkPad 760 CD includes software that can turn the Mwave into a speakerphone and a digital answering machine. It feels odd using a computer as a speakerphone, but if your hotel room's phone doesn't have one, it works well.

The battery powered ThinkPad can run for between 2 and 8 hours without recharging; actual battery life depends upon how someone uses the ThinkPad. Of course, the ThinkPad also plugs into a standard wall outlet. Finally, the ThinkPad uses an infrared link to provide wireless data transfers between ThinkPads.

All this resides in a package less than 12 inches wide. The ThinkPad is a little over 8 inches deep and about 2 inches high. With the diskette drive and battery pack installed, it weighs 6.1 pounds. For operating systems, it supports PC-DOS, Microsoft Windows, Microsoft Windows 95, and OS/2. Other operating systems also may run on the ThinkPad 760 CD, but IBM supplies these directly.

The IBM PC Server 310

The IBM PC Server 310 is a low-cost floor-standing system suitable for use as a file, print, or code server. It just under 1.5 feet tall and deep, and it is 6 inches wide. It uses a 75 MHz Intel Pentium processor with 256 KB of 15-nanosecond cache. The PC Server 310 comes standard with 16 MB of 70-nanosecond parity main memory, which can expand to 192 MB. It does not support SMP.

For I/O, the standard PC Server 310 includes a 132 MBps PCI bus and a SCSI-2 fast adapter. This leaves one PCI bus slot open for high-performance adapters. A buyer can specify the I/O bus to be either AT bus or MCA; either way, the I/O bus has five slots, of which three are available. One of these remaining three slots can be occupied by a network adapter. The PC Server 310 comes standard with a 1 GB SCSI hard disk drive, but it connects up to 9 GB of disk storage to the system. It does not support RAID drives in the standard configuration. The PC Server 310 also comes standard with a CD-ROM drive, which is useful for installing new software onto the system.

All of IBM's PCs designed to support servers come with **NetFinity** software. NetFinity lets a LAN administrator collect hardware configuration information or schedule events, such as backups. It also can use a modem to dial out to a pager, alerting an administrator of a problem. Finally, with some IBM disk drives, NetFinity's **Predictive Failure Analysis** can tell an operator or administrator that a disk drive failure is about to occur. This normally gives 24 to 48 hours' notice, so someone can ensure backups are good and give users warning of impending downtime. While disk failure is uncommon, it is best to have warning of a failure.

The PC Server 310 supports popular file and print servers, such as IBM's LAN Server, Novell's NetWare, and Microsoft's Windows NT. Other operating systems or file and print server products may also work on the system.

The IBM PC Server 520-PCI/Micro Channel with 100 MHz SMP

The IBM PC Server 520, shown in Figure 4.5, is the next step up in Personal Computers designed to support servers. The top of the line PC Server 720 uses a more advanced technology, and it supports up to 6 faster processors in an SMP configuration. Both the 520 and the 720 use a larger tower package than the 310; the 520 stands 24.5 inches high, and is nearly 30 inches deep.

The IBM PC Server 520 uses one or two Intel Pentium processors running at 100 MHz in an SMP-capable configuration. The SMP hardware allows the remaining processor to continue if one processor should fail. It comes standard with 32 MB of ECC memory and 512 KB of 15-nanosecond cache memory. Main memory expands to 256 MB.

For I/O, the PC Server 520 supports a PCI and an MCA bus, with two PCI slots and 6 MCA slots available for expansion. The 520 goes beyond the 310 in disk subsystem performance; it supports either a fast/wide SCSI-2 disk controller or a RAID controller. The RAID controller supports RAID levels 1 and 5, and uses fast/wide SCSI hot-swap hard disks. So, if a drive fails, someone can replace it while the system continues to operate. It can support up to 18 drives with a total capacity of 40 GB in a RAID configuration. Like the 310, the 520 comes standard with a CD-ROM. Finally, IBM offers a model of the 520 that includes a four-port full duplex Ethernet adapter, providing up to 80 Mbps of theoretical network throughput.

Like the 310, the 520 supports NetFinity. It also supports common file and print servers. In general, the 520 is a more reliable, more robust,

Figure 4.5. The IBM PC Server 520.

faster system. It offers better data integrity than the 310 in a more expandable package. Of course, it also costs more.

Attaching IBM Personal Computers to Networks

IBM provides many ways to attach personal computers to networks, including ATM, Ethernet/802.3, token-ring, FDDI, and wide area networks. They can use all major transport protocols, including SNA, APPN, OSI, and TCP/IP. IBM's offerings revolve around a PC's expansion bus and the intended use. For example, a card best suited for a server system might have several LAN attachment ports. In contrast, cards for a ThinkPad would use the small PC Card form factor, and cards for client systems would have one port at a low cost.

Personal computer and laptop users attached to a LAN can run "diskless," loading their operating systems from a centralized file server. IBM's **Remote Program Load (RPL)** feature allows this, reducing the burden of updating operating systems on every personal computer when new versions come out. Generally, RPL works better with desktop machines than with mobile computers.

Token-ring is IBM's preferred LAN type, especially when users value fairness and predictability. Generally, designers can build larger subnetworks using token-ring than using Ethernet, possibly reducing costs for internetworking devices such as routers. Also, token-ring's built-in management reduces diagnostic and repair times. IBM supports all of its major higher-level protocols, including SNA, APPN, APPN/HPR, TCP/IP, and NetBIOS over both token-ring and Ethernet.

Many of IBM's adapter card products work both on IBM Personal Computers and IBM RISC System/6000 computers. We'll cover all possibilities for Personal Computers here. When we investigate the IBM RISC System/6000 family, we'll refer back to this section often.

Attaching IBM Personal Computers to WANs

IBM produces several modems suitable for use with personal computers. The **IBM 7851 Model 001** is an external, V.32bis-compatible 14.4 Kbps data and fax modem. It also includes V.42bis and MNP level 5 data compression. Some modems support higher speeds, but the 7851 can support either leased or dialup lines. With compression, the 7851 Model 001 can reach speeds of 57.6 Kbps, given an ideal input bit stream. IBM also packages the 7851 with software suitable for DOS- or Windows-based personal computers. It is compatible with the industry leading Hayes modem command set, and it supports the IBM command set as well.

IBM also supplies a Digital Signal Processor, the **IBM DSP Modem and Audio Card**. It sits in a 16-bit AT bus slot and connects a personal computer to a telephone, an optional full duplex speakerphone, and to speakers. It transmits data and faxes at 14.4 Kbps line speed, plays audio compact discs and MIDI files, all at the same time. Because it has an onboard processor, it can do work like this in the background, and run other personal computer applications. With the optional Telephone Enhancement upgrade, the DSP Modem and Audio Card can handle voice mail, putting messages into voice mailboxes on the PC's hard disk. It provides caller ID, if available in your area, and it distinguishes between incoming voice, fax, and data calls. Because the DSP Modem and Audio Card works with an onboard processor and a digital signal processing chip, simply loading new software changes its capabilities.

For attachment to synchronous, wide area networks, IBM supplies the **Wide Area Connection (WAC)** adapter. With it, a PC can attach to a WAN link, at up to T1 speeds, and the software running with the WAC adapter will determine the WAN protocols the link supports. For example, the WAC adapter and IBM's **RouteXpander for OS/2** software attaches an OS/2 system to a frame relay network. Or, it connects to an X.25 network as a DTE. The WAC card understands many protocols. With IBM's **Communications Manager** software for OS/2, a user might choose to run SDLC and SNA over this connection. With RouteXpander for OS/2, then it might run, say, APPN and TCP/IP over separate virtual circuits on the same physical connection.

The **IBM WAVERUNNER Digital Modem** adapter uses one 64 Kbps N-ISDN channel on a BRI to connect personal computers with a N-ISDN WAN. It can also use N-ISDN to communicate with existing analog modems or fax machines. This capability is unique to the WAVERUNNER. It lets your designers mix and match different devices, some analog, some ISDN, within a network. The WAVERUNNER is based on IBM's Mwave signal processing technology, so IBM can upgrade the WAVERUNNER using a software update. IBM makes WAVERUNNER digital modems for the AT bus and for Micro Channel PCs running MS-DOS, Windows, or OS/2.

For personal computers acting as communications servers, IBM provides the **IBM ISDN Primary Rate Adapter**. Installed in a Micro Channel–based Personal Computer, this adapter becomes an ISDN communications server. It can connect several client systems using either Basic Rate ISDN or Switched 56 Kbps services. Each adapter can support up to 23 user sessions, but this number may vary depending on how clients use the network. Figure 4.6 shows how a firm might use IBM's LAN Distance software, WAVERUNNER Digital Modems, and the IBM ISDN Primary Rate Adapter to support telecommuters.

Attaching IBM Personal Computers to Ethernet LANs

The most unusual card IBM makes to attach PCs to Ethernets is the IBM Ethernet Quad PeerMaster Server Adapter. It promotes microsegmentation and bridges or switches traffic between segments without server system intervention. Of course, it also attaches the server system to each segment. Some Micro Channel–based server systems can support up to 6 network cards; using Ethernet Quad PeerMaster Server Adapters, one server system could attach to 24 Ethernet segments. The Ethernet Quad PeerMaster Quad-BT Server Adapter attaches to 10 Base T LANs; the Quad-B2 version attaches to 10 Base 2 coaxial cabling. These cards can find use in systems

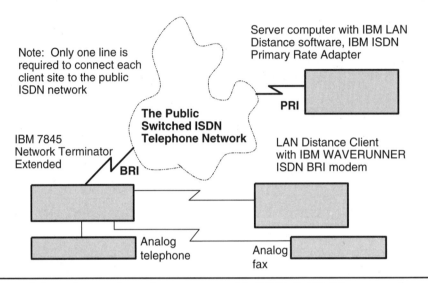

Figure 4.6. Supporting telecommuter with IBM's LAN Distance software, WAVERUNNER Digital Modems and the IBM ISDN Primary Rate Adapter.

running either IBM's OS/2 LAN Server or Novell's NetWare file and print server software.

For PCs with a 16-bit MCA bus, the **IBM LAN Adapter/A for Ethernet** connects to Ethernet LANs. This card is suitable for personal use, but isn't quick enough for use, say, in a file server. There, a 32-bit MCA bus and Ethernet card makes more sense.

PCs based upon the 32-bit MCA bus can also use the **IBM Dual EtherStreamer MC 32.** This card provides two full duplex Ethernet ports, making it suitable for use on server systems with several network connections. Full duplex Ethernet provides speeds of up to 20 Mbps when used with certain switching hubs; however, it also supports standard Ethernet/802.3 in "half duplex mode." This card uses RJ45 connectors. The **IBM EtherStreamer MC 32** provides a one-port version for server systems with fewer network connections. It connects to 10 Base T or co-axial Ethernet LANs. Both EtherStreamer cards run at full Ethernet media speed, 10 Mbps.

Today's newest PCs use the PCI bus. To connect these machines to an Ethernet LAN, IBM supplies the **IBM PCI Ethernet Adapter.** This 32-bit, single-port card is suitable for both client and server system use because it provides solid performance at a low cost. It supports SMP systems, so it can accommodate the largest PC server system's needs. It also supports Plug and Play hardware installation and full duplex Ethernet.

Client or server systems with the EISA bus can use the **IBM EISA Ethernet Adapter** to attach to Ethernet networks. This adapter also supports full duplex Ethernet. It provides one port, and does not explicitly support SMP systems.

Five IBM adapters connect PCs using the older AT bus to Ethernet networks. The first three adapters are IBM's first generation AT bus adapters. The **IBM LAN Adapter for Ethernet TP** supports 10 Base T connections only, using an RJ45 jack. The **IBM LAN Adapter for Ethernet CX** supports coaxial connection to 10 Base 2 Ethernet LANs. Finally, the **IBM LAN Adapter for Ethernet** supports all common Ethernet wiring environments.

Recently, IBM announced a second generation of AT bus adapters. The **IBM EtherJet 10 Base-T ISA Adapter** has only one RJ45 connector, suitable for connecting to twisted pair Ethernet LANs. The **IBM EtherJet ISA Adapter** sports three connectors, one 10 Base T, one 10 Base 2, and one 10 Base 5. With an appropriate Ethernet transceiver, the EtherJet ISA Adapter also connects to optical fiber–based Ethernets. Both adapters function identically and support SMP computers, full duplex Ethernet, RPL, and Plug and Play installation.

ThinkPad users can connect to Ethernet networks based upon 10 Base T and 10 Base 2 wiring with the **IBM Ethernet Credit Card Adapter II**. Another PC Card device, the **IBM Home and Away** card, contains an Ethernet connection for the office and a data/fax modem for use on the road. Since most ThinkPads only have two PC Card slots, combining two common functions into a single card frees the second slot for another use. The IBM Home and Away card even works with a cellular phone.

Connecting IBM Personal Computers to Token-Ring LANs

IBM makes several token-ring adapters for personal computers that use an MCA bus. The **IBM Dual LANStreamer MC 32 Adapter**, like its Ethernet counterpart, provides two media speed connections to a 4 Mbps or 16 Mbps token-ring LAN for 32-bit Micro Channel bus machines. It automatically senses the ring speed, adapting to the correct speed. It also senses if you're using UTP or STP and adapts accordingly. This adapter is particularly well suited to server applications, if the network's structure allows several connections to a server. It includes a priority channel, making it suitable for networked multimedia applications. Possible applications might include fast file servers, image servers, or even a lightly used video server for a small workgroup. When teamed with a full duplex token-ring switch such as the IBM 8272, the Dual LanStreamer MC 32 Adapter is also enabled for full duplex token-ring.

A single-port version of this card, called the **IBM Auto LANStreamer MC 32 Adapter,** provides similar performance and characteristics, including full duplex token-ring support, at a lower cost. It is suited for fast personal computers and servers supporting smaller workgroups. Finally, the **IBM Auto LANStreamer MC 16 Adapter** provides similar function for 16-bit Micro Channel computers, except it does not support full duplex token-ring.

The LANStreamer cards provide improved performance, but they do use more memory in the personal computer than older cards. This isn't a problem for OS/2 or other 32-bit, multitasking systems, but personal computers running DOS or Windows may find themselves running out of usable memory. For Micro Channel systems running DOS, a better adapter might be the **IBM Auto 16/4 Token-Ring MC Adapter.** It uses less memory and provides adequate performance for the DOS or Windows user. Like the LANStreamer cards, the Auto 16/4 Token-Ring MC Adapter sense the ring's speed and wiring type, adapting accordingly. It also supports full duplex token-ring.

AT bus users have a simpler choice to make. For them, the **IBM Auto 16/4 ISA Adapter** is the best token-ring attachment card. The Auto 16/4 ISA Adapter also comes enabled for full duplex operation, RPL is standard, and it automatically determines and sets the correct ring speed, eliminating potential network down time. Finally, this adapter is fully compatible with the new Plug and Play specifications being put forth by Intel, Microsoft, and others in the personal computer industry.

For IBM ThinkPads or other laptops with a PCMCIA slot, the **IBM Token-Ring Auto 16/4 Credit Card Adapter** fits the bill. It can attach to both UTP and STP wired networks, using a single cable. It senses the wiring type, and adapts accordingly. Like its cousins for desktop computers, it also senses ring speed automatically. It supports RPL, and it also supports the ThinkPad's Suspend/Resume function. The adapter fits into a PC Card, found on ThinkPad and other laptop computers.

Finally, IBM also has two token-ring cards for personal computers that use the PCI bus. The **IBM Auto LANStreamer PCI Adapter** is a single-port card. It has the same features as the other Auto LANStreamer adapters, including automatic ring speed selection, and it also supports full duplex operation. The **IBM Triple LANStreamer PCI Adapter** has three ports, supporting similar functions. This card is suitable for a server system attached to a switched token-ring or to a microsegmented token-ring LAN. For server hardware or high end power users, these cards match any PCI user's needs.

Attaching IBM Personal Computers to 100 Mbps LANs

PCI-bus-based personal computers can attach to a so-called "fast Ethernet" LAN with one 32-bit IBM adapter. The **IBM 100/10 PCI Ethernet Adapter** supports standard half duplex Ethernet and full duplex Ethernet at 10 Mbps. A second mode supports 100 Mbps operation in either half or full duplex mode. Of course, this assumes the adapter is directly connected to a capable full duplex switch. The adapter tracks the specifications for Fast Ethernet as it is being defined by the IEEE 802.3 standards committee, called 100 Base TX. It uses a single RJ45 connector. As is typical today, this adapter supports Plug and Play hardware installation, and it includes device drivers for DOS, OS/2, DOS/Windows, and Novell NetWare.

The other common 100 Mbps LAN is FDDI. IBM PCs with a Micro Channel bus can attach to FDDI LANs, as can PCs with ISA or EISA buses. Designers build FDDI LANs using UTP, STP, or optical fiber cabling. IBM's FDDI adapter family is based upon the bus type and the cable connection required. For PCs with Micro Channel architecture, choose the **IBM FDDI Adapter/A** for optical fiber cabling. For Category 5 UTP or STP copper cabling, the **IBM UTP5 FDDI Base MC Adapter** will work in a Micro Channel PC. Similarly, the **IBM UTP5 FDDI Base ISA Adapter** works in AT-bus-based PCs, and the **IBM UTP5 FDDI Base EISA Adapter** is for EISA bus PCs.

All of IBM's FDDI adapters provide the latest synchronous FDDI support. This makes them suitable for situations where nearly guaranteed bandwidth and response time is required. A few applications use this feature. All of these adapters also support standard FDDI network management commands. These adapters are for Single Attached Station (SAS) use only; to attach a PC to both FDDI rings, your firm must request a price quotation from IBM for dual attached station adapters. Typically, though SAS is acceptable for most PCs.

Using IBM Personal Computers in ATM Networks

IBM supplies four ATM adapters for use in PCs. Again, they vary by bus type. The slowest such ATM adapters, operating at 25 Mbps over UTP Category 3 cabling, install into an AT bus or a Micro Channel slot. The **IBM TURBOWAYS 25 ATM ISA Adapter** works along with an IBM 8282 supports a 25 Mbps interface. Because it uses UTP cabling, it can be at most 100 meters away from the switch or concentrator. It is intended for use within client systems, but it has all of the features of its more capable cousins. The **IBM TURBOWAYS 25 ATM MC Adapter**, shown in Figure 4.7, is a similar adapter for use with Micro Channel bus systems. It provides device drivers for OS/2 version 2.11 and above, including OS/2 Warp. To date, though, it enables only the TCP/IP protocol, providing Classical IP support, as specified by the IETF.

IBM's next fastest ATM adapter runs at 100 Mbps over multimode optical fiber cabling. The TURBOWAYS 100 ATM MC Adapter works with OS/2 LAN Servers or with NetWare server systems that use the Micro Channel bus. It also supports RISC System/6000 computers. When used in a RISC System/6000 computer, it uses the IETF's Classical IP TCP/IP emulation over ATM. When used in a PC, the device drivers use the ATM Forum's LAN Emulation scheme. It connects to an IBM 8260 or similar ATM switch at 100 Mbps. Because it uses optical fiber, it can be positioned farther away from the switch.

IBM's latest, and fastest, ATM adapter is the **IBM TURBOWAYS 155 ATM Adapter**. It installs in Micro Channel bus computers, and operates at 155 Mbps over multimode optical fiber cabling. All the IBM TURBOWAYS adapters support the ATM Forum specification for ATM Adaptation Layer 5, and they all support the Forum's User to Network Interface (UNI) specification 3.0. This includes both permanent and switched virtual circuit support. All of these cards support NetBIOS, SNA, Novell IPX/SPX, and TCP/IP protocols when used with OS/2 Warp or NetWare.

Figure 4.7.   IBM TURBOWAYS 25 ATM MC Adapter.

IPX/SPX, and TCP/IP protocols when used with OS/2 Warp or NetWare. With AIX, they all support Classical IP.

Remote LAN Attachment Software for Mobile Users

Mobile users (fondly called "road warriors") have different concerns than do people who are wired into a LAN. As a mobile user, I want to use my modem connection as if it were my LAN connection. That way, my software works the same way in the office or from a hotel. Of course, when I'm on the road, it works more slowly, but that's expected.

A few years ago, IBM, Microsoft, and others agreed upon a way to share a PC's network card between protocols, such as TCP/IP or SNA. This **Network Device Interface Specification (NDIS)** split the adapter's software, called a **device driver**, into three main pieces. The first piece of NDIS defines a clean interface to higher layer protocols, like TCP/IP or SNA. The second part physically runs the card. The third, called the **protocol manager**, acts like a traffic cop, directing requests for service to the right place. Figure 4.8 shows how NDIS allows a personal computer with two higher layer protocols to run over a single LAN adapter. Many software and adapter suppliers support NDIS.

Novell developed a competing approach, called ODI. NDIS and ODI are not compatible with each other. However, "shim" software can convert Novell's ODI to NDIS (or vice versa). Normally, the hardware-oriented NDIS or ODI device drivers come from a network adapter's vendor, typically packaged with the card. The higher-layer drivers usually come from the LAN software vendor. Either firm can supply the protocol manager.

With its **LAN Distance** software, IBM uses a client/server approach to providing LAN services for remote users. IBM modified the client's NDIS device driver's lower layers to run over an ISDN link or an RS-232 asynchronous serial link instead of over the LAN. The server uses a PC with IBM communications cards. It runs up to 23 simultaneous remote connections at 56 or 64 Kbps with one server. LAN Distance offers road warriors flexibility because it supports many different protocols, perhaps simultaneously. For example, one of my colleagues can run four protocols, TCP/IP, SNA, APPN, and NetBIOS/SMB, concurrently from his LAN Distance client at home.

The **IBM 8235** is a different answer to the road warrior's networking challenges. It uses a specific program to redirect packets from higher-layer software to the RS-232 asynchronous link. It is a complete package of hardware and software, and it supports SNA, APPN, IPX/SPX,

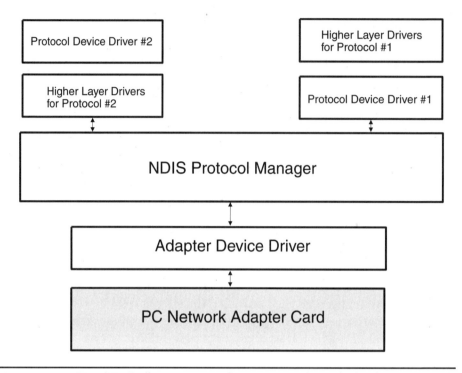

Figure 4.8. How NDIS allows a personal computer with two higher layer protocols to run over a single LAN adapter.

NetBIOS/SMB, and TCP/IP with minimal configuration and fuss. Although it lacks the flexibility of LAN Distance, it offers other advantages. Physically, the 8235 Server is much smaller than the equivalent LAN Distance server, and the 8235 fits easily into a standard rack. IBM has announced its intentions to build a model of the 8235 that will support ISDN connections.

The IBM RISC System/6000 Family

The IBM RISC System/6000 family of computers is a fast computer originally oriented toward scientific and graphical computing. Common applications for RISC System/6000 computers include Computer Automated Design (CAD), geological analysis, molecular chemistry simulations, and scientific visualization. For example, with a RISC System/6000 computer, a chemist might see a simulated reaction taking place, molecule by molecule. The most recent applications of RISC System/6000 technology have been in business. There, the RISC System/6000 performs economic analyses, mines retail sales data for buying patterns, and performs similarly intense computations.

The RISC System/6000's Architecture

The IBM RISC System/6000 can meet many firm's needs, from the desktop to large data center computers. A RISC System/6000 computer uses one of three RISC processors, all of which are based upon IBM's POWER architecture. Some models use older POWER processors, but more recently introduced models use the newer PowerPC and POWER2 processors. The PowerPC models use single-chip processors; the others use a multiple-chip implementation. These processors use a CMOS fabrication process, and they are clocked at various speeds, depending upon the model's target cost.

The RISC System/6000's processor usually performs better than an equivalent Intel processor at the same clock speeds. This is because the PowerPC and POWER2 architectures are highly superscalar; a POWER2 processor can decode and execute up to eight operations in one clock cycle. The actual number of operations that occur depends upon the kind of application being run and the compiler's sophistication. The RISC System/6000's main processor performs best in complex calculations, particularly those that use "double precision floating point" numbers. New RISC System/6000 models support SMP, with up to 8 main processors in a complex. The RISC System/6000 SP2 processors support up to 512 processors in a highly parallel configuration.

The RISC System/6000 uses ECC memory for data integrity. The smallest models use 16 MB of main memory, and the largest models can use 2 GB. Virtual memory for RISC System/6000 computers is a huge 4 TB (trillion bytes). All models have caches of varying sizes, typically between 0.5 and 2 MB. Mechanically, RISC System/6000 computers span the gamut from a notebook computer (the Model N40) to computers that use several dozen racks.

Most RISC System/6000 computers use a Micro Channel bus as an I/O bus, and they use a separate processor-to-memory bus. Larger models use one or more enhanced Micro Channel buses, capable of running at 160 MBps. However, IBM has yet to announce adapters to support these higher speeds. Some newer, smaller models use PCI or AT buses for I/O.

Most RISC System/6000 computers don't have as much I/O capacity as, say, an AS/400 or a System/390, but they outrun most PCs. The RISC System/6000 SP2 systems are exceptional; they can have up to 512 Micro

Channels, one per processor complex. Most RISC System/6000 computers are sufficiently fast to be a server system for a moderate number of users. They can also fulfill the role of a traditional, time sharing system, using inexpensive character mode terminals.

For long-term storage, the RISC System/6000 can use SCSI, RAID, or **Serial Storage Architecture (SSA)** disks. SSA is a new kind of disk controller, and it runs faster than any kind of SCSI controller. Today, it can attach over 1 TB of disk storage to a single RISC System/6000. With IBM's new **7133** disk drives, this trillion bytes of disk storage fits into two 19-inch-wide racks.

Groups of RISC System/6000 computers can work together using a new kind of channel, called the **Fibre Channel**. IBM, Hewlett-Packard, Sun Microsystems, and other firms originally developed Fibre Channel as a high-speed channel technology to attach CPU, I/O, and mass storage devices together. As such, it can provide LAN-like services as well, supporting speeds of 133 Mbps to over 1 Gbps over optical fiber cabling. This makes Fibre Channel links suitable for high-throughput I/O processing. Fibre Channel also implements the SCSI command set, so Fibre Channel attaches compatible disks to RISC System/6000 computers. Fibre Channel uses a switch to direct traffic over the channel.

The AIX Operating System

The RISC System/6000 family of computers uses the **Advanced Interactive eXecutive** (AIX) operating system, IBM's enhanced version of the UNIX operating system. IBM has made a number of contributions to UNIX. The most important of these are a more reliable file system, an extensible disk management system, and a core, or kernel, that lets the system load and unload device drivers dynamically.

To change earlier versions of UNIX, someone needed to completely recompile and rebuild the kernel, shut the system down, and restart it. With AIX, an operator simply fills out a screen that describes the new device to be added, removed, or changed. With earlier versions of UNIX, if a file system overflowed, a technician made a complete copy of the existing data, carved out a new, larger area of disk, and then restored the data. With AIX, an operator tells the system to extend the file system. AIX is a commercial-strength UNIX system.

AIX is also a friendlier UNIX system. With some UNIX systems, users must memorize cryptic commands to configure and manage the system. AIX provides the **System Management Interface Tool (SMIT)** instead.

SMIT lets users fill out onscreen forms, gives hints along the way, and includes a complete help facility. While SMIT makes UNIX accessible to ordinary mortals, AIX as a whole is UNIX for the rest of us.

Specific RISC System/6000 models

As of this writing, the RISC System/6000 family has over 25 basic models. This doesn't include IBM's POWERparallel systems. We'll discuss three models in detail.

The RISC System/6000 Model 390

The RISC System/6000 Model 390, shown in Figure 4.9, is a fast desktop machine, using a POWER2 processor at 67 MHz, along with an optional 0.5 or 1 MB cache. Because it uses the POWER2 processor, it can execute up to eight operations in one clock cycle. To quote a colleague, "this baby really screams."

The Model 390 comes standard with 32 MB of main memory and 2 GB of SCSI-2 internal disk storage. It allows main memory to expand to up to 512 MB, and internal disk storage up to 9 GB. It comes with an integrated SCSI-2 fast/wide controller. The controller has two ports, one for

Figure 4.9. IBM RISC System/6000 Model 390.

internal devices, and one for external drives. It also comes with a CD-ROM drive. IBM also provides a complete set of documentation for AIX on CD-ROM, along with software to read it.

For I/O expansion, the RISC System/6000 Model 390 has four open Micro Channel slots. This is sufficient for a client machine on a LAN. If, for example, the machine is to be used as a CAD client, one slot might hold a graphics processor and another might contain a controller for a stylus and pad. A couple of slots are still available, say, to put the Model 390 onto a fast network such as FDDI or ATM.

The Model 390 is also large enough to use as a server platform for a small workgroup. Disk expansion is limited, though, by the number of slots. It is also suitable for use a time shared system for small businesses. Typically, such firms would buy a software package that runs on the RISC System/6000. Depending upon the application, transaction rates, and response times required, the Model 390 could support up to 50 character mode terminal users.

The RISC System/6000 Model J30

The Model J30 is a RISC System/6000 SMP system. These systems use processor cards with two PowerPC processors each. These processor cards also include 1 MB of cache. Today, the processors are PowerPC 601 models, the earliest PowerPC processor, clocked at 75 MHz. However, IBM has announced a free upgrade for all 601-based SMP machines to the more recent PowerPC 604 processors. Mechanically, the J30 is meant to sit on the floor, beside a desk.

The SMP systems all have slots for global memory, shared between the processors. The J30 has four such slots. It comes standard with 64 MB of global memory in one slot. Memory can expand to 2 GB. IBM ships the J30 with one dual processor card; the J30 allows up to three more cards for a total of eight PowerPC processors. Like the other SMP RISC System/6000 systems, the J30 uses three buses. The first bus is the Micro Channel, for I/O, and the second is the processor to memory bus. The third bus is called the "snoopy bus"; it ensures that the caches on the various processor cards maintain coherent values. This three-bus design is unusual in the industry, as most SMP designs use only one or two.

For I/O, the system includes a 1.44 MB diskette drive, an integrated SCSI-2 controller, and a CD-ROM drive. The J30 has seven Micro Channel slots for expansion. All of the disks supplied with the J30 can be changed without powering down the computer—they are "hot pluggable." If 7 slots aren't enough, the IBM RISC System/6000 PowerSMP Model J01 expansion cabinet adds 8 more Micro Channel slots and 14 bays for disk or tape drives. Constructed like the J30, the J01 also provides hot pluggable disk bays. With I/O features like this, the J30 is well suited for duty as a departmental server. It could also support up to 250 or so users as a time sharing system.

The IBM RISC System/6000 SP2 Systems

The most powerful RISC System/6000 systems, shown in Figure 4.10, use a highly parallel approach. These computers can use up to 512 **nodes**, packaged in frames suitable for use in a data center. Each node contains a processor, memory, and Micro Channel I/O slots; each node also runs a copy of AIX. These nodes reside in tall, floor-standing frames, suitable for a data center environment.

Two kinds of nodes exist. A "wide" node is roughly equivalent in capability to a RISC System/6000 model 590 or 590H computer. It contains 8 Micro Channel slots for I/O expansion. Up to 8 wide nodes fit into a single frame. The second node type is a "thin" node; up to 16 of these fit into a frame. Each thin node is roughly equal in capability to a RISC System/6000 Model 390 or 390H. IBM lets firms mix and match wide and thin

Figure 4.10. A large IBM RISC System/6000 SP2 system.

nodes in a frame as they see fit.

In the bottom of each frame is a special, high-speed switch. This switch is capable of making connections between any pair of nodes in the SP2 system. Each connection can run at a sustained 32 MBps. This is using special "lightweight" device drivers. Without special programming, ordinary TCP/IP connections can sustain up to 12 MBps between nodes. That's faster than an FDDI connection, with much less delay incurred. Programmers can also use the switch as a fast memory-to-memory connection when designing and building highly parallel software.

The SP2 systems can handle many UNIX workloads that would challenge ordinary SMP systems. They also can serve as an easily managed collection of servers. Instead of using separate systems with separate management utilities, the SP2 systems provide a single, more coherent configuration and management interface. For example, due to lower support costs, using an SP2 system instead of several smaller systems as a database server makes sense. The SP2's highly parallel approach also provides high availability: If one node fails, a spare node can be configured to boot and take over its tasks.

Attaching RISC System/6000 Computers to Networks

Because most RISC System/6000 computers use Micro Channel buses for I/O, IBM can offer the same Micro Channel cards for use in PCs and RISC System/6000 computers. However, because the RISC System/6000 uses a different operating system (AIX) than PCs, IBM must write a new, AIX-compatible device driver for each adapter used. Sometimes, IBM writes AIX device drivers before drivers for other operating systems; sometimes, it is the other way round. This depends upon customer demands. For example, IBM's first ATM adapters ran at 100 Mbps, used the Micro Channel, and ran under the AIX operating system. Over time, IBM added drivers for PC operating systems so that the same card would work in Micro Channel PCs.

Attaching RISC System/6000 Computers to WANs

RISC System/6000 systems find themselves more often attached to LANs than to WANs. Many times, the computers themselves are attached to the LAN, and then a multiprotocol bridge or router takes care of moving traffic between sites. So, the RISC System/6000 systems only have a few options for WAN links.

IBM's PCs are ordered differently than other IBM computers. With PCs, each product has its own name. With IBM's other computers, a product might have a name or only a four-digit feature code. This reflects the idea that the adapter modifies the functions of the main machine; hence, it is a machine feature.

For high-speed WAN connections, the RISC System/6000 systems use the **IBM Realtime Interface Co-processor Portmaster Adapter/A** (feature #7006). The Portmaster can drive up to eight ports at 64 Kbps, or a single port at up to T1 or E1 speeds. To connect to X.25 WANs, RISC System/6000 computers use the IBM X.25 Interface Co-Processor/2 adapter. This is the same card that PCs can use, but the RISC System/6000 refers to it as feature #2960. This adapter's functions are also available for use with the AT bus (feature #2961). They provide low-speed (up to 64 Kbps) X.25 connectivity. The **IBM 4 Port Multiprotocol Communications Controller** (feature #2700) provides up to four Bisynchronous or SDLC links at up to 64 Kbps each; the **1 Port Multiprotocol Communications Adapter** (feature #2959) provides a single 19.2 Kbps link suitable for Bisynchronous or SDLC use. Except for the X.25 Interface Co-Processor/2 adapter for the AT bus, all of these WAN adapters are for Micro Channel use.

Attaching RISC System/6000 Computers to LANs

The RISC System/6000 family of computers is "LAN friendly." Indeed, several models come with built-in Ethernet ports. Because some users need additional connectivity, though, IBM supplies expansion adapters for Ethernet, token-ring, FDDI, and ATM networks.

For ATM connectivity, the IBM TURBOWAYS ATM 100 MC Adapter (feature #2984) and its 155 Mbps sibling work with the RISC System/6000. On the RISC System/6000, instead of LAN Emulation device drivers, they work only with the TCP/IP protocol, using the IETF's Classical IP specification. These adapters work with Micro Channel–based RISC System/6000 computers.

For FDDI LAN users, the FDDI-Fiber Single-Ring Adapter (feature #2724) provides a SAS optical fiber connection; the FDDI-Fiber Dual-Ring Upgrade (feature #2723) changes this into a DAS connection. For STP connections, feature #2725 provides a SAS connection, while #2726 supports DAS usage. Similar adapters exist for FDDI over UTP Category 5. These are Micro Channel adapters, as well.

IBM offers several token-ring adapters. The most recent adapter is IBM's premier offering. The **IBM Auto Token-Ring LANstreamer 32 MC Adapter** (feature #2972) works like its PC counterpart, automatically sensing the correct ring speed. It uses a single RJ45 connector, suitable for UTP cabling. It includes an adapter cable for use with STP wiring as well. This is a Micro Channel adapter; for AT bus systems, feature #2971 attaches to either 16 or 4 Mbps token-ring LANs.

For Ethernet users, besides the built-in adapters in some models, three adapters exist. The **Ethernet/FDX High Performance AUI/RJ-45 MC Adapter** (feature #2992) attaches to all types of Ethernet, including full duplex Ethernets, using a transceiver or directly to Ethernets using twisted pair cabling. The **Ethernet High Performance BNC MC Adapter** (feature #2993) attaches to 10 Base 2 LANs directly. These adapters use EtherStreamer technology and provide media speed performance. Finally, the **Ethernet High-Performance LAN Adapter** (feature #2980) also connects RISC System/6000 computers to 10 Base 5 or 10 Base 2 Ethernet LANs; with appropriate transceivers it also can attach to 10 Base T or optical fiber cabling. These are all Micro Channel adapters. For AT bus systems, feature #2981 attaches the RISC System/6000 computer to Ethernet LANs with any kind of cabling.

Attaching the RISC System/6000 to Switched LANs

The RISC System/6000 attaches to switched LANs, such as a switched Ethernet or switched token-ring LAN, using standard Ethernet or token-ring adapters. It also connects to ATM networks using the TURBOWAYS adapters described earlier.

On the RISC System/6000, ATM currently supports the TCP/IP protocol suite only. This is because the TCP/IP community, through the IETF, defined a way for IP to run over ATM before the ATM Forum devised a more general scheme. The IETF's approach is called **Classical IP**, and the ATM Forum's method uses LAN emulation. The ATM Forum is also working on a newer scheme, called MultiProtocol Over ATM (MPOA), due out late in 1996.

Because of these multiple specifications, a computer attached to an ATM network using Classical IP might not be able to talk with another computer on the same ATM network. If the second computer isn't using

Classical IP, then a machine, usually a router, must convert the data from one approach to another. This is inconvenient and messy, but that's what the marketplace requires today. UNIX systems tend to use Classical IP; PCs tend to use LAN Emulation.

As this is written, the RISC System/6000 uses Classical IP, and almost all of IBM's other products use ATM Forum–compliant LAN Emulation. New device drivers for AIX should allow firms to use the same ATM hardware while supporting either Classical IP or LAN Emulation. Until this occurs, be aware of the differences.

Fibre Channel is available for specialized LAN applications using RISC System/6000 computers and other compliant machines. IBM supplies the **Fibre Channel Switch 16/1063**, mostly targeted to RISC System/6000 and POWERParallel system users. This works along with the **IBM RISC System/6000 Fibre Channel Adapter/1063**. Along with the adapter card, IBM supplies device drivers for the TCP/IP protocol, or programmers can write drivers directly for the card. As an example, IBM uses these cards to build clusters of RISC System/6000 systems for specialized applications. Fibre Channel offers high speeds, but it is also defined to provide low latencies, as would be required for an interconnect for mass storage to CPU transfers. However, Fibre Channel doesn't scale like other technologies, especially ATM, to WANs. So, it is likely to see use in small but important environments.

IBM TURBOWAYS ATM Adapters for Sun Microsystems Computers

The IBM RISC System/6000, due to its UNIX heritage, is likely to see service in multivendor UNIX networks. So, IBM also supplies TURBOWAYS adapters for Sun Microsystems computers with Sun's SBus.

The SBus is an I/O bus, like a Micro Channel. These adapters run at 25 or 155 Mbps and offer support for both of SUN's main operating systems, Sun OS and Solaris. The **IBM TURBOWAYS 25 SBus Adapter** works with either UTP or STP cabling, subject to typical 100-meter distance limitations. Like the other 25 Mbps IBM ATM adapters, this card expects to work either with an IBM 8282 ATM Workgroup Concentrator or a 25 Mbps ATM switch, such as the IBM 8285. The **IBM TURBOWAYS 155 ATM SBus UTP5 Adapter** offers 155 Mbps performance over UTP or STP cabling. Finally, the **IBM TURBOWAYS 155 ATM SBus Multimode Fiber Adapter** runs at 155 Mbps over optical fiber cabling.

The IBM Enterprise System/9000 Family

The IBM Enterprise System/9000 (ES/9000) family of computers is the successor to IBM's successful line of mainframe systems. Today, however, ES/9000 computers can fulfill several roles. They can still perform traditional batch processing and transaction processing for tens of thousands of block mode terminal users. They can also be superservers, providing file, print, transaction, and database services for a entire campus of users. With IBM's new **OS/390** or Open Edition software, today's ES/9000 computers can even run software designed for UNIX systems. If an application needs I/O capacity, the ES/9000 packs IBM's biggest punch. If an application needs the fastest possible single-task throughput or quick response times for many users, the ES/9000's speed and capacity are right for the job.

The System/390 Architecture

Today's System/390 system packages one to eight main processors into a single, powerful computing unit. IBM fabricates System/390 (S/390) processors using bipolar and CMOS processes. Each bipolar processor runs faster, but bipolar machines must be liquid cooled. S/390 computers use up to 256 channels for I/O processing; each channel can process I/O requests without involving the main processors.

A Brief Look at System/390 Processors and Memory

System/390 processors have several unique capabilities. For example, systems programmers can partition them to look like several smaller mainframe systems. This is done with the integrated **Processor Resource/System Manager (PR/SM)**. The first way to use PR/SM is **Physically PARtitioned mode (PPAR)**, where a large, multiprocessor mainframe behaves as if it were two discrete systems, or "sides." This capability is only available on the largest bipolar models, but it is useful where security is paramount. Using PPARs also can reduce costs; for example, one eight-processor ES/9000 Model 982 is less expensive than two four-processor systems. Finally, using PPARs can enhance availability, because one processor side can continue to operate even if the other is completely powered off.

Another System/390 PR/SM mode is **Logically PARtitioned mode (LPAR)**. LPARs are used more often than PPARs, partly because they are more flexible. The largest single-sided systems divide into as many as 10

LPARs. Each LPAR behaves like an independent computer, with its own operating system, memory, and I/O paths. This is useful, say, to run multiple System/390 operating systems, such as VM/ESA, OS/390, or VSE/ESA, on the same mainframe or to separate test and production hardware. Finally, to run older System/370 software and operating systems on the larger systems, a systems programmer must create an LPAR and define it to be a System/370 mode partition. This eliminates the need for a native System/370 mode in the larger mainframes. Smaller S/390 processors include a native S/370 mode.

Several large models of ES/9000 computers support vector processors or cryptography processors. **Vector processors** are useful in high-speed scientific computations because they perform many calculations in parallel. The cryptography processors are specialized hardware devices that encrypt and decrypt information to improve data security. They can encrypt data to be stored on disk or to be transmitted over networks. The **Integrated Cryptographic Feature** uses tamper-detecting packaging, so even if someone tries to physically break into the unit, your operations staff can tell. However, because the encryption technique these processors use is powerful, the U.S. government regulates their export.

System/390 computers can support up to 10 GB of main memory. Up to 2 GB of this is main storage, and up to 8 GB is used as **expanded storage**. Expanded storage uses slower chips than main memory; however, it is still much faster than disk storage. Most System/390 operating systems use expanded storage for temporary storage, like virtual memory paging, temporary files, and so forth. Finally, the largest models also include standard hardware assisted data compression. This reduces the amount of data that must be transferred over networks, sent over channels, or stored on disk. Some studies show a 10 to 50% savings of disk storage space versus uncompressed data, although the exact amount of compression achieved varies. This capability can be very useful, particularly if your network uses expensive WAN links outside of North America.

An Overview of the System/390 I/O Subsystem

The System/390 I/O subsystem is IBM's most powerful. S/390 systems use channel processors, and they use two main kinds of channels for I/O processing. The first channel type is called a **parallel channel**. It uses two thick wire cables and first found use on the System/370 computer family. To reduce radio emissions, each wire in each cable is separately isolated and insulated. That's partly why they are thick. One cable, the **bus cable**, carries data. The other, the **tag cable**, carries control signals. These channels are called parallel channels because they transfer data several bits at a time, in parallel. Parallel channels carry data at speeds between 40 KBps and 4.5 MBps, and they can span 400 feet. Parallel channels can each address up to 256 devices, although the number in practice is usually lower.

The second kind of channel, the **Enterprise Systems CONnection Architecture (ESCON)** channel, uses optical fiber cabling. It actually contains two subtypes, the basic ESCON channel and the ESCON eXtended Distance Feature (XDF) channel. Basic ESCON channels run at 10 MBps (80 Mbps); ESCON XDF channels run at 17 MBps (136 Mbps). ESCON channels use a much thinner optical fiber cable.

Parallel channels use a bus topology, daisy-chaining controllers along the channel. ESCON channels, though, can only attach one control unit directly to the channel processor. This control unit, however, can be an **ESCON Director**, which is an "ESCON switch." It can then connect up to 32 I/O control units and 256 devices. An ESCON Director allows any attached ESCON channel to access any attached control unit. The ESCON Director 9033 Model 1 is a tabletop unit, providing 8, 12, or 16 ports. Each port can attach to an ESCON channel or to a control unit. The ESCON Director 9032 Model 2 supports 28 to 60 ports. Systems programmers and operators use a personal computer to configure and manage an ESCON director. IBM also provides ESCON converters to attach older, bus and tag devices to an ESCON channel. In this case, a single ESCON channel, running at a degraded speed of 4.5 Mbps, can attach up to 8 I/O control units.

ESCON channels provide improved reliability and availability because of the ESCON Director's switching function. What isn't immediately clear, though, is that ESCON channels also divide workload more evenly. If channel 1 is idle, it can handle an I/O activity request on behalf of channel 2 if they are both attached to the same ESCON Director or to the control unit itself. This gets information into central storage more quickly.

The **ESCON Multiple Image Facility (EMIF)** shares ESCON channels among multiple LPARs. Previously, each LPAR had its own channel set. EMIF reduces the number of ESCON channels, ESCON Director ports, and control unit channel interfaces needed for multiple LPAR systems. A single ESCON I/O controller can thus appear to be attached to multiple LPARs in the same physical machine.

Operating Systems for System/390 Computers

IBM provides several operating systems for S/390 computers. Of these, some have significant presence inside specific industries. For example, IBM's **Trans-**

action Processing Facility (TPF) is a high-speed operating system used for only the most difficult of transaction processing environments. It might find use, for example, in an airline computer reservation system. A typical TPF environment might have over 100,000 terminals, and it could handle several thousand transactions per second.

MVS/ESA and OS/390

Three general-purpose operating systems exist for the S/390 architecture. IBM's premier operating system for System/390 computers is the **Multiple Virtual System/Enterprise Systems Architecture (MVS/ESA)** system. MVS/ESA grew from a batch-oriented system into a system capable of batch, transaction, and interactive processing. Today, it is compatible with most UNIX software as well.

MVS, as its name suggests, supports virtual memory. It has evolved along with IBM's Enterprise Systems, moving from a 24-bit memory scheme to 31-bit scheme early in the 1980s. In the 1990s, IBM extended MVS to support multiple 31-bit address spaces. Today, IBM S/390 systems support up to 10 GB of real memory and much more virtual memory. Memory, both virtual and real, is allocated and deallocated as needed.

MVS/ESA supports IBM's most sophisticated and most complex software easily. It gets more batch work and transactions completed per hour than any other IBM operating system. It supports the largest system complexes, handles more disk and tape storage, and expands almost limitlessly. With **MVS Sysplex** software, built into new versions of MVS/ESA, firms can tie together many S/390 systems into a computing system that appears as a **single system image**. This simplifies the configuration, management, and operation of a large computing complex.

The name MVS/ESA might not be around for long, though. Unlike, say, OS/400 or OS/2 Warp Connect, MVS/ESA is a more barebones system. To add time sharing to it, IBM sold the **Time Sharing Option/Extensions (TSO/E)** separately. Similarly, for batch processing, one of IBM's **Job Entry System (JES)** packages came separately. IBM's **Resource Access Control Facility (RACF)** provided solid security, but as a separate package. Your staff then integrated and tested these components before placing them into production. This was quite a task.

Late in 1995, IBM announced it would take about 30 of these products, and integrate them into a common offering, called **OS/390**. OS/390 reduces the amount of integration required to run a complex, multiple workload mainframe environment.

OS/390 also adds some facilities we'll discuss in more detail in Chapter 5. Many of them explicitly relate to building client/server programs. For example, one is a **Remote Procedure Call (RPC)** facility that is compatible with the OSF's RPC. The second is IBM's object oriented enabling software, called SOM. SOMobjects will be included in S/390.

MVS and OS/390 take full advantage of IBM's new S/390 parallel processing hardware. In fact, IBM's **Parallel Sysplex**, where several discrete S/390 computers appear as one large processor, depends heavily upon MVS' capabilities. We'll discuss the Parallel Sysplex more when we consider the IBM 9674, below.

VSE/ESA

IBM's **Virtual Storage Extended/Enterprise System Architecture (VSE/ESA)** operating system is best suited to small and medium-sized S/390 computers. It supports these comfortably and easily. VSE/ESA also provides superior features for unattended, remote operation of S/390 computers.

Unlike MVS/ESA, which supports all S/390 processors, including the largest water cooled SMP systems, VSE/ESA only directly supports models with one processor. It operates in Basic S/390 mode. One exception to this broad statement exists: With IBM's CMOS parallel S/390 computers, VSE/ESA can dispatch work within a single **Central Electronics Complex (CEC)**. We'll discuss the hardware details later. Of course, with LPAR support, firms can partition a larger S/390 computer into what appear to be several uniprocessor models. Also, using VM/ESA, also discussed later, VSE can operate as a guest operating system. A single VM/ESA system can, in principle, support dozens of VSE/ESA guests.

Like MVS, VSE has evolved from a 24-bit memory system to a multiple address space 31-bit virtual memory system. Unlike MVS, however, VSE used a series of simple, static **partitions** to allocate memory. Only with VSE/ESA have dynamic partitions become available. Static partitions exist permanently; they accept work as POWER, VSE's batch job entry subsystem, assigns work to them. Dynamic partitions come and go as needed. Each partition can be up to 2 GB, and a system can handle over 100 partitions. VSE/ESA can support up to 2 GB of real central memory, and its design limit for virtual memory is 90 GB. For I/O, VSE/ESA supports up to 256 parallel or ESCON channels.

VSE/ESA is at heart a batch-oriented system, using POWER. It also uses IBM's **Customer Information Control System** transaction processor. With CICS, it shares software with MVS/ESA; CICS runs on both operating systems. Similarly, IBM'S SNA software for mainframes, the **Virtual Tele-communications Access Method**, runs under both MVS and VSE.

VSE/ESA offers a simpler product set than MVS/ESA. It makes medium-sized mainframe systems straightforward to manage, but it lacks some of the sophistication that MVS provides. As one example, although VSE supports SNA and APPN, if your organization needs native TCP/IP support, VSE/ESA doesn't provide it. Instead, it works with gateways that convert TCP/IP to SNA, or with VM/ESA, which supports TCP/IP directly. As another example, with ESCON channels, VSE/ESA can't directly configure an ESCON Director. VSE/ESA also doesn't grow, or **scale**, as well as MVS/ESA because it doesn't directly support the largest S/390 computers. Similarly, it doesn't provide a capability equivalent to the MVS Sysplex.

Some firms use a centralized MVS/ESA complex for highly available, high-throughput, high-transaction-rate computing. Then, they tie many distributed VSE/ESA systems into this complex. In such a system, the MVS/ESA staff can configure, manage, and update the VSE/ESA systems from the central site. Finally, VSE/ESA data center users who outgrow the system find that many of their skills, hardware components, and software applications transfer easily into an MVS/ESA environment.

VM/ESA

We discussed VM briefly in Chapter 1. IBM's **Virtual Machine** system makes each user believe they have a complete mainframe system to themselves. It includes a **Conversational Monitor System (CMS)** that accepts commands that users type on a keyboard, and executes them. VM and CMS together feel very much like a flexible time sharing system. Many firms use VM/ESA and VSE/ESA together to provide a simple system for batch, transactional, and interactive use.

VM/ESA is different than most operating systems, though, in how it handles disk I/O. Since VM's paradigm is to emulate a complete computer, it provides each user with one or more **minidisks,** or virtual disks. So, unlike PC-DOS or UNIX, many VM/ESA systems do not have a single, hierarchical file system. Recently, VM/ESA did add support for such a file system, but most software for VM/ESA assumes minidisks.

VM/ESA is excellent for time sharing and for testing S/390 products and applications. It has a limited batch and transaction processing capability, though. It can't keep up with either VSE/ESA or MVS/ESA in either batch throughput or transaction processing speed. Indeed, one of VM/ESA's most common uses is to share hardware with a VSE/ESA guest; VM provides time sharing, and VSE handles the batch and transaction processing load.

One application in particular occurs frequently in VM/ESA installations: IBM's OfficeVision/VM. This software can automate scheduling, electronic mail, document management, and more across an enterprise. It is mostly oriented toward 3270 block mode terminal users. Nevertheless, for many firms, including IBM, it continues to provide a stable, reliable office automation environment.

Specific System/390 Models

System/390 computers range in size from devices that look like a PC to room filling machines. We'll examine two models of the S/390 computer. One is a large, water cooled system, using bipolar circuitry. The second is a medium-sized building block depending upon low-cost CMOS processors running in highly parallel systems for its performance. Both are capable of acting in the roles of batch system, transaction processor, and server, depending upon the software used. Finally, we'll look at a special-purpose S/390 computer, the IBM Coupling Facility 9674, as a way to introduce IBM's Parallel Sysplex.

System/390 computers use many techniques to avoid failures that cause down time. As an example, S/390 computers not only use ECC memory, but they have spare memory chips in each array. The hardware tracks where bit errors occur over time, and during a scheduled machine startup, it swaps the failing chip for one of the spares. This can forestall a repair until it is convenient. Similar fault-tolerant engineering exists elsewhere as well; many models support the repair of a failed unit, say, an I/O channel, while the rest of the computer continues to work normally. Although the S/390 is not capable of completely redundant operations, it is clear from the S/390's design that high availability is a major goal for these computers.

The IBM Enterprise System/9000 9021 Models

IBM's largest and fastest S/390 models are IBM 9021 computers. IBM produces eleven 9021 models, the largest of which is the Model 9X2. Figure 4.11 shows a 9021 Model 9X2. The 2 at the end indicates that the 9X2 has two sides, an A side and a B side. So, a firm can physically partition the Model 9X2. The 9 indicates the relative capability of the processor, with 9 being highest. The X indicates 10 processors; other models have a 1 through an 8 in this position. So, a 9021 Model 952 is quite powerful, has two sides, and has five processors.

The Model 9X2 can have up to 10 bipolar main processors. It comes standard with 512 MB of main memory, and can expand up to 2 GB of main memory and 8 GB of expanded storage. The 9X2 expands to include up to 10 Vector Facilities and two Integrated Cryptographic Features.

For I/O, the 9X2 comes standard with 64 channels per side, of which 16 per side must be ESCON channels. The 9X2 expands to 256 total channels, but only 96 can be parallel channels. The rest must be ESCON channels. IBM's Open Systems Adapter attaches to the 9X2 in lieu of a channel processor, a possibility we'll discuss in more detail below. The Model 9X2 attaches up to 24,576 I/O control units, and it provides standard S/390 data compression.

The ES/9000 9021 models can also participate in an MVS Parallel Sysplex. They can run IBM's **Integrated Coupling Migration Facility** software, or they can use **Coupling Links** to communicate with another S/390 running the Coupling Facility. The ICMF software is mostly for testing purposes; IBM advises firms to use the Coupling Facility 9674 for production. In a Sysplex, the 9021 must use Coupling Links to communicate with the 9674. The Model 9X2 can contain up to four Coupling Links, two per side. When Coupling Links are used, the maximum number of channels drops to 124 per side.

Two kinds of Coupling Links exist. Both use connectors compatible with Fibre Channel, but one uses 50-micron multimode fiber, and the other uses 9-micron single-mode fiber. The multimode version transmits signals

Figure 4.11. IBM ES/9000 9021 Model 9X2.

up to 1 kilometer, and the single-mode Coupling Link can go up to 3 kilometers.

The IBM S/390 Parallel Enterprise Server Type 9672

IBM's newest S/390 computer models belong to the **IBM S/390 Parallel Enterprise Server** family. These machines, one of which is shown in Figure 4.12, use the S/390 architecture, but they use lower-cost CMOS components in a much more parallel configuration. If your firm's workload consists mainly of batch jobs that must be executed one after another, these processors won't speed them dramatically. However, many workloads, such as transaction processing, database searches, and even some batch jobs, can be performed well in parallel.

In the past, upgrading a large computer system to a newer, faster model was an expensive proposition. Not only did the system's cost increase, but ongoing costs went up as well. When few models existed, each jump between models was expensive. The new systems allow much more granular changes to the computer's configuration, and each change is less costly.

Figure 4.12.   IBM S/390 Parallel Enterprise Server.

Today, IBM offers 12 models in the 9672 CMOS S/390 line. These models use similar chips clocked at two different speeds. The R2 line uses the slower chips; the R3 line gets the faster ones. The R2 line uses between 1 and 7 processors, and the R3 line starts with 5 processors, moving up to a 10-processor model. Each 9672 uses shared memory between these processors; the combination of the processors and memory is referred to as a Central Electronics Complex, or CEC. The R3 models can use up to 4 GB of memory, configured as either main memory or expanded memory; the R2 models only accept up to 2 GB. Unlike larger S/390 processors, main and expanded memory uses the same types of chips, so reconfiguration is simpler.

For I/O, the 9672 models use ESCON or parallel channels. The R2 models support between 3 and 96 parallel channels, and between 4 and 128 ESCON channels. Similarly, the R3 models support between 3 and 96 parallel channels, and between 4 and 192 ESCON channels. Because the 9672 is a small package, it cannot physically accommodate more parallel channels. Finally, a standard IBM 9672 can have up to 12 Coupling Links to attach the 9672 into an MVS Parallel Sysplex.

IBM produces three specialized machines based upon 9672 technology. The first is the IBM Coupling Facility 9674, discussed later. The second is the **IBM Parallel Transaction Server**. As its name implies, it is best at high-volume, highly responsive transaction processing. The third is a machine whose software is optimized around searching relational databases, the **IBM Query Server**, which uses up to 48 processors. Both of these applications are solid uses of IBM's new, lower-cost parallel processing technology.

The IBM Coupling Facility 9674 and the Parallel Sysplex

The **IBM Coupling Facility 9674** comes in three models, the C01, C02, and C03. It uses the same basic technology as the 9672 models. The Model C01 CEC provides between one and six CMOS processing units. The Model C02 uses components like the 9672 R2 models, whereas the Model C03 uses 9672 R3 technology. So, the Model C03 supports hot-pluggable channels and Coupling Links, repair of many parts during operation, and both types of Coupling Links. The model C03 allows up to 4 GB of main memory. The Coupling Facility software runs on several models of S/390 computers, but the 9674 is optimized for this task. The Coupling Facility handles all the locking and coordination within the Parallel Sysplex.

A Sysplex allows multiple Coupling Facilities, so if one fails another can continue. Similarly, it permits redundant Coupling Links between the Coupling Facility and the other processors in the Sysplex. Since the Model C03 supports up to 32 Coupling Links, it links up to 32 separate MVS systems in a Parallel Sysplex. With redundant Coupling Links, the maximum number of systems attached drops.

So, what does a Parallel Sysplex do? It increases system availability, and it gets around three impediments to computer system growth. One way to grow is to use faster processors. As we've seen, this is expensive, and it has a limit. A second way to grow is to add processors, sharing memory. This causes a bottleneck eventually, because the processors must share the memory and its memory controller. The third way adds complete computer systems, but then someone must administer each system separately.

Instead, the Parallel Sysplex allows growth by making up to 32 MVS systems, using both air and water cooled processors, look like a single computing system. For example, Parallel Sysplex software performs load balancing across Sysplex components for certain workloads. So, if a Parallel Sysplex' large processors are busily doing batch jobs, an operator needn't do anything special to redirect some requests, such as CICS transactions or DB2 queries, to less heavily used computers. It simplifies the administration of multiple computing systems, letting a systems programmer "clone" systems as needed to increase capacity. This approach also provides higher availability: the failure of one computer doesn't affect MVS' ability to get work done in a Parallel Sysplex.

Parallel Sysplex software shares data and devices across members of the Parallel Sysplex. MVS/ESA's Parallel Sysplex software coordinates the locking and other administration required to enable this sharing. A Sysplex Timer, the IBM 9037, precisely synchronizes time across all computers within the Parallel Sysplex. So transactions on one computer don't interfere with other transaction within the Parallel Sysplex. The Parallel Sysplex philosophy is to let MVS/ESA manage the workload within the Parallel Sysplex. That way, it can react more quickly to changes in workload, processor availability, and so forth than any staff member. This increases uptime.

Connecting System/390 Computers to Networks

IBM offers ways to connect mainframe systems to networks using the **IBM 3172 Interconnect Controller**, the Open Systems Adapter, the **IBM 3745 Communications Controller**, and the **IBM 3174 Establishment Controller**.

Because the 3745, 3746, and 3174 are more general purpose devices, we'll describe them later. We'll consider the 3172 and the Open Systems Adapter here.

The IBM 3172 Model 3 Interconnect Controller

The IBM 3172 Model 3 Interconnect Controller provides LAN speed connections into IBM mainframe processors. To connect to the processor, this rack mounted device supports both parallel and ESCON channels. The 3172 Model 3 supports token-ring, Ethernet, FDDI, ATM at 100 and 155 Mbps, wide area frame relay, and SDLC. With different software, this controller can provide SNA, TCP/IP, or server connections to users.

The first purpose for the 3172 was to provide a high-speed connection into the mainframe for TCP/IP users. Two software methods exist to provide TCP/IP connectivity. The first, the **3172 Interconnect Controller Program** (ICP), uses more mainframe resources when using TCP/IP, but it runs faster. It supports SNA and APPN/ISR connectivity, working with VTAM on the mainframe. IBM has also announced that it plans to support DLU/R and DLU/S services over the 3172. The second possibility, the **TCP/IP offload feature** software, runs slightly more slowly and only supports TCP/IP, but it conserves mainframe CPU cycles. Using the offload feature reduces the effects of host TCP/IP processing by 30 to 50%.

The 3172 also works with IBM's **LAN File Services/ESA (LFS)** software for VM and MVS. LFS provides file services from the mainframe to users on Ethernet or token-ring LANs via the 3172; we'll discuss it further in Chapter 5. IBM's **LAN Resource Extension and Services (LANRES)** software also works with the 3172. It lets Novell NetWare clients use mainframe disk space and printers. LANRES can also distribute data and software through a LAN, and it can administer NetWare servers from the mainframe.

Finally, the 3172 Model 3 is also useful for WAN communications. The **SNA Communications Program** supports up to 32 SDLC lines and gives those lines direct channel attachment into the mainframe. Using the Wide Area Connection (WAC) adapter and RouteXpander for OS/2 software, the 3172 can attach to a frame relay network or an X.25 network as a DTE, transporting both SNA and TCP/IP traffic. A single 3172 can run the TCP/IP offload feature, the RouteXpander for OS/2 software, and the SNA Communications Program at the same time.

The IBM S/390 Open Systems Adapter Feature

The S/390 **Open Systems Adapter (OSA)** is an optional hardware feature for newer S/390 computers. It attaches a S/390 processor to several different LAN types, including Ethernet, token-ring, and FDDI. IBM has also stated it intends to add ATM to this list, using speeds of up to 155 Mbps. The OSA comes in two models. The first is more expensive and larger, but it includes facilities to offload processing from the main computer. The second model simply provides connectivity from the computer to the LANs. Comparing the OSA with the 3172, the 3172 is supported with nearly all models of S/390 computers, whereas the OSA only works with the most recent models.

Software that uses the OSA implements services based upon SNA, APPN, TCP/IP, NetBIOS, and Novell's IPX protocols. It is useful for ordinary SNA, APPN, and TCP/IP processing, or for disk and file serving with the right software. We'll discuss this software, including LANRES, LFS/ESA, and the NFS option for TCP/IP, more fully in the next chapter.

Like the 3172 Model 3, one model of the OSA can offload TCP/IP's protocol processing. This uses S/390 processor cycles more efficiently, which is particularly important with larger, bipolar processors. The OSA uses software within it, and the **S/390 Open Systems Adapter Support Facility** provides a simple way to update the OSA's software. It also shares the OSA's ports across different LPARs in a large S/390 environment. In some cases, applications can share individual OSA ports.

The OSA is implemented as a new kind of channel, so it attaches directly to the S/390's internal data paths. To software, it looks like a channel attached I/O controller, so the S/390 model of I/O remains intact. The OSA is likely to see service in 9021, 9121, and 9672 processing environments. Older processors can't support the OSA; they must use the 3172. The OSA is fast enough to compete with PC-based file and print servers, and it adds to a PC's data the traditional S/390 strengths of security, backup and recovery, and data integrity. Because the OSA provides LAN connectivity without a separate physical frame, ongoing environmental costs are reduced, as is data center floor space.

Physically, the OSA can attach many LAN segments to a S/390. The OSA's Ethernet and token-ring features each have five LAN ports, and the FDDI feature uses one dual attached station port. ES/9000 9021 models can support up to 80 Ethernet or token-ring ports and up to 32 FDDI ports. Smaller ES/9000 9121 models have half this capacity. Depending upon the model, the 9672-based processors support up to 40 Ethernet or token-ring ports, or up to 18 FDDI ports. Smaller 9672 models support half this much. At any rate, the OSA lets a S/390 system scale from a small LAN node to a highly connected, large server system.

The IBM Application System/400 Family

In 1964, IBM united its computer hardware offerings into the mainframe systems that eventually became the S/390 series. For smaller firms, another division of IBM, based in Rochester, Minnesota, developed the System/3 series of minicomputers in the late 1960s. During the 1970s and early 1980s, IBM Rochester extended the System/3 design into the System/32, System/34, and System/36 computers.

In the late 1970s, though, IBM Rochester introduced a revolutionary design, the System/38. Most computers use a standard processor architecture or an approach based upon Application Programming Interfaces. Instead, the S/38 used a **Technology Independent Machine Interface** that formally defined all interfaces to the computer system for the operating system and for most applications. Some have nicknamed this "TIMI," but most refer to it as the "MI," or the machine interface. The MI is the boundary between anything that must know about the hardware's details, and anything that doesn't. This means that a part of the S/38's operating system resided below the MI. With the MI, IBM could extend the computer system's architecture in a way appropriate for applications, hiding all details below the MI.

The AS/400's Architecture

The **Application System/400 (AS/400)** uses the S/38's techniques to isolate applications from the computer's details. Even more important, the AS/400 is designed to make it impossible to "get around" the MI. So, all applications use the same interfaces to the computer. Instead of multiple security interfaces, say, one for memory and another for files, applications use one interface built into the MI.

Because of this, AS/400 applications are independent from the underlying hardware technology used. Even moving from 48-bit CISC processors to 64-bit RISC processors requires no source code changes to existing applications. On day one, applications for the older CISC AS/400 systems could immediately exploit the new RISC processors. This transition has occurred nowhere else in the computer industry. AS/400 systems also allow coprocessors; one example is feature code #2620, a cryptographic processor. The cryptographic processor, and an optional tamper evident security interface unit, feature code #4754, encrypts and decrypts data communications securely.

Memory on the AS/400 is unique. Whereas most virtual memory systems assign memory on a user by user basis, the AS/400 works like the original Atlas design. It uses virtual memory as a single "pool," available to all users. This approach requires a tightly integrated security system to be effective, and most computers can't provide this. Because of the MI, though, the AS/400 defines a object oriented view of security. Users have various attributes that define their security profile; memory, devices, and other system objects have corresponding profiles. If the user's profile allows the use of a device, an area of memory, or any object within the system, the MI grants access. So, the single pool of virtual memory works.

Today, the largest AS/400 computers can have up to 4 GB of physical, main memory. Available virtual memory is over 4 TeraBytes (TB). Because of the MI's design, when this becomes insufficient, the AS/400's architecture can expand beyond this, with no changes required for most applications.

For I/O, AS/400 computers use a bus design called the **SPD** bus. This was named after an IBM division that was supposed to unite IBM's midrange computers onto a common hardware design. The project failed. Now, the SPD itself doesn't exist any more, but the bus lives on. It is a 32-bit bus, with four parity bits to ensure data integrity. Unlike most other buses, it is asynchronous; it uses no clock. This allows it to accommodate a wide variety of devices with a longer overall bus length. SPD buses on CISC-based AS/400 systems transfer data at 266 Mbps; RISC-based AS/400s have SPD buses that transfer 1 Gbps. SPD buses can't be as long as S/390 channels, but they can be longer than most PC or UNIX system buses.

A single AS/400 system can have up to 19 SPD buses. Most have between 1 and 7. The first SPD bus is copper, and any additional buses use optical fiber links. Using optical fiber links allows increases in speed and distance compared to a copper bus.

The SPD bus communicates with I/O Processors (IOPs). Each IOP is an independent computer, complete with a specialized operating system, memory, and processors. So, somewhat like a channel, the processors hands off responsibility for most I/O operations to the IOP. When the IOP is done, it interrupts the main processor. Unlike a S/390's ESCON channels, though, the IOP and bus design links an IOP to a specific SPD bus. Redundancy, where needed, is achieved using redundant SPD buses, redundant IOPs, redundant cabling, and specialized software built into the operating system. ESCON's switch-based approach is more elegant and scalable, but the AS/400's I/O subsystem meets the needs of many businesses.

Operating System/400

It is difficult to speak of an AS/400 system without **Operating System/400 (OS/400)**. In theory, another vendor could supply an operating system for the AS/400, but this has not occurred. OS/400 is a highly integrated operating environment that comprises most of the operations an AS/400 user would need. For example, OS/400 includes integrated security, a relational database, systems management tools, and many other components that would be optional on other systems. When a user asks for help, it displays information based upon the current application, screen, and field. If a user is unsure what to put into a field, OS/400 can prompt for valid choices.

For an AS/400 user, this integration is paramount. It simplifies operations, eases training, and makes a firm's staff more productive. Because of this, the AS/400 is one of the most inexpensive computers in the world to operate. When considering overall costs of ownership, the AS/400's hardware may appear expensive at first, especially compared with a couple of PCs. The AS/400's ongoing costs, though, are far below PCs and many UNIX-based systems.

OS/400 contributes to the AS/400's stability and high availability. For example, it performs RAID storage control operations, along with IOPs, and handles mirroring. So, if a storage device fails, a technician can replace it while OS/400 continues to run. OS/400 also works along with the uninterruptible power supply and battery backup in some AS/400 models to reduce the effects of power problems and outages.

Finally, the **File System I/O Processor (FSIOP)** and OS/400 integrate file, printer, and database servers into the AS/400's traditional interactive and transactional processing. Now, one computer, with a simple, manageable operating system, can support many software servers for a few users, or for a thousand. If your firm uses traditional, textual applications, and needs PC file and printing services, the AS/400 is a solid choice. For database users and applications, the AS/400's integrated database makes it simple to have textual applications share structured data with PCs. Because IBM has done the integration work, people without pocket protectors can operate and use the OS/400 system.

Specific AS/400 Models

IBM makes several models of AS/400 computers. We'll concentrate on the most recent ones, which use RISC processors. AS/400 computers come in two main forms, the 9402 series and the 9406 series. Within each, IBM offers either an Advanced System configuration or a server configuration. For firms that use the older System/36, an AS/400 predecessor, IBM also supplies an updated, RISC-based processor.

The IBM AS/400 Advanced 36

IBM's System/36 users have proven a dedicated lot. For them, IBM provides the **Application System/400 Advanced 36** series. These computers use IBM's PowerPC AS processor, fabricated using CMOS. They run S/36 applications between two and eight times faster than older models. To use this new RISC processor, existing S/36 applications need not change. The Advanced 36 models also use less floor space and air conditioning than earlier S/36 models. This reduces ongoing costs.

These computers are designed for firms that use System/36 processors today, and whose existing applications work well for them. These firms can continue using their applications while pursuing a migration, at their own pace, into AS/400 applications. Because the S/36 is also often used as a remote, unattended processor, the Advanced 36 also contains features for unattended operations, such as remote power-on and shutdown. This allows personnel at a central site to control the Advanced 36 over an SNA network.

The AS/400 Advanced 36 comes in three packages, the Entry, Growth, and Large models. Each comes with the main system processor and 32 MB of main storage; the Large model can expand up to 96 MB. The Advanced 36 uses a bus for I/O, along with a separate Multi-Function I/O Processor. Because of this dual processor approach, one main processor and one for I/O, the Advanced 36 is less expandable than larger AS/400 computers, which can have up to 19 buses.

The AS/400 Advanced 36 allows one to eight WAN communications lines, and it supports up to 80 block mode terminals. The Advanced 36 can attach up to two LANs, either of which can be Ethernet or 16/4 Mbps token-ring. If these LANs contain PCs, the Advanced 36 supports PC file and printer sharing, along with a simple database query facility for PC users. For storage, the Entry model uses a single 1 GB disk, and the Large model uses up to four 1 GB disks. All models use a 2.5 GB quarter-inch cartridge tape drive for backups.

For compatibility, the AS/400 Advanced 36 runs an older, simple operating system called the System Support Program (SSP). It also supports both SSP and OS/400 within the same computer. So, firms can run existing S/36 applications, adding new AS/400 applications or converting existing applications from S/36 to AS/400. For those users of the hundreds of thousands of S/36 computers today, the AS/400 Advanced 36 should be a simple swap with immediate savings.

The IBM AS/400 9402 Model 400

The AS/400 9402 Model 400, shown in Figure 4.13, puts the integrated openness of OS/400 into a compact package. It uses a CMOS PowerPC AS microprocessor. This RISC processor is a version of the PowerPC architecture optimized for commercial computing. It runs all AS/400 software with better performance and greater capacity than earlier AS/400 compact models.

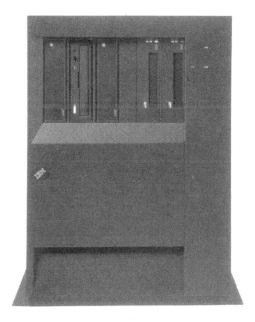

Figure 4.13. IBM AS/400 9402 Model 400.

IBM measures the performance of AS/400 models against each other, comparing each to a base model with a performance designated as 1. If a model has a performance of 2, it is twice as fast as the base model. Depending upon the processor feature chosen, the Model 400 performs between a 4.1 and a 10.9 in IBM's testing. Of course, performance on specific applications will vary.

The Model 400's main memory sizes start from a base configuration of 32 MB, and goes up to 224 MB. All the Model 400 computers use one bus for the system's I/O. Because the Model 400 is a compact model, it doesn't have as much room as other AS/400 models for I/O expansion. However, nearly 24 GB of disk storage attaches to the system. The Model 400 comes standard with a 650 MB quad speed CD-ROM drive for software distribution.

The Model 400 processors can support up to 280 block mode terminal users, but performance considerations might reduce that number in practice. The Model 400 has six slots available for feature cards, such as communications processors, fax I/O processors, or terminal I/O controllers. LAN adapters, including 16 Mbps token-ring, 4 Mbps token-ring, or Ethernet LAN adapters, can occupy up to two of these slots. For communications over a WAN, the Model 400 can support up to 20 lines.

The IBM AS/400 9406 Advanced Series with PowerPC AS

The Advanced Server 53S is IBM's most powerful AS/400 system optimized for use with server software. Figure 4.14 shows this computer. The 53S shares hardware with the Advanced System 530, but the 530 is oriented toward more traditional applications such as transaction processing. The 53S, for example, attaches only seven terminals, whereas the 530 can physically handle up to 7000 block mode terminals. The 53S's relative processor rating for interactive work is a mere 8.3 compared with the 530's 119 and the model 400's maximum of 10.4. In a client/server workload, though, the 53S rates a relative value of up to 101.4.

The 53S and 530 use up to four BiCMOS PowerPC AS processors, which improves performance by up to 330% over older models. Because BiCMOS runs hotter than CMOS, it needs more cooling; the 53S or 530 would likely see service in a data center environment as a result. Each system contains between 256 MB and 4 GB of ECC memory, and a battery backup system keeps the contents of memory valid during power outages of a day or two.

Figure 4.14. IBM Advanced Server 53S.

For I/O, the systems accept up to 19 System I/O buses, each of which can run at either 266 Mbps or 1 Gbps; up to 237 feature cards (usually I/O Processors) can attach to these buses. Up to 16 of these IOPs can be LAN adapters, and the 53S comes with at least one LAN adapter. In addition, these models accept up to 200 WAN lines, providing a large communications capacity. The 53S or 530 also manage up to 520 GB of disk storage.

Clearly, these systems can become large I/O engines, although they don't have the I/O capacity of the biggest mainframe systems. The need for large, fast I/O is typical of commercial processing. It is also typical of much client/server processing. Consider, for example, what file, printer, fax, and database servers do: They move data around more than they calculate. This I/O capacity, along with OS/400's low operational costs, make the AS/400 a good hardware platform for many common servers.

Connecting IBM AS/400 Systems to Networks

Attaching AS/400 computers to networks is somewhat different than for PCs or mainframes. PCs attach to LANs more than WANs, and mainframes tend to have communications controllers to handle these tasks. By contrast, networking features tend to be integrated directly into the AS/400. This is because AS/400 systems can function either as a central site or as a remotely operated computer. Your designers might choose to attach an AS/400 directly to one or more WAN links, or they might prefer to attach it to a LAN, using a different device for WAN connectivity. Specific designs will vary.

Connecting IBM AS/400 systems to WANs

For WAN connectivity, the AS/400 Advanced Series has several possibilities; we won't cover all of them here. The AS/400 sorts WAN speeds into three "brackets." Low-speed lines run at 19.2 Kbps or slower, and use the EIA 232/V.24 interface. Medium-speed lines run between 19.2 Kbps and 64 Kbps, using V.35, X.21, or ISDN interfaces. High-speed lines run at up to T1/E1 (2.048 Mbps) and use either V.35, V.36/RS-449, or X.21 interfaces. High-speed lines use an adapter, feature code #2666, as an IOP. This IOP only supports one line; to use multiple T1 lines, an AS/400 system needs multiple #2666 cards.

Low- and medium-speed WAN options use an IOP, feature code #2623, to control them. One #2623 can control between two and six lines. Because most AS/400 systems come with at least one WAN line for electronic customer support, most sites don't need to add another #2623 IOP right away. Figure 4.15 shows the low and medium speed connectivity options available.

Feature Code	Description
#2605	ISDN Basic Rate Interface Adapter
#2609	EIA 232/V.24 Two-Line Adapter
#2610	X.21 Two-Line Adapter
#2612	EIA 232/V.24 One-Line Adapter
#2613	V.35 One-Line Adapter
#2614	X.21 One-Line Adapter
#2654	EIA 232/V.24 Two-Line 20E
#2655	EIA 232/V.24 Two-Line 20
#2656	X.21 Two-Line 20
#2657	EIA 232/V.24 Two-Line 50E
#2658	EIA 232/V.24 Two-Line 50
#2659	X.21 Two-Line 50

Figure 4.15. Low and medium speed connectivity options.

The numbers after the description, if present, refer to the kind of cable supplied with the adapter; 20 refers to a 20-foot cable, and 50E refers to a 50-foot enhanced quality cable. If no number appears after the description, IBM assumes your firm will provide needed cables.

Using these cards, the AS/400 supports several datalink protocols, including SDLC, IDLC (for ISDN), X.25, and BiSynChronous (BSC). Over these, the AS/400 supports SNA and APPN directly. It also emulates job entry devices, so an AS/400 can act like an RJE or NJE device in a mainframe network. Most often, though, AS/400 computers will be linked by APPN protocols. That way, AS/400s can talk as peers across the network without necessarily going through a central site.

Connecting AS/400 Systems to LANs

AS/400 systems connect to LANs as they do to WANs; each LAN type has an appropriate feature code. However, two specialized processors exist in addition to typical Ethernet or token-ring adapters. One is for Apple Macintosh users, and it provides an adapter that is compatible with Apple's LocalTalk network. LocalTalk is a 230 Kbps network built into almost every Macintosh ever made. The second is the AS/400 File System IOP (FSIOP), which puts a PC style file and printer server onto a single feature card.

AS/400 systems have used several Ethernet and token-ring adapters over the years. Some of oldest of them, particularly the oldest Ethernet cards, are slow in today's client/server environments. In Advanced Server and Advanced System models, these oldest cards won't physically fit. So, we'll ignore them here. Figure 4.16 shows the optional LAN connectivity features available.

The first four of these adapters mostly connect as you'd expect. The Ethernet adapter uses an AUI connector; IBM doesn't supply the transceiver. This approach provides the flexibility to attach to any kind of Ethernet physical medium, such as ThinWire, optical fiber, or twisted pair.

The LocalTalk Workstation Adapter implements Apple's LocalTalk specification, providing a 230 Kbps LAN. Each adapter uses a CSMA/CA (Collision Avoidance) scheme and can attach up to 31 Macintosh computers or LaserWriter printers to an AS/400 system. Because LocalTalk operates at such a low speed, though, it is unusual to have that many devices attached. IBM recommends fewer than 20 active, concurrent sessions over this adapter due to LocalTalk's low speeds. With this adapter and Client

Feature Code	Description
#2617	Ethernet/IEEE 802.3 CSMA/CD Adapter
#2618	FDDI Adapter
#2619	16/4 Mbps Token-Ring Adapter
#2665	SDDI (Shielded Twisted Pair FDDI) Adapter
#8054	Workstation Adapter (LocalTalk)
#6516	16 MB One-Port FSIOP
#6517	32 MB One-Port FSIOP
#6518	48 MB One-Port FSIOP
#6519	64 MB One-Port FSIOP
#6526	16 MB Two-Port FSIOP
#6527	32 MB Two-Port FSIOP
#6528	48 MB Two-Port FSIOP
#6529	64 MB Two-Port FSIOP

Figure 4.16. Optional LAN connectivity features.

Access/400 software, Macintosh users can log onto the AS/400 as a block mode terminal and the AS/400 can use Apple printers.

From a client PC's perspective, the FSIOP looks like an ordinary IBM file server. It is compatible with IBM's LAN Server software. Indeed, the FSIOP works in conjunction with IBM's LAN Server/400 software. The advantage of the FSIOP, though, is that this apparent file server is integrated into all of the other data on the AS/400 system. AS/400 applications can access the FSIOP's file system; networked TCP/IP and APPN applications will also work with it. The two-port FSIOP features have two LAN ports; the amount of memory need varies based upon how users and applications might use the FSIOP.

The FSIOP performs up to eight times better than earlier AS/400 file servers. This makes its performance competitive with standalone PC file servers. With the tight integration and low operating costs that the AS/400 and OS/400 provides, the FSIOP's performance provides a good argument to use an AS/400 as a file server. If your firm uses AS/400 applications, say, for transaction processing, using an AS/400 as a file server is likely to prove more effective than using a separate PC.

Finally, IBM supplies specialized devices, such as the IBM 6250 X-Windows display. This display attaches to either Ethernet or token-ring LANs, using TCP/IP and X-Windows protocols. If your firm uses both AS/400 and UNIX-based systems, this is a very useful terminal. With it, a user can run X-Windows applications, and log onto AS/400, UNIX, and other character mode systems. In the Open Systems Center, the 6250 gives visitors an awakening; people walk away saying "I didn't know the AS/400 could do that."

IBM's Components For Building Networks

Now that we've examined IBM's four computer families, we can discuss specific ways to link them into networks. We'll cover IBM's networking products from the wires on up. Sometimes, specific software works in conjunction with a hardware device, such as IBM's Network Control Program (NCP) with the IBM 3745 Communications Controller. When this occurs, we'll discuss the supporting software along with the device itself.

IBM's Hardware for Building Subnetworks

IBM provides many products to help your firm build subnetworks of any size and scope. We'll first consider a sampling of WAN products, including IBM's ATM offerings for WAN use. Next, we'll look at IBM's hubs and bridges for all kinds of LANs. Then, we'll consider IBM's new family of ATM products for campuses and buildings.

Hardware Building Blocks for Traditional WAN Links

IBM supplies many Physical Layer products for WAN links, including modems, CSUs, DSUs, and muxes. We won't go into the details of most of them here. Instead, we'll discuss a few representative samples.

IBM produces many modems. Some models stand alone, with power supplies, while others slide into rack mounted chassis. They also support different network management methods. Some support IBM's **Link Problem Determination Aid (LPDA)** or LPDA-2 protocols, directing alerts to a mainframe's **NetView** network management system. Those modems that support LPDA-2 often report performance information such as line quality and bit error rates to NetView for logging and possible analysis. This can help an operations staff to diagnose performance problems without the telephone company's help.

IBM produces several modems for use with personal computers. These offer little or no network management support and provide speeds of up to 115 Kbps, given optimal data compression. They have capabilities similar to the data/fax modem built into the ThinkPad that we discussed earlier. Mostly, these modems provide asynchronous data and fax support at moderate speeds and synchronous data support at low speeds. To configure them, a user or packaged software sends commands to them from a PC. Modems like these are designed mostly for low cost.

In contrast, the **IBM 7857** V.32bis modem is intended for purely data transmissions, offering no fax support. It also aids network management by supporting IBM's LPDA-2 command set. It runs at 19.2 Kbps over both dialup and leased analog lines, and it includes compression, so actual through-put should be higher. The modem can handle both synchronous and asynchronous transmission modes. It is designed to provide high reliability with a very high mean time between failure, making it suitable for applications like automatic teller machines where availability is key. An operator or systems programmer can configure the IBM 7857 from the operator panel, from a DTE using the Hayes AT command set, or from a mainframe running NetView using LPDA commands. In some circumstances, NetView can configure both a local modem and a remote modem from a central site.

The last modems we'll discuss are microprocessor-based devices operating up to 19.2 Kbps, with one to four ports. Some models of the **IBM 7861** modem support multipoint or multidrop analog unconditioned leased lines; others support fan-in to a central point. All support Switched Network Back Up, a feature that dials through a backup path if the primary line fails. These modems are also compatible with NetView, and your staff can configure them from NetView or from the modem's keypad. They are also compatible with the LIC5 integrated modem in the IBM 3745 Communications Controller. So, an IBM 3745 or 3746 can use the smaller, integrated modems at a central site, and IBM 7861 modems at remote facilities will work with them.

IBM sells and services the IBM **Integrated Digital Network eXchange (IDNX)** series of TDM bandwidth managers; NET, another firm, produces the devices. The IDNX integrates data, voice, image, and video onto leased telephone lines at T1, E1, and higher speeds. A mainframe NetView console operator can manage an IDNX network, reconfiguring the muxed network as traffic needs change. For example, some firms don't need as much voice capacity after hours; NetView could reconfigure the IDNX to allocate that bandwidth to data instead. The IDNX also can dynamically reroute voice and data traffic around failures in a network with alternate routes. The disadvantage of muxes like the IDNX is that ultimately they waste bandwidth because each link is only allowed a specific capacity at any point in time.

IBM provides several N-ISDN products. For example, the **IBM 7845 ISDN Network Terminator Extended** allows a personal computer equipped for basic rate ISDN to share a single digital phone line coming into a home or business with standard analog telephones. The telephone uses one of the two 64 Kbps channels; the PC uses the other. The 7845 also provides advanced services to the telephone set, including speed dialing, last number redial, call hold, call retrieve, call waiting, return of the last incoming call, and three- to six-way teleconferencing. It can even arrange for analog telephone service to continue during a short power outage, because it contains a backup battery. The 7845 gives a home or a small business a way to use the new digital network while continuing to use existing analog telephone equipment.

Finally, IBM also supplies specialized WAN devices, such as the **IBM 9471 High Speed Inverse Multiplexer**. Instead of muxing several lower-speed links onto a single higher-speed line, an inverse mux reverses the process. This is useful when the next increment in speed is large and expensive, such as from T1 to T3. For only two or three T1s worth of required capacity, it may be less expensive to use three T1s than a T3. With the 9471, attaching devices need only one high-speed port; the 9471 distributes the load from that port across the less expensive T1 lines. Indeed, some carriers require that firms provide matching inverse multiplexers at both ends of a fractional T3 service. The 9471 supports up to 12 Mbps of traffic, using two to eight dedicated T1 links.

Advanced WAN links: The IBM 2220 Nways Broadband Switches

The newest WAN product family from IBM is the IBM 2220 Nways Broadband Switch. Figure 4.17 shows a larger 2220 model. The 2220 is available in three models, the Model 300, Model 500, and Model 501. These switches support two kinds of fast packet switching, ATM and Packet Transfer Mode (PTM). PTM is an IBM developed fast packet switching technique that switches variable sized frames rather than fixed size cells. It is particularly useful in networks that value WAN capacity; using PTM instead of ATM on a WAN link can save up to 45 percent of a line's capacity. Your staff can configure each port on the 2220 appropriately; if you should decide to use ATM instead of PTM, someone just needs to reconfigure the port.

Figure 4.17. IBM 2220 Nways Broadband Switch.

The 2220 connects at speeds up to 155 Mbps per port. The models differ in total switching capacity; the Model 300, for example has 2.1 Gbps of capacity, while the Model 500 can handle up to 4.2 Gbps. Devices such as these might function as an enterprise ATM switch, or they might concentrate traffic from other sources, such as T3 or frame relay links.

While one of ATM's strengths is that it is useful in both WANs and in LANs, the two environments still need different characteristics in an ATM switch. LAN users don't care much about the 2220's voice compression abilities, but WAN users do. For many firms, voice traffic is an ongoing and increasing expense, and compressing conversations well saves money.

The 2220 is optimized for use in a WAN that carries ATM, frame relay, fax, voice, video, and other data traffic. The switch can emulate leased line circuits, like T1 or T3 lines, permitting it to carry constant bit rate traffic as well. It can act as a frame relay frame handler, performing frame switching and relaying functions for attached frame relay DTEs. These capabilities make the 2220 more of a WAN switch.

The 2220 is capable of building a reliable, global network carrying voice, data, and video transmissions. IBM's Global Network relies upon it to deliver ATM and other services to most major cities worldwide. Because IBM developed these switches with carriers in mind, they are packed full of features to enhance uptime, such as hot-swappable cards, multiple hot-swappable power supplies, and so forth. A technician can reconfigure the switch while it is running. One option even offers a seismic hardened rack, for use in earthquake prone areas.

The 2220 can guarantee quality of services to various applications, because IBM built bandwidth allocation into its hardware and software. These Network BroadBand Services (NBBS) address areas that the ATM Forum has yet to standardize. NBBS corresponds well with APPN/HPR; these switches can act as DCEs for many mainframe or server DTE systems.

Unlike many firms, IBM is a source for ATM technology; IBM designs and fabricates its basic ATM components. The 2220 is based on IBM's 16-port "ATM switch on a chip" technology. IBM has stated its intention to scale the 2220 line to as large as 51 Gbps; the switch technology was designed for devices as large as this.

In March 1996, IBM announced a joint development, manufacturing, and sales agreement with Cascade Communications for WAN-oriented switches. Cascade is a leader in the carrier switch marketplace, and is known for multifunction switches. The IBM 2219, 2225, and 2230 switches are the outgrowths of this agreement.

The IBM 2219 Nways Frame Relay Switch Model 250 is a switch for frame relay permanent virtual circuits. It is designed for high uptime, offering completely hot-swappable components. It is a six-slot device, with one slot taken by the main processor. It lets your staff monitor the performance of any PVC in the switch, and allows your firm to build completely private frame relay networks, or a network based on a hybrid of private and public services. Each port on the 2219 can be a DCE, a DTE, or a Network to Network Interface (NNI). The 2219 supports speeds up to T1 and E1.

The IBM 2225 Nways Multiservice Switch offers switching for several WAN services, including frame relay, ATM, and Switched Multimegabit Data Services (SMDS). It comes in two models, the Model 400 and the Model 450. The Model 450 is a sixteen slot device, with one or two slots given over to a Control Processor and a redundant Control Processor, if desired. The Model 400 is an 8 slot device, leaving six slots available for port modules. The 2225 supports speeds up to T3 and E3, and permits ATM on the high speed ports. As an ATM device, the 2225 is a DTE, using the ATM Forum UNI specification to communicate with the rest of the ATM network.

The IBM 2230 Nways ATM Switch comes in two models, the Model 600 and Model 650. The Model 600 has a switching capacity of up to 2.5 Gbps, while the Model 650 offers up to 5 Gbps. The 2230 is designed for

ATM-only networks; it lacks the port density, voice capabilities, and low speed ports that the 2220 offers. The 2230 offers ports speeds at T3/E3 and OC3 (155 Mbps).

Hardware for Building Shared Medium LAN Subnetworks

IBM is one of the world's largest suppliers of LAN components. Many think of IBM in light of token-ring networking, which IBM successfully commercialized, but IBM also supplies Ethernet/802.3, FDDI, Fast Ethernet, and 100 Base VG networking components. We've covered most of IBM's adapter cards earlier in this chapter; here we'll concentrate on hubs, and later we'll cover devices, such as bridges and routers, that forward data between subnetworks.

IBM's Ethernet/802.3 Hubs

IBM provides a wide range of Ethernet/802.3-compatible hardware. IBM provides a simple, unintelligent Ethernet/802.3-only hub called the **IBM 8222**. It works best for small workgroups when the LAN isn't attached to many other LAN segments. An 8222 Model 008 hub provides eight 10 Base T ports as well as an AUI connection. The Model 016 supplies 16 10 Base T ports. The AUI port attaches an 8222 to another kind of wiring, such as 10 Base 2. The **IBM 8224**, shown in a stack of five units in Figure 4.18, is a stackable Ethernet/802.3-only hub that is well suited to small workgroups and remote sites. Because up to ten of these hubs stack neatly, with minimal "spaghetti wiring," a small network can grow easily as needs change. Each 8224 contains sixteen 10 Base T compliant ports and one optional expansion port. If your site has an existing 10 Base 2, 10 Base 5, or 10 Base F network, the 8224 can attach to it via the expansion port.

The 8224 comes in two models. The Model 001 is a "managed" hub; to manage it, a Simple Network Management Protocol (SNMP) manager must exist somewhere in the network. (We'll discuss SNMP managers later, in the chapter on designing and managing your client/server system.) The Model 002 is a "managing" hub; it can manage itself and up to nine Model 001 hubs. A stack of 8224s can also divide into several independent LAN segments. This can give your designers greater control over how traffic on the segments interact. Finally, pairs of 8224 10 Base T ports can act as redundant links; this offers better reliability than most Ethernet/802.3 hubs can provide. IBM also supports Ethernet/802.3 in its **8250** and **8260** hubs,

Figure 4.18. IBM 8224 Ethernet/802.3 stackable hubs.

but we'll consider them in a later section because they support other LAN types as well.

IBM's Token-Ring Hubs

IBM makes several token-ring hubs. The first, the **IBM 8228 Multistation Access Unit**, is the original, passive wiring concentrator for token-ring. In early token-ring LANs, the hub wasn't powered; it only contained relays to let stations onto the LAN. When token-ring LANs went to 16 Mbps, the 8228 worked well without alteration; only the adapters changed. One model of the 8228 supports STP wiring and the IBM Cabling System; a second uses RJ45 ports and supports UTP cabling. The 8228 gives the lowest cost per port, with no port level security and without supporting 16 Mbps token-ring over Category 3 UTP wiring.

The next hub, the **IBM 8230 Controlled Access Unit**, is a token-ring-only, single-segment, intelligent hub. It provides per-port security and management, keeping potential intruders off the LAN. Token-rings built using 8230 hubs "heal" better than those with 8228s, and the 8230's active components can drive 16 Mbps signals over Category 3 UTP. The 8230, along with LAN Network Manager, can track some of a network's assets. The 8230 supports up to 80 ports, using up to four **Lobe Attachment Modules (LAMs)**. Each LAM contains 20 ports. The 8230 CAU also includes either copper or optical fiber repeaters. IBM's LAN Network Manager software or a SNMP management station can manage the 8230. Figure 4.19 shows an 8230.

One model of the 8230, the Model 003, allows more flexible wiring than earlier models. With the Model 003, network designers can mix UTP and STP, and RJ45 and IBM Cabling System connectors, easily. It also permits 8228 hubs as "fanout" devices, and "remote" LAMs, up to 100 meters away from the main hub, which can lower costs. The Model 003 can use LAMs from earlier 8230 models, making it an easy upgrade. Like other intelligent token-ring hubs, it detects an adapter inserting into the ring at the wrong speed. With an 8228, a rogue adapter can bring down the segment until it is located and removed; with earlier 8230 models, it would disrupt ring operations briefly while the hub threw the offending adapter off the ring. An SNMP manager, a LAN Network Manager, or a dialup port can all manage the 8230 Model 003. The dialup port helps if your firm's management center is at a different site than the hub; if a line goes down, operations staff can still manage the hub remotely during the outage.

The **IBM 8226** provides eight ports suitable for use at 4 or 16 Mbps. At first glance, this seems like the 8228, but the 8226 offers a "splitter" capability, whereby the 8226 can connect up to eight devices to a single port of another hub. The 8226 supports UTP, STP, and Foiled Twisted Pair (FTP) cabling. Like the 8228, it is an relatively unintelligent device, aimed at a low price point. Other devices, such as the 8230 or 8238, are smarter.

IBM's latest token-ring hub is a stackable model, the **IBM 8238 Nways Token-Ring Stackable Hub.** The base unit includes 16 ports along with SNMP

Figure 4.19. IBM 8230 Controlled Access Unit.

and Remote MONitoring (RMON) management agents. Up to seven additional 16-port units can sit atop the base unit, for a total of 128 possible
ports. Because a single management entity exists, the stack looks like a
single hub to network management software. The stack can work with active ports, passive ports, or a combination. Passive ports cost a little less, but
active ports support greater cable lengths from the hub to a computer. This
hub is suitable for use in smaller workgroups or at remote locations, where
the security, high speeds, and flexibility of a large hub aren't required.

Finally, the IBM 8250 and 8260 hubs also support several token-ring
segments within the hub. Because these hubs have many functions, we will
consider them in a separate section.

The IBM 8244 FDDI Hub

IBM provides an FDDI managed hub, the **IBM 8244 FDDI Workgroup Concentrator**, shown in Figure 4.20. This concentrator, available in six models,
attaches up to ten devices to an FDDI network using UTP Category 5, STP,
or multimode optical fiber cables. Each model also uses two ports to attach
the hub to the FDDI Ring In and Ring Out; thus, the largest model contains
12 ports. The 8244 supports both SNMP and ANSI's **Station ManagemenT**
(**SMT**) protocols directly. It also includes an SNMP **Proxy Agent** program,
which converts SMT protocols to SNMP protocols. Of course, your SNMP
management station must understand these frames. If the network goes down,
operations staff can dial into an RS-232 port to manage the hub. The 8244
supports both dual and single attached stations, and is suited for small, high-

Figure 4.20. IBM 8244 FDDI Workgroup Concentrator.

performance workgroups and for other applications that might need a fast, data-only LAN.

The IBM 8285 Nways ATM Workgroup Switch

The **IBM TURBOWAYS ATM-Workgroup Concentrator Model 001** was IBM's first 25 Mbps ATM concentration device. The 8282 is not a switch; it concentrates traffic onto a 100 Mbps ATM optical fiber link to another switch, usually in an IBM 8260 Intelligent Hub. Recently, IBM announced a true 25 Mbps switch, the **IBM 8285 Nways ATM Workgroup Switch**. Unlike the 8282, the 8285 needs no external switch; the switch is within the 8285. The 8285 also includes a 155 Mbps optical fiber ATM connection to other ATM switches, including other 8285 switches. This makes the 8285 suitable for connecting ATM workgroups throughout a campus.

The 8285 base unit contains 12 ports, and can work with Category 3 UTP or better, or STP cabling. By adding 12 port cards to slots in the 8285 chassis, the 8285 can grow to support up to 48 users. Even when fully populated, the 8285 can support all 48 users at media speed. The 8285 includes ATM Forum compliant LAN Emulation (LANE) inside the switch. So, your existing Token-Ring or Ethernet LAN based software, when configured with appropriate 25 Mbps TURBOWAYS device drivers, will work with the 8285.

The 8285 is important not just because of its technical abilities. IBM took analysts by surprise with its pricing; 25 Mbps ATM competes well with switched LAN technologies. Compared with, say, switched Ethernet, the 8285 offers higher speeds, ATM Quality of Service guarantees, and lower delays. One model of the 8285, the model 00P, is packaged as a bundle. Here, IBM offers consistent pricing, on a per-port basis, for configurations of 12 to 48 ports. This bundle also includes 25 Mbps TURBOWAYS adapters, either for a PCI bus, or for an AT bus. So, with the 8285 Model 00P, you simply tell IBM the number of ports you need and the kind of bus your PCs use, and IBM ships you the switch and the adapters.

Meet the IBM 8250 and 8260 Intelligent Hubs

IBM makes two intelligent hubs capable of supporting several kinds of LANs: the **IBM 8250**, shown in Figure 4.21, and the **IBM 8260**, shown in Figure 4.22. IBM calls the 8250 a "multiprotocol intelligent hub," and its partner,

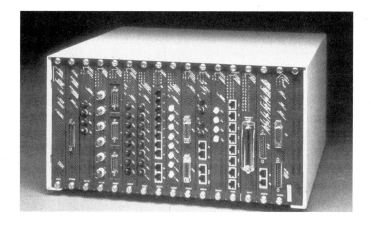

Figure 4.21. IBM 8250-017 Multiprotocol Intelligent Hub.

Figure 4.22. IBM 8260-A17 Multiprotocol Intelligent Switching Hub.

3-Com, calls it "multimedia," but both terms already have several meanings. We'll follow a trade press trend and call these IBM's superhubs. They adapt to UTP, STP, and optical fiber wiring, and they support several token-ring, Ethernet, and FDDI segments simultaneously. The 8260 also supports ATM. Designers can build redundant LAN hardware using these hubs, and technicians can change almost every card "on the fly" while the units continue to run. Both units fit neatly into a standard 19-inch rack.

The 8250 is the older of the two devices. It can handle up to seven Ethernet, three token-ring, and four FDDI segments, or smaller numbers of each in combination. It comes in two main sizes, one with 6 slots, and the larger with 17 slots. One 6-slot model, the 8250/6PS, comes with an embedded Personal System/2. This device is ideal for a branch office that needs a hub and a file and print server or a communications server in a small space. Figure 4.23 shows the 8250/6PS hub.

IBM supplies several kinds of Ethernet, token-ring, and FDDI cards for any of these models. Some cards work with optical fiber cabling, others with copper wiring; some handle 25-pair telco connectors, others use RJ45 connectors. If a site needs high availability, the 8250 supports redundant power supplies, controller modules, and hub management modules. For a high-availability Ethernet LAN, IBM provides transceivers with redundant optical fiber or copper links back to the hub. For sites with SNA block mode terminals, such as IBM 3270 displays, the 8250 offers a card that emulates a small IBM 3174 controller; for sites with ASCII terminals such as Digital's VT series, another card puts a LAT- and TCP/IP-capable terminal server into the hub.

The 8260 also comes in two main models, one with a 10-slot chassis, the other with a 17-slot chassis. The 8260 fits into a standard rack as does the 8250, but it is much taller. The 8260 accepts the 8250's cards along with

Figure 4.23. IBM 8250-6PS Multiprotocol Intelligent Hub.

its own. The 8260 goes beyond the 8250 in providing both token-ring and Ethernet port switching; the 8250 only supports port switching for Ethernet users. With port switching, a technician can assign devices to one Ethernet segment or another using software, without making physical changes in a wiring closet. Just as important for network managers looking at increasing segmentation in the short term, the 8260 supports more LAN segments in a single chassis. For example, whereas the 8250 supports three Ethernet segments, the 8260 provides eight. Finally, the 8260 supports a new Ethernet blade that provides per-port security, eliminating promiscuous mode eavesdropping without authorization.

Both the 8250 and 8260 provide high port densities. Compared to most hubs, 8250 or 8260 hubs fit more ports in a square foot of rack space. Also, because the 8250 and 8260 use advanced electronics to rejuvenate signals and control jitter, designers can specify larger token-ring segments. Of course, the 8250 and 8260 provides flexibility; if token-ring users today want to use FDDI or ATM tomorrow, the whole hub needn't change, just a card or two. IBM also designed the 8250 and 8260 for reliability; technicians can swap a card, a power supply, or even a management module while the hub continues to operate.

The 8260 also supports ATM switching. The 8250 wasn't designed with ATM switching in mind, so the switch hardware won't fit into the 8250. Today, devices attach to the switch using 100 Mbps or 155 Mbps connections. The switch itself doesn't have as much capacity as the largest 2220 models, but it can handle 4.1 Gbps. A single 8260 chassis permits up to two ATM switches, for a combined capacity of up to 8.2 Gbps. A single 8260 allows a maximum of 56 ATM ports.

Just as the hardware can change "on the fly," operations staff can also change these hubs using a management station. The 8250 and 8260 are unusual in the industry because software manages everything in the hub. An SNMP manager, such as **IBM's NetView for AIX**, with the **IBM Intelligent Hub Management Program**, views and changes hub settings. The Intelligent Hub Management Program can manage several hubs and depicts each managed hub graphically. An operator points and clicks on each port or card of interest.

With a LAN management module in the hub, the hub also supplies performance statistics for the various LAN segments it contains. For example, an Ethernet Management Module gives Ethernet collision and frame count statistics for all Ethernet segments in the hub, but it cannot supply token-ring statistics. Similarly, the Token-Ring Management Module supplies token-ring–specific statistics. Since software manages everything in the hub, an operator can do nearly every hub operation except swapping cards remotely. Nearly every card 8250 card also fits into the 8260, allowing a smooth transition into the world of high-speed, switched networking.

IBM's LAN Switches

LAN switches are a hybrid of a hub and an internetworking device. For example, LAN switches can replace bridges in some cases. Indeed, it is impossible to distinguish some kinds of LAN switches from fast, multiport bridges. In other situations, the LAN switch simply acts as a hub with more capacity than a shared medium LAN.

IBM supplies two LAN switches today, and has announced its intention to provide at least two more. Today's switches provide eight ports each, together with a Universal Feature Card (UFC) slot; the promised models, called the 216 models, will provide 16 ports and two UFC slots. These switching devices operate in either a store and forward mode, when faced with error-prone segments, or in a "cut-through" mode. In cut-through mode, they can switch a frame from one port to another in under 50 microseconds. In store and forward mode, it takes between 100 and 4000 microseconds to switch a frame; the actual delay depends upon the frame's length. Most of today's LANs can operate in cut-through mode and take advantage of the better performance that results. IBM's switches adapt, choosing cut-through unless errors reach a particular threshold. Then, when errors occur, it changes to store and forward mode for greater reliability. As errors lessen, it can revert to cut-through mode automatically.

The **IBM 8271 Nways Ethernet LAN Switch Model 108**, shown in Figure 4.24, provides eight switched, full duplex Ethernet/802.3 ports. Each port operates at either 10 Mbps in standard Ethernet mode or at a maximum or 20 Mbps in full duplex mode. Each port may be dedicated to a single device, or it may attach to an Ethernet segment with many attached devices. IBM supplies the 8172 with either RJ45 ports for 10 Base T connections, or with AUI ports for use with transceivers. To monitor traffic inside the switch, IBM includes an EtherProbe port. This separate port "mirrors" the traffic on one of the switch's ports, allowing a technician to attach a LAN trace tool. Total Ethernet-to-Ethernet switching capacity within the 8271 is up to 40 Mbps, depending upon traffic patterns. With a UFC, total capacity increases.

The **IBM 8272 Nways Token-Ring LAN Switch Model 108** creates switched token-ring LANs, also using full duplex adapters for each connection. The 8272 allows either UTP or STP wiring. It operates at 4 and 16 Mbps, with full duplex mode available for a total possible bandwidth of 32

Figure 4.24. IBM 8271 Nways Ethernet LAN Switch Model 108.

Mbps per port. The 8272 also includes a feature called Source Route Switching, which enables it to replace several source routing bridges, with better overall performance. The 8272's standard token-ring–to–token-ring switching capacity is up to 64 Mbps. If either a UFC or many full duplex connections are used, then the switch's aggregate capacity can jump to 128 Mbps, and if both are used, then it can easily pass 128 Mbps. The 8272 includes a TokenProbe port, which operates much like the EtherProbe port on the 8271.

The Universal Feature Cards available let customers build LANs with switched Ethernet or token-ring segments close to users, connecting to, say, a building or campus ATM backbone segment. A UFC might also attach servers to a smaller workgroup. Universal Feature Cards announced to date include those given in Figure 4.25.

Finally, IBM has announced an agreement with Bay Networks to sell and service larger switches produced by a Bay Networks subsidiary. Sometimes, in a large network, using a larger switch may be less expensive than combinations of 8271 or 8272 switches.

IBM's Hardware for Interconnecting Subnetworks

Here, we'll cover IBM's products that connect subnetworks together. A given subnetwork might be a LAN or a WAN link of some sort. The subnetworks might be alike or not. First, we'll cover a LAN-oriented approach, bridging. Bridges extend LANs, sometimes across WAN links. Next, we'll discuss alternatives that are based upon TCP/IP services, including IBM's multiple protocol routers. Finally, we'll consider products based upon SNA and APPN services, including IBM's Communications Controller products.

Datalink/LAN Type	Ports	Device
155 Mbps ATM	1	8271/8272
100 Base TX (Twisted Pair)	1	8271
100 Base FX (Fiber Optic)	1	8271
100 Base VG	1	8271
Ethernet/802.3 10 Base T	4	8271
Ethernet/802.3 10 Base FL	3	8271
Token-Ring UTP/STP	4	8272
Token-Ring Fiber Optic	2	8272
Token-Ring/Ethernet Bridge	1	8272
FDDI (Twisted Pair UTP5)	1	8271/8272
FDDI (Dual Attached Fiber)	1	8271/8272
FDDI (Single Attached Fiber)	1	8271/8272

Figure 4.25. Universal Feature Cards.

Figure 4.26. IBM 8229 Model 002 Bridge.

IBM's Bridges

IBM makes and sells mostly token-ring bridging products, although IBM also supplies products for Ethernet and other environments. For example, the **IBM 8229 Model 002**, shown in Figure 4.26, provides translational bridging between Ethernet and token-ring segments. This capability should be used carefully, and lends itself well to higher layer protocols like SNA and NetBIOS. The 8229 also supports IPX/SPX (for NetWare) and TCP/IP, but customers with large networks tend to route these protocols between disparate MAC layers rather than bridge them. As described earlier, the 8272 switch can also accept a UFC that translates from token-ring to Ethernet.

IBM's Token-Ring–to–Token-Ring Bridge

The **IBM 8229 Model 001** acts as a local token-ring–to–token-ring source routing bridge. It forward frames at media speeds across all frame sizes. The 8229 mounts into a standard 19-inch rack and uses no monitor or keyboard. A technician configures the 8229 using a configuration program on a personal computer elsewhere on the token-ring. It also comes in a WAN version, the **IBM 8229 Model 003**, which provides a remote bridge over leased line at speeds up to T1 or E1.

The **IBM Local Token-Ring Bridge/DOS** program runs on a PC and provides a local token-ring–to–token-ring source routing bridge. Its performance depends on the token-ring adapters used, the computer's processor, the bus type in the computer, and the number of filters configured into the bridge. It can forward frames at media speed given the correct supporting hardware. The personal computer won't fit as easily into a 19-inch rack, and it needs a monitor and keyboard. Some installations use racks for the processors and keyboards, switching a single display between the bridges. In contrast to the 8229, the PC-based program lets a technician build sophisticated filters. Also, if your network changes so the bridge isn't needed, your firm still has a personal computer and two perfectly serviceable token-ring adapters.

IBM also makes several other bridges, meeting various needs for performance and connectivity. The **IBM LANStreamer Token-Ring Bridge/DOS** works similarly. It provides media speed performance across all frame sizes using the IBM LANStreamer 32-bit Token-Ring Adapter. The **IBM Remote Token-Ring Bridge/DOS** program works like the local version, but it works with a leased line at speeds up to T1 or E1. IBM also supports the older **IBM Token-Ring Network Bridge Program** version 2.2.4. To configure and manage these bridges, operations can use the **IBM LAN Bridge Manager/2**. It centralizes bridge software distribution in a large token-ring subnetwork, and so a single person can install, configure, and modify all of the bridges in a token-ring subnetwork.

IBM's multiprotocol routers also can act as token-ring source routing bridges. The IBM 6611 and 2210 Nways Multiprotocol Routers can bridge token-ring traffic between LAN segments. The 2210 can bridge token-ring traffic over PPP WAN links. The 6611 can also handle remote bridging along with the IBM Remote Token-Ring Bridge/DOS, providing a simple way for several remote sites to bridge into a multiport central site. The 6611 has one more remote bridging method, using frame relay links. It can work with other 6611 multiprotocol routers or with IBM's **RouteExpander/2** software. RouteExpander/2 is software that runs on an OS/2 system, often with a file and print server or a communications server. It connects to frame relay WAN links, and it routes and bridges traffic. It is entirely compatible with the 6611 Nways Multiprotocol Router, so it can easily be a remote site bridge on a frame relay network.

The **IBM Frame Relay Token-Ring Bridge/DOS** program runs on a dedicated machine and provides source routing bridge services over a frame relay or a leased WAN line at up to T1 or E1 speeds. This bridge interoperates with IBM's RouteXpander/2, the IBM 6611 Network Processor, and other IBM Frame Relay Token-Ring Bridge/DOS bridges. If other vendors implement the IETF's RFC 1294 "Multiprotocol Interconnect over Frame Relay Specification," the IBM Frame Relay Token-Ring Bridge/DOS should work with their devices also.

IBM's Ethernet-to-Ethernet Bridges

Both the IBM 2210 Nways Multiprotocol Router and the IBM 6611 Nways Network Processor, described later, can act as transparent bridges. These devices support transparent bridging between LAN segments; they support WAN links also, using the **Point-to-Point Protocol (PPP)** as a Datalink protocol for WAN bridged traffic. The 6611 further allows transparently bridged traffic over frame relay links. Transparent bridging in a routed network is particularly useful for NetBIOS and Digital's LAT protocols, since they have no Network Layer and therefore cannot be routed like most connectionless protocols.

Managing Bridged LANs

We'll discuss systems and network management more in Chapter 6, but the subject deserves a brief mention here. IBM's **LAN Network Manager** helps to monitor and manage all aspects of a token-ring subnetwork. It manages token-ring adapters, monitors which adapters are inserted into the ring, manages port-level security on 8230 hubs, and maintains a database of the assets that make up a token-ring subnetwork. It can also monitor how heavily a ring is used so that designers know when to split a ring if it's too busy.

LAN Network Manager also performs a rudimentary security function. If someone enters the ring without authorization, LAN Network Manager can force them off. This way, if a new user (or someone who has moved offices) hasn't told your operations staff about the new connection, they can find out and manage it accordingly. LAN Network Manager also provides links to other network management programs, such as NetView on a mainframe or NetView for AIX. As a result, it is part of an enterprise wide network management approach.

IBM's Multiprotocol Routers: TCP/IP-Based Internetworking

Although IBM is known for building large, mission critical networks with its SNA and APPN protocols, IBM also builds networks using multiprotocol routers. Sometimes, both SNA- and TCP/IP-based internetworking devices are appropriate in a network. We'll look at the multiprotocol router viewpoint in this section.

Your designers might use routers in a network for one of several reasons. First, routers help if a subnetwork is running out of addresses. In a TCP/IP network, for example, some classes of addresses only allow 254 TCP/IP systems on a bridged network. To add the 255th computer, a TCP/IP router must route packets between two different TCP/IP network numbers. This is a common, and solid, reason to use routers.

Next, routers with **DataLink Switching** (DLSw), an IBM developed technique described in RFC 1434, can help designers to overcome the seven-hop limitation of most existing token-ring cards and bridges. Also, using routers in strategic locations can filter traffic going onto WAN links, using WAN capacity more efficiently. Again, this is a good reason to use routers.

Finally, routers can also block broadcast storms caused at the Datalink Layer, although routers can cause storms themselves if they are misconfigured. Broadcast storms within a campus are often cited as cause to microsegment a LAN with many routers; this is poppycock in most networks. Most switched or bridged LANs can easily handle hundreds of devices before broadcast storms become a problem.

Most firms these days need routers for several protocols and prefer to use one box to provide similar functions for these protocols. Cisco Systems built the first commercially successful many protocol router; Wellfleet Communications, Proteon, and IBM followed. Multiprotocol routers are most effective when routing connectionless Network Layer protocols, such as TCP/IP, IPX/SPX, AppleTalk, and DECnet.

If a router cannot route a protocol, it usually bridges it. Some use DLSw or other, proprietary techniques, to translate connection-oriented protocols such as SNA and APPN to a "routable" (read connectionless) protocol, such as IP, and back. This is less effective than using, say, a 3745 or a 3746 when routing SNA or APPN. Multiprotocol routers typically incur more variable delays than connection-oriented devices such as the 3745 and 3746. They also don't fill WAN links as well because they rely on TCP/IP and its congestion management techniques, which aren't as effective as SNA or APPN.

However, on frame relay WAN links, a designer can assign one virtual circuit to the routed protocols and a second virtual circuit to connection-oriented protocols, such as SNA and APPN. This is becoming a more common way to consolidate multiple protocols onto a single WAN line, especially for branch offices. IBM's **RouteXpandeR/2 (RXR/2)** is useful in this way, routing connectionless protocols, and concentrating both connectionless and connection oriented traffic onto frame relay lines. We'll talk about RXR/2 more later.

IBM's multiprotocol routers are most effective when firms want to route SNA and NetBIOS traffic over a TCP/IP-based infrastructure. Early attempts by other vendors to route SNA and NetBIOS traffic met with failure because these connection-oriented protocols expect smaller variations in delay than connectionless, adaptive routed networks can provide. So, when networking topologies changed or when traffic grew, SNA and NetBIOS sessions would be interrupted because the routers would lose traffic. Also, NetBIOS tends to be a "chatty" protocol, causing unnecessary WAN traffic. IBM invented DataLink Switching (DLSw) to fix these problems, then made it available as a published specification to the rest of the industry. Several other vendors now support DLSw, and IBM's multiprotocol routers should interoperate with them, although IBM hasn't tested all the possible combinations.

IBM also fully supports APPN networks with APPN Network Node software on their 6611 family of multiprotocol routers. Because some customers want their SNA and APPN traffic to have priority over other traffic, IBM has also defined a flexible priority management scheme, with class of service names. This further ensures your mission critical transaction processing traffic gets through the TCP/IP network as quickly as possible.

The IBM 6611 Nways Multiprotocol Router

IBM's first router was the **IBM 6611 Nways Multiprotocol Router**, sometimes called the **IBM 6611 Network Processor**. It was originally built on the IBM RISC System/6000 hardware platform, using the desktop and freestanding CPUs. These devices, the models 140 and 170 respectively, were withdrawn from marketing in late 1994, but they are still compatible with the newer models of the 6611 Network Processor family. The software that runs on all of the IBM 6611 models is called the IBM **MultiProtocol Network Program (MPNP)**.

The next Model 6611 is the 6611 Network Processor Model 120. It is a fixed-configuration, moderate-cost device. The Model 120 offers all of the possibilities of the 6611 line in a low-cost, fixed configuration. The IBM 6611 Model 125 is a recent addition to the 6611 Nways line. It is a two-slot model, allowing a configuration that changes over time. The Model 145, shown in Figure 4.27, contains four slots for adding intelligent adapters, and the Model 175 has seven. These devices can be rack mounted and reduce significantly the amount of space needed compared to their predecessors, the Models 140 and 170. For example, the Model 175 uses 62 percent less space than the Model 170. Figure 4.28 shows the maximum capacities of each device for LAN or WAN devices. Most real-world configurations would use a combination of LAN and WAN connections, reducing these maximum numbers.

Figure 4.27. IBM 6611 Model 145 Network Processor.

6611 Model	Maximum WAN Links Attached	Maximum LAN Segments Attached
120/125	8 SDLC or 4 high-speed serial lines	4 token-ring or Ethernet
145	16 SDLC or 8 high-speed serial lines	8 token-ring or Ethernet
175	28 SDLC or 14 high-speed serial lines	14 token-ring or Ethernet

Figure 4.28. Maximum Capacities for LAN and WAN Devices.

The 6611 line uses intelligent adapters to connect to LAN and WAN links. These cards have a RISC microprocessor on board, along with memory for routing tables, software, and packets in transit. LAN adapters for the 6611 include two ports; two token-ring ports, two Ethernet ports, and one token-ring port with one Ethernet port. The main processor of the 6611 supports network management with the Simple Network Management Protocol (SNMP), and processing router-to-router updates. It also handles DLSw processing. All other processing occurs in the distributed, intelligent cards.

The 6611's WAN adapters can provide several ports per card as well. One combination supports four SDLC ports and two high-speed serial ports. The SDLC ports are low-speed lines, intended to connect older 3274 and 3174 display controllers to the 6611. The 6611, with its DLSw support, switches SNA traffic over the TCP/IP network to another 6611 router, which then takes the traffic off the TCP/IP network and resends it as SNA traffic. DLSw can consolidate traffic from several older SNA PU Type 2 devices onto a single PPP line or Frame Relay line. Another WAN adapter supports two high-speed serial ports, each capable of operating at T1 or E1 speeds.

In late 1994, IBM announced combination adapters. These cards support one LAN port and one or more WAN ports. These cards are useful in considering the needs of remote sites. Figure 4.29 shows the characteristics of these cards.

Across these LAN and WAN lines, the IBM 6611 family routes several protocols. The 6611 supports all routing protocols over both token-ring and Ethernet LAN interfaces, along with frame relay and PPP WAN interfaces. The SDLC links support only SNA and APPN PU Type 2 or PU Type 2.1 nodes. Transparent bridging only works on Ethernet LAN segments, as expected, and source route bridging only works for token-ring segments. Translational bridging, compatible with the IBM 8229, works over token-ring, Ethernet, frame relay, and PPP. Figure 4.30 summarizes the 6611 family's protocol support.

The IBM 6611 Network Processor family running the MPNP supports most of the protocols in use in large organizations today. For TCP/IP,

LAN Port	WAN Ports	WAN Port Speeds
One Ethernet	One X.25	T1/E1
One token-ring	One X.25	T1/E1
One Ethernet	Four SDLC	19.2 Kbps per SDLC port
One token-ring	Four SDLC	19.2 Kbps per SDLC port
One Ethernet	Two multi-interface serial	T1/E1
One token-ring	Two multi-interface serial	T1/E1

Figure 4.29. 6611 Combination Adapter Characteristics.

it supports the most common router to router protocols as well, including OSPF, RIP, RIP-2, and EGP. The OSPF and RIP implementations have been tested to interoperate with those from Bay Networks, Proteon, and Cisco.

Just as important, the 6611 can be managed by a Simple Network Management Protocol (SNMP) management station, such as IBM's **NetView for AIX**. The SNA and APPN capabilities of these routers are also available for a mainframe's **NetView** to manage. Most customers will choose to use NetView for AIX as the main management station for a multiprotocol network, but we'll discuss the various options available in Chapter 6.

Although any SNMP management station can see into the IBM 6611 family of multiprotocol routers, the best and easiest way to manage the IBM router family is using the **IBM Router and Bridge Manager/6000**. It offers a simple, graphical interface into IBM's routers. It can manage a network of routers from a central site, monitor protocol specific performance data, and monitor 6611 processor usage. It runs on only RISC System/6000 systems,

Protocol	Token-Ring	Ethernet	Frame Relay	PPP	X.25	SDLC
TCP/IP	yes	yes	yes	yes	yes	no
XNS	yes	yes	yes	yes	no	no
IPX	yes	yes	yes	yes	yes	no
AppleTalk	yes	yes	yes	yes	no	no
DECnet	yes	yes	yes	yes	no	no
Banyan Vines	yes	yes	yes	yes	no	no
SNA	yes	yes	yes	yes	yes	yes
NetBIOS	yes	yes	yes	yes	yes	no
APPN	yes	yes	yes	yes	yes	yes
Source route bridging	yes	no	yes	yes	no	no
Transparent bridging	no	yes	yes	yes	no	no
Translational bridging	yes	yes	yes	yes	no	no

Figure 4.30. Protocol Support for the 6611 Family.

and shows an operator the complete status and topology of protocols such as APPN and DLSw, unlike most SNMP management software. It can further display the status of any source route bridge or transparent bridge ports. The Router and Bridge Manager/6000 maintains historical performance data, and supports performance thresholds; if a threshold is exceeded, it generates a trap to NetView for AIX.

The **IBM 6611 Configuration Program and System Manager** works with the Router and Bridge Manager/6000 to create and modify router configurations. This is useful, say, if a designer wants to change the network's topology, or add some new filters to manage traffic. With these tools, your staff can manage changes more effectively in a network of IBM 6611 routers.

The IBM 2210 Nways Multiprotocol Router

In late 1994, IBM introduced another router family, the **IBM 2210 Nways Multiprotocol Router**, a newer model of which is shown in Figure 4.31. This smaller, less expensive device is suited for small offices, branch offices, and expanding an enterprise multiprotocol network to suppliers and customers. It interoperates with the 6611 family and with RXR/2. It runs using the **Nways Multiprotocol Router Network Services** software, not the MPNP, and offers TCP/IP, IPX, SNA DLSw, and AppleTalk support. IBM has announced it will add bridging, Banyan VINES, NetBIOS via DLSw, and DECnet Phase IV support as part of a "product preview."

The 2210 comes in eight models. Each fits into a standard 19-inch rack, and is about an inch and a half thick. They are summarized in Figure

Figure 4.31. IBM 2210 Nways Multiprotocol Router Model 24E.

4.32. The variations between models are based on the LAN type supported, whether or not ISDN links are supported, and how much flash memory and RAM the routers have. More flash memory allows the 2210 to support more protocols; more RAM provides more buffer space. Until recently, the configurations for each model were fixed; upgrading these devices implied swapping boxes. Now, IBM permits RAM changes as needed with the 8 MB memory expansion feature. This upgrades a 2210 with 4 MB to the maximum 8 MB allowed.

All of the models in the 2210 series come preloaded with the IBM Nways Multiprotocol Routing Network Services, and the hardware comes installed from the factory. A technician simply bolts it into a rack or sets it down and begins the software configuration process. IBM has worked to make this as simple as possible: The configuration and software is stored in flash memory, so no complex configuration is required. The **IBM 2210 Configuration Program**, which can run on a DOS/Windows, OS/2, or AIX system, sets up the 2210. Any RISC System/6000 in the same TCP/IP network can download new configurations to a 2210.

The 2210 series differs from the 6611 series in several key ways. For example, the 2210 supports frame relay, PPP, X.25, and SDLC on its WAN ports, although it only supports SDLC for downstream PU Type 2.0 or Type 2.1 controllers. The 6611 only supports frame relay, PPP, and X.25. The 2210 also supports dial-on-demand and dial backup links using its PPP and ISDN ports. Next, the 2210's AppleTalk support only interoperates with the 6611 series using PPP as a WAN datalink. Finally, the 2210 uses a different way to ensure fairness over PPP WAN links called Bandwidth Reservation. Although it differs from the 6611's priority queuing, the two can be intermixed in a network.

Model	Dual Serial T1/E1	Token-Ring	Ethernet	Flash Memory	RAM	ISDN BRI Support
121	yes	yes		2 MB	4 MB	
122	yes		yes	2 MB	4 MB	
12T	yes	yes		4 MB	4 MB	
12E	yes		yes	4 MB	4 MB	
125	yes	yes		2 MB	4 MB	yes
126	yes		yes	2 MB	4 MB	yes
127	yes	yes		4 MB	4 MB	yes
128	yes		yes	4 MB	4 MB	yes

Figure 4.32. The 2210 Series.

In a series of product previews, IBM has indicated the general direction for the Nways Network Processor and the Nways Multiprotocol Router families. First, they will become more tightly integrated with the next generation of SNA and APPN support, with such features as Dependent Logical Unit Requestor (DLUR) support. This will allow older, non-APPC traffic to flow over an APPC session in an APPN network. Another feature both families will add is support for RFC 1490 Boundary Access Node (BAN) and APPN over a frame relay network. This will provide a standardized way to support connectionless and connection oriented protocols on a common WAN link for these processors. Both families will also add support IBM's next generation network layer protocol, APPN/HPR. The 2210 Nways Multiprotocol Router will add features the 6611 Nways Network Processor already has, like bridging over frame relay networks, Banyan VINES and DECnet Phase IV support, DLSw for NetBIOS, and support for the IBM LAN Network Manager token-ring management station. Most of these changes should occur during 1996.

IBM's Nondedicated Routing Products

The last members of the IBM family of multiprotocol routing products are combinations of hardware and software called the IBM RouteXpander/2 and the IBM **X.25 Xpander/2**. RXR/2 runs on an OS/2 version 2.0 or later operating system, and provides, in software, a two-port local bridge/router or a one-port local-to-remote bridge/router. When RXR/2 interfaces onto a WAN, it is usually onto a frame relay network, although RXR/2 supports leased line point-to-point interfaces as well. An IBM Wide Area Connector card inside a personal computer can attach to the WAN link. By adding **IBM Multiport Support/2** software, RXR/2 Version 2 can concentrate up to four downstream routers into a single, higher-speed line.

RXR/2 can use an existing OS/2 system, say, a file and print server, to route and bridge packets. If IBM's **TCP/IP for OS/2** and **Communications Manager/2** software reside on the system, RXR/2 can manage TCP/IP, SNA, and APPN traffic. Finally, RXR/2 can look like a source routing bridge with up to 9 ports. It can communicate with another RXR/2, or with a 6611, say, at a central site. If the OS/2 system is running Communications Manager/2, then RXR/2 can also route or bridge APPN and SNA packets onto the frame relay network. If a site already has an OS/2 file server or communications gateway, RXR/2 is an inexpensive way to get it "on the air" quickly.

The IBM X.25 Xpander/2 works along the same lines as RXR/2, only it interfaces into an X.25 WAN instead of frame relay for remote access.

Both products can work with additional, optional support products; for example, **RouteXpander LNM Support/2** lets a LAN Network Manager workstation see "through" a RouteXpander network and manage a token-ring LAN on the other side.

IBM's Communications Controllers: SNA- and APPN-Based Internetworking

Many firms, particularly in the United States, where carrier fees are relatively low, believe strongly in multiprotocol routers based upon TCP/IP. These devices are particularly useful if your network has many protocols, such as Banyan Vines or AppleTalk, that aren't as common as, say, Novell's IPX/SPX, but that require routing.

Other firms prefer to use SNA or APPN as their main communications protocol. SNA and APPN use WAN bandwidth frugally, and they provide highly predictable performance. In addition, these firms usually need to transport TCP/IP- and LAN-oriented protocols such as NetBIOS and IPX/SPX over their WAN links.

The IBM 2217 Nways Multiprotocol Concentrator and AnyNet

For needs like these, IBM has developed an answer: the AnyNet series of transport gateways. AnyNet software transforms, say, TCP/IP, into APPN, or vice versa. AnyNet software is included within OS/2 Warp Connect and VTAM, and other IBM communications software. It is available as a separate product for RISC System/6000, DOS, and "ordinary" OS/2 Warp users.

AnyNet supports SNA/APPN or TCP/IP as a main WAN protocol, and it can transform SNA/APPN, TCP/IP, IPX/SPX, and NetBIOS into one of these two protocols. Unlike most other approaches, the transformation can be one way or bidirectional. So, AnyNet software could tunnel, say, TCP/IP and NetBIOS traffic through an APPN backbone, or it could transform, say, SNA traffic into TCP/IP for use with a particular application. To achieve this, IBM defined a series of common transport semantics. These APIs, which X/Open has standardized, permit the mix and match networking that AnyNet exploits.

AnyNet's performance depends upon the amount of data being transferred and the links over which the transfer occurs. Over moderate speed (up to T1/E1) links, SNA and APPN's improved line efficiency contributes to better performance. Over faster links, SNA and APPN's improved congestion control gives them a slight edge over TCP/IP when transferring large files. Indeed, in tests, IBM found that large files transferred about 10% faster using AnyNet/6000 over APPN than using standard TCP/IP.

IBM has also taken the AnyNet principle and developed it into a hardware offering, the **IBM 2217 Nways Multiprotocol Concentrator**. The 2217, shown in Figure 4.33, is designed for firms that have a large volume of SNA or APPN traffic, or that have mission critical applications that depend upon SNA or APPN. Today's version of the 2217 uses APPN as a WAN protocol; IBM has announced its intent to provide an APPN/HPR version in the future. At that point, the 2217 will be an edge device in an ATM/HPR network, suitable for use, say, in branch offices.

The 2217 supports SNA, APPN, IPX/SPX, TCP/IP, and NetBIOS protocols. It supports three datalinks on the WAN, frame relay, SDLC, and X.25. It doesn't channel attach, and it has two WAN ports and one LAN port. The WAN port supports frame relay at speeds up to 2 Mbps (E1), SDLC up to 64 Kbps, and X.25 at 64 Kbps. When used at up to 2 Mbps, only one of the two WAN links can run faster than 64 Kbps. The LAN port can either be Ethernet/802.3 or token-ring operating at either 16 or 4 Mbps. For sites with mid-sized bandwidth needs and an interest in SNA or APPN, the 2217 can help to reduce ongoing costs.

The IBM 3174 Establishment Controller

The **IBM 3174 Establishment Controller** has been a workhorse in SNA networks for many years. It began life as a simple SNA display controller. Most early models either attached to a mainframe using a parallel channel or attached to a 3725 or 3745 Communications Controller using an SDLC WAN line. IBM 3270 block mode displays attached using RG62/U coaxial ca-

Figure 4.33. Five IBM 2217 Nways Multiprotocol Concentrators in a rack.

bling, a single purpose wiring scheme. Early 3174s could support speeds up to 64 Kbps.

Over the years, IBM has changed the 3174 little by little. Today, it provides SNA, APPN, and TCP/IP connectivity for Ethernet, token-ring, and coaxially attached devices. Early models only supported up to 32 displays, but today up to six 3174 controllers mount in a single rack, supporting up to 384 Model 3270 displays. Today's 3174s come with between 2 and 6 MB of main memory, and use diskettes or hard disks to store configurations and microcode. The mainframe attached models support either S/390 parallel channels or ESCON channels. Figure 4.34 shows a rack-mounted series of 3174s.

Today's 3174 attaches 3270 displays to networks, using coaxial or twisted pair cabling, and it concentrates and routes traffic from LANs to WAN links. Also, with the correct microcode and optional hardware support, some models can support asynchronous ASCII terminals and printers, such as Digital's VT series of terminals. Different 3174 models provide different numbers of ports, as shown in Figure 4.35.

The 3174 communicates over WAN lines at up to 256 Kbps, using SDLC, X.25, BSC, ISDN, or frame relay links. In some BSC and SDLC configurations, the 3174 supports multidrop links. Several main classes of 3174 models exist; the models with an R at the end are remote, and those with an L are channel attached, or local. The WNM is the Workstation Networking Module, and it is designed to fit into either an IBM 8250 or 8260 intelligent hub.

Figure 4.34. IBM 3174-21L Establishment Controller.

3174 Model	Local	Rack Mount	Remote	Maximum 3270 Ports	Maximum ASCII Ports	LANs Supported
2XL	Yes	Yes		64		Token-ring 16/4; Ethernet
2XR		Yes	Yes	64		Token-ring 16/4; Ethernet
1XL	Yes			64	32	Token-ring 16/4; Ethernet
1XR			Yes	64	32	Token-ring 16/4; Ethernet
WNM		In 8250 or 8260 hub	Yes	32		Token-ring 16/4
6XR			Yes	16	8	Token-ring 16/4; Ethernet
9XR			Yes	8		Token-ring 16/4; Ethernet

Figure 4.35. The 3174 Models.

Today, the IBM 3174 not only supports SNA, but also APPN and TCP/IP. We'll go over the SNA and APPN capabilities first, and then cover the TCP/IP features the 3174 offers.

In a subarea SNA network, the 3174 performs many roles. First, it can act as a display controller, attaching 3270 terminals to mainframes running VTAM or to AS/400 computers. Those models that support ASCII terminal attachment convert the ASCII keyboard sequences to the equivalent 3270 data stream and send this to the host system. When output comes back, the 3174 translates the output data stream into the appropriate VT escape sequences to paint the screen correctly. The 3174 can perform this role no matter how it is attached.

A channel attached 3174 (local models) can support up to 254 downstream PUs in this way; usually these are attached via a LAN. Unlike the 3745, discussed later, the 3174 does not perform the SNA boundary function between peripheral nodes and subarea nodes; VTAM, using a mainframe's processor, must do this when a 3174 or a 3172 acts as an SNA gateway.

A 3174 can also be an APPN Network Node. It provides **Dependent LU Requestor (DLUR)** and **Dependent LU Server (DLUS)** support, enabling older SNA devices to attach seamlessly to an APPN network. If your network contains personal computers running non-APPN 3270 terminal emulators, then the 3174's DLUR/DLUS support allows them to participate in an APPN network as well. APPN gives dynamic routing from 3270 displays and printers to applications. This reduces the time needed to define the network. APPN chooses the best available route and finds backup and alternate routes automatically. These capabilities can help many sites as they change their mission critical networks from hierarchical SNA to APPN.

IBM 3270 or ASCII terminals attached to a 3174 can log into remote TCP/IP systems using the TCP/IP Telnet application. This is useful if your network contains systems like an IBM RISC System/6000, another UNIX-based computer, or a system like a DEC VAX running VMS. The 3174 converts the 3270 display's keystrokes into appropriate VT series inputs and interprets the output accordingly. Of course, a VT series terminal doesn't need this translation when going to an ASCII-based computer, so the 3174 simply provides a standard TCP/IP Telnet service. The 3174 also supports printers in an SNA environment; its TCP/IP support lets TCP/IP computers running standard remote spooling software print on these devices as well. Finally, the 3174 supports SNMP, making it visible to SNMP management stations elsewhere in the network. Mainframe NetView can also manage 3174s in an SNA or APPN network.

The 3174 supports SDLC, X.25, ISDN, and frame relay WAN lines. Up to 255 frame relay connections provide direct communication through the frame relay network to as many as 255 hosts or to other 3174s. The 3174 uses the IETF's RFC 1490 to carry multiple protocols over frame relay links; it interoperates with the IBM 3745 and other devices that support this specification. On frame relay links, the 3174 routes TCP/IP and APPN. It can also act as a source routing bridge, creating a highly reliable, low-delay bridged LAN. If multiple WAN lines exist between two sites, perhaps supporting bridged traffic on one, SNA or APPN on another, and TCP/IP on a third, the 3174 can to consolidate these networks onto a single, less expensive frame relay line.

Finally, the 3174 provides several features that make managing a network of controllers simpler. For example, it supports IBM's **Response Time Monitor (RTM)**, software that measures the how long it takes a computer and the network to respond to a user's input. If your firm has service-level agreements with your users, RTM can verify if you are meeting these response time goals. The 3174 also receives and installs new revisions of microcode when **NetView Distribution Manager (NetView DM)** sends them; NetView DM can also change the 3174's configuration. NetView can even restart the controller remotely, activating the new configuration at a specific time. The 3174 maintains information regarding vital product data, like model numbers and serial numbers of attached displays, simplifying asset management.

The IBM 3745 Communications Controller

The **IBM 3745 Communications Controller** controls data communications between modem attached, directly attached, IBM token-ring LAN attached terminals and mainframe host processors. It also works with Ethernet LAN attached IP workstations. The 3745's predecessors functioned as subarea SNA, WAN-oriented controllers. The 3745 retains this orientation, but it is more flexible today. It performs SNA networking functions, such as routing and the boundary function, that otherwise would be done by a mainframe, which reduces costs. It uses communications lines very efficiently, keeping ongoing line costs low. Although it supports both Ethernet and token-ring, other devices, such as the 3172, the Open Systems Adapter, and the 3746 Model 900, provide greater subarea SNA LAN–to–mainframe capacity. As a WAN controller and as a frame relay DCE, only the 3746 exceeds the 3745's capabilities.

The 3745 controllers attach to up to eight parallel channels. Normally, these channels attach to more than one mainframe processor. This provides a backup configuration. The 3745s use specialized processors as their Central Control Units. The larger 3745 models have two CCUs; smaller models have one. The fastest 3745 models use bipolar chip technologies in the CCU, but most use CMOS components. Configured correctly, one CCU can back up the other in case of failure. For memory, each CCU supports up to 16 MB of main storage.

The 3745 is designed for high availability. Most of its hardware components can be changed while the controller continues to operate. Each 3745 has its own service processor and console; it can even report problems automatically to IBM if unattended. If the problem reported is in the machine's microcode, and if a fix exists, IBM can immediately send the fix to the controller. The 3745 then informs the operations staff via a mainframe NetView alert that the fix has been received and is waiting to be activated.

Twelve models of 3745 exist today. They differ in traffic bearing capacity and in the numbers of LANs and lines they can attach. Several models work together with the 3746 Model 900 (3746-900) expansion unit, and provide ESCON channels, higher-speed token-ring LAN adapters, more connectivity, and greater frame relay processing capacity.

For example, the 3745 Model 170 (3745-170) has one CMOS CCU and supports up to 8 MB of memory. It supports up to two 16/4 Mbps token-ring LANs, up to two high-speed lines, up to four Ethernet or LAN connections, up to four parallel channels, and four low- to mid-speed line controllers. This is a relatively small 3745, suitable for remote locations, such as a campus with two or three hundred terminal users.

As another example, consider the 3745 Model 61A, shown in Figure 4.36. It can work with the 3746-900. Unlike the 170, it contains two bipolar CCUs. It accepts up to 16 MB of memory per CCU. With the 3746-900 expansion, also shown in Figure 4.36, it supports up to 9 ESCON channels, up to 20 media speed token-ring ports, up to 18 high-speed lines, and up to 540 lines at speeds up to 64 Kbps. These are maximums; when mixing port types, practical maximums will be smaller. The 3746-900 itself contains up to ten processors. The 3745-61A along with the 3746-900 is a formidable, enterprise capable SNA and APPN controller.

The 3745 runs software called the **Network Control Program (NCP)**. NCP runs on a 3745's CCU. So, the Model 17A has one NCP running in it, whereas the 61A has two. NCP performs many tasks in a subarea SNA network, such as error detection and correction, pacing, polling, and so forth. NCP also detects broken and impaired lines, rerouting traffic around them automatically. NCP works well when lines are slow or unreliable. Then, hop by hop error detection and correction is mandatory.

Because the 3746-900 is an expansion device, it doesn't run an NCP itself. Instead, it relies upon the NCP software in the 3745. The 3746-900's adapters assume modern digital lines, so they are much faster. They don't need to perform nearly as much error checking and correction. As an example, the 3746-900's token-ring adapters run at media speed, three to four times faster than the older 3745 token-ring adapters. Using a 3746-900 also removes processing from the main CCUs of the 3745. In a token-ring environment, this can remove up to 70% of the CCU's load; in a communication line environment, it can reduce the load on the CCU by up to 50%. As

Figure 4.36.   IBM 3745 Model 61A with four expansion units.

another example, each Communication Line Adapter on the 3746-900 can switch about 3000 frame relay frames a second, eight times the 3745's capacity.

NCP has also become simpler to administer and change. This improves a controller's uptime. At first, a systems programmer statically configured NCP. To change NCP, an operator had to restart the 3745. Today, though, NCP makes most configuration changes dynamically. NCP, along with the 3746-900, implements frame relay frame handling. This "DCE" works well with many frame relay DTEs, including the IBM 3174, the IBM 6611 and IBM 2210 multiprotocol routers and RouteXpander/2. IBM has used the IETF's RFC 1490 formats to achieve this frame relay support, so non–IBM-supplied devices supporting this RFC should also work with the 3746/3746.

When used with the 3746 Model 900, the 3745 can form what IBM calls a "Composite Node." Such a device can act as an APPN Network Node at the same time as it is an ordinary SNA controller. IBM intends this capability as a means to simplify the migration from hierarchical SNA networks to APPN and APPN/HPR. Without this, existing devices would become obsolete overnight. As a Composite Node, the 3745/3746-900 acts as an APPN Network Node, routing APPN over the attached links. It also supports Dependent Logical Unit Requester (DLUR) to allow older 3270 terminals and controllers to work over the APPN network. In this way, an existing hierarchical SNA network metamorphoses into a peer-to-peer APPN network.

The IBM 3746 Nways Communications Controller

IBM's newest Communications Controller, the **IBM 3746 Nways Communications Controller**, sometimes known as the 3746 Model 950, supports APPN only, so it doesn't run NCP. It is independent of any mainframe processor. IBM can upgrade the Model 900 into a 950 in the field without swapping frames. While the 900 as part of a Composite Network Node depends upon NCP, and, ultimately, a mainframe's VTAM, for its APPN control point support, the 950 executes APPN directly. It has an APPN Network Node Processor built in that performs all the APPN control point's functions. It also has its own service processor, like the 3745 and the 3746-900, and it shares their high-availability characteristics. Figure 4.37 shows the 3746-950.

The 950 is designed for high-speed networks, such as APPN/HPR and ATM. Like the 3746-900, the 3746-950 contains up to ten processors. At

Figure 4.37. IBM 3746-950 Nways Communications Controller.

this writing, it supports only 120 medium-speed lines, but IBM describes this as a temporary limitation. In other regards, it physically connects to LANs and lines much like the 3746-900. The 950 works with SDLC, X.25, or frame relay lines, and token-ring LANs. Unlike the 3745, the 3746-950 has no Ethernet/802.3 support to date.

In large APPN networks, such as networks of AS/400 computers, OS/2 servers, or S/390 mainframes, the 3746 offloads the Network Node processing from these machines. It is suitable for use in a centralized data center, or at, say, regional concentration points in a large or global network. It can concentrate traffic from several small lines into a single, higher-capacity line. Often, this reduces line charges. Because it provides frame relay frame handling, the 3746-950 can shape multiprotocol traffic. By allocating multiple virtual circuits within a single physical frame relay line, your designers can control the bandwidth each virtual circuit uses. If any bandwidth is left, the 3746-950 allocates it to any virtual circuits that need it.

The 3746-950 is IBM's enterprise controller for the future. Because it is designed to accommodate APPN/HPR and ATM, it will grow as WAN capacities increase. Because it is designed with a distributed, multiprocessor architecture, it can scale to meet these needs. Because it runs APPN and APPN/HPR, it separates the network from a given mainframe's VTAM. This provides flexibility, both now and into the future, without sacrificing SNA's efficiency and predictability.

5

Software for Building Client/Server Applications

To choose the right software for your client/server solution, you must understand the reference models, the functionality required by your users, the available technology and products, your current environment, and the skills within your organization. Chapter 2 presented the client/server reference models developed by IBM to help you structure your client/server systems. This chapter uses those reference models to examine the technologies that you can use for client/server computing. Our grouping is somewhat artificial because you can use some of these technologies in several models, but it is useful to explain the functions provided by the technologies. Although our intent is not to be exhaustive, we will also describe some of the IBM products providing these functions.

Many of the technologies discussed in this chapter are standards or specifications defined by various organizations, some of which have a significant impact on the software for client/server computing. Figure 5.1 provides a brief description of the organizations and standards referred to throughout.

Organization	Acronym	Members	Goal	Standards
American National Standards Institute	ANSI	National standards body		Programming languages
International Standards Organization	ISO	International standards body		Reference model Programming languages X.500 Directory Services SQL
Object Management Group	OMG	Consortium of vendors and users	Define specifications to promote software interoperability	CORBA
Open Software Foundation	OSF	Consortium of vendors and users	Promote inter-operability of different comput-ing systems	Motif Distributed Computing Environ-ment Distributed Manage-ment Envir-onment
SQL Access Group	SAG	Consortium of vendors and users	Promote standards for database access	Call Level Interface
X/Open Company Limited	X/Open	Consortium of vendors, users, and other stand-ards bodies	Develop Common Application Environment and promote its implementation	X/Open Portability Guide

Table 5.1. Standards and organizations of client/server reference models.

Before going through the reference models, we will explore the software development tools that can be used to develop your applications. Some of these tools can be used to develop standalone applications as well as client/server applications. Most of them are being presented here because they have specific features for the development of client/server applications.

Software Development

You can buy off-the-shelf products to implement parts of your client/server applications; however, it is often necessary to write additional software. This is particularly true for mission-critical applications, because they typically reflect your specific business processes. The development tools you choose and their integration will be critical to the success of your projects.

As you evaluate the development environment that your team will use, you must consider many factors. Foremost on this list are the skills of the team members and any existing application code that must be integrated. Other considerations for the tools might be ease of use, platforms supported, connectivity supported, portability of the generated code, and cost.

Integrating Existing Applications

Businesses have a large investment in applications written in 3GLs such as COBOL, FORTRAN, PL/I, and others. It is likely that you will need to integrate some of these programs, since many client/server applications enhance access to existing data and applications. Figure 5.2 shows the languages and the systems that IBM supports. In addition to the compilers, IBM has many other useful products for client/server development efforts.

Language Environment/370 (LE/370) provides a common runtime environment for PL/I, COBOL, and C applications on MVS, VM, and VSE systems. A major benefit of LE/370 is the ability to easily and quickly call applications written in different programming languages. This facilitates the use of existing programs in your client/server applications.

The **CoOperative Development Environment (CODE/370)** is a companion product for editing, compiling, and debugging COBOL/370, C/370, and VS COBOL II applications running in the LE/370. CODE/370 can be purchased as a standalone host-based tool or as an OS/2 tool. The advan-

Operating System	PL/1	Pascal	RPG	BASIC	COBOL	C	FORTRAN
MVS	X	X	X	X	X	X	X
VM	X	X	X	X	X	X	X
VSE	X		X	X	X		
OS/400	X	X	X	X	X	X	X
AIX		X		X	X	X	
OS/2	X	X	X	X	X	X	X

Figure 5.2. Systems supported by CSP.

tage of using OS/2 is the ability to use its GUI. CODE/400 provides similar capabilities for OS/400.

Many programming languages include support for client enabling software. This support facilitates the development of client/server applications. IBM includes this kind of support in several development tools. **CO-BOL for OS/2** and **COBOL for AIX** are visual programming tools providing this kind of support. Similarly, **PL/I for OS/2** and **PL/I for AIX** provide visual programming environments for PL/I programmers. They can develop applications that access IBM's **Customer Information Control System (CICS), Information Management System (IMS),** and members of the **DATABASE 2 (DB2)** family. This is accomplished with client enabling software such as the CICS for OS/2 client, Distributed Data Connection Services, and IMS Client Server/2. We'll talk more about these product families later.

VRPG CLIENT/2 for AS/400 is a visual programming tool for RPG. It runs on OS/2 Personal Computers (PCs) and provides a GUI builder and communication services to access DB2/400.

Some existing applications may be written in a 4GL. IBM's **Cross System Product (CSP)** is an example of a 4GL. The systems supported for application development are listed in Figure 5.3 with the systems supported for execution. **VisualGen** is a new 4GL that helps programmers develop companywide client/server applications. CSP code can be imported into VisualGen and used to generate COBOL or C++ code. In this way, VisualGen can be used to integrate existing CSP applications.

VisualGen's development environment runs on OS/2 and provides visual programming capabilities. During development, the visual capabili-

Operating System	Development	Execution
MVS	X	X
VM	X	X
VSE	X	X
OS/400		X
OS/2		X
DOS		X

Figure 5.3. Systems supported for application development.

ties of the tool can help a programmer see the relationships among the components of the program. With VisualGen you select the target system for execution, so the generated source code is specific to that environment. The source code can be generated in either COBOL or C++. Today, Windows, OS/2, and AIX are supported as clients. The target systems can be MVS/ESA, VSE/ESA, OS/400, AIX, or OS/2. Depending on your configuration, clients can use TCP/IP, APPC, 3270 emulation, or named pipes to communicate with servers. VisualGen also provides support to access various databases.

Object Oriented Design

In Chapter 2 we mentioned that many people hope that object oriented design and programming will increase the reuse of existing code. Object oriented design differs greatly from existing methods and therefore is difficult for current designers to learn. Since not many tools are available yet for the design stage, it is even more important for designers to be well trained and if possible mentored for their first object oriented effort.

Object Oriented Programming Languages: C++ and Smalltalk

New programming languages have been developed to support object orientation. These languages are often called **Object Oriented Programming Languages (OOPLs)**. C++ and SmallTalk are the most widely used OOPLs. Currently, two SmallTalk products are available: **SmallTalk for OS/2** and **SmallTalk for Windows**. In addition, IBM has announced their intent to provide SmallTalk for MVS.

IBM's **VisualAge** is an object oriented programming tool for writing client/server applications that is available for OS/2 and Windows. **Smalltalk** is included with VisualAge. VisualAge hides the complexity of manipulating databases, communicating over different networks, and programming the user interface. It provides a library of reusable parts. With VisualAge programmers can incorporate C and COBOL programs, thereby allowing existing applications to be reused or expanded. The tool provides access to members of the DB2 family, as well as OS/400 services and objects. It also includes support for **System Object Model (SOM)**, and the OS/2 version supports Distributed SOM which we'll discuss soon.

Programmers can use IBM's family of VisualAge C++ products to develop C or C++ applications. **VisualAge C++ for OS/2** includes a set of C++ class libraries called the IBM Open Class Library. These libraries provide classes for a variety of common purposes like basic input/output and string manipulation. There is a GUI builder, graphical debugger, and subroutine call trace facility. Using a new technology called **Direct To SOM (DTS)**, SOM objects can be developed with this tool. VisualAge C++ is also available for OS/400 and can be used to develop OS/2, OS/400, or client/server applications. Development of client/server applications is eased by using the Access Class Library. The Access Class Library provides classes for accessing OS/400 data. It also includes the IBM Open Class Library. IBM is planning a version of VisualAge C++ for Windows, and OS/2 for the PowerPC. VisualAge C++ is the next generation of C Set ++ products for these platforms. A version of **C Set ++** is available for AIX, Solaris, and MVS. The Solaris version is based on the AIX product. C Set ++ for MVS builds on the existing C compiler for MVS.

Distributing Objects

An important consortium in this field is the **Object Management Group (OMG)**. They are working on standards for object orientation. OMG's approach is similar to the OSF's approach; both are using available object technology to produce an architecture and specifications. The intent is to promote the implementation of this architecture by many vendors so that object oriented applications will be reusable, portable, and interoperable. OMG defined the **Common Object Request Broker Architecture (CORBA)**. CORBA specifies how objects will communicate. It includes standards for managing objects (naming and locating them), invoking actions on objects, passing parameters, and handling issues like security and errors.

In concert with OMG, IBM defined the **System Object Model (SOM)**. The SOM addresses the problem of reusing an object class defined in one programming language in an application developed with another programming language. To provide that capability, SOM allows objects to be built using an independent specification language. Basically it is a way to package objects for reuse. A runtime library holds this information, and programs written in different languages can use it. IBM's family of developer toolkits called SOMobjects can be used to create SOM objects. The toolkits are currently available for Windows, OS/2, AIX, OS/400, and MVS. As mentioned previously, the new DTS technology also allows direct development of SOM objects from VisualAge C++.

This is an extremely important capability because it allows developers to create class libraries or frameworks that can be sold as a package to businesses that want to build applications based on the existing objects. They only need to sell the runtime library for the framework. Then, their source code for the objects remains proprietary.

IBM has also introduced **CommonPoint Application System for OS/2** and **CommonPoint Application System for AIX**. CommonPoint is a result of work done by Taligent, a company originally formed by IBM and Apple Computer. These two products provide over a hundred frameworks to help developers build object oriented applications. The frameworks include support for text editing, compound documents, graphics editing, database access, real-time collaboration, distributed object computing, heterogeneous communications, multimedia, and others. These frameworks are C++ objects. The frameworks can be extended by using the **CommonPoint Application Development Toolkit.**

Distributed SOM (DSOM) is the component of SOM that allows objects to be distributed across systems and provides the means to access and use them. DSOM is CORBA compliant. It is provided with all of the **SOMobjects** toolkits except the MVS version. However, IBM has made a statement of direction that DSOM will be supported in MVS.

Managing the Development Environment

Once the source code is written, it must be compiled and linked with any other object code that it requires. This is called the **build** process. There are tools available to help with the build process and managing source code. These tools allow the programmer to select the components to be built. Source code management can be very important during client/server development efforts because typically large, cross-functional teams are involved. The better versions of software are managed, the less trouble you will have during testing. It can also help you support the application better after roll-out by documenting and tracking changes.

Configuration Management and Version Control (CMVC)

An IBM product providing these services is **Configuration Management and Version Control (CMVC)**. It is a client/server tool that can be used for project management, design specifications, code management, and documentation. CMVC servers can be AIX, HP/UX, SunOS, and Solaris systems. The databases supported vary by server platform but include DB2, Oracle, Informix, and Sybase. OS/2, Windows, AIX, HP/UX, SunOS, and Solaris systems can be clients. CMVC provides an audit trail to determine who made changes, statistics to monitor application quality, tracking of code changes, and access control to limit who can make those changes.

TeamConnection for OS/2

CMVC was used as the basis for **TeamConnection for OS/2**. It supports teams of programmers by providing facilities for code management, electronic software packaging and distribution, change control, and problem tracking. TeamConnection controls access to source code and maintains different versions of components, or objects, in the repository. A hierarchy, called a build tree, is used to manage different configurations, or versions, of the objects in the repository. This capability facilitates reusing objects in different applications. It will also be used to compile and link, or build, applications based on different versions. These applications could then be packaged for distribution using IBM's **NetView Distribution Manager/2 (NetView DM/2)**. Since NetView DM/2 provides systems management functions, it is discussed in Chapter 6. TeamConnection for OS/2 has been incorporated in the Team version of several development tools. For example, there is a Team version of SmallTalk, VisualGen, and VisualAge.

Testing Applications

Because of the complexity of today's software, testers use tools to generate and run their test cases. This helps them to be more productive because they can run more test cases in a shorter period of time and they can keep better track of the tests that are used. These tools also serve other purposes besides testing. For example, they can be used to create demos or simulate users for performance measurements. A programmer can also use them to help debug a problem.

The **Workstation Interactive Test Tool (WITT)** family of products helps with this step in the process. The tool allows a tester to record the actions and inputs used for a particular test case as a script. During testing the script is played back to simulate the user interaction. Playback can be done interactively or in a batch mode. WITT is available for OS/2, Windows, and X-Windows environments.

Summary

Many new technologies are changing how client/server and traditional applications are developed. Your client systems will probably have a graphical user interface, perhaps Microsoft Windows, IBM's OS/2 **Presentation Manager (PM)**, Apple's Macintosh interface, or X-Windows. Your programmers may use object oriented design techniques and tools to create the applications. Their development tools will have a GUI and may themselves be object based. The programmers will also need to use some client enabling software to provide the communication between clients and servers.

The Client/Server Reference Models

Chapter 2 presented six reference models: Resource Sharing, Process-Driven, Remote Presentation, Front End, Distributed Logic, and Staged Data. Here we will illustrate how these examples could be implemented.

Resource Sharing

First, let's look at the Resource Sharing Model. Usually this model gives clients transparent access to remote resources. Transparent access means the client uses the remote resource as if it were a local one. Shared resources might be files, disks, printers, or other peripherals such as fax machines. Sometimes, the shared resource might be a database accessed using client enabling software from the database vendor. The products can be categorized by the services that they provide: disk and file sharing, printer sharing, database sharing, and groupware.

Disk and File Sharing

Today, many reasons exist for a group of people to share files. This group might include people from the same department on the same floor of a single building or might consist of people from disparate units around the world. In either case, files, such as spreadsheets or word processing documents, often must be shared in a way that provides integrity and reliability.

With **disk sharing,** the data on the remote device is written using the client's format for data, files, and directories. In other words, the disk server software doesn't change the structure of the data as it reads and writes it. This implies that only clients with an understanding of that structure can read or write data stored on the disk server. For example, a Macintosh uses a different structure to store data on a disk than a PC running OS/2; without translation a Macintosh can't read data stored on a disk server using OS/2 storage structures. With **file sharing,** the data on the remote device is written using the server's format for files and directories. The server then interprets and translates any requests when communicating with clients using different formats. In this way, many different types of clients can share the same data. This is a less restrictive means to share disk storage, so most products provide file sharing.

Depending on their origins, some file sharing products provide better support for a particular networking protocol, even if they support several others. For example, Novell's NetWare was originally developed for Novell's IPX protocol, IBM's LAN Server for NetBIOS, and Network File System (NFS) servers for TCP/IP. Most of them support other networking protocols as well. Many of these products also provide additional capabilities such as printer sharing, application sharing, and others either directly or through add-on products.

Personal computers usually access file servers by using redirection. **Redirection** assigns a local resource to a remote one. For file sharing, a PC disk drive is assigned to some storage location on the file server. This may be an entire drive on the server or a specific subdirectory on a drive. Access to the redirected drive is the same on the PC as if it were a local drive; hence, it is also referred to as a **virtual drive.** However, the client enabling software intercepts the commands to access the drive and sends, or redirects, them over the network to the server. The server's software receives the commands and performs them on its disk storage as if they were being done on the server system. This technique is also used for other kinds of resource sharing, such as printer sharing and modem sharing.

It is important for you to understand that using your network to share resources puts an additional load on the network, as well as the client and the server. You should carefully consider the size of the hardware supporting your servers, making sure that there is enough CPU speed, memory, and disk storage to support all of your clients. Where you place your servers in the network also affects the load on your network. As the server moves farther from the client, the client's requests must traverse more internetworking devices. Each internetworking device adds some delay, and each request adds some load onto the internetworking device. There should be a balance between the hardware your client software uses, the network, and the hardware your server software uses.

IBM's LAN Server

IBM initially made **OS/2 LAN Server** available on the OS/2 operating system. It provided file and printer sharing for DOS, Windows, and OS/2 clients. These clients run either the OS/2 LAN Requester or DOS LAN Requester software. Later, IBM added support for Macintosh clients with **LAN Server for Macintosh (LSM)**. There is also an implementation of LAN Server for AIX. The AIX version does not support Macintosh clients.

LAN Server was initially based on Microsoft's LAN Manager. So were several other file server products such as Digital Equipment Corporation's PATHWORKS. Although there are some similarities between the various implementations, the vendors have implemented different extensions to their products. An important component of OS/2 LAN Server and Microsoft LAN Manager is the use of domains. A **domain** is a logical grouping of servers in the network. A user logs into the domain and can then get to any of the resources that the user is authorized to use on any server in the domain. This feature makes it easier for end users to get to resources on different LAN Servers because they don't have to know exactly where the resources are located.

Applications can be developed in several different ways using capabilities provided with LAN Server. There are APIs (Application Programming Interfaces) for NetBIOS and for LAN Server. Because the NetBIOS API is at a lower level in the OSI reference model, it is more difficult to use than the LAN Server API. The LAN Server API provides functions to perform specific activities such as managing users, groups of users, and resources. However, it also provides an interprocess communication facility called **named pipes**. (By interprocess communication facility we mean a way for an application on one system to communicate with another application on the same system or on a different system.) In this environment, named pipes appear to be file resources, so data is exchanged using functions to open the named pipe, read from it, write to it, and close it.

Many corporations have significant investments in large, shared systems and disk storage, and need to use these resources in a LAN environment. IBM has provided OS/2 LAN Server integration with IBM System/390 systems through the **LAN File Services/ESA (LFS/ESA)** and **Workstation LAN File Services/VM (WLFS/VM)** products. We will refer to both products as "LFS" in this book. These products use a mainframe host as an extension of OS/2 LAN Servers. They also provide a Network File System (NFS) Server so that NFS clients can take advantage of the host resources. These clients can then share files with OS/2 LAN Requesters. We'll explain more about NFS later. The exact capabilities provided by these products depend on the operating system (MVS/ESA, VM/ESA, or VM/SP). Basically, LFS allows the host to act as a file server. It also provides ways to exchange data stored on host disks with a LAN Server.

The ability to use the host as a file server is crucial for many companies because their host systems normally provide massive disk and tape storage capacity. This also provides a way to manage critical business data using proven techniques and operational procedures. For example, most shared-system sites insist on regularly scheduled backups, complete with off-site tape storage. This lets them recover critical business data in case a disaster destroys their primary data storage location. Most server administrators today do not exercise the same care with LAN-based data as their large system counterparts. Unfortunately, data stored on smaller servers may be just as critical to your business. This is an example where the discipline of large, shared systems can benefit your business in a client/server environment.

IBM announced a similar product to LFS for the AS/400 called **LAN Server/400**. One difference from LFS is that LAN Server/400 is a software and hardware solution. It adds an AS/400 hardware feature called the **File Server I/O Processor (FSIOP)** along with the OS/2 LAN Server software. The FSIOP uses a fast Intel processor to allow most of the server processing to be done in the FSIOP. This means that there is little impact on the main AS/400 processor. Today LAN Server/400 only provides file serving. The key component that has enhanced the AS/400's ability to act as a file server is the Integrated File System (IFS). The IFS allows the AS/400 to support many different file structures besides its native structure. These file structures provide compatibility with DOS, Windows, OS/2, UNIX-based systems, and other products derived from Microsoft LAN Manager.

Novell NetWare

Novell's NetWare holds the largest market share for file and printer sharing products. NetWare servers are supported on IBM-compatible PCs. Many NetWare servers today are running NetWare version 3 software. NetWare version 4 provides many new capabilities but also requires many changes to user's environments. For example, NetWare version 4 has a new directory scheme, called NetWare Directory Services, for finding resources in the NetWare environment. Novell provides a NetWare for OS/2 server that is a version of Novell's network operating system that will run on OS/2. Because of OS/2's multitasking ability, the OS/2 system can provide NetWare plus additional services if needed. There is also a version of NetWare for UNIX based systems. AIX is one of the supported systems with IBM's **NetWare for AIX**.

Similar to LFS, IBM offers **LAN Resource Extension and Services (LANRES)** for VM and MVS. LANRES is like the LAN Server mainframe extensions because it lets NetWare clients use mainframe resources. However, LANRES provides disk sharing rather than file sharing. The NetWare clients communicate with NetWare servers, which then talk to the LANRES host to access disk storage or printers. With LFS, the clients talk directly to server software on the host. This software understands the requests that they make and handles them directly. In either case, it is transparent to the end user. However, LANRES provides an additional capability that LFS does not provide. It allows a NetWare client to print using mainframe printers. Similarly, mainframe users and programs can print using NetWare printers. LANRES also allows authorized mainframe users to manipulate files and directories controlled by NetWare. These users can also perform LAN administration tasks.

Later, IBM made LANRES available for OS/400. This product is now being superseded by an OS/400 feature called **OS/400 Integration for Novell NetWare**. This allows a licensed copy of Novell NetWare to be loaded in the FSIOP. The OS/400 integration with NetWare includes IFS support and increased printing capabilities.

Client Access/400

PC Support/400 was available before IBM introduced LANRES, LFS, and LAN Server/400. **PC Support/400** provided file sharing and other services for OS/400 users. IBM changed the name to **Client Access/400**. Client Access/400 supports PCs running DOS, Windows, or OS/2 as clients and

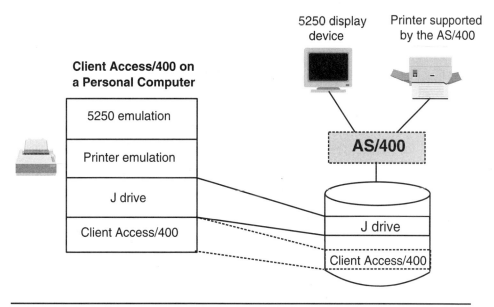

Figure 5.4. Client Access/400.

AS/400 systems as servers. It includes many capabilities: terminal emulation, printer emulation, file sharing, printer sharing, software distribution, and APIs. Some of these capabilities are shown in Figure 5.4.

With **terminal emulation** a PC can **emulate**, or look like, an AS/400 5250 display device. So, the PC is treated by the AS/400 just like any other 5250 display device. Users can log on and work on the system the same way they would from a directly connected terminal. Printer sharing allows printing in both directions: from the PC to printers attached to the AS/400 and from the AS/400 to PC printers. Printing from the AS/400 to the PC is similar to terminal emulation. The PC emulates an AS/400 printer. When users log on to the AS/400 system, they can print from that system to the printer attached to the PC. The AS/400 thinks that the printer is directly connected. Printing from the PC to the AS/400, the PC has a printer port redirected to a printer attached to the AS/400. In this way, users print using their PC applications and printers on the AS/400.

Client Access/400 includes a facility called **shared folders**. This feature allows the AS/400 to act as a file server for PCs. As you can see in Figure 5.4, the PC has a J drive. The PC has been redirected through the Client Access/400 software to disk storage on the AS/400, so users can access the J drive just as they would a local disk drive. Client Access/400 also provides an additional **transfer utility** to exchange data between shared folders and the native AS/400 database. Using this utility, the AS/400 users without PCs can share information with the PC users.

An important component of Client Access/400 helps you manage the version of the product that is installed on the PCs. You can set up the client software to check for new files on the AS/400 and to **update** them on the PC. This process keeps the latest version of software on all of your users' systems.

In addition, programmers can use Client Access/400's APIs to ease the development of client/server applications between PCs and the AS/400. Applications on the PC can make SQL calls to AS/400 databases. Using this capability, PC applications can work directly with data stored on the AS/400. ODBC calls can also be used for database access. Windows and OS/2 users can use **RUMBA/400**, now provided with Client Access/400, to take advantage of the PC GUIs for terminal emulation, file sharing, and printer sharing. Using RUMBA/400, users have sophisticated capabilities such as hot links, hot spots, and user definable buttons. A hot link makes a connection between a PC application and information from the AS/400, so when the information is changed on the AS/400, it is updated in the application. A hot spot allows a user to click somewhere in an emulation session and have an action performed based on that click. For example, a user can click on a PF key listed at the bottom of the screen and it is as if the PF key was pressed on the keyboard. The Quick Step Pad feature allows a user to assign system-provided or user-defined actions to a button. When the button is clicked, the action is performed.

Network File System

Sun Microsystems originally developed the Network File System (NFS) to share files between UNIX-based systems using a TCP/IP network. This differs from LAN Server and NetWare, which vendors originally developed to support PCs. Today, both LAN Server and NetWare also support UNIX clients because you can buy additional products to add NFS servers to them. NFS servers exist for many other systems also: IBM provides NFS servers on MVS, VM, OS/400, AIX, and OS/2.

To authenticate users and systems in an NFS environment, Sun Microsystems also developed **Network Information Services (NIS)**. NIS is a distributed way to manage user IDs and passwords throughout the network. Like NFS, Sun developed NIS for UNIX workstations. A master server maintains the database and distributes this authentication information to other slave servers. On UNIX systems, a user ID is associated with a number called the UID. For NIS, the UID for a single user must be the same on all of the systems within a given security domain. In this context, a domain is a logical grouping of devices in a TCP/IP network authenticated by an NIS server. This implies that system administrators must cooperate when adding new user IDs to systems. If NIS is added to an existing environment, then you must suddenly change existing user ID and UID associations to provide consistency.

Researchers at Carnegie Mellon University developed the **Andrew File System (AFS)**, a new file sharing scheme not targeted to a specific operating system. This scheme also addresses performance issues. Whereas NFS, like LAN Server and NetWare, works well on LANs, AFS also works well over WAN links. AFS caches information on the client for future use to eliminate unnecessary requests to the server. AFS also provides better support for large networks, although huge AFS networks do not yet exist. It also offers tighter security via a Kerberos security server. The OSF chose AFS for the Distributed File Service in its **Distributed Computing Environment (DCE)**, and Kerberos was its choice for the DCE Security Service. We will talk more about DFS, DCE, and Kerberos later.

It is important to note that NFS is widely available and AFS is available mostly on UNIX systems. Because of the openness and popularity of DCE, it is likely that AFS will become available on more systems over time.

Differences Between File Sharing Products

For simple file and printer sharing, OS/2 LAN Server and NetWare provide similar functions. Third parties develop add-on features for both systems. Many of these add-on features in the NetWare environment are written as NetWare Loadable Modules (NLMs). Good NLMs are difficult to write because they must cooperate closely with the NetWare software. For example, a poorly behaved NLM can monopolize the processor or even crash the network operating system. Novell is managing this issue by certifying NLMs. On the other hand, add-on features for OS/2 LAN Server can take advantage of all of the inherent features of OS/2, such as multitasking and memory protection. Developers can also use all of the various programming tools available for OS/2.

IBM and Novell advocate different ways to develop client/server applications. IBM has stated its intent to integrate OS/2 LAN Server with the OSF's DCE and DME. When completed, this will integrate OS/2 LAN Server with anyone's DCE and DME software. So far, IBM, Hewlett-

Packard, Digital Equipment Corporation, every major UNIX vendor, and most third-party developers have announced their intent to support DCE. Novell, on the other hand, has announced that NetWare, AppWare, and UnixWare comprise their distributed strategy. For example, they are using NetWare Directory Services rather than the DCE Directory Services to manage and locate resources in the environment. Similarly, NetWare 4.0's authentication is a proprietary implementation whereas OS/2 LAN Server is using the OSF's authentication specification.

Client Access/400 differs from LAN Server and NetWare because besides file sharing, it provides features such as terminal emulation and APIs for application development that are specific to the integration of PCs with OS/400. Many of the same features are also available in the LAN Server and NetWare environments through add-on products. For example, the **NetWare for SAA** gateway can be used for 3270 and 5250 terminal emulation from NetWare clients. Similarly, Communications Manager/2 can be used with OS/2 LAN Server.

NFS differs from OS/2 LAN Server and NetWare because NFS only provides file sharing. For NFS, the administrative tasks are done manually by editing files or entering commands. With OS/2 LAN Server and NetWare these tasks have a menu or graphical interface. NFS does not provide sophisticated administrative functions. For example, a user can have read only or read/write access to a file system with many NFS servers. OS/2 LAN Server and NetWare provide many more levels of access. With OS/2 LAN Server, access can be defined as no privileges, read, write, create, execute, delete, attributes, and permissions. So administrators have more flexibility with the levels of access that can be given to a user.

Extending File Sharing: Code Sharing and Software Distribution

In medium and large organizations, managing the use of software is very complex. It is particularly difficult to manage the number of licenses purchased and the version levels used. This is important for many reasons. First, you can enjoy cost savings through site licenses or volume purchases. Next, if all of your users have the same version of software, then it is easier and less costly for your help desk staff to support them. Last, you can ensure that all copies of a product are legitimate. For these reasons, some vendors have extended file sharing technology to code sharing and software distribution.

Many vendors will negotiate a sitewide or multiple-user license with you. You can then install the software on a file server. If clients run the application from the server, then they are using **code sharing**. Here, the software is loaded into the client's main memory as needed. This implementation makes heavy use of the network each time the application starts, but the support staff does not have to install the software on every client.

If clients install the application on their system's hard disk from the server, then they are using **software distribution**. Here there is less network activity because the software resides locally and it is only loaded from the server when a new version becomes available. You can extend this idea by creating a hierarchy of distribution servers, perhaps with a "super" server at the main location and "sub" servers at remote offices. Software distribution works well for mobile devices, like ThinkPad computers.

In either of these cases, the server manages the number of copies in use to ensure that they do not exceed the number of licenses. Also, administrators are assured that all end users have the same version of the software. Some servers also let you distribute your own software applications so that you can similarly manage applications developed in-house. This area is discussed further in Chapter 6.

IBM's **Network Door/2** (**NetDoor**) provides application sharing services. A NetDoor server on OS/2 can use OS/2 LAN Server or NFS. OS/2 and Windows PCs can act as NetDoor clients; however, Windows clients can only access OS/2 LAN Server NetDoor servers. Menus show clients the applications that are available through the NetDoor. These might be internally developed applications or software purchased from a vendor. The applications might also be available over the network via other communication services provided by the server. Figure 5.5 shows a hospital administrator's OS/2 system with the NetDoor client. The administrator can get to local applications, server applications, and mainframe applications through the NetDoor. Since the administrator has an OS/2 system, multiple applications could be up and running at any given point in time. In this example, a patient registration application that runs on a System/390 MVS system is in the list of available applications. Communications Manager/2 allows the NetDoor server to provide this option.

Extending File Sharing: Multimedia

The term **multimedia** refers to data or applications that incorporate some combination of text, image, audio, and/or video. Multimedia hardware and

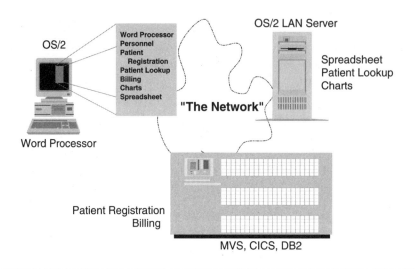

Figure 5.5. A network view with NetDoor.

networks must support **isochronous,** or time-dependent, traffic. Motion pictures consist of many separate frames played in sequence; VCR-quality images run at 24 to 30 frames per second. Consider the scenario in which a server houses a collection of movies that client systems can play. The network must consistently transfer the movie to the client at the correct speed. If it is sent too rapidly, the huge amount of data will overrun the client's buffers. (A **buffer** is an area in memory where data can be stored temporarily.) If it is sent too slowly, the playback will stop momentarily, resulting in noticeable jerkiness, or flicker. Because multimedia files are large in size, being able to compress and decompress them is very important. Compressed multimedia objects require less disk storage and network bandwidth. Rapid technology changes in networking, compression techniques, storage systems, and image processing are paving the way for multimedia, requiring vendors to develop new file sharing products to support multimedia.

IBM **LAN Server Ultimedia** allows DOS, Windows, and OS/2 clients to store and play back multimedia data, both audio and video, without compromising the quality of the presentation. The server sends the multimedia data to the client. In token-ring networks, the built-in priority scheme maintains transmission quality. In Ethernet networks, more restraint must be used to ensure that the LAN can transport the multimedia objects in the time required for smooth playback. The IEEE has approved a type of Ethernet, called isochronous Ethernet or IsoENET, designed to make multimedia more feasible in Ethernet networks.

Suppose there were a training video for each step in the production of a product. There might be a PC at each station on the manufacturing line. If the videos were stored on a LAN Server Ultimedia system, then anyone working on the manufacturing line could start the video over the network to answer questions about a specific part of the process. In the meantime, someone at another station could be viewing another segment of the same video or a completely different one.

One very difficult capability with images is to be able to search and sort through images by their content. Suppose you had a library of images that were used in a mail order catalog for women's clothing. How would you find all of the images that pictured red dresses? Hitherto, you might have had to view all of the images or descriptive information with each image for a search. IBM's Ultimedia Manager allows you to search for images using image content and descriptive information. So, if your descriptive information included the type of clothing, then you could pick the shade of red you wanted and you could pick dresses. It would then search through the images to find all red dresses. Ultimedia Manager supports many common image formats (Audio Visual Connection images, OS/2 and Windows bitmaps, TIFF, GIF, and Kodak Photo-CD). These images can be stored in DB2/2 or DB2/6000 databases. The Ultimedia Manager Client Search feature supports OS/2 and Windows clients.

Besides being able to store and play back multimedia objects, tools are required to create the multimedia objects. **Ultimedia Services for AIX** provides many tools for multimedia application developers: compression/decompression algorithms, audio and video editors and players, and support for a variety of multimedia file formats. OS/400 **Ultimedia System Facilities** registers and manages multimedia objects stored in shared folders or on optical libraries accessible by the AS/400. These facilities must be used in conjunction with the **Client Access/400 Ultimedia Tools** on OS/2, which can be used to build the multimedia objects.

Extending File Sharing: Archiving and Backup

Heavy reliance on file sharing has resulted in widely distributed data. Predominantly, the data has proliferated through end user organizations rather than through the traditional Information Systems staff. Often, inexperienced users have access to data that is critical to the operation of the business. But is it treated with the same care given to other critical data? For many reasons, the answer is probably not. Sometimes, the administrators of the file servers are not trained in the intricacies of backup and recovery. Even if they are, they may not be disciplined with their procedures. For example, they might not do backups on a regularly scheduled basis, test backups to ensure that they can be recovered, or store tapes at another location. In many cases, these administrators perform these duties on a part-time basis besides their normal responsibilities. It might not be feasible to expect them to spend their time doing these tasks.

Many large corporations want these backups to be done on their mainframes because, as mentioned previously, they have known and proven systems management disciplines in that environment. Suppose there were an earthquake, flood, fire, or other disaster at one of your locations. Would you be able to retrieve backups from the critical systems there? Most often, the system management procedures for a shared system include off-site storage of tapes. Tapes are stored off-site so that if there is a disaster, the tapes can be retrieved from the other location. This allows you to recover from a disaster. These procedures also include well-labeled tapes along with an archive so that the proper tapes can be easily restored. In addition, these shared systems support large, fast disk and tape drives.

IBM's **ADSTAR Distributed Storage Manager** (ADSM) product provides the ability to backup client machines to servers. Figure 5.6 shows the supported ADSM clients and servers in addition to the protocols that each system can use. ADSM allows an administrator to schedule backups so that they are automated and unattended, keeps track of archived data, and provides facilities to restore files.

Printer Sharing

People need to share printers and other peripherals just as they share files. High-quality and color printing devices are expensive resources. A single user does not constantly print documents. So, by sharing the printer, the expensive resource gets more use.

On a shared system, printers by definition are shared resources. In these environments, vendors developed robust printing management techniques over time. For example, in the financial industry, it is very important to know whether a check printed correctly or not. These print management systems usually include control and error recovery mechanisms that monitor every step of the printing process. It is important to note that in this environment error recovery is as automated as possible.

Operating System	Client	Server	Administration	Backup/Archive	Protocol(s)
DOS/Windows	X		X	X	TCP/IP, 3270
OS/2	X	X	X	X	TCP/IP, APPC, 3270, Net-BIOS, IPX/SPX
Apple System 7	X			X	TCP/IP
AIX	X	X	X	X	TCP/IP, APPC, IPX/SPX, NetBIOS
Ultrix	X		X	X	TCP/IP
SCO UNIX	X		X	X	TCP/IP
SunOS or Solaris	X		X	X	TCP/IP
HP-UX	X		X	X	TCP/IP
NetWare Server	X			X	TCP/IP, APPC
OS/400		X	X	X	TCP/IP, APPC
VSE		X			APPC, 3270
VM	X	X	X		APPC, TCP/IP
MVS	X	X	X		APPC, TCP/IP

Figure 5.6. Platforms supported by ADSM.

In a network of PCs, shared printers seem directly connected to a user's PC. Actually, the local printer port is redirected to a remote printer, so the user and applications are unaware that the printer is connected to a server or directly connected to the network—it is a virtual printer. Users encounter such problems as the printer being offline or out of paper, and formatting trouble. Managing printers in this environment is very time-consuming because the software and the printers aren't very sophisticated.

Some print servers will notify the user when their print job is done. Some will notify the user or an administrator if there is a problem with the printer. In most cases, the result is that someone has to physically go to the printer to fix the problem.

Printer sharing is a complex area that is greatly underappreciated. This complexity stems from the many different computing systems, printing devices, and file formats in use today. Technological advances and additional user requirements only add more complexity. Often, printed documents could be viewed online, saving time and paper. Since users have more powerful processors for the desktop, faster display adapters, and higher resolution displays, viewing documents in their composed form is possible. Besides viewing them, they need to easily search through them and move around in the document. The more sophisticated printing architectures also provide for viewing documents.

The Printing Process

On a shared system, the printing process starts with a file in a format generated by a user's application. The user spools the file to the printer either directly from the application or indirectly via an operating system command. The term **print job** is sometimes used to refer to the file to be printed. **Spooling** allows multiple print jobs to be sent to a single printer simultaneously. Spooling lets the user continue with other processing when the print job finishes spooling to the queue. A **queue** is a holding area, usually kept on disk storage. Here, it is a holding area for print jobs. Writing the print job to the queue is faster than sending it directly to the printer and also prevents different users' print jobs from going to the printer simultaneously and being printed intermingled with each other!

Some systems allow different priorities, based on such characteristics as the size of the job or the class of the user, to be assigned to print jobs. From the queue, a printer driver translates the file into the data stream required for the printer and sends that data stream to the printer. The printer driver dictates how much control you have over the printing process. For example, some printers can rotate documents, print multiple copies, or use different fonts. The printer driver must manage these capabilities. The most expensive printers and best printer drivers manage the entire process with minimal communication between the drivers and the printer, and little operator intervention.

Document Formats and Printer Data Streams

Many different formats and many different data streams are in use today. PostScript is a popular formatting language owned, defined, and published by Adobe Systems. Another common formatting language is owned, defined, and published by IBM: **Mixed Object Document Content Architecture for Presentation (MO:DCA-P)**. Some common data streams are IBM's **Intelligent Printer Data Stream (IPDS)** and Hewlett-Packard's **Printer Control Language (PCL)**. In many cases, there are different versions of these formatting languages and data streams. For example, there are two levels of PostScript: Level 1 and Level 2. Hewlett-Packard's PCL is now in its fifth generation (PCL5). This adds more complexity to printing because there can be incompatibilities between applications, printer drivers, and printers due to version differences.

Printing on a Personal Computer

On a PC, a user specifies from an application to print a document. The application creates a formatted document and the print function puts it in the printer's queue. The printer driver must translate the formatted document to a data stream that the printer understands. Then, the printer can print the document. This process is illustrated in Figure 5.7. In this example, the word processor generates a formatted document using PostScript and the print function sends it to the printer queue. Many printers understand PostScript and can directly print a PostScript document sent to them, but the printer in this example does not and cannot, so the printer driver translates the PostScript to the Intelligent Printer Data Stream (IPDS), which the printer does understand.

OS/2 LAN Server and NetWare Printing

Most PC products that provide file sharing also let you share printers. As mentioned previously, OS/2 LAN Server and NetWare both provide printer sharing. As in file sharing, the remote printers appear to the local system as if they were directly attached. This transparency allows the users to print to the remote device just as they would to a local one. The communication port for the printer is redirected so that output sent to the printer gets spooled over the network to a queue on the print server, which then

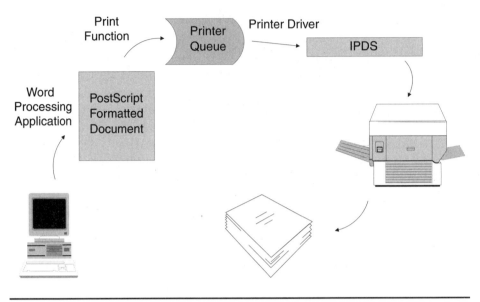

Figure 5.7. Printing translation.

handles the coordination of printing files from multiple users. Frequently, the server can notify the user when the printing has completed or if there is a problem. Although users are thus made aware of the problem, the user or the server administrator must often intervene manually to fix it.

Line Printer Daemon

The printing services defined for TCP/IP are **lpr** and **lpd**. A client uses the lpr command to spool output to a system running the lpd print server. Lpr and lpd do not include any translation facilities. Lpr spools the file as is to the lpd print server. So, on the lpd print server, the printer driver must be able to interpret the file correctly.

Because this protocol originated in the UNIX world, it usually provides an awkward command line interface. Some TCP/IP products simplify this by providing integration with the system's inherent printing features. For example, TCP/IP for OS/2 provides an lpr port daemon. This daemon, or server, listens for requests to a printer port and routes them to the appropriate TCP/IP system running the lpd print server. To make this even easier to use, you can define the printer to the OS/2 Workplace Shell. You specify a special remote communication port for it rather than a local one.

When you drag a document to that printer icon, the system uses the lpr command to send it to the remote system for you.

Advanced Function Printing

IBM has defined a set of architectures that form its **Advanced Function Printing (AFP)** strategy. The **AFP Data Stream (AFPDS)** defines the format of documents, and the Intelligent Printer Data Stream (IPDS) defines the printer data stream. IPDS provides bidirectional communication between the printer driver and the printer itself. This allows the software to be notified of printing errors so that it can attempt to overcome the errors and complete the print job. IPDS also allows you to define resources such as fonts and form definitions. The Mixed Object Document Content Architecture for Presentation (MO:DCA-P) is a subset of the AFPDS. As new requirements evolve, IBM modifies the architectures to address them. For example, the ability to view documents on your display with the same appearance that they have when they are printed has been added to the architecture.

Print Services Facility

AFP is supported by the IBM family of printing products known as the **Print Services Facility (PSF)**. PSF is available for OS/2, AIX, OS/400, VM, VSE, and MVS. Figure 5.8 shows the printing formats and data streams supported by PSF/2 and PSF/6000. The other members of the PSF family can use PSF/2 to support print data streams and protocols that they do not support natively. The Distributed Print Function provides this capability. Print jobs are downloaded from the originating system to PSF/2 and then printed. PSF/2 provides the necessary conversion to the supported printer data streams. Also, PSF/2 is very flexible because it can also use TCP/IP, NetBIOS, IPX, and SNA to communicate with other printers on the network as well as those directly connected to the PSF/2 server. All PSF products provide system management, resource management, and error recovery and reporting.

   PSF/2 provides a resource library where IPDS resources such as fonts, images, overlays, and form definitions can be stored. This is relevant for print jobs that are downloaded from MVS and VSE using the Distributed Print Function. If a resource in the library is required by a print job, it is retrieved from the library and does not have to be transmitted with the

Supported Printing Formats	AIX	OS/2
AFPDS	X	X
MO:DCA-P	X	X
EBCDIC line printer data		
ASCII	X	X
Metafile		X
PostScript Level 1	X	X
DBCS ASCII	X	X
IPDS	X	X
Supported Data Streams		
IPDS	X	X
PPDS	X	X
PCL4	X	X
PCL5	X	X

Figure 5.8. Printing formats supported by PSF/2 and PSF/6000.

print job. Thus, the print job can be printed faster because it requires less transmission between the host and PSF/2 server.

The **AFP Workbench for OS/2** and the **AFP Workbench for Windows** allow these clients to access, view, annotate, and print documents stored on a large, shared system. They can access VM or MVS systems using PCOM/3270 or OS/400 systems using Client Access/400.

Managing Printers

As mentioned previously, printing is very complex in an environment with many different types of printers, print management software, and computing systems. When these are also distributed throughout an enterprise, it is very difficult to manage the environment. IBM's **Printing Systems Manager for AIX (PSM)** allows remote administration and management of printers. Some of the functions that administrators can do are defining printers, examining or changing printer characteristics, checking the status of print jobs, changing priority on print jobs, and reassigning queues. PSM uses services provided by DCE to provide this functionality. It can work in conjunction with PSF/2 to support a greater number of printers and data streams. PSM supports OS/2 and Windows clients to submit print jobs, check the status of print jobs, receive notification on completion, and many other useful functions.

Extending Printer Sharing: Other Peripherals

The idea behind printer sharing has also been extended to other peripheral devices. The most common instance of this is shared modems. Since modems are relatively expensive devices, it does not make sense to have one for every person that needs to use them. Instead these devices can be controlled by a server and used by everyone that needs to use them. OS/2 LAN Server provides native support for shared modems.

Fax machines are also relatively expensive devices, so rather than sharing an actual fax machine, you can use a fax server. A fax server can accept outbound faxes over the network and queue them to be sent. It can accept inbound faxes and route them to the appropriate people. **FaxRouter/2** is a fax server that works with OS/2 LAN Server to send, receive, manage, and print faxes using an OS/2 or Windows client workstation.

Database Sharing

Beyond file and print sharing, the Resource Sharing Model can be used for databases. IBM's Research Division was the birthplace of relational database technology. The research resulted in the development of System R. From these origins, IBM created DATABASE 2, which spawned an entire family of products.

In a relational database, data is represented in **rows** or **records** containing **columns** or **fields** of information. A collection of such data is a **table**, and a collection of tables is a **relational database**. In Figure 5.9, the entry in the employee table for Alfred Smith is a row or record. The list of names is a column or field in the table. The organization database consists of the employee table and the department table.

IBM also originated **Structured Query Language (SQL)**—one major reason why relational databases have become so popular. Using SQL statements, you can create powerful queries against relational databases. A **query** asks for information from the database. Using the same example from Figure 5.9, we could query the employee table for all of the employees in department 890. The corresponding SQL statement represents our question in a format used to extract the appropriate information from the database. The ANSI and the **International Standards Organization (ISO)** have standardized SQL. This is important because ANSI SQL queries written against one vendor's relational database are the same as queries written against another vendor's relational database given the same database structure. In practice many vendors add additional capabilities to their

Organization Database

Employee Table

Name	Department	Job Identifier
Alfred Smith	890	300010
Ellie Jones	324	209991
John Fields	890	103367

Row → (points to Alfred Smith row)

Column ↑ (points to Name column)

Department Table

Department	Dept Title	Manager
890	Graphics	Harry Wells
324	Advertising	Sally Matthews
555	Sales	David Cronin

Question: Who are all of the employees in department 890?

SQL Statement: SELECT NAME FROM EMPLOYEE WHERE DEPARTMENT = 890

Figure 5.9. A relational database.

versions of SQL, creating private extensions to the standards. A group of vendors has also created a consortium called the SQL Access Group, which has defined the **Call Level Interface (CLI)**. This specification was also adopted by X/Open. Microsoft's **Open DataBase Connectivity (ODBC)** is based on the CLI with extensions. It is a layer above SQL that is intended to mask implementation differences from applications.

A **DataBase Management System (DBMS)** must provide the ability to define, update, query, and manage databases. In addition, many other features can be provided by a DBMS, several of which are important in a client/server environment. Our example database consists of two tables, an employee table and a department table. The employee table has name, department number, and job identifier fields. The department table has department number, department title, and manager name fields. From Figure 5.9 it is easy to see that these two tables are related, as both have a department number field. Suppose there has been a reorganization, department 890 is eliminated, the record in the department table for department 890 is deleted, and the employee table is not updated. The employee table will contain records that reference a nonexistent department. To prevent this kind of inconsistency, some DBMSs provide a feature called **referential integrity**. Figure 5.10 shows how the department number fields in the two tables can be defined as related fields. When a new employee is added to

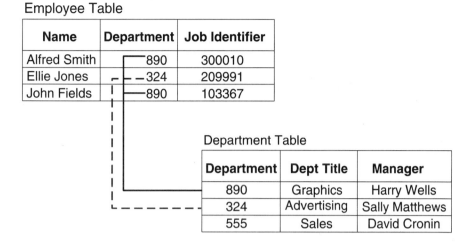

Figure 5.10.   Referential integrity.

the employee table, the department number must exist in the department table. Similarly, a department cannot be deleted if there are records in the employee table that refer to it.

Another important feature in client/server solutions is **stored procedures**—programs controlled by the DBMS. Depending on the implementation, the stored procedure might be a program written in a 3GL using SQL statements or might be SQL only. A client application can call a stored procedure; basically, the client is asking the DBMS to perform some function for it. The client can pass parameters to the stored procedure and receive results.

Stored procedures have several benefits. A single stored procedure could be used by many different client applications because parameters can be passed. This allows programmers to reuse code that has already been developed and tested. It also provides consistency, since applications accessing the same data can use the same stored procedure. If a change to the stored procedure must be made, this is done in one place and the client applications do not have to be updated.

A significant advantage of stored procedures is that they can reduce the amount of network traffic generated between the client and server. Suppose that the function to be performed consists of three SQL statements. Without stored procedures, the client would send three SQL requests across the network and the server would return three results. With a stored procedure, the client would make one request across the network and the server would return one result. Depending on the scenario, this could result in large savings in network bandwidth and the amount of time it takes to receive the final result.

Triggers are like stored procedures in that they are controlled by the DBMS. However, rather than being called by a client application, they are event driven. A **trigger** specifies that when a certain condition or threshold is met then some action is to be taken. Depending on the situation, the action might even be to invoke a stored procedure.

Meet the DB2 Family of Relational Databases

Initially, IBM made DataBase 2 (DB2) available for the MVS operating system. Eventually IBM provided it on VM and VSE as **Structured Query Language/Data System (SQL/DS)**. IBM changed the name on VSE; today the product name is DB2/VSE.

OS/400 has a relational database structure built in to the operating system. IBM has enhanced the capabilities and changed the name to DB2/400. The DB2/400 Query Manager and SQL Development Kit are follow-on products to SQL/400, which now supports the major SQL standard specifications and provides an SQL optimizer for better performance. Other new features that are important in the client/server arena are referential integrity, stored procedures, triggers, two-phase commit, and support for other SQL access methods such as Microsoft's Open DataBase Connection (ODBC). We'll talk about the two-phase commit protocol later in "Distributed online transaction processing" section.

As corporations distribute more powerful machines throughout the enterprise, the need to store and manipulate data on those machines has risen. IBM has provided versions of DB2 for OS/2 and for AIX, **DATABASE 2 OS/2 (DB2/2)** and **DATABASE 2 AIX/6000 (DB2/6000)** respectively. To meet customer requirements for support of DB2 on other systems, IBM has also provided versions of DB2 for the HP-UX, Solaris, Windows NT, and SINIX operating systems. Version 2 of DB2 on these platforms is referred to as common Server because the functionality is common across these platforms while leveraging the native operating system services.

Common Server–based products provide significant database technology enhancements for client/server solutions. Users can define their own data types and functions. IBM built on the capability to create these user-defined types and functions to create a set of commonly used database extenders. The database relational extenders are for text, image, audio, video, and fingerprint information. There are new multimedia data types and support for large (up to 2 GB) binary objects. Object oriented extensions have also been added. Later we'll talk about IBM's **Distributed Relational Database Architecture** and the **DRDA** capabilities that these products provide.

DB2/2 comes in a single-user version and a server version. The single-user version allows you to create and use databases on a single system. It also allows that system to be a client to other DB2/2 servers on the network. The server version gives clients read and update access to multiple databases on the server system. This version comes with the needed OS/2 database client software for DOS, Windows, and OS/2 systems.

The **DB2 Software Developer's Kit** provides developers with tools to build applications that access and manage databases. The kits are available for DOS, Windows, OS/2, and AIX. IBM also plans on making kits available for Macintosh, HP/UX, Solaris, and Windows NT. All of the kits allow programmers to write programs using embedded SQL, the DB2 CLI, or the DB2 administrative APIs. The DB2 CLI incorporates most of the X/Open SQL CLI and Microsoft's ODBC Version 2 specifications.

IBM recently announced a version of DB2/6000 called **DB2 Parallel Edition for AIX/6000**. This product can support as many as 128 RISC System/6000 nodes, providing the power to maintain and query very large databases. The appearance to client applications is as if there is a single database server because all of the benefits of parallelism are transparent to the client. However, this implementation is based on DB2/6000 version 1 rather than the version 2 Common Server implementation. The client/server technology enhancements described above as part of the Common Server are not yet included in DB2 Parallel Edition.

Distributed Database Connection Services

The evolution of client/server computing has brought with it the need to provide more sophisticated means of communication between database products on different systems. **Distributed Database Connection Services** is available for OS/2 (**DDCS/2**) and for AIX **DDCS/6000**. DDCS provides a gateway from an OS/2 or AIX system to DB2 databases. It also provides support for stored procedures for databases that support them, for example, DB2/MVS, DB2/400, and DB2 Common Server platforms (OS/2, AIX, HP/UX, and Solaris).

The **Client Application Enabler** products provide runtime environments for PCs to reach DB2/2 databases. Client Application Enabler is available for DOS, Windows, OS/2, AIX, HP/UX, Solaris, and Macintosh clients. With the assistance of a DDCS/2 or DDCS/6000 gateway, these systems can also use databases on other systems in the DB2 family. The CAE products support a variety of protocols including IPX/SPX, NetBIOS, TCP/IP, and APPC, depending on the configuration. CAE for Windows and CAE for OS/2 support the X/Open Call Level Interface (CLI), which includes support for Microsoft's ODBC Level 1 specification and most of the Level 2 functionality. Applications written to Microsoft's specification can use this client enabling software.

Groupware

A different class of resource sharing software has emerged, called groupware. **Groupware** is used to facilitate collaboration between users. Hence, it is also referred to as collaborative computing. Lotus Notes is an example of groupware. It uses a file server such as OS/2 LAN Server or NetWare to provide resource sharing, but provides additional functions such as electronic conferencing, electronic mail, databases, and forms processing. IBM also offers OS/2 LAN Server, Lotus Notes, along with OS/2 Warp in an integrated package called OS/2 Warp Server. IBM also plans to make a version of Lotus Notes available to run on the AS/400 FSIOP like LAN Server and NetWare.

Lotus Notes can also integrate with other software packages to provide alternatives to its own functions. For example, it can use Lotus cc:Mail rather than its own internal mail mechanism. Basically, groupware acts as an integrator of different applications and makes it easier for end users to work with the software as well as each other.

Resource Sharing: Order Entry for Global Plumbing Supplies

In Chapter 2 we talked about Global Plumbing Supplies, Inc. (GPSI) and how resource sharing might help them. Let's look at a typical order processing scenario, as The House of Home Improvement calls GPSI to place an order for valves. They aren't sure of the part number, but they know what the existing valve looks like. A customer service representative in the New York office, Nick Zielinski, answers the phone. He uses the multimedia server's parts catalog to review different valves and faxes two promising part images to the customer. Once The House of Home Improvement agrees that the second fax is the correct part, Nick quotes a price and a shipment date for the order. The House of Home Improvement confirms the order, but Nick notes they are one day behind in paying an existing invoice. He mentions this to the customer, and chooses to place the order instead of holding the process until GPSI receives payment.

Figure 5.11 specifies the products GPSI used. Note that two servers are running on the OS/2 system, the OS/2 LAN Server and the OS/2 LAN Server Ultimedia. Although there is only one physical computer, there are multiple software applications providing different services. This is only possible on multitasking operating systems, because all of the servers must be running concurrently to handle client requests at any time. Also, because of the transparency of the Resource Sharing Model, Nick did not know where the server stored the images for the valves or the order confirmation template. Nick logged on to the server when he booted his system, and then it appeared as if everything was local to his system.

In most client/server applications, there will be some interaction between the new application and existing applications, databases, or other components. GPSI's customer and inventory records already existed in a

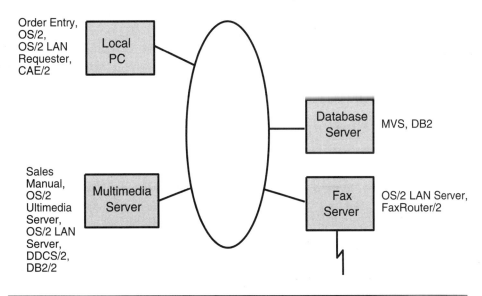

Figure 5.11. Resource sharing at GPSI.

DB2 relational database on their MVS mainframe. The DB2 data is also used by other mainframe applications. Since Nick only needs to query these databases, the existing applications need not change. Because Nick must create a new order to be placed in the existing order database, more care must be given to the development of this part of the application. The client software must be able to add new orders, cancel orders, and modify orders in such a way that it will not disturb existing applications on the mainframe while maintaining the integrity of the data.

The client OS/2 systems can reach the DB2 data on the mainframe via the DDCS/2 gateway. Essentially, this solution provides database sharing. The mainframe acts as the database server, and the PC is the client. To the order entry application the database appears to be local, so the SQL calls in the application are the same as if they were being made to a database directly on the PC. The CAE/2 software passes those SQL requests to the gateway that sends them to the mainframe for processing. The mainframe sends the return codes back through the gateway to the CAE/2 software, which returns them to the application. The order entry application was developed using VisualAge; this masked the communications and database access complexities from the programmers.

VisualAge was also used to develop the only other application built for this solution, the sales manual interface. Nick uses this application to search for products based on different criteria, manipulate the images, and check prices. Notice that there are only two applications that had to be developed in-house for this solution. All of the other function is provided by off-the-shelf products. Even if the sales manual application did not use a client/server approach, it still would have had to have been developed as a new application.

Figure 5.12 shows how the various software components fit together to provide the functions for this example. The OS/2 Ultimedia Server provides images for the "View the Sales Manual" function. This is a simple two-tiered approach using resource sharing. The "Create Confirmation" and "Fax Confirmation" functions also use two-tiered resource sharing; however, there is different client and server software for each case. Both queries and updates to the mainframe database are provided via the CAE/2 and DDCS/2 software. Notice that in this case, a three-tiered approach is used to share the database resource.

As you can see from this example, it is possible to use different types of resource sharing in one solution (file/image, print, fax, and database), and to use both two-tiered and three-tiered approaches in one solution. As you can tell from the figures, many software components are required for this solution. Other software combinations may also work in this scenario.

View the Sales Manual

| Sales Manual Application |
| OS/2 LAN Requester |
| NetBIOS |
| Token-Ring |

OS/2 LAN Server	OS/2 Ultimedia Server
NetBIOS	
Token-Ring	

OS/2 Client —————————— OS/2 LAN Server

Create Confirmation

| Word Pro |
| OS/2 LAN Requester |
| NetBIOS |
| Token-Ring |

| OS/2 LAN Server |
| NetBIOS |
| Token-Ring |

OS/2 Client —————————— OS/2 LAN Server

Fax Confirmation

| |
| OS/2 LAN Requester |
| NetBIOS |
| Token-Ring |

| FaxRouter/2 |
| OS/2 LAN Server |
| NetBIOS |
| Token-Ring |

OS/2 Client —————————— FaxRouter/2 Server

Query Credit, Query Ship Date, Create Order

| Credit Check |
| Client Application Enabler/2 |
| NetBIOS |
| Token-Ring |

Dist'd Data Connection Svcs/2	
NetBIOS	SNA
Token-Ring	

| DB2 |
| SNA |
| Token-Ring |

OS/2 Client —————————— OS/2 LAN Server ————— Mainframe

Figure 5.12. GPSI's sharing functions.

Summary

In many cases, resource sharing can be used to carry out client/server solutions with products that are readily available. In simple cases, resource sharing solutions do not require additional programming. You can install and configure them as provided, because they provide you with the necessary access to the remote resource. Since file servers and print servers have been available for quite a while, resource sharing is a very widely understood method for client/server solutions. Usually, it is used in two-tiered solutions. However, it can also be used for three-tiered solutions. Resource sharing provides cost savings because it allows many users to use expensive resources (disk storage, printers, fax machines, modems, databases, etc.).

Client/Server Communications

By definition, any client/server solution will require some form of communication between the client and the server. Some client/server solutions split application logic between clients and server. These kinds of solutions typically use three main ways to accomplish the needed communication: conversations, remote procedure calls, and messages. The Process-Driven and Distributed Logic models by their nature use this division of labor. Before we discuss these reference models, we need to review the communication models.

When you need to talk between distributed systems, your solutions can use these communication models. It takes forethought to decide which model best fits your needs. Sometimes you may need to use more than one model. This is particularly true if you are using a three-tiered solution: One model may be used between tiers one and two, and another model between tiers two and three. It is important to know the differences between the models so that you can understand why one model fits a particular client/server reference model better than another.

Conversations

As shown in Figure 5.13, the **conversational model** is like a telephone call. Just as you would dial a phone number to call someone, one system calls the other system using some form of identification. When that system answers, the connection is established. If you are using the telephone, you know when to speak and when to listen; each person follows a protocol. Similarly, networked software follows a protocol during a conversation. Once the conversation is finished, both sides hang up. The communications using this model are synchronous; each side of the conversation depends on the other. If there is a communications error during the conversation, both sides eventually hang up, and the caller tries again.

Advanced Program-to-Program Communications

Advanced Program-to-Program Communications (APPC), a standard published by IBM, is an API for writing applications using the conversational model in an SNA environment. The API consists of verbs representing the actions that a program can use for conversations. Some important functions provided by APPC are security, commitment control, and error han-

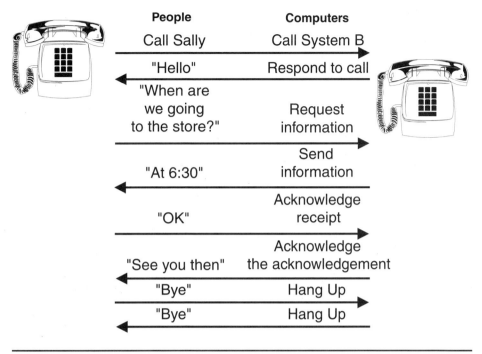

	People	Computers
	Call Sally	Call System B
	"Hello"	Respond to call
	"When are we going to the store?"	Request information
		Send information
	"At 6:30"	
	"OK"	Acknowledge receipt
	"See you then"	Acknowledge the acknowledgement
	"Bye"	Hang Up
	"Bye"	Hang Up

Figure 5.13. Communication models—conversations.

dling. When a conversation is established, a user ID, password, and profile are used to validate that the calling system is authorized to access the called system and the requested resources. We'll talk about transactions a little later, but for now you should be aware that there are verbs that allow you to commit requested changes or to undo changes that have been requested. The commitment is also known as a syncpoint, and the undo is also known as a roll back or back out. In the event of an error during the conversation, there is a verb to send an error message to the other side of the conversation. These capabilities are important because they allow programmers to develop robust applications more easily. The API provides these functions so that the programmers don't have to write extra source code to do it in their programs! IBM provides implementations of APPC for each of its operating systems. Some products use APPC for their implementations; one example is Client Access/400. Many other vendors have also implemented APPC for their operating systems.

Although most implementations of APPC provided the same basic capabilities, their APIs were not exactly the same. Those differences hindered application portability and required additional training for programmers to learn the different interfaces on each system, so IBM designed the **Common Programming Interface for Communications (CPI-C)**. CPI-C provides a consistent programming interface for applications across systems— the commonality needed to enhance application portability. However, the intent of CPI-C is to provide portability for applications, not only between systems, but also between network protocols. Eventually, if you have a program using CPI-C, you will be able to use it over different types of networks (e.g., TCP/IP, SNA, OSI). Typically only APPC is supported, and therefore SNA is the only network protocol supported. However, Encina for AIX allows CPI-C to be used with TCP/IP and IBM has licensed CPI-C to X/Open, which is incorporating CPI-C into their Common Application Environment (CAE). Novell, Apple, and others have also licensed CPI-C.

Berkeley Sockets

Berkeley sockets, or **sockets** for short, are a de facto standard. They were developed at the University of California at Berkeley as part of a government funded research project. Sockets are designed to support conversations over several different network protocols: TCP/IP, XNS, and OSI. The sockets' API was modeled after the UNIX file I/O functions. Therefore, you perform functions like open, read, write, and close on sockets. IBM provides implementations of sockets for the operating systems shown in Figure 5.14.

Operating System	Product Providing Sockets
MVS	TCP/IP for MVS
	Sockets interface for CICS
	Sockets interface for IMS
VM	TCP/IP for VM
OS/400	TCP/IP for OS/400
AIX	AIX
OS/2	TCP/IP for OS/2
DOS	TCP/IP for DOS

Figure 5.14. IBM's implementation of sockets.

UNIX workstation   MVS mainframe

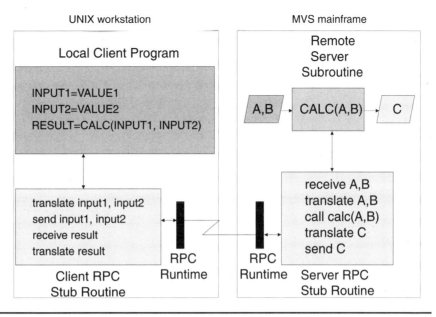

Figure 5.15. Communication models—RPCs.

Remote Procedure Calls

Remote Procedure Calls (RPCs) are function calls that appear local but run on a different system. Figure 5.15 shows a UNIX workstation making a call to the CALC function. CALC is actually a function call defined on an MVS mainframe. CALC requires two input parameters and returns one result. The local system passes two parameters, INPUT1 and INPUT2, and expects the calculation to be returned in RESULT.

Each system has a **stub routine** that is created from your input and output specifications for the function. You define the specifications in an **Interface Definition Language (IDL)**. The IDL provides a standard way of defining variables for functions across many platforms. It is also used to give the function an identity in the network. The IDL is then compiled for the particular platform that you are using and linked together with your RPC client and server.

The client stub routine translates the two input parameters to a common or network data representation and sends them to the remote system via the RPC runtime. Here, the translation is required because the UNIX and MVS systems represent numbers differently. The RPC runtime actually handles all of the necessary communications between the two systems.

The server stub routine receives the input parameters and translates them into the format required for the MVS system. It then makes the call to the CALC routine. When the result is returned, the server stub routine translates it into common data representation and sends it to the other system. The client stub receives the result and translates it back into the format for the UNIX workstation. RPCs are easy for programmers to learn because they are an extension of something that is already very familiar to them, the function call.

The communications using this model are also synchronous. However, in the event of an error, usually the calling program will handle any necessary recovery.

Network Computing System

Vendors have specified several kinds of RPCs. The **Network Computing System (NCS)** from Hewlett-Packard is one example. It was chosen by the OSF to be included in the DCE. NCS uses **Network Data Representation (NDR)** to eliminate differences between data representations on communicating systems. For example, one system might use ASCII to store characters and another might use EBCDIC. NDR uses a philosophy in which the receiver handles any necessary data conversion. So if two similar systems are using NCS then there is no data conversion necessary.

Open Network Computing

Sun also defined an RPC, the SunRPC. It is licensed by Sun as part of **Open Network Computing (ONC)**. The SunRPC uses **eXternal Data Representation (XDR)** to coordinate the exchange of data between different systems. It requires that both systems convert to XDR before sending data over the network. In the case where both systems are of the same type, this adds unnecessary overhead.

Named Pipes

Earlier, we mentioned named pipes in a LAN Server environment as a form of interprocess communication. Named pipes can be used to implement the conversational model. When used in this manner, a protocol defines how information will flow between the client and server. Read and write calls are used to receive and send information between the systems. Named pipes can also be used to implement RPCs. Two different kinds of calls can be made with named pipes. The "transaction" function makes a request over an opened pipe and waits for a response. The "call" function opens a pipe, uses the "transaction" call to execute the request and receive a response, and closes the pipe.

Messages

The **messaging model** queues messages and processes them as required. A message consists of information that is being exchanged between applications. The format of the message is dictated by the applications. Applications only know the names of the queues that they use; they do not know where they are located or how the message gets there. The underlying messaging system handles moving the messages between systems. Typically, a **store and forward** mechanism is used to move messages from system to system until it arrives at its destination. Queue managers ensure that messages are delivered so the communications are also reliable.

As you can see in Figure 5.16, a single system may have multiple queues monitored by different applications. The application monitoring a queue does not have to be running when a message is stored in the queue.

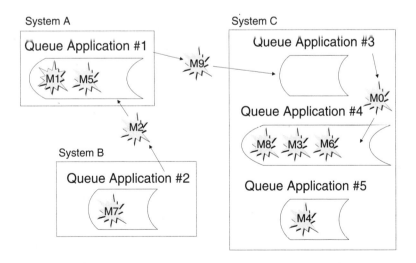

Figure 5.16. Communication models—messages.

Therefore, the communications in this model are normally asynchronous. Messages can be sent between queues on the same system or on remote systems. If there is an error during the transmission of the message, then the error is handled by the messaging system itself. Messages can be removed from a queue in several different ways. They can be removed First In, First Out (FIFO), Last In, First Out (LIFO), or based on a priority. Different messaging systems provide different capabilities.

Message Queueing Interface

IBM's **Message Queueing Interface (MQI)** is an example of communication services that use the messaging model. MQI features a simple interface for sending and receiving messages, recoverable queues, a standard message format, and message tracking. Message exchange is asynchronous, but delivery of a message can be implemented using a syncpoint. This capability provides a means for recovering messages in the event of a system failure.

Mail Systems

Mail systems are based on messaging. Microsoft's Messaging Application Programming Interface (MAPI), Lotus's Vendor Independent Messaging (VIM), and Novell's Message Handling Interface (MHS) are several popular specifications for messaging. These specifications are used by electronic mail software. For example, MAPI is used by Microsoft Mail, VIM is used by Lotus Notes and cc:Mail, and MHS is used by da Vinci's e-MAIL and Beyond Corporation's BeyondMail.

Which Model Is Appropriate?

Your distributed applications can use many different APIs, so how do you choose one? In an ideal world, technology would dictate the most appropriate model to use in a particular situation. However, reality requires that in the current environment, programming and support staff skills and product availability be considered as well. Here we provide some generalizations that can be helpful to better understand the differences between models and why one model might be more appropriate than another.

Processing a transaction, like withdrawing money from a savings account, often requires multiple requests and responses. These interactions follow a protocol defined by the business process that you want to automate. For example, when you use an Automated Teller Machine (ATM) to withdraw funds from your savings account, you first identify yourself with a Personal Identification Number (PIN). The system verifies that you entered the correct PIN. Then you specify that you want to withdraw money from your savings account. Next, you enter the amount to be withdrawn and the system ensures that you have that amount in your account. The specified amount is subtracted from your account, and the system dispenses the cash to you. Each of these steps depends on the execution of the previous step. The ATM shouldn't let you withdraw money if you didn't enter the correct PIN or dispense cash if you don't have enough in your account. As a user of the ATM, you want all of this to happen in "real time." You wouldn't want to ask for money and come back at a later time to pick it up!

Here a conversational model is the most appropriate to use. One side initiates the conversation, and the data exchange continues until it is no longer needed. You can think of this as the "interactive" communication model. For an interactive session, an end user logs on, does some processing, and logs off when finished. For a conversation, a system connects, does some processing, and disconnects when finished. This approach reduces the number of times that a connection has to be established: It is only created once for each conversation. It also simplifies acknowledgments because they are done during the course of the conversation. If there is an error during the communications, however, you are out of luck, because your transaction cannot be completed. You have to come back at some later point in time to try again or find another ATM. This is analogous to a client using a different server in the event of a failure. A message-passing facility that provides synchronized interactions, like IBM's MQI, also would work well.

For processing intensive requests or an occasional request and response, the remote procedure call model is the most appropriate to use. When used for processing intensive requests, the remote system is usually more powerful than the local system, so the request is processed more quickly on the remote system. Sometimes remote systems have access to a resource (data, peripheral, or processing capability) that the local system does not have and cannot get to directly. Remote procedure calls allow the local system to use that resource also. For each RPC, the client enabling software must create a connection, send the data, wait for the response, and close the connection. Generally, the client software is blocked while it waits for a response; it cannot continue processing. An exception to this is if the system supports threads. On such a system, a single process can have multiple subprocesses, or **threads**, within it. Several of a process's threads may be executing at the same time. Therefore, if a program needs to do multiple RPCs, it can execute each as a separate thread. While one thread is suspended, other processing can continue. This is only appropriate if the RPCs do not have to be executed sequentially.

The connection setup and shutdown add a certain degree of overhead to each RPC. For example, if you compare using five RPCs to using a single conversation, you see that four additional connections are established and closed with the RPCs. That is one reason why RPCs work best for infrequent requests and responses. If you must make multiple requests in a specific sequence, then the conversational model fits better. It might also perform better.

If the sequencing is not important, then the messaging model might be more appropriate. The messaging model works best when each request is autonomous and generally does not require an immediate response.

Process-Driven Computing

As mentioned in Chapter 2, the Process-Driven Model generally requires a manager to control the flow of processes. This is the **workflow manager**. IBM is participating in the Work Flow Management Coalition, a group of vendors that are developing specifications for the interoperability of workflow managers.

IBM's MQSeries of Messaging and Queuing Software

The Process-Driven Model works well with the messaging communication model because distinct processes execute independently. IBM's **MQSeries** products use the messaging model. They let an application reliably send a message to another application's queue. At some point, the other application will check the queue and act on the message. This occurs asynchronously; after writing the message to the queue, the sender can continue processing. The sender just needs to know the name of the queue where the message should be written. Then, a message coordinator handles all of the networking details to deliver it to the receiver.

MQI is implemented by the products in the MQSeries from IBM. MQSeries is provided on the following platforms: MVS, VSE, OS/400, AIX, various UNIX-based systems, OS/2, Tandem Guardian Himalaya, DEC VMS, S/88, Solaris, and NCR UNIX. There are some differences between the MQSeries products on various platforms. For example, some of the MQSeries products include integration with CICS on their platforms and some implement triggers. The AIX and OS/2 products support DOS, Windows, OS/2, and AIX clients. The OS/2 product provides a single point of administration for MQSeries Version 2 products and MQSeries for MVS. A unique feature of MQSeries for AIX is support for queue names in DCE Directory Services. Recently, IBM has also integrated MQSeries support as an optional component of Lotus Notes. You can also use MQSeries in distributed logic applications. This is particularly true when you use it with CICS software.

FlowMark and FormTalk

IBM's **FlowMark for OS/2** and **FlowMark for AIX** are workflow managers. FlowMark consists of development, runtime, and administrative functions. The development environment runs on OS/2 today. For runtime, FlowMark supports Windows, OS/2, and AIX clients. FlowMark supports business process management in many different industries. The process models can be defined graphically as a network of activities. Each activity is identified by the person or people that use it in the process, the application that performs the activity, and the data required by the application to execute. Once the model has been created, FlowMark provides a facility to simulate execution to test and validate the model. During actual execution of the process, FlowMark tracks the status of the work, keeps statistics about the execution, and maintains an audit trail. For example, you can find out how long the entire process took for a specific piece of work or how long it took for each of the activities. **FlowMark for MVS** currently provides the ability for MVS to initiate processes on OS/2 and AIX FlowMark servers. In the future it will also include the ability for MVS to be a FlowMark server.

The **FormTalk** family of products provides simple workflow capabilities. With FormTalk, forms can be created, completed, and routed online. Routing is accomplished by using a MAPI-enabled mail system like Microsoft Mail or a VIM-enabled mail system like Lotus Notes or cc:Mail. FormTalk is available for OS/2 and Windows.

A Process-Driven Example: Acme Roadrunner Traps Company

In Chapter 2 we presented a process driven example using a workflow manager to order office supplies at the Acme Roadrunner Traps company. Figure 5.17 shows the business process flow for this example. Instead of filling out a paper form, an electronic form is used and processed electronically according to the normal procedures. Suppose that a staff member, Fritz Payling, needs an ergonomic chair due to back problems. Fritz fills out the electronic order form, asking for the chair. Because it is an expense of more than fifty dollars, it has to be approved by a manager. Once Will Warner, Fritz's supervisor, approves the expense, the chair is ordered, and notification is sent to Fritz.

Figure 5.17 also shows the software that Acme used to manage this process. Most staff members at Acme use PCs running PC-DOS and Microsoft Windows. From the "To Do" list on his Windows system, Fritz chooses the task "order supplies." This task displays a graphical order form that looks just like the paper form previously used. A programmer created it in Lotus Notes, running on a RISC System/6000 with AIX. When Fred finishes entering the data, the form goes into a Notes database on the AIX Notes server. If the total field on the order form is greater than fifty dollars, the workflow manager, FlowMark for AIX, sends a note to Will for approval. Will uses an OS/2 system. When the mail arrives, an approval request appears in his "To Do" list.

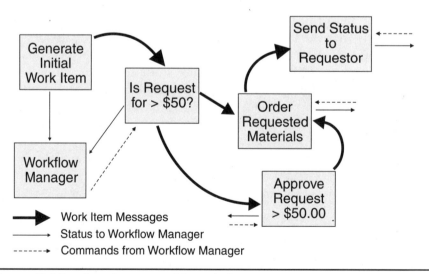

Figure 5.17. Acme's process-driven design.

Unfortunately for Fritz, Will is attending a conference on reducing workplace accidents, and forgot to check his mail. After 24 hours, FlowMark for AIX routes Fritz's request to Will's administrative assistant, Fred Brewer, for approval. Fred knows that Fritz's request is valid because Fritz tests Acme's roadrunner traps (a very hazardous job). Eventually Fred approves the request. FlowMark for AIX then starts a CICS transaction on a CICS for AIX server. The transaction creates an order based on the information in the Notes database and faxes it to the vendor. Then FlowMark for AIX sends a Lotus cc:Mail message to Fred, Fritz, and Will indicating approval, order completed, and the chair's expected delivery date.

Summary

The Process-Driven Model is most often used to ensure the sequencing of well-defined and autonomous tasks. The tasks might be distributed across an enterprise or handled within a department. Although ordering office supplies requires human intervention for several steps throughout the process, this model can also be used for tasks that might not involve any human intervention.

Front Ends

Front ending tools come in several different varieties: screen scrapers, GUI tools, and tools specific to a particular hardware or software system. You can use most of these approaches to migrate from a traditional computing environment to a client/server environment.

Screen scraping uses an existing application's screen displays to "scrape" off the information that the user needs to see and present it to them in a friendly, graphical interface. IBM's **VisualLift** provides this ability for MVS, VSE, and VM systems. You develop the VisualLift interface using the Application Development environment on OS/2. The Application Development environment uses a "What You See Is What You Get" (WYSIWYG) window editor to create the interface. This makes it very easy for developers to define the GUI. You can run the application using the VisualLift runtime environment on either OS/2 or Windows clients.

Using this approach, the existing applications do not have to be modified. This has the added benefit of allowing end users with nonprogrammable terminals to continue to use the application while allowing PC users to take advantage of their GUI when using the application. VisualLift allows logic to be added to the GUI so that simple editing checks for input can be done at the workstation before transmitting the information to the application. The new interface will probably be easier for end users to learn and can therefore reduce training time.

For firms with MVS and IMS, **IMS Client Server** is an API provided to simplify interactions with **IMS Data Communications (IMS DC)** or **IMS Transaction Manager (IMS TM)**. It is available for OS/2 and Windows. This product uses a 3270 data stream API available with the Communications Manager/2 interface. The IMS Client Server/2 APIs are simpler for a programmer to use than the native Communications Manager/2 interface. With this facility, an OS/2 or Windows client can call existing IMS transactions. This is particularly useful in an environment where PCs and nonprogrammable terminals must coexist. It still allows you to use the GUI and processing power of PCs.

A Front End: Jones' Happy Travel's Reservation System

In Chapter 2 we discussed Jones' Happy Travel's need to use a front end to two reservation systems. In our example, the reservation application that the Jones agency uses is owned by an airline. The agency can't change the reservation system because it is a service provided to them by the airline. However, by using front ending techniques the agency can make it easier for agents like JoLynn Betts to get the necessary travel information.

The front end consists of graphical software that looks to the main computer like a person using a terminal. Put another way, the client application and the enabling software grab JoLynn's mouse movements, menu choices, and other inputs from the graphical interface. Then, they translate these into the strings of text and the networking protocols the main computer expect. Figure 5.18 shows that the agency chose VisualLift to develop the GUI and to communicate with the airline system. VisualLift, in fact, works well with applications like this.

Sometimes the front end's designers hide the session with the main computer from the user. Here, since experienced agents know how to use the reservation systems, the developer wanted to expose several screens. This lets an agent enter unusual or complex requests directly. With VisualLift, the developer simply didn't make changes to these transactions. In any case, the main computer system and its software need not change. The only change the reservation system would see is the return of the now unused terminals.

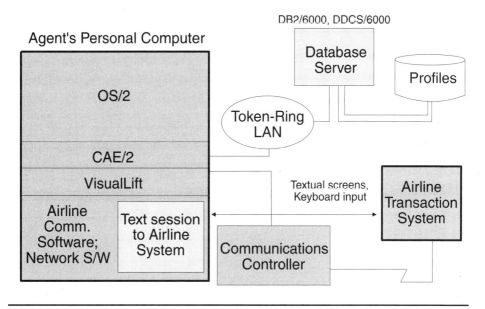

Figure 5.18. Jones' Happy Travel's front end.

Maintaining profiles for the agency's customers requires a local, shared database. This database provides JoLynn with the data she needs to make her discussions with clients such as Alan Marchesseault seem more personal. The agency's office manager, Anna Sue Kingsley, also uses the information to target promotional material more accurately and to validate operational decisions. The agency chose to use the DB2/6000 relational database, running on a RISC System/6000 system, because it scales well as business needs changed. Each agent's OS/2 system uses Client Application Enabler/2 and the Distributed Data Connection Services/6000 gateway to access the data contained within DB2/6000.

Summary

This technique can be used to familiarize end users with GUIs while creating an infrastructure for client/server technology. The tools to provide front ends are becoming increasingly friendly so the investment to implement this model is relatively small. Although front ending provides a prettier and easier to use interface for older applications, the basic functionality of the application remains the same.

Remote Presentation

The World Wide Web

As mentioned in Chapter 2, access to the **World Wide Web** via a Web browser is a form of remote presentation. The Web server that you access from your Web browser (or client) uses HTML to describe what the pages will look like. Your browser formats the HTML that it receives. Information is exchanged between the client and the server using HTTP.

IBM's Internet Connection family of products includes both browsers and servers. The browsers are **WebExplorer for OS/2 Warp** and **WebExplorer for Windows**. There are also plans for an AIX browser. IBM has Web servers for OS/2 and AIX called **Internet Connection Server for OS/2 Warp** and **Internet Connection Server for AIX**. There is also a Web server for OS/400 called **WebConnection for OS/400**. IBM has also announced plans to provide a server for MVS.

The OS/2 and AIX Web servers can act as a **proxy** for Web browsers. A proxy acts on the behalf of another system. For example, suppose you have an AIX Internet Connection Server with your home page available on your internal network and on the Internet. The AIX system has two connections: one on your private network and another to an Internet access provider. If you need to access home pages on the Internet from your Web browser, then the AIX Internet Connection Server can act on your behalf to access the information from the Internet and transfer it to you. The OS/2 and AIX Internet Connection Servers can also act as proxies for FTP and Gopher. Gopher is similar to WWW except that the information is textual only; FTP is the Internet's File Transfer Protocol.

One of the largest concerns regarding the WWW is security. The Internet is accessible by anyone with a PC and a modem. The issue then is how to provide secure access to your servers and how to ensure that no one can enter your internal network from the Internet. An extension to the HTTP was developed called **Secure-Hypertext Transfer Protocol (S-HTTP)** as was the **Secure Sockets Layer (SSL)**. These protocols provide an added degree of security by encrypting and decrypting transmitted data. These protocols can be used with the IBM products by using the **Internet Connection Secure Server**. The Secure Server is available for OS/2 Warp and AIX. The Internet Connection family also includes two secure Web browsers: **Secure WebExplorer for OS/2 Warp** and **Secure WebExplorer for AIX**. IBM also provides a firewall called the **Internet Connection Secured Net-**

work Gateway. A firewall allows authorized users on your internal network to access specific kinds of resources on an external network. It also prevents access to your internal network from the external network.

Accessing Other Information from the Web

Another Web specification is the **Common Gateway Interface (CGI)**, which describes how external applications can be accessed by web servers. IBM has created two other Internet Connection family members that provide a CGI. Both products can also use the Internet Connection Secure Server to enhance security.

One is the **DB2 World Wide Web Connection**, which allows a Web server to access DB2 databases on OS/2, AIX, and MVS. The access is through normal HTML and SQL. When the DB2 WWW Connection is used in a three-tiered environment with DDCS or DataJoiner, it can provide access to numerous other DBMSs. We'll talk more about DataJoiner later. With this product, an authorized user can use any Web browser supporting HTML to access the relational data that you want them to see.

Similarly, the **CICS Internet** gateway allows a user with a standard Web browser to access CICS 3270 applications. The gateway generates HTML for these applications, so no changes to existing applications are required. Initially, the gateway is available for OS/2 and AIX. A CICS client is required, as is a Web server. A similar capability is included with the WebConnection for OS/400 to allow access to existing OS/400 applications.

X-Windows

The X-Windows protocol is another example of remote presentation. Figure 5.19 shows the systems for which IBM provides an X-Windows client, server, or both. An X-Windows client (X-client) is the system executing the application logic and making the X-Windows function calls. An X-Windows server (X-server) is the system providing the display services. Different levels of X-Windows are defined; the current level is X11 Release 5. For the best results, your X-Windows servers and clients should be at the same level of the specification. Many vendors have added extensions to the X-Windows specification and defined proprietary fonts and colors. If a particular X-server does not support a font or mapping specified by an X-client, then the X-client will receive an error. Some X-servers allow you to

Operating System	Product	X-Windows Client	X-Windows Server
MVS	TCP/IP for MVS	X	
VM	TCP/IP for VM	X	
OS/400	TCP/IP for OS/400	X	
AIX	AIXwindows Environment/6000	X	X
OS/2	TCP/IP for OS/2		X

Figure 5.19.   IBM client/server support for x-windows protocol.

define aliases to avoid this problem. Aliases allow the X-server to use a supported font or mapping instead of the one requested by the X-client.

The X-Windows specification does not define guidelines for the "look and feel" of the X-Windows. IBM's TCP/IP for OS/2 provides an X-server for OS/2 called PMX. PMX stands for Presentation Manager X-server. PMX uses the windows support of OS/2, Presentation Manager, to control and present the X-Windows. Other X-servers also use native windowing capabilities. For example, several products available for Microsoft Windows manage X-Windows with the normal Windows style. However, standards organizations have created guidelines for X-Windows and provided toolkits to enforce them. For example, OSF has defined the Motif interface to provide a common appearance of X-Windows in different applications. Motif also includes a window manager. The window manager can provide the windowing support if there is no native support on the X-Server, or if you want to use the Motif standard.

Remote Presentation: A Doctor Using X-Windows

Dr. Dale Nemati at Cripple Creek Community Hospital has a patient, Jerry Gant, with a broken leg. When Jerry got to the emergency room, information was taken regarding his identity, insurance coverage, and medical history. All of this information is stored in DB2 on an MVS mainframe. After Jerry has X-rays taken, Dr. Nemati will need to examine them before setting the leg. Radiology uses a Digital Equipment Corporation VMS system to store the X-rays. The doctor will also need to prescribe medication to relieve the pain. A Hewlett-Packard HP-UX system is used by the pharmacy for its prescription system.

Using AIX on a RISC System/6000 running the AIXwindows Environment/6000, Dr. Nemati has a customized desktop with icons representing the different systems he may need to use. Figure 5.20 shows icons for the patient information application, the prescription application, and the radiology application. Dr. Nemati does not know that X-Windows is the magic providing access to the needed applications, nor does he know that different network protocols are being used to transmit information between the various X-clients and their X-server. (TCP/IP is being used to communicate with MVS and HP-UX; DECnet is being used to communicate with VMS.)

The doctor can start the patient information application by double clicking on the icon. An X-Window appears with a graphical interface based on Motif that allows the doctor to find Jerry's information. Dr. Nemati now knows the patient identifier for Jerry and whether he has any allergies or past medical history that would preclude a certain type of medication. While the patient information is still being displayed within the X-Window, Dr. Nemati can start the radiology application to look at Jerry's X-ray. He can verify the patient identifier from the patient information

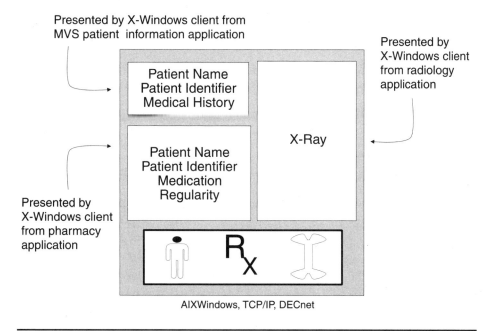

Figure 5.20. Cripple Creek Community Hospital's remote presentation.

X-Window and the radiology X-Window. He can be certain that he is looking at the appropriate X-ray. Once Dr. Nemati determines the extent of the damage, he can start the pharmacy application in another X-Window to prescribe some pain relievers and antiinflammatory medication. He can cut and paste between all of the X-Windows as necessary.

The example shows that even though different network protocols were used to get to the various systems, it was transparent to Dr. Nemati. All of the X-Windows could be active at the same time, so it was easy for the doctor to use information from all of them.

Summary

The X-Windows protocol is important because it eases application portability. X-Windows clients are portable because the functions to display and manipulate windows are the same on all systems supporting the X-Windows interface. This feature also allows the programmer to create a GUI based on the capabilities of X-Windows rather than the capabilities of a particular display device or family of devices so that any device that supports the X-server can support any X-client application. However, the capabilities of the device will dictate the quality of the presentation.

The WWW is very important because of the global reach of the Internet, the easy-to-use Web browser interfaces, the volume of information available, and the enormous potential for commercial applications. The Web interface can also provide an easy way of disseminating information within your company. For example, Material Safety Data Sheets required by OSHA or information on benefits might be made accessible via a Web server. In any event, this area has already experienced explosive growth and should continue to grow well into the future.

Distributed Logic

The Distributed Logic Model puts part of the application processing on two or more systems in the network, which requires that the application use one, or possibly several, of the communication models. A prominent technology in the industry for distributed logic is the Distributed Computing Environment (DCE). IBM provides DCE as well as several other product families for distributing application logic: Customer Information Control System (CICS), MQSeries, **Distributed Application Environment (DAE)**, and **LAN Distributed Processing (LANDP)**. The sections that follow describe differences between the technologies. These differences have four main causes. First, the families use different communication models. Second, some are more suited for a particular industry segment. Sometimes the protocol specifications are standards based; other times they are proprietary. Last, some products are available on more systems than others including non-IBM systems. Before describing these technologies, we will define some important terms and explain functionality that can aid the implementation of a distributed logic solution.

Distributed Online Transaction Processing

To understand transaction processing, let's consider a business transaction: buying on credit. If you purchase something with a credit card, the store must validate your account number, check your credit, debit your account, and obtain your signature. All of those steps must be taken to complete the transaction. However, if you went on a spending binge last month and didn't have enough credit left to buy that home theater, the transaction would be voided! In computing, a **transaction** consists of several business actions, all of which must be done in order for the transaction to be completed. The collection of actions comprising a transaction is a **Unit of Work (UW)**. The term "unit" illustrates that the separate components in a transaction together form a single entity: the transaction. When a transaction completes, it is **committed**, just as you are when you sign on the dotted line and commit that you will pay your credit card bill. If for some reason a step does not finish, the transaction is voided. The transaction is backed out or **rolled back**.

    Distributed transaction processing occurs when different systems execute the steps comprising a unit of work. If there are two systems, then it is a **Remote Unit of Work (RUW)**. If there are more than two systems, then it is a **Distributed Unit of Work (DUW)**. It is easier to ensure that all steps have been completed when they all run on the same system. This verification is much more complex when there are more systems involved. Obviously, there must be some coordination between the systems to synchronize the execution of the transaction. This synchronization is normally done with a **two-phase commit** protocol. The first phase of the protocol consists of a coordinating system asking all of the other participating systems if they are ready to commit. When the coordinator receives all positive responses, the second phase occurs, in which the coordinator tells the participants to make the commitment. If any piece of the protocol fails, then the actions are rolled back on all systems to void the transaction.

Distributing Relational Data with DRDA

Synchronizing databases to maintain integrity across the enterprise and coordinating transaction execution are critical success factors for client/server applications. Both the Distributed Logic and Data Staging models require coordination of database updates between distributed systems. IBM's **Distributed Relational Database Architecture (DRDA)** is one method to provide the needed coordination. DRDA defines three basic types of remote database access: Remote Unit of Work (RUW), Distributed Unit of Work (DUW), and **Distributed Request (DR)**. In this context, a unit of work will contain SQL statements to manipulate data in one or more databases. Figure 5.21 shows three locations of a corporation. Each location has a database managed by a different DBMS. A RUW is a unit of work that uses one remote DBMS. In the RUW example, the UW consists of three SQL statements; each statement uses the Employee Database from System A. When a unit of work accesses multiple remote DBMSs, it is a DUW. Here, the DUW requires the use of all three databases, but each is reached with a separate SQL statement. A DR allows a single SQL state-

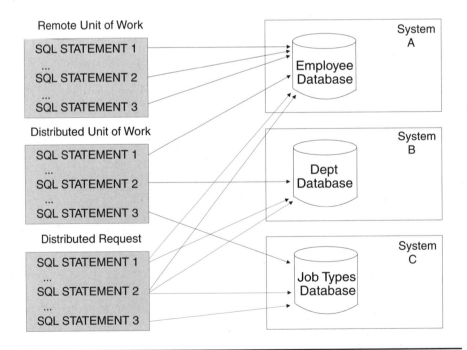

Figure 5.21. Distributed database access.

ment to access multiple remote databases. The DR in the figure has three SQL statements. The first uses the Employee database and the Department database, the second uses all three databases, and the last only uses the Job Types database.

IBM has been implementing DRDA in phases. Most of the DB2 family already do, or will, support RUW for both client and server. The terminology used in DRDA for client and server is **application requester** and **application server**. IBM has also announced that most of the DB2 family will also support DUW clients. OS/400 and DB2 support both clients and servers for DUW. For quite a while, OS/400's **Distributed Data Management (DDM)** has provided the ability to do a RUW if the remote system was also an AS/400. IBM recently announced that OS/400 version 3 will support DUW.

OSF Distributed Computing Environment (DCE)

The OSF created the Distributed Computing Environment to make it easier to build applications using heterogeneous systems. Figure 5.22 illustrates that the DCE architecture consists of several interrelated layers. Five of these components are considered core technologies: threads, RPCs, and directory (naming), security, and time services.

Figure 5.23 shows the technology contributor for components of DCE. The OSF uses an open process to select the best technologies for its standards. This process starts with a Request for Technology that specifies the types of services required. Anyone can respond with a technology if a working implementation exists. Then, the OSF evaluates the responses and a technology is chosen. Because of this approach, the components for DCE originate from various sources. The OSF must then combine them into a cohesive package, called a reference implementation. Member companies can then license the technology to incorporate it in their products. The OSF chose IBM to create the reference implementation for DCE, so IBM integrated the various technologies on the RISC System/6000.

DCE Core Technologies

Threads. Threads are necessary for all of the layers above them because they provide a means for one process to concurrently handle multiple events. Each thread executes a different set of instructions to accomplish some

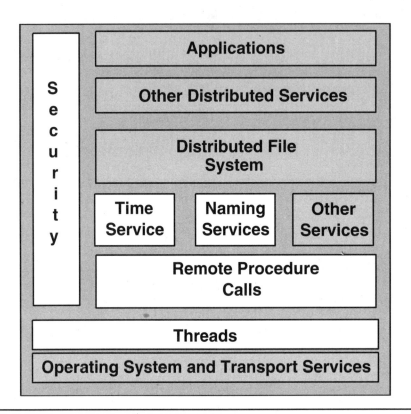

Figure 5.22. DCE architecture.

DCE Components	Contributor(s)	Technology
Threads	DEC	Concert Multi-thread Architecture
RPC	HP and DEC	Network Computing System
Distributed Time Services	DEC	DECdts
Security Services	MIT and HP	Kerberos
Distributed Naming Services	DEC and Siemens	DECdns and DIR-X
Distributed File Service	Transarc and HP	Andrew File System

Figure 5.23. Technology contributor for DCE components.

task that the process needs to do. There is less overhead when using threads than there is to create a new process for each task. Sometimes, the operating system provides threads natively; for example, OS/2 provides threads. However, if the operating system does not provide threads, then some other product must include the OSF's specification for threads.

RPCs. Earlier we discussed RPCs as a communication model. Here it represents an implementation of that model based on the Network Computing System (NCS). You will remember from our discussion of the RPC model that an RPC is a synchronous process; the calling program must wait for the response from the remote system. Consequently, threads are crucial to the implementation of DCE. One program can concurrently make multiple RPCs using threads, so if the program needs to make multiple queries to different databases, then each thread in the program can handle a separate query.

Directory Services. In a distributed environment it is virtually impossible to know where all of the resources are located. Also, you might want to move resources to different places over time. So it is necessary to have a directory that maintains all of the pertinent information about resources in the environment. When you need a resource, it can be found. You can think of the directory as a networkwide telephone book. DCE Directory Services use a distributed approach as shown in Figure 5.24. A **cell** is a logical collection of named resources in the distributed computing environment. It is a grouping made for easier management and adminis-

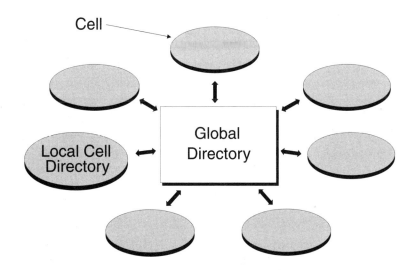

Figure 5.24. DCE directory services.

tration of the environment. A local directory contains information about a cell. You can think of the local cell directory as the phone book for your area. The collection of cell directories located throughout the environment comprises the global directory. This is comparable to calling information to get a phone number for someone outside of your area. So, there are two components: Cell Directory Services and the Global Directory Services. Resources not known by the local cell directory can be found via the global directory. The global directory can use either the OSI X.500 standard or the TCP/IP-based Domain Name Services to communicate with the cell directories.

Security Services. Once the directory locates a resource, DCE Security Services authenticate the user and verify the user's authority to do the requested action. Security Services provides the necessary functions to do both authentication and authorization. Authentication uses encrypted passwords.

Time Services. On a single system, it usually is not important that the time be exact. However, in a distributed system where events happen on systems with different clocks, it can be much more important. For example, an administrator might schedule events to occur at a certain time or a trace tool might use timestamps to record events in a trace. Consider trying to debug a problem using a trace with timestamps from two different systems with a difference in time of 20 seconds. It could be very difficult to understand the sequence of events! Any application that uses a timestamp easily proves the need for time synchronization. The DCE Time Services synchronize clocks on systems across the environment.

As shown previously in Figure 5.23, there are two other components besides the core components: Distributed File Services and Diskless Support. The Andrew File System discussed previously is the basis for Distributed File Services. Diskless Support allows a diskless workstation or PC to load its operating system from another system in the environment. This is also called remote boot or remote Initial Program Load (IPL). Figure 5.25 shows the DCE components that IBM provides for IBM systems and for Microsoft Windows. You will notice that sometimes there is only client or server function. An X shows that the system has both functions.

IBM's Customer Information Control System (CICS)

IBM's Customer Information Control System (CICS) is an online transaction monitoring system used by many corporations to run their crucial business systems. It is by far the market leader for transaction processing. CICS

DCE Components	MVS	VM	OS/400	AIX	OS/2	Windows
Threads	X	X	X	X	X	X
RPC	X	X	X	X	X	X
Time Services			X	X	Client	Client
Security Services	X	Client	Client	X	Client	Client
Cell Directory Services	X	Client	Client	X	Client	Client
Global Directory Services				X		
Distributed File Services				X		

Figure 5.25. DCE components for IBM systems and Microsoft Windows.

has been available for many years on MVS and VSE. More recently, CICS has become available for OS/400, AIX, and OS/2. Now, other vendors are providing CICS for their systems (e.g., Hewlett-Packard's HP-UX and Digital Equipment Corporation's Digital UNIX). These CICS servers are based on CICS/6000. CICS clients are available for DOS, Windows, OS/2, Macintosh, AIX, and Solaris systems. Various protocols are supported for communication between the client and the server (APPC, TCP/IP, and NetBIOS). The protocol that can be used in a particular environment depends on the client and server platforms being used. There are common APIs on all of the systems, so IBM has made it possible for you to port CICS applications between systems and to use existing programming skills on different systems. More important, you can now easily build distributed transaction processing applications using these dissimilar systems.

There are many reasons why CICS has such widespread use. Predominantly it is because of its ability to effectively administer, secure, execute, and manage transactions. CICS also has many capabilities for distributed transaction processing. In CICS, the term **InterSystem Communications (ISC)** is used as a synonym for interprocess communications. Intersystem Communications consists of transaction routing, function shipping, Distributed Transaction Processing (DTP), and Distributed Program Link (DPL). Let's look at each of these and see how they relate to the communication models described earlier.

Transaction routing allows a terminal logged on to one CICS system to initiate a transaction on another CICS system. This is done transparently to the programmer and to the end user. In a client/server environment this is useful if the transaction exists on a remote system connected through

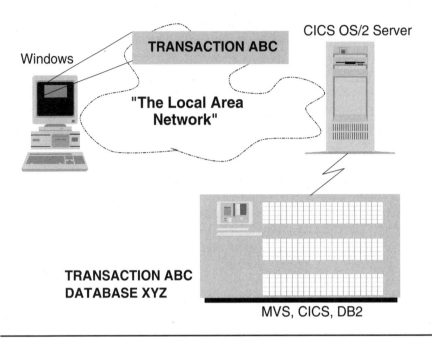

Figure 5.26. CICS transaction routing.

a WAN, as shown in Figure 5.26. Suppose the clients do not have direct connectivity to the remote system but the server does. Transaction routing allows the clients to start the transaction on the remote system. In this scenario, the CICS OS/2 client is using a CICS OS/2 server and the remote system is an MVS system with a DB2 database. The client could start a transaction through the CICS OS/2 server on the MVS system to get to and process data in the database. Using transaction routing, the client seemingly starts the transaction on the CICS OS/2 server, but actually it is executed on the remote system. At a minimum, the definition of the transaction on the CICS OS/2 server specifies the name of the remote system and the transaction to execute on that system. Transaction routing is an implementation of the RPC communication model, where parameters cannot be passed between the two systems.

Function shipping provides a different approach. CICS resource managers use the remote resources on behalf of the application. Therefore, the data location is transparent to the programmer and to the end user. Figure 5.27 shows the CICS OS/2 client initiating a transaction that executes on the CICS OS/2 server. Through function shipping the transaction can manipulate data (files and queues) on the remote MVS system. This is done

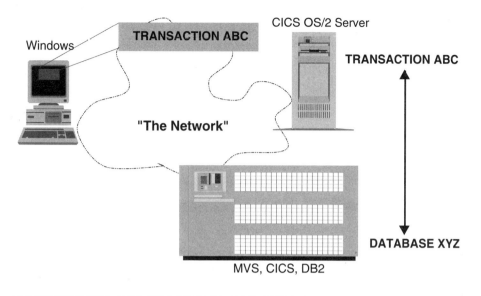

Figure 5.27. CICS function shipping.

with a request to a mirror transaction on the remote system. The mirror transaction accesses the resource and responds to the CICS OS/2 server. The CICS OS/2 server has definitions defining the resource, the remote system, and the mirror transaction. So, function shipping is also an implementation of the RPC communication model but provides access at the resource level rather than at the transaction level. With transaction routing, end users start remote transactions only. With function shipping, a single transaction can call many mirror transactions to access different remote resources.

CICS also provides the ability to use the conversational model of communication with APPC or sockets. Any system that supports APPC can hold a conversation with a CICS transaction. This includes many non-CICS systems and many non-IBM systems. Figure 5.28 shows a Windows client using Networking Services/DOS to provide the underlying network support for APPC. Then the Windows client runs a program that talks directly with an APPC transaction on the mainframe to complete the required request. Figure 5.29 shows an alternate, three-tiered solution in which the CICS OS/2 server is using Communications Manager/2 (CM/2) and Network Transport Services/2 (NTS/2) to have a conversation with the mainframe using APPC. Here, the Windows client starts a transaction on the CICS OS/2 server and the server conducts the conversation with the

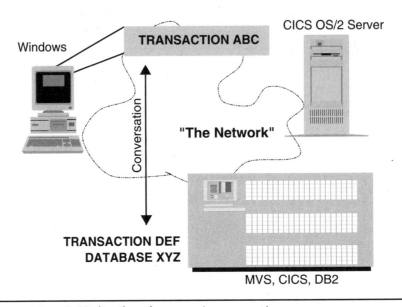

Figure 5.28. CICS distributed transaction processing.

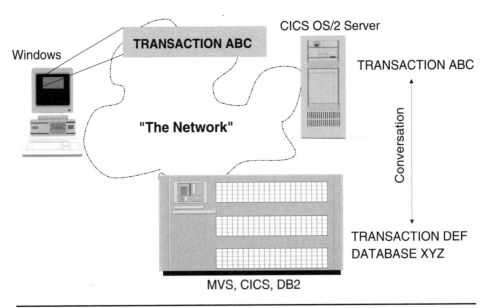

Figure 5.29. Three-tiered CICS distributed transaction processing.

MVS system. This alternative simplifies configuration, since an administrator defines one server rather than multiple clients. It also reduces the amount of software required on the client. However, it does add additional processing to the server. Similarly, any client that supports sockets can hold a conversation with a CICS transaction. The **Sockets Interface for CICS** feature allows CICS transactions to be clients or servers. Typically, CICS acts as a server.

Distributed Program Link provides more function than transaction routing and function shipping. Using this method a transaction on one CICS system can be "linked" to a remote transaction on another CICS system. The systems exchange data using a Communications Area that appears shared. In Figure 5.30, the CICS OS/2 server transaction links to the MVS CICS transaction and shares data via the communications area. This approach is basically a CICS Remote Procedure Call. One transaction calls a remote transaction and passes data in the communications area. The remote transaction returns results to the calling transaction in the communications area also. The CICS clients have an extension to this feature called the **External Call Interface (ECI)**. ECI allows a non-CICS client program to call a CICS transaction. To the CICS program, the call looks like a DPL from another CICS transaction.

Besides the native distributed transaction processing capabilities, CICS on MVS can also use IBM's MVS implementation of the Message Queueing Interface to distribute application logic. So a CICS transaction can use the message queueing APIs to send a message to other systems or receive a message.

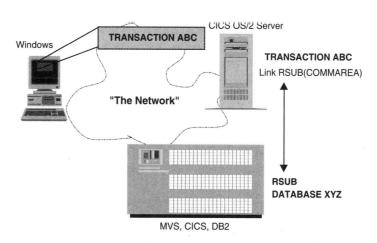

Figure 5.30. CICS distributed program link.

DCE, CICS/ESA, and IMS/ESA

As mentioned previously, a large volume of mission critical business applications use IBM's CICS transaction monitor today. There are also a large number of applications using IBM's IMS transaction monitor. Many businesses want to maximize their investment in these applications by providing access to them from distributed systems with minimal or no change to the applications. One method is to use IBM's **OpenEdition Distributed Computing Environment Application Support MVS/ESA (OE DCE Application Support)**. OE DCE Application Support allows clients to make DCE RPC calls to transactions on the MVS system. The DCE Directory Services can be used to determine the location of the host subsystem and transaction. Security is provided by the DCE Security Services.

DCE and CICS/6000

IBM's DCE for AIX provides the basic DCE services. It also includes a DCE Manager function. The DCE Manager is used to monitor one or more DCE cells. DCE Manager dynamically discovers changes in the DCE topology. It can also monitor all DCE core servers and DFS servers. Another unique function in DCE for AIX is the NFS to DFS Authentication Gateway for AIX. This gateway allows NFS clients to access DFS server resources.

Transarc Corporation, a wholly owned subsidiary of IBM, uses DCE, along with their enhancements, to provide better support for OLTP in a distributed environment. Some of their enhancements are Transactional C and X/Open Transactional RPC (TxRPC), a structured file server, and a monitor. Transactional C and TxRPC provide programming support for transaction processing. The structured file server supports additional file structures to allow for data integrity. Administrators use the monitor to perform administrative tasks on the system. The monitor can ensure that servers are running and, if not, can start them. Transarc packaged these additions to DCE as **Encina**. IBM licensed the Encina technology to create Encina for AIX and later purchased Transarc Corporation. Encina for AIX also includes a gateway for SNA access to mainframe CICS systems. This gateway is unique because it provides two-phase commit. So database updates can be done across the platforms with integrity. IBM also has an Encina client for OS/2. This product includes the Encina Base client, which is used for development of Encina applications, and the Encina Monitor client. You can also use this client to administer Encina Base servers.

IBM's Distributed Application Environment (DAE)

IBM's Distributed Application Environment is a middleware solution consisting of APIs and management functions for the development of distributed applications. Because DAE originated as part of the computer integrated manufacturing architecture, it provides the necessary support to communicate with many tools and devices on the shop floor. However, there is nothing that would limit DAE's use to manufacturing environments. DAE uses the messaging communication model and is available on DOS, OS/2, AIX, VM, and Sun's SunOS. The APIs are consistent across all of the systems. They have evolved and now include support for DCE services and standards.

IBM's LAN Distributed System (LANDP)

IBM's LAN Distributed System (LANDP) products evolved from IBM's Financial Branch System Services (FBSS) products. Since they originated in the finance industry, they include support for specialized devices such as magnetic card readers or Personal Identification Number (PIN) keypads.

LANDP is available for DOS, Windows, OS/2, OS/400, and AIX. It uses the underlying communication facilities of networking products available for those systems. LANDP provides a common API for writing distributed applications on the supported systems. In addition, it provides several important systems management capabilities. The System Manager provides user administration, NetView alerts, logs, date and time synchronization, and application program maintenance. It works with NetView Distribution Manager (NetView DM) for software distribution.

Distributed Logic: Selling Tickets at a Kiosk

Earlier we described SpeedyTix kiosks, where spectators purchase tickets to a concert or ball game. The customer uses a touch screen to search through upcoming events, find seats, and purchase tickets. Purchases can be made with either a debit or credit card. Once payment has been validated, tickets are dispensed from the kiosk.

The design of the system allows some processing to occur at the kiosk because it contains a PC; the kiosk is a client. For example, there might be a local database of upcoming events so a "window shopper" can see what's happening over the next month without requiring any remote communications. This is important to the owners of the kiosks because they are paying for the communication costs on a usage basis. Because the upcoming events are maintained locally, window shoppers do not generate any traffic to the central site. Therefore, window shoppers do not cost SpeedyTix anything. Since window shoppers sometimes buy tickets and sometimes don't, this is very advantageous.

As mentioned previously, the kiosk cannot maintain all of the data locally. The central site maintains the status of seating for events because department stores, sporting goods stores, and other ticket agencies sell tickets throughout the city. When a buyer swipes a credit card in the kiosk to make a purchase, the kiosk sends the transaction to the central system. The central system must now also do some processing to validate and record the credit purchase. You can see that the Distributed Logic Model fits this scenario well. Furthermore, the system cannot sell duplicate tickets and must have complete recovery in case of failure. These requirements demand a distributed online transaction processing system.

In Figure 5.31, CICS provides transaction processing services. The central system here is an AS/400 with CICS/400 and DB2/400. IBM PCs with touch screen displays are in the kiosks, running OS/2 with DB2/2 for the local database and the CICS/2 client to interact with CICS/400.

For SpeedyTix, CICS' ability to roll back incomplete transactions on multiple systems is crucial to customer satisfaction. Consider a teenager,

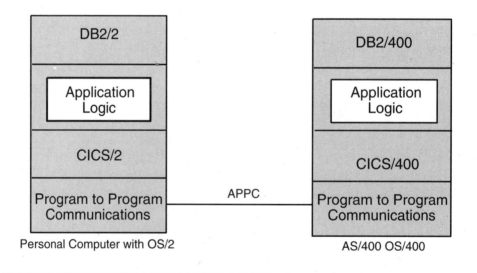

Figure 5.31. Distributed logic at SpeedyTix.

Lenny Hinton, who uses the kiosk to purchase concert tickets. After browsing through the upcoming events, he selects the concert that he wants to attend. After carefully selecting front row seats, he swipes a credit card through the system. Selecting the seats will put a lock on them in DB2/400 so that no one else can try to purchase them at another kiosk. A message appears to verify that the purchase is about to be completed. Before Lenny can touch the screen, Mom appears. Quickly Mrs. Hinton realizes that her 14-year-old son is buying tickets to the Unholy Rockers concert that she asked him not to attend. He's doing it with her credit card! Mom abruptly reaches over and cancels the transaction. The system now has to release the lock on the seats and roll back the credit record. This can be accomplished using standard CICS roll back facilities.

Summary

As mentioned earlier, Distributed OLTP is a vital technology for mission critical client/server applications. It is the coordinator of all of the components comprising the environment and ensures the reliability and integrity of transactions. Distributed OLTP systems also aid the development of client/server applications. They provide a base level of functionality to the programmer. Otherwise, the programmer would have to provide the same functions in the application. The more work that the system software can reliably handle, the less work that you have to worry about!

CICS has been available for many years and therefore provides rich and robust features for distributed OLTP. As CICS is being provided on more and more systems, it is becoming an extremely important tool for client/server development. Mission critical implications in this new world of client/server computing can use proven technology for their implementations.

Because of its genesis, DCE is an open architecture; as such, vendors have put it, too, on many systems. Eventually, it will probably become as widespread as TCP/IP. DCE is practical in environments where TCP/IP is already in use or where there are plans to use it for the integration of several heterogeneous systems.

Although technologies like DAE and LANDP can be used in any industry, they are still best suited for the manufacturing and financial industries respectively. For example, their support for specialized devices is extremely important to both of those industries. Environments using these products should take advantage of their standard interfaces where appropriate.

Data Staging

The Data Staging Model distributes data from a centralized database to other locations. These other locations might only read the data or they might also update it. Figure 5.32 shows a headquarters location where information about Five and Dime Import's customers is in a customer table. Five and Dime has different geographic regions defined by the region table. The figure shows excerpts from these tables. Each region has a copy of the customer table. Every night there is a refresh of the table. A **refresh** is a copy of the entire table. Each region has control over its customer information. So if Lily Monroe got married, the Eastern region could make the appropriate change to Lily's name. Each day at the close of business, each region sends any changes to the customer table back to the headquarters location. Sending only changes to a table is an update. It should be obvious to you that this model requires very careful design and implementation to ensure that the integrity of the data remains intact. IBM's DRDA, mentioned earlier, and Information Warehouse both play key roles in the IBM solutions for data staging.

Customer Table

Name	Number	Address	City	State	Zip
Carl Bryantt	890	1 Elm Ln.	San Francisco	CA	98403
George Mann	324	80 Carter Blvd.	New York	NY	10112
Lily Monroe	121	45 Main St.	Brick Town	NJ	08723
Sue Holbrook	645	12 Espana Ct.	Point Pleasant	NJ	08711
Tim Marlow	788	3300 Lark Dr.	Brick Town	NJ	08723
Mickey Farlow	902	790 Mission Dr.	Rochester	MN	76550
Ron Grier	034	860 Circle Dr.	Los Angeles	CA	90123

Headquarters Site

Region Table

State	Region
MN	Central
NJ	East
NY	East

Figure 5.32.   Data staging.

IBM's Information Warehouse

Have you ever tried to find a piece of information that you know is out there somewhere, but you aren't quite sure where to get it from or how? Perhaps you could find the information in many places, but you aren't sure which one is the most current. Once you decide where to get the data, you have to find a tool that can get to it. Then, you have to figure out how to use the tool or else request that someone else get the information for you. Once you finally get to the information, is it accurate or does it conflict with other reports? IBM defined and published the architecture of the Information Warehouse to address common data access problems like these. The primary goal of the Information Warehouse is to make it easy to get to data anywhere in the enterprise. The idea behind the Information Warehouse is to provide a framework for your information needs. Once you understand the framework, you can use it to choose and integrate the products required for your environment. So, let's look at the components of the Information Warehouse.

Figure 5.33 shows the major building blocks of the Information Warehouse. The Applications building block simply represents applications that end users work with to access data. Perhaps programmers developed the applications internally or perhaps the company purchased them from a

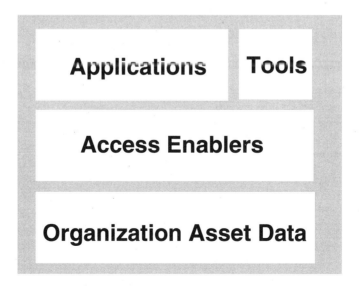

Figure 5.33. The IBM Information Warehouse.

vendor. They include traditional business applications and ad hoc query managers. The Tools building block represents various utilities, including copy management tools and systems management tools for data. Copy management tools allow you to refresh and update databases. Systems management tools for data allow you to define access authorization and perform various other administrative functions. Both building blocks use the Access Enablers to get to the data. The Access Enablers include traditional file access mechanisms such as **Virtual Sequential Access Method (VSAM)** in addition to SQL APIs, object APIs, and any other APIs that provide access to data. The Organization Asset Data consists of not only the data but also the **metadata**. Metadata is a description of data. The data might be kept in files, hierarchical databases, relational databases, or object databases. Finally, the Infrastructure building block provides data management, systems management, and workflow management.

IBM development is focusing on four areas of the Information Warehouse architecture: informational applications, the information catalog, access to data, and copy management. We are discussing them here because of their potential impact and benefit in client/server solutions.

Informational Applications

Informational applications are part of the Applications building block. People typically use these applications to evaluate or analyze data, so they include query tools, decision support systems, report generators, and spreadsheets.

The Visualizer family is a set of informational applications. They are client/server tools that you can use to query, analyze, and present data from relational databases. Figure 5.34 shows the currently supported client systems. The servers can be members of the DB2 family, Oracle, SQL Server (Sybase and Microsoft), Ingres, and Informix DBMSs. The chart shows the additional client enabling software needed for each scenario. The Visualizer family consists of several members. The Visualizer Query tool is the basis for the Charts, Procedures, Plans, Statistics, Ultimedia Query, and Development tools.

Information Catalog

The information catalog is really part of the metadata. It is the part that is important to the end user because it describes the data in understandable

Client	DB2	DB2/VSE	SQL/DS	DB2/400	DB2/6000	DB2/2
OS/2						X
OS/2 with DB2/2	X	X	X	X		X
OS/2 with CAE/2 and DDCS Gateway	X	X	X	X		X
OS/2 with Client Access/400				X		

Figure 5.34. The Visualizer family—client systems.

terms. Names and business-related descriptions are associated with the metadata. It also tells where to find the data (e.g., the table, view, or file containing the data). End users can search or navigate through the information catalog to find the information that they need. The catalog can relate, or group together, pieces of information so the user can logically and easily find them. Once found, the user can pass the data to an informational application.

IBM's **DataGuide** family of products make it easy for the end user to find information because they provide an information catalog. The user can search the information catalog for files, tables, queries, and other items using business related titles. Once a specific item is found, DataGuide can initiate an application to act on that item. As corporations distribute more information across the enterprise, end users can get to the right data more easily with a tool like DataGuide. DataGuide clients exist on Windows, OS/2, and Lotus Notes. DataGuide/2 can act independently, without DataGuide/MVS, or can provide a GUI for it through DDCS/2.

DataAtlas for OS/2 provides a capability similar to DataGuide but is intended for developers and database administrators. Data definitions used in existing programs and databases can be stored, managed, and queried with DataAtlas. New definitions can be added and maintained. Having this kind of information easily accessible can be important during client/server development to ensure that everyone uses 20 characters for last names or a MM/DD/YYYY format for a birth date.

Access to Data

SQL. Earlier we described SQL as an important standard to query relational databases. Here programmers can use SQL for relational data and for nonrelational data, wherever it may be. SQL can get to nonrelational data by using **SQL mappers** to convert the SQL statements to the equivalent nonrelational calls. The SQL mappers make the proper conversion by using a relational view of the data in the nonrelational system. Although this approach works for read access to data, researchers have proven that there are cases where this approach would not provide consistency to update nonrelational data. However, the nature of informational applications is such that the access is primarily read only for nonrelational data.

DataJoiner. DataJoiner is IBM's product providing read only query capability to multiple databases. A client can join data from multiple distributed DBMSs using a single SQL statement. DataJoiner will also allow a client to update a single remote database, so it implements part of the DRDA Distributed Request capability.

One way to describe DataJoiner is as database middleware, since it acts as the interface between client database requests and the database servers. Another term used to describe DataJoiner is "multiaccess server," since it allows access to multiple databases. Supported databases include the DB2 family, Oracle, and Sybase. DataJoiner can also be used in conjunction with other vendors' database access products to allow it to access other DBMSs. For example, databases using CLI can be accessed via Intersolv's Q+E product. Other databases, including nonrelational databases, can be accessed via relational gateways with support for the RISC System/6000 such as Cross Access and EDA/SQL.

DataJoiner allows views to be defined that span multiple DBMSs. DataJoiner uses DB2/6000, so any clients that can access DB2/6000 can use DataJoiner. This product provides a unique feature called compensation. If a client tries to use SQL functions against a database that does not support the function and DB2/6000 does support the function, then DataJoiner uses the capabilities of DB2/6000 to provide the function. Similarly, if the database supports a function not supported by DB2/6000 then DataJoiner uses pass-through to pass that request on to the other DBMS so that it can provide the function.

Optimization is an important capability for DBMSs. IBM is a leader in optimization techniques and implementations. DataJoiner takes advantage of IBM's technological prowess in optimization to provide a global optimizer for these kinds of queries and to compensate for deficiencies in other DBMS's optimizers.

Copy Management

The copy management component of the Information Warehouse provides the ability to do data staging. Three tools offer refresh and update functions for different environments: DataPropagator Relational, DataPropagator NonRelational, and DataRefresher. **DataPropagator Relational** provides the ability to refresh and update data between members of the DB2 family. There are two components: capture and apply. The capture component obtains data to be replicated, and the apply component performs the replication. Depending on the actual DB2 platform that you are using, either or both components may be supported. **DataPropagator NonRelational** allows you to coordinate changes between IMS and DB2 databases. An update can be unidirectional or bidirectional. It can also be synchronous or asynchronous. You can even automate it to occur at predetermined intervals. **DataRefresher** provides the ability to extract data between many source and target databases. It provides a user exit to allow you to use it for other databases that are not natively supported.

DataHub provides the ability to administer multiple members of the DB2 family, Oracle, and Sybase databases from a single OS/2 or Unix (AIX, Solaris, or HP-UX) system. The interface to each database is the same on DataHub. By providing a single image appearance, DataHub makes support and administration of the distributed databases easier. This may translate to less administrative staff and lower training requirements. DataPropagator Relational, DataPropagator NonRelational, and DataRefresher can integrate with DataHub. If you install them on the same system, then the DataHub interface can coordinate the functionality of all of the products. Database management tasks can be automated using DataHub's built-in scheduler or by using it in conjunction with IBM's FlowMark. These automated tasks are performed by "watchdogs." The watchdogs are based on your business policies and can take corrective action.

IBM's replication solution is comprised of all four of these products: DataPropagator Relational, DataPropagator NonRelational, DataRefresher, and DataHub. Together they form a powerful, flexible, and manageable way of replicating data in an enterprise.

The **IMS Client Server Object Manager for OS/2 (IMS CSOM)** product also provides a form of data staging. IMS CSOM enables an OS/2 client to access DB2 and IMS data using a standard set of classes. Programmers can use any language supporting SOM and DSOM with the IMS CSOM. The data from IMS and DB2 is staged to an OS/2 server with DB2/2. The clients access the data from this server. They can also update data and the server can pass the updates to the MVS system.

Data Staging: Customer Information for Five and Dime

Five and Dime Imports keeps the centralized copy of the customer information database on an MVS system in DB2. Each region has a subset of the database kept on an OS/400 system in DB2/400. The region's subset consists of only the customers in that region. Therefore, the customer information can only be changed by the region that owns it. All of the regions update the central database nightly so that headquarters has a list of customers that is current to the previous day. Figure 5.35 shows how the records in the central database are owned by the different regions.

As shown in Figure 5.36, there is an OS/2 system at headquarters running DataHub and DataPropagator Relational. With this configura-

Customer Table

Name	Number	Address	City	State	Zip
Carl Bryantt	890	1 Elm Ln.	San Francisco	CA	98403
George Mann	324	80 Carter Blvd.	New York	NY	10112
Lily Monroe	121	45 Main St.	Brick Town	NJ	08723
Sue Holbrook	645	12 Espana Ct.	Point Pleasant	NJ	08711
Tim Marlow	788	3300 Lark Dr.	Brick Town	NJ	08723
Mickey Farlow	902	790 Mission Dr.	Rochester	MN	76550
Ron Grier	034	860 Circle Dr.	Los Angeles	CA	90123

Headquarters Site

Region Table

State	Region
MN	Central
NJ	East
NY	East

Figure 5.35. Five and Dime's customer information by region.

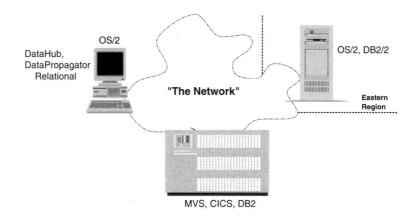

Figure 5.36 Replicating Five and Dime's customer information.

tion, the database administrators are all located at the central site. They can remotely administer the DB2/400 databases in the regions. With DataPropagator Relational, the region's nightly updates can also be scheduled from the central site. The regional and headquarters staff use the Visualizer family of products to analyze the customer information.

The example here is relatively simple. Data ownership is clearly defined, and updates are only made in one direction, from the regions to the headquarters site. Also, the databases used in all locations are from the same family and products are available to propagate changes between them. Data staging becomes more complex as you realize that the ownership of data may not be so easily defined. Some changes may need to be propagated in both directions, existing databases might not be from the same family, and tools may not be readily available to provide the necessary services.

Summary

Data staging is very beneficial in environments where there is local authority of data that is also kept at a central site or where there are a large number of read only requests to data. By having a local copy of the needed data, response time can be improved. However, this approach by definition requires duplicate data so there are greater disk storage requirements and synchronization issues that must be addressed.

IBM Software Servers

Just as we went to print, IBM announced the IBM Software Servers. These integrated software packages combine Lotus and IBM technology for OS/2, Microsoft NT, and AIX server platforms. This simplifies installation, configuration, and administration. In this regard, IBM is making client/server software simpler, just as greater integration in OS/400 and OS/390 simplifies building and operating client/server systems.

The seven IBM Software Servers include:

- Lotus Notes

- IBM Internet Connection Server

- IBM Database Server

- IBM Communications Server

- IBM Directory and Security Server

- IBM Systems Management Server

- IBM Transaction Server

As discussed above, Lotus Notes is comprehensive workgroup, workflow, and synchronized collaboration software. Notes can exploit information stored and maintained by other Software Servers, making it easily accessible to a workgroup cooperating on a project. IBM also announced it would make Notes compatible with the leading World Wide Web technologies, such as the Java programming language. These Internet related enhancements are due in the third quarter of 1996.

The IBM Internet Connection Server is a full-feature World Wide Web server. As this book is written, the standard version is available for free download. This version doesn't include additional security features required for secure commerce over the Web, like authentication and encryption. The Secure Connection Server offers these capabilities for an additional fee.

The IBM Database Server is based upon DB2, and it packages several database administration tools into the server. While these tools don't replace DataGuide, DataHub, or similar enterprise tools, they do simplify the administration of DB2 databases for smaller groups. The server can manipulate multimedia data, objects, and traditional data types.

The IBM Communications Server takes the older Communications Manager and AnyNet products, combining them into a single server. It supports SNA, APPN, APPN/HPR, and TCP/IP protocols directly. Like AnyNet, it lets you deploy applications more flexibly, whether your network is based upon SNA technologies or TCP/IP.

The IBM Directory and Security Server uses the DCE components for directory and security services discussed above. Of course, it also contains the prerequisite DCE services, such as RPC and time services. It simplifies the administration of security and permits flexible placement of applications and servers, especially in far flung enterprises.

The IBM Systems Management Server is based upon IBM's SystemView software, which we'll discuss more in the next chapter. It also will incorporate, over time, software from a newly-acquired IBM subsidiary, Tivoli Systems. Exactly how the Tivoli merger will proceed will be more clear when you buy this book than as I write it; IBM completed the acquisition of Tivoli in March 1996. Tivoli's reputation in the industry is as a leading edge technologist. Combined with IBM's enterprise focus, the Systems Management Server should bring topnotch abilities to client/server computing systems. This should ease operations and reduce long term costs for client/server applications.

Finally, the IBM Transaction Server is based upon IBM's CICS and Encina transaction managers. By combining these into a single product, IBM offers a single way to connect transaction processing into Notes and the Internet. As IBM further develops and deploys Internet commerce products, having a single transaction manager will reduce complexity, and ultimately, the costs of transactions. Firms using the Transaction Server will have fewer integration and configuration tasks.

The IBM Software Servers work together, and have already found use in applications in several industries. Not all the Software Servers are available immediately; all seven are available today for AIX, five for OS/2, and two for Windows NT. The remaining Software Servers will become available on OS/2 later in 1996, and the NT Software Servers will follow.

Where Do I Go From Here?

This chapter has reviewed various technologies in the context of the client/server reference models, and some of the IBM products implementing those technologies. The number of different technologies can seem overwhelming, but we hope this examination of them has made it easier to understand their similarities, differences, and uses. The next chapter will provide you with some design techniques and tools to use in designing and operating an application for your business.

6

Designing and Managing Your Client/Server Applications

Albert Einstein once said, "make it as simple as possible, but not simpler." Chapters 1 to 5 have looked at several models for client/server computing and have discussed many possible components that might go into your client/server computing designs. Next, we look beyond the parts to the whole, so you can make sound, economical decisions and operate your client/server system successfully.

A key to operational success is to heed Einstein's advice. Most competent teams of technicians today can design and build a working client/server system. Far fewer can design, build, and operate a client/server computing system that meets your business objectives. Sometimes the system doesn't perform as required. Maybe it cost much more than anticipated to build and modify. Perhaps the designers didn't properly estimate support and operations costs.

In this chapter, we'll consider the costs of client/server computing, particularly ongoing costs, and we'll discuss ways to evaluate client/server computing's appropriateness. Then, we'll discuss a design approach that helps to minimize costs while meeting your business objectives. Then, we'll review systems and network management techniques and products that should help you to control your costs. Next, we'll briefly look at some of IBM's services for client/server computing analysis, design, and operations. Finally, we'll revisit our hypothetical companies, showing their final client/server computing designs.

Support Costs: Client/Server Computing's 800-Pound Gorilla

You've undoubtedly heard the old joke, "Where does an 800-pound gorilla stand? Anywhere he wants." Clearly, when a sizable issue won't go away with the usual poking and prodding, you work around it. It turns out that client/server computing has one such issue: support costs.

In comparing the costs of software on shared systems with client/server implementations, most people underestimate the costs of supporting many PCs. Usually, these costs are hidden throughout a company, so they are hard to find. Until recently, most firms weren't looking beyond their I/S organizations, so they underestimated their overall costs to support PCs, whether networked or standalone.

Industry Studies of Client/Server Computing Costs

In 1994, the Gartner Group conducted a widely reported study. It estimated the 5-year cost of one networked PC in a large firm at between $50,000 and $65,000. Other studies have put the cost of supporting a networked PC at two to three times the cost of a mainframe terminal user. At first blush, this seems wrong, given that PC hardware and software seem so inexpensive compared to mainframes. However, considering the total cost of ownership and operation, these figures become credible.

The study found that internal labor can account for over 70% of life-time costs of a networked PC. Someone keeps the software up to date, replaces broken hardware, maintains backups, answers questions when users have problems, diagnoses problems, and reports software bugs to vendors. Over a third of these labor costs are outside a firm's central I/S budget. These folks are secretaries, local PC enthusiasts, and others, who do not report to an I/S organization but who keep users productive by helping wherever they can. The study also found that a typical "LAN Administrator" spent 95% more time than expected in supporting a LAN, including file and print servers.

Personal computer users, being an enthusiastic and helpful lot, also spend time helping other PC users. According to a survey by SBT Accounting, workers waste, on average, 5 hours a week tinkering with their desktop computers. Nolan, Norton and Company, in a study of 10 large U.S. companies (quoted by *The Wall Street Journal* in November 1992), estimated that each worker spends between $6,000 and $15,000 of productive time annually tweaking their PCs' configurations or helping other PC users.

Of course, your organization might be much more or less efficient than those studied. However, comparing the costs to support many PCs with traditional, shared systems, one would expect higher ongoing costs for PCs. Your staff is installing, configuring, monitoring, and changing many more components per user supported. That's why blindly downsizing shared system applications to PCs usually fails to deliver business value.

Client/Server Computing's Financial Considerations

Two business reasons exist to consider a client/server computing application. First, client/server computing can share hardware and software better among existing PCs, an option evaluated on the basis of costs alone. Second, a new client/server application can replace an existing application or a manual process. This may be harder to justify, because it depends upon increasing revenue, improving quality, or increasing productivity to offset likely increased costs.

Sharing Among Existing PCs Improves Your Bottom Line

The first approach reduces costs by sharing hardware, software, and data, reducing duplicated assets and support tasks where possible. File servers, fax servers, database servers, and printer servers usually fit here. Another, less obvious sharing method uses code servers to centralize executable software. Reducing the number of times software or data is duplicated on different PCs streamlines support operations.

If your firm uses PCs now, these "sharing" approaches assume the existing PCs are already justified by improved personal productivity. Usually, applications such as electronic spreadsheets, word processors, and other personal productivity tools justify PCs. Sharing helps you operate these existing PCs more effectively.

Adding a Code Server to Workgroups

Using a file server to share a pool of licensed software among a workgroup's users can save money. Some vendors regularly sell software licenses in "pools" like this. Others sell licenses based on the number of people who might use it at one time. Some will negotiate special terms and conditions. A code server exploits how most people use software: Not everyone in a workgroup uses a given package at the same time. If a 60-person workgroup only needs to use 30 copies at once, 30 concurrent-use licenses may cost less than 60 machine-based licenses.

Most code servers are file servers, like IBM's LAN Server, that can also run metering software. When a user invokes an application, the metering software checks how many licenses are in use and adds one to the count. Then, the code server sends the software over the network into the client machine's memory for execution. When the user is done, the metering software returns the license to the pool. Metering software helps your firm to comply with license agreements more easily. Sometimes, the application itself checks the number of licenses in use.

Code servers need fast, scalable hardware and networks. The relative slowness of WAN links makes code serving to mobile laptops impractical. Although fast, low-delay server hardware and LANs aren't cheaply acquired, lower ongoing license fees and support costs often justify this approach. Your mileage may vary, but code serving is an attractive alternative to installing, configuring, and maintaining software on many PCs.

Using Large Systems to Serve Many Needs

Some firms with large campuses and many workgroups centralize their servers onto one or two large machines. This works when the machine's hardware architecture "scales" well. The System/390, with its channel-based I/O architecture, and the AS/400, with numerous buses and IOPs, scales well to meet large I/O needs, whereas a PC based server does not.

A larger, scalable system can act as a file, print, database, and code server for many workgroups on a campus. Using IBM's parallel mainframe as an example, IBM's Open Systems Adapter attaches up to 40 workgroups to an IBM 9672 system. Each workgroup has its own LAN segment, avoiding excess traffic between workgroups. Each workgroup also has a low-latency path into the server system. Once inside, DB2 and LAN Server for MVS software provide file, print, database, and code services. This works like LAN Server and DB2 for OS/2 software on an IBM PC, but it scales better, reducing ongoing costs per user. Figure 6.1 shows a schematic of how such an environment might look.

This approach can offer technological and financial advantages over using several smaller servers. With MVS/ESA or OS/400 systems, both the

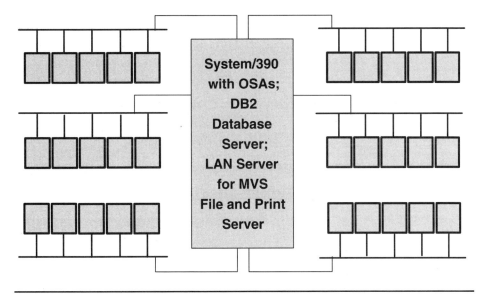

Figure 6.1. Using a campus server.

hardware and software are more robust than their PC counterparts. RISC System/6000 servers and PowerParallel systems also provide best-of-class reliability. By using these systems as a server platform, this engineering comes as part of the bargain. Security is tighter, disaster recovery is simpler, and operational automation is better. During off-shift periods, operational responsibility can switch to other facilities, maintaining a "lights out" system.

Financially, this approach works best with many users; for one or two small workgroups, it may not be competitive with a single, PC-based server. Thoughtful capacity planning decides its feasibility. If your environment is a good match for servers on a large system, you'll spend more on hardware and software, but your operations and support staff should be smaller. Your savings will come from reduced operational costs, and you'll lower your ongoing risks of doing business.

If your firm already uses textual applications on a robust, commercial system, such as an IBM mainframe or AS/400, using it as a server also reduces risks. Your staff needs little retraining, and existing operational procedures are more quickly adapted to the server's new missions. Your uptime should be higher, and it is easier to integrate new applications with your existing portfolio.

Costs and benefits of single-site sharing

To calculate the possible benefits of sharing, your designers should find the following costs and risks for each user:

- Lifetime hardware acquisition and maintenance costs

- Lifetime software acquisition and maintenance costs

- Existing software support costs

- Number and cost of hardware changes over lifetime

- Number and cost of software changes over lifetime

- Cost to provide "help" for the user

- Costs/risks of lost, stolen, compromised, or corrupted data

- Possible costs and risk of natural disaster or fire

Here, "lifetime" refers to the life of the hardware and software. Hardware lifetime is based on your accounting practices; PCs, for example, may have a lifetime of 1 to 5 years. Software lifetime refers to the expected life of the application, usually 5 years or more.

Finding accurate numbers for support costs and risks is challenging. Your staff and key users might keep a diary for a few weeks, recording how they spend their days, particularly during a change or an upgrade. Estimates are likely to be optimistic; get hard data wherever possible. For the last three items, you might interview users and managers to verify the costs of downtime. Unfortunately, most firms don't know the cost of a failure before it occurs. If this is the case, someone might have to make a scientific wild guess.

Now, you can consider the added costs of a networked, client/server configuration. Again, you and your designers should consider these costs per user over the anticipated life of the system. They could include

- Networking hardware and maintenance for each PC

- Networking software and maintenance for each PC

- Software telephone/onsite support costs

- The network's hardware, software, and maintenance (includes routers, hubs, switches, and so forth)

- Client application and enabling software for each PC

- Installing data grade wiring, if not already in place

- Antivirus software for each PC, if not already in place

- Server hardware (including disks, tapes, printers, etc.)

- Server software

- Pooled software costs (if considering using code servers)

- Systems and network management software costs

- Support staff training costs

Your vendors should give you expected lifetime costs of hardware and software maintenance. Due to differing terms and conditions, software maintenance costs vary significantly from vendor to vendor. Some vendors include free bug fixes, telephone support, and other services for a period of time following purchase, others don't. Depending on uptime requirements, you may want more or fewer vendor support services, and these will affect your software maintenance costs.

Finally, you should calculate the value of productivity and cost benefits of using a client/server system. You should be able to define the value to your firm of

- Improved user productivity

- Better data security and integrity

- Cost savings of pooled software versus separate licenses

- Hardware and maintenance costs avoided

- Better PC software support staff productivity

- More consistent software use and PC training

- Reduced time copying files to and from diskettes or tapes

- Reduced time transferring data by hand

- Reduced cycle time

A less obvious benefit of sharing is reduced business risk. File servers tend to be backed up more carefully than individual PCs. Code servers and metering software reduce your exposure to litigation after a software piracy audit, and server-based or site licenses can avoid these issues completely. With these costs and benefits defined, a decision to use client/server computing or not should be easy for a single site. Multiple site systems, though, need additional thought.

Financial Considerations of Multisite Client/Server Sharing

In a multiple site system, designers place data, servers, and staff carefully, optimizing performance and network usage. Using sharing techniques with laptop computers, particularly, requires care. Most often, one server and its associated hardware per site is less costly than using a fast telephone line to transport data to a centralized server, but circumstances vary. Adding a server entails at least the following costs:

- Acquisition and maintenance costs of server hardware

- Acquisition and maintenance costs of server software

- Added local support costs

- Additional staff training costs

These items argue against adding servers. The cost for additional servers of the same type is less than the first server's cost; many client/server costs result from increased complexity at the client and additional staff training. Once you've decided to use a client/server approach, these costs are fixed for each client system. The following items argue in favor of adding servers:

- Better performance, leading to increased user productivity

- Revenue or profit gains due to increased responsiveness

- Ongoing cost of faster data networking lines

- Productivity gains due to faster, onsite problem resolution

- Costs and risks of down time due to network failure

A local server at each site improves the reliability and responsiveness of a client/server system. Sometimes, the application's needs make this the only reasonable alternative. Other times, adding WAN capacity will provide sufficient responsiveness. If adding more WAN capacity is an option, then the matter becomes a financial decision; is the WAN capacity cheaper than the hardware, software, and support costs?

An Example of Multisite Sharing: Global Plumbing Supplies, Inc.

Let's look again at Global Plumbing Supplies, Inc. (GPSI), which decided to give its sales staff new, PC-based applications. GPSI could equip each PC with a large disk, a tape drive for backups, and suitable software for each user. Instead, GPSI uses server systems running IBM LAN Server and LAN Server Ultimedia software. In the San Francisco office, GPSI upgrades its mainframe system to an IBM 9672 with 4 Open Systems Adapters. It runs LAN Server for MVS software to support San Francisco's 750 users.

In New York and Rome, IBM PC Server 720s, with RAID disks, a tape drive, and IBM LAN Server software provide adequate performance for the 150 users per site. Compared to supporting many PCs, this approach lowers hardware capital and maintenance costs, and it improves data integrity. It also improves operational productivity, since only one person at each site worries about backups. Finally, by ensuring proper backups, when a device fails or someone deletes an important file accidentally, GPSI recovers from the failure more quickly. Because LAN Server also includes printer server software, GPSI shares a few fast printers per site instead of buying a printer for each user.

In Chapter 2, we mentioned that GPSI decided to use file, code, database, image, and fax servers. Now, GPSI's I/S staff must decide where to place them. They could place servers at each site or centralize them. GPSI has three main sales sites, connected to San Francisco by T1 and E1 lines.

These lines support voice and data traffic today, using a small mux at each site. Today, 128 Kbps is available on each line for SNA data traffic to and from the mainframe; the rest is allocated to voice traffic. Their manufacturing sites use slower lines but incur less traffic. To each, 64 Kbps is available for data applications today.

For GPSI, a centralized file, code, or image server will be about 30 times less responsive for remote users than for local users. If two users at the same remote site simultaneously viewed different 1 Mb images, sending then would take at least 20 seconds at 128 Kbps. Telephone sales staff can't wait that long. A local token-ring LAN transports them in under half a second. Similarly, it isn't unusual for executable code and printer output to exceed 1 Mb or more in size. So, it seems impractical to centralize code, file, printer, and image servers. Centralizing fax services also appears to be a poor choice; GPSI's long distance telephone charges would likely increase.

For e-mail, if GPSI's users include attachments, like spreadsheets and documents, to their messages, then one e-mail server per site makes sense. If GPSI's e-mail only consists of short, textual notes, one e-mail server might perform adequately and be simpler to administer. However, if GPSI's staff sends lots of e-mail, 128 Kbps and 64 Kbps will quickly seem small.

One server remains unplaced: the relational database server. The application is textual and requires quick response times. Because the inventory, customer, and order databases reside on GPSI's MVS-based mainframe in San Francisco, and because other, existing applications use them, the data should stay on the mainframe. For San Francisco users, that works well. For New York and Rome, because the database queries and responses are small, the WAN link doesn't inhibit performance as badly as it does for, say, the image server. GPSI used VisualAge to build parts of the application, and instead of putting DDCS/2 software on each client, it used one gateway per site. For New York and Rome, this software resides on the same OS/2 system as the LAN Server and LANServer Ultimedia software.

So, GPSI has decided upon a topology similar to that shown in Figure 6.2. Each site has a file and print server. This same server downloads code to PCs on demand, meters usage, and in New York and Rome, it provides fax and image services. E-mail services remain in San Francisco, along with the mainframe, pending an audit of usage patterns. The San Francisco e-mail server also provides fax services. The relational database remains in San Francisco, with a gateway at each site. After performance analysis and testing, GPSI determined that a PC Server 720 would suffice in New York and Rome; if transfer frequencies increased during use, a second PC Server would be required to meet demand.

The client systems run OS/2 and use OS/2 and Windows applications. So, GPSI's staff must understand OS/2, MVS, Windows software, and networking to support the new application properly. Each client system also has 3270 terminal emulation software. This allows knowledgeable users to run GPSI's other mainframe applications.

New Applications Improve Productivity and Revenues

New client/server applications support four main business themes today. First, firms use client/server applications to extend their reach, marketing and selling in new ways. Second, client/server software can control processes more closely, improving quality. Third, products such as Lotus Notes or IBM's Flowmark enable quicker, closer cooperation between people who may be located in many places. And last, techniques like data staging enable new ways to mine information from existing data. Successful applications give users autonomy with quick access to information stored on shared

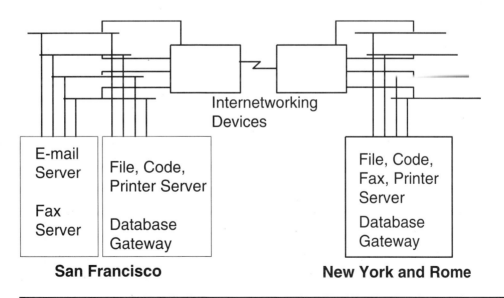

Figure 6.2.   GPSI's server and site topology.

systems while controlling support costs and WAN charges. New client/server computing applications must also work smoothly with existing software.

When considering a new client/server application, you're really making two decisions. First, you're deciding whether to automate a process. Second, you're determining if client/server computing is the most appropriate technology to use. Sometimes, it makes sense to use traditional software on shared systems instead of client/server software.

Next, we'll discuss how to evaluate the costs and benefits of building new client/server applications. We'll then justify a hypothetical new client/server application and cover some guidelines regarding when to use traditional software and when to use client/server software.

Costs and Benefits of Building New Applications

It's harder to define a "cookbook" approach to quantify possible costs, gains, and savings for a new application. That's because only you can quantify the value of a new application to your business.

A new application's business success relates directly to its performance, WAN usage, and support costs. If a newly deployed application performs badly, expected gains in productivity or reduced cycle times don't occur. If the application uses the WAN incorrectly, it drives costs higher, and the expected gain still doesn't occur. To evaluate these costs fully, you need an initial design.

First, your design staff gathers the system's operational and business requirements. Instead of talking about a PC's graphical I/O performance, they understand how users hear, read, and interpret information presented to them. They also observe how automated tasks might fit into the user's work. Good designers ask many questions that delve into your business processes, such as

- How quickly must each computerized operation complete?

- Is it a bottleneck in the process today?

- Will it become such a bottleneck over the software's life?

- When is the computer used, compared to other tools?

- Must users interrupt their usual flow of operations to use an input device such as a keyboard, mouse, or scanner? How much more efficient would another input method, such as voice recognition or annotation, be?

- Would greater efficiency here lead to greater production or efficiencies later in the process? How big would they be?

- Would a change here lead to improved product quality?

- What happens when the application isn't available? Can the data be queued for later transmission if the network or the back end system fails, or will it become stale?

- How long must the data be maintained?

When asking questions like these, the best designers talk to the system's users, avoiding technical language to find the truth. Once they find answers, they should be able to quantify the results. With this, you should be able to document the anticipated value of the application. Ideally, this should show the application's value on a year by year basis. You must decide if the application will

- Improve productivity

- Improve revenues

- Reduce inventory on hand or work in process

- Reduce accounts receivable

- Reduce cycle times or increase a process' flexibility

- Improve your product or service's quality

- Increase customer satisfaction or customer retention rates

- Let your firm raise prices due to greater perceived value

- Protect an existing revenue stream

At some point, you can assign an annual monetary value to the new application. You might also want to consider an "optimism factor," giving you a range of values. This might be based upon the track record of the person or organization giving you the figures. If they tend to be overly optimistic, make the "optimism factor" higher, and subtract it from the application's value.

Your designers should then produce an initial design that sketches the system's components, functions, and performance. It is important to define performance requirements here, since the application's performance determines if the required benefits occur. Now, they can estimate costs and savings for the following items:

- Hardware and maintenance for each user, if any

- Added PC networking hardware, software, and maintenance, per user

- Added software telephone/onsite support costs

- Added network hardware, software, and maintenance (includes routers, hubs, switches, muxes, and so forth)

- Reduced hardware maintenance for replaced equipment, if any

- Client application and enabling software for each PC

- Installing data grade wiring, if not already in place

- Antivirus software for each PC, if not already in place

- Additional server hardware and maintenance

- Server software and client enabling software

- Client application software

- Added systems and network management software costs

- User and support staff training costs

- Operations support costs

- Lost opportunity costs during training, installation

- Systems integration, testing, and quality assurance costs

- Installation and configuration costs

- Worst-case additional WAN line or dialup costs

The first new client/server application will be the hardest to justify, because it absorbs most of your staff's "learning curve." It also must absorb wiring, test lab, systems and network management, and LAN infrastructure costs. Sometimes, you may want to apply a "newness factor"; if your staff has little experience with a particular technology, their estimates will probably be wrong.

Now, you should know if application is viable. If the waters are still murky, you may want to assign risk factors to each figure and build a likely range of costs and benefits. Perhaps additional, intangible benefits exist when changing the application to client/server. Maybe some costs can be amortized over two or three related applications. Next, you make a decision to pursue a more detailed design or to stop the project.

When assessing an application's fit for a client/server implementation, both you and your design team should consider the following alternatives:

- A shared system with textual or graphics terminals

- Networked shared systems

- Standalone PCs

- A manual system different from your current system

- An outsourced system

Without evaluating these alternatives, this step in the design process isn't complete. Few things are worse than realizing you've designed and built a system more complex and expensive than necessary—after it's done.

SpeedyTix: Flexibly Reaching Customers

Sometimes, the initial justification is almost obvious. As noted in Chapter 2, SpeedyTix wants to use PC-based kiosks to expand their ticket distribution network. Without a new application, SpeedyTix must find other ways to increase revenues. So, it must only decide if client/server computing best matches its needs. An alternate approach uses a shared system with a textual user interface. SpeedyTix rejects this because customers wouldn't like it. They also might become confused, and a confused customer slows transactions, creates long lines, and thereby discourages sales.

Today, SpeedyTix wants to use kiosks, but later, it might want to use the Internet, telesales, direct mail sales, or other methods. Instead of building or buying a different application for each kind of sale, SpeedyTix could use one new application. Eventually, it could have a kiosk client, a mail sales client, an Internet sales client, a telesales client, and a direct sales client. Each client would use a different user interface, but each would work with a common server. With this flexibility, SpeedyTix can add new sales channels quickly and easily. A client/server application appears viable here.

SpeedyTix adds a $3.00 service fee per ticket sold, and it believes each kiosk will sell 100,000 tickets over five years, for $300,000 per kiosk in revenues. The plan calls for 20 kiosks, or $6 million in sales. At SpeedyTix' current margin of 16%, that would normally mean a profit of $1 million. To outperform this, the kiosks should cost less than $5 million to acquire and operate. Because client/server computing is new to SpeedyTix, it chooses an optimism factor of 20% and a newness factor of 20%, lowering the target cost to $3 million. The firm expects each kiosk to last for five years, and it will write the software expense off immediately. So, the 20 kiosks and the new client/server application should cost less than $3 million to acquire and operate for 5 years. Initial estimates of hardware and software costs, $1,7 million, are encouraging.

Evaluating possible designs, SpeedyTix notes three things that define the application's profitability. The number of kiosks, the WAN costs, and the cost of changes, either to the software or the kiosk's data, determines if the application is viable or not. The distributed application logic design that SpeedyTix chooses achieves low normal WAN usage, but software and data changes need about 56 Kbps of capacity. At $200 a month per kiosk, ISDN lines meet these needs easily, making WAN costs over five years $240,000. Added to the $1.7 million initial outlay, this makes about $1.95 million, leaving just over $1 million available to cover support costs.

Unfortunately, this is $500,000 below the firm's support cost estimates. SpeedyTix' inexperience in client/server computing drives up training and support cost estimates, and also increases risk, which they reflect in their newness factor. If SpeedyTix could tap outside experience, they would reduce risk and get some ideas to reduce support costs. Then, the application would likely be profitable. We'll see how SpeedyTix resolves this problem at the end of this chapter.

Considering Existing Shared System Applications

So far, we've assumed a completely new application. With existing applications, however, you have additional matters to consider. Fundamentally, you must decide if your firm will derive advantage from changing the way the application interacts with its users. Deciding this stops an insidious practice: justifying a new application based on an older one's problems. It also decouples a business decision from a technological decision. The first decision becomes: "Should I replace this application?" If the answer to the first decision is yes, then you ask: "Should the new application have a nontextual user interface?" Sometimes, replacing a textual application with another, more effective textual application may prove the better choice, because it avoids added support and WAN costs.

Textual and Client/Server Applications at Cripple Creek Community Hospital

Let's look again at Cripple Creek Community Hospital (CCCH). They used several applications and needed to improve physician productivity. A designer could conceive a grand scheme to integrate all Cripple Creek's data, with a graphical front end, but this isn't realistic. It would also become a nightmare to maintain, since it is likely to be unique to CCCH. The hospital's physicians needed a graphical interface, though, to view radiological images. New applications, such as viewing lab test results online, also would use graphics. Having many single-use terminals scattered about isn't helpful; CCCH prefers standardized bedside and general-purpose devices. So, a client/server approach clearly is needed for some applications.

CCCH watched how physicians and nurses used their existing systems. They decided that improving access to these systems would result in sufficient productivity and intangible gains to justify a new client/server infrastructure. It didn't make sense, though, to rework all the existing HIS applications, since these were mostly textual. CCCH decided the existing textual software met departmental needs and decided against wholesale change. This decision reduced anxiety and introduced change at a rate CCCH staffers and physicians alike would accept. That's why CCCH decided to use the X-Windows approach; it meets the needs of their graphical applications, it offers multiple terminal emulators, and, with slight customizations, it provides an easy to use "launch pad" to CCCH's applications.

So, CCCH now has a portfolio of applications, some textual, some client/server. It also has a common user interface, via X-Windows, and a vehicle to change applications one at a time, as business needs dictate. Finally, by changing access to existing applications, CCCH has met its business goal of improved overall system responsiveness and physician productivity. Many firms choose, like Cripple Creek Community Hospital, to augment or change their applications portfolios gradually.

Managing the Client/Server Design Process

Once you spot what may be a viable client/server application, someone must analyze and design the best system for your users. You could contract someone to design the system, or your firm could design it. Whether your staff, a consultant, or a systems integrator designs the system, the next few sections should give you a better understanding of what you're buying.

Client/Server Design, Step by Step

To design a large, complex, or mission critical system, a design team follows several steps. First, they understand your users' business needs and develop an initial design, as described earlier. Then they translate these needs into technical design goals. Next, the team defines performance budgets for each component in the system. Then they design and verify a technically valid solution. Finally, they analyze the life cycle costs of realizing the design.

To achieve a sound design, it isn't uncommon to iterate through this process a few times. Performance or uptime targets that seemed reasonable at first may appear unreachable toward the end of the process. Perhaps the initial design's server placement created overly high WAN costs, so the design must be changed to reflect different server placements. Quick iteration is desirable; newer design philosophies emphasize parallelism in the development process. Our description of steps in the process doesn't prescribe or preclude any specific process. However, these steps must all occur when producing a design for a predictable, reliable system of moderate or greater complexity.

Define the Design's Technical Goals

The first step in any system design is to define the business problem and justify a possible solution. We've already walked through that process. Next, designers translate business needs into specific technical goals, such as response times, uptime, data integrity requirements, and disaster recovery needs. Then, they map each of these against the business needs that support them, and verify this mapping with your users before proceeding further. This step also verifies that a client/server design is appropriate for the application.

Understanding client/server system responsiveness can become complex if someone hasn't yet designed how the application interacts with the user. For example, if a transaction must be completed and committed within three seconds, the business requirement seems simple. But, a single transaction might require several database lookups and a database write before it is done. Then, each interaction within the transaction must finish more quickly to meet the three-second business need. Your designers and vendors should consider these kinds of technical design goals for each operation the application encompasses. Sometimes, the work is simple and obvious, almost tedious. Other times, a solution eludes the design team. When they understand all the operations, they can ensure that their specific technical design goals match each business need identified earlier.

Many designers overlook an application's operational needs. They should define goals for the system's uptime, security, and integrity. For example, it is reasonable to require estimated times between failures, expected times needed to diagnose problems, and anticipated times needed for repairs to occur. Scheduled maintenance, data recovery, disaster recovery, and component failures all deserve consideration here. They'll also need to consider the data's confidentiality and value to the business. Then, they can decide how they wish to protect it.

These goals affect how much you'll spend on hardware features, hardware maintenance, software support, and consultation. If your new system can only be down for two hours, you wouldn't want to use, say, a networking vendor with an overnight hardware replacement policy. Instead, you'd want spares that are onsite and tested, ready for use. Similarly, your team might partially judge software quality based upon how long a staff member sits "on hold" waiting for help.

After these steps, your technical staff should assess the reasonableness of these goals, especially in light of the application's business justification. Now you should feel confident about each number in the justification and the design. If not, then the design probably won't meet your business goals. The team should probably feel comfortable placing a small part of their compensation at risk if they can't achieve the design's technical goals. After all, that's what you and your firm's stakeholders are doing.

Define Performance and Reliability Goals for Each Component

Novices and apprentices of client/server design overlook this step. Since most designers and programmers have built software on a single system, they aren't likely to think about how delays across systems and networks can accumulate. The problem is, what runs well on a single system can become unacceptably slow when two or more systems are joined by a network, sometimes even a fast network.

The responsiveness of a client/server system is made up of a series of delays. For example, your network has delays in each bridge, line, router, or gateway between a client and its servers. Servers have delays when reading or writing files, or queuing output to the network. Client machines cause delays when they must interpret and display information obtained over the network. When the application is built, if these combined delays exceed the technical design goals for the application, it feels unresponsive to the user.

To control the application's responsiveness, your design team can define a range, or a performance budget, describing how much delay it can tolerate at each point. Usually, the system's shared parts, the servers and the network, especially WAN links, introduce the greatest delays. Delay also varies according to the load offered to a component at any instant. Smoothing this offered load improves consistency, possibly at a higher overall average delay. Sharp designers understand the trade-offs between predictability, cost, and raw performance.

Performance budgets are important for several reasons, but the most important is simple: They give designers concrete, quantified goals for larger client/server systems. Without them, you have no evidence before implementation that the system is reasonable and viable. Performance budgets also take technical information and put it into an economic context. If your designer can't quantify a design's performance, you should consider building a design prototype or evaluate the risks of failure before proceeding much further.

Similarly, designers must consider the reliability of each component and how it influences the system's reliability. A heavily shared component usually demands better reliability than a lightly shared one. Similarly, placing components in a string, one after another, hurts reliability. Put another way, a system with three devices between a client and a server will fail more often than a system with one intervening device. If your application needs such a string of components, then each component must be more reliable to compensate.

Design and Verify the New Client/Server Application

Now the "craft" of system design begins. Others have written entire volumes discussing the design process. Suffice it to say that someone must produce a credible design document that shows someone else how to build the system as described. This distinction is important; even if the designers and builders are the same people, they must document the design clearly. Since software has a long life span, it may outlive the careers of the people who designed and built it. Those who follow will appreciate good design documentation.

Now is also the best chance to simplify the design. Does anything appear shaky? Does it contain many single points of failure? If a failure occurs, will it be easily and quickly diagnosed? Is the design tolerant of faults when they occur? A few "thought experiments" with your support staff may cause them to reconsider a complex design in favor of greater simplicity, perhaps even at additional initial expense. If not, then the design is likely to be "as simple as possible" to meet your business needs. Knowing this should give you confidence in a design.

Finally, your staff, or your contractor, should build a prototype of the system to ensure that it will function as planned. A prototype can test how the system interacts with users, measure its performance, and verify empirically how it will use expensive resources such as telephone lines. It can help to define the training your staff and users will need before deployment. It can even test your operational procedures for effectiveness.

Verifying and Controlling Your System's Operating Costs

Some managers leave the verification and cost analysis steps out of the process. They sometimes preside over "runaways," where costs spiral out of control. Other times, the system doesn't deliver what it promised. When the designers and implementors are different staffs, or worse, different firms, recriminations can result. Verification and cost analysis are tedious, non-technical steps, but they help to build quality into the system. If you or your contractor has built a prototype, then these verification steps become simpler.

A client/server design must meet three objectives before implementation. First, your staff should be able to support the system as designed. According to a study done by IBM's **Consulting Group** in 1993 and 1994, the biggest cause of failure in a client/server system is to design and build a system mismatched to a staff's capabilities. Among the firms surveyed, a client/server project's success or failure could be predicted within 85% accuracy. Information systems infrastructure, management expertise, and the development approach being used were key variables in what the study calls "process readiness." If your firm's process readiness matches a project's complexity, then the project is more likely to succeed.

Second, your staff—or an outsourcer—must support the system within budget. When controlling costs, nobody has a better incentive than an outsourcer. Contracting an outsourcing firm to estimate ongoing costs is one way you might verify the design's viability.

Third, verify your telecommunications costs over the life of the software. This task can be simple or difficult. For example, a typical textual e-mail message poses no problem for an analog line with modems. However, if the sender embeds a color image or a video clip into the message, then it can take minutes to hours to retrieve the message. Can you train your users to use these features carefully? Sometimes, to get acceptable responsiveness across a representative range of user behaviors, firms find they should buy faster WAN links than originally expected.

Common Pitfalls in Designing Client/Server Systems

Analysts, designers, and managers make several common mistakes when considering client/server systems. Sometimes, these errors result from inexperience, poorly defined business requirements, or badly defined design goals. Other times, office politics and hidden agendas conspire to torpedo the best intentions of technicians. You probably don't need unforeseen alligators to make you their lunch while you traverse unknown waters. Here, then, is a quick guide to the bayou.

Overcombining hardware. When considering the costs of servers and networks, a common temptation is to combine hardware as much as possible. Unfortunately, this approach often results in poor performance for users. For example, if a file server also routes frames between LAN segments and responds to SQL database requests, users making requests to the database may well experience highly variable response times. To avoid this tendency, it is better to assume separate hardware for each kind of server, at least early in the design. Later, when your design team knows how individual servers perform, they can optimize hardware for particular workgroups.

Configuring too many users. A second common mistake designers make is to configure too many users for each server or for each network link in the system. The other obvious mistake is to overdesign the system intentionally. Since client/server computing is new to many, these problems in defining the environment's scope are to be expected. Avoiding this usually requires outside help. Simulations and experiments using capacity planning tools can help designers see how specific changes will alter the cost and performance of a system under test.

Server placement. Another common error is defining a system topology that doesn't fit the work required. For example, usually a good design places file servers and print servers as "close" to your users as possible. This provides the best performance and reliability. To share a server between workgroups, many designers use a topology like that shown in Figure 6.3. This typically slows responsiveness by 10 to 30%, enough to possibly eliminate your savings. It also requires a larger, more expensive internetworking device. Using a topology like that shown in Figure 6.1, where possible, shares file and print servers between workgroups without compromising users' productivity. It can also reduce your capital costs.

To avoid unnecessary delays between users and servers, it helps to divorce an application's logical design from its physical manifestation. Designers can centralize servers for a single site while still maintaining a server's presence "on segment." Assuming the logical design in Figure 6.4, two ways exist to build it physically. The first way is the obvious way, depicted in Figure 6.4. This approach causes added operational expense because the servers are distributed within a site. Figure 6.5 shows a better way. Note that Client Y and Server B are on the same logical LAN segment in this figure; only a repeater separates them. Since simple repeaters are faster and cheaper than switches, bridges, or routers, this optimizes performance and reduces costs. This approach thus obtains the operational advantages of centralized servers and avoids the performance penalties of a hop through a router, bridge, or other internetworking device.

Unrealistic scheduling. It is easy to let time pressures, development tool features, or hardware and communications infrastructure considerations force a solution. Your business, staff, and users can only absorb change at a

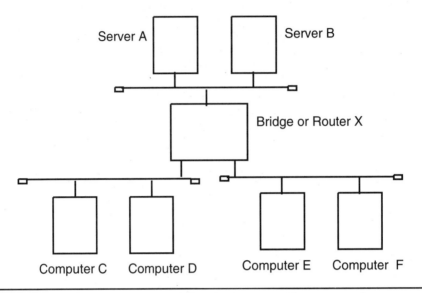

Figure 6.3. A common approach for sharing servers between workgroups.

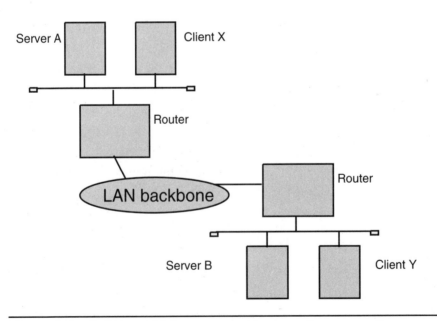

Figure 6.4. Building multiple segments with servers "on segment."

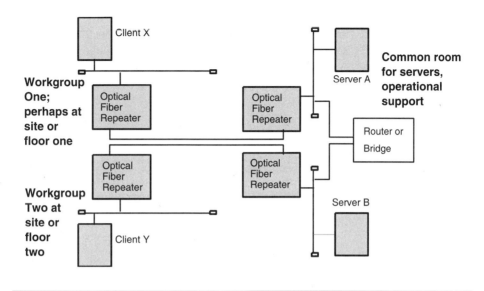

Figure 6.5. Building multiple segments with centralized servers "on segment."

given rate, so don't push unrealistic deadlines upon them unless you also bring in outside help. Remember, too, that your staff must keep existing systems running well while designing and building new applications.

This is where outside experts can give you a "leg up." Their technicians see many client/server development programs, while your staff may not have nearly as much experience. By bringing others in to help, your staff gains some of their experience, while you reduce the risks of a failed project.

Force fitting. Equally problematic as an unrealistic schedule is force fitting an application to a particular tool or programming style. If an application is well suited to messaging and queuing, for example, forcing it to work under a conversational style of communications will probably fail. Similarly, a project might use a relational database for keyword updates when a free-form text search tool, such as IBM's **Search Manager/2**, would fit the application better. Because of this, adding new data would be much more difficult than necessary. So, the system would not be used as much as it could be.

To solve this problem, be flexible. Technicians often use only what they know; your job may be to let them appreciate other viewpoints. Have many tools in your firm's belt. When you see nails, use a hammer; when you see plumbing fixtures, use a pipe wrench.

Not thinking through failures. Many teams design systems without considering what a firm must do when something breaks. Perhaps you've heard tales of firms with generator backup systems that ran out of fuel before power was restored. Or, consider the staff member sitting on hold, listening to music, while users can't get work done because of an unusual software failure. Maybe a key vendor's nearest parts depot is on the other side of a washed-out bridge. Your servers and networks deserve hardware maintenance, software support, and staff training that matches their business value.

Sometimes, a failure doesn't matter much; maybe a print server is down, but a similar device, down the hall, is available. On the other hand, errors in complex network configurations can cripple key business processes for a ten-thousand-user campus. To avoid unpleasant surprises, consider the value of defining and testing a temporary, manual workaround in case of catastrophic failure. Force your design team to think beyond technology, to logistics, process analysis, and team building.

For example, consider a system that can tolerate a failure but needs quick repairs; a one-minute outage is annoying, but a two-hour failure is costly. Many systems behave this way. Such a system demands speedy diagnosis and repair. Investing in staff training, buying and testing onsite spare parts, and drilling operations staff in failure procedures is time and money well spent. Designing redundant hardware components into the system isn't. Redundant components increase complexity, which in turn increases diagnostic times. So, spending money on redundant components could reduce, not increase, such a system's likely business value.

Going it alone. A common tendency among firms is to try to solve problems themselves. Unfortunately, if your staff is inexperienced, they will spend too much time thrashing through a problem and may not find a solid answer. The result is regularly a fragile system delivered behind schedule and over budget.

You should share the risks of designing and building critical or complex client/server systems. The idea is to reduce the risks of implementation by ensuring the integrity of the design process. For internal systems, before you settle on a design, ask veterans of prior campaigns for their advice. These foot soldiers may work on your staff, but a third party's opinion may be more valuable. A formal design review, including experts outside your design team, can help find flaws in a proposed system.

You can sometimes also make the designers stakeholders in your application's success. This works better if outside firms design your system; you can define the terms and conditions of the design contract to meet your needs. Specific performance guarantees are expensive, but using the design team for fixed price consultation during deployment and initial operation is sensible and less expensive. If they mess up, their time and productivity is at stake. This approach also gauges your designers' commitment to your success. If they won't share the operational and economic risks in the design, they shouldn't ask you to accept them. If they wouldn't want the phone calls at two in the morning, you probably don't want them either.

Listening to people with no stake in your success. This is common today. Because our industry is severely fragmented, people rely upon trade newsletters, magazines, consultants, and others (even book authors) for advice. Unfortunately, most writers and speakers are just as often wrong as right, and nobody audits their advice for accuracy. It's easy for our industry's generals to discuss nifty systems on paper; a subindustry has grown around vacuous claims based on shreds of preannounced rumor. It's another matter to make theory practical, as the foot soldiers will attest. Beware of advisors who don't know your business well and who lose nothing if your new application fails to deliver the expected business results.

IBM's Open Blueprint

In designing a new client/server system, especially a new application, your staff might wonder how all the parts fit together best. In response to questions like this, both within IBM and from users, IBM has defined an Open Blueprint, shown in Figure 6.6. This blueprint is an architectural framework that shows how IBM believes the parts of client/server computing fit together. It is based upon international standards, when available, and upon consortium specifications and IBM specifications when international standards are absent or unfinished.

You'll note that many parts of the Open Blueprint might be present in each client/server application. For example, the blueprint includes RPC-, conversational-, and message-based communications. Most applications would only use one of the three. Similarly, most applications wouldn't use both TCP/IP and APPN/HPR. IBM includes reasonable possibilities—such as RPC, conversations, and messaging—for each function (e.g., communicating between programs). The blueprint doesn't require that all be used.

IBM uses the Open Blueprint internally as well. This means that IBM's products correspond to the blueprint. If your applications make use of the techniques and interfaces defined in the Open Blueprint, then they are more likely to work in harmony with IBM's products. Similarly, vendors besides IBM can use the Open Blueprint as a way to build more compatible applications and products.

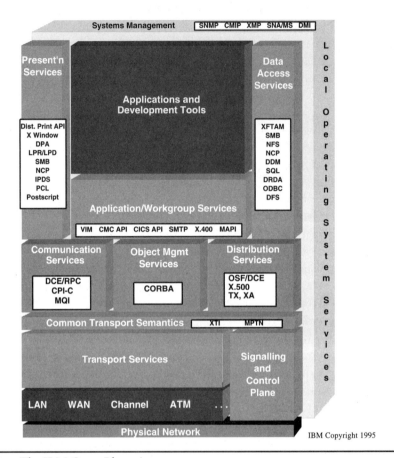

Figure 6.6. The IBM Open Blueprint.

Operating Open Client/Server Systems Effectively

Automating your client/server computing environment's management is critical in keeping ongoing costs low. In centralized computing today, systems and network management is assumed. It's also an easier task: Proprietary peripherals, like printers, tend to be tightly yoked to the shared systems they support. IBM mainframes tended to have IBM or compatible printers, disk drives, and terminals. In early distributed computing environments, customers also tended to operate common equipment and software. If your firm used several AS/400 systems, IBM had systems management, software distribution, network management, and other products available to meet your needs. DEC, Hewlett-Packard and other systems vendors also provided products to support their systems and software.

In a shared system, 1 to 10 vendors might contribute components to a major, complex application. A complex open client/server computing environment might use a hundred products from 10 to 50 vendors. Before individual vendors could write specifications for their products, but today vendors, international standards bodies, user groups, and others jockey for position in the marketplace.

In the next few pages, we'll discuss what causes good systems and network management. Then, we'll go over technologies available for managing networks of computers. Next, we'll cover IBM's products for managing client/server environments. Finally, we'll look at one example of how these products worked together to manage a sample multivendor client/server environment.

What Causes Good Systems and Network Management?

Companies that operate large shared systems know the costs and the value of predictable, reliable computing. They insist on understanding how new releases of software or new hardware will affect existing workloads before they install new products. They perform simulations and live tests to verify their opinions as much as possible before they alter an existing production environment. They continuously improve their operating procedures, planning carefully to minimize the time needed for outages, updates, and configuration changes. They design these systems with their operation in mind. Client/server computing systems are no different.

Start with a good design. First, effective systems and network management starts with a good design. No amount of discipline, software, skill, and money will make a poor design work well. Also, if the products used aren't designed to be managed automatically, no amount of retrofitting will help make your operations more efficient over time. A GUI or menu-driven user interface is nice for a single user or administrator, but in a large, complex environment, automated systems and network management are more effective in keeping your systems running well.

Use only a few vendors. A better managed, more economical system more often stems from buying products from fewer vendors. Here, you replace individual products that might have the latest gee-whiz features with products proven to work together. Clearly, any product you choose must meet your design's requirements, but some products might be more manageable, whereas others may be "sexier."

Especially in your first client/server computing designs, you should ignore the siren song of features, since you're wrestling the 800-pound gorilla of support costs. In a mission critical environment, taking support and downtime costs into account, the admired feature or the initial price break might not be worth it. By reducing your vendor count, you're also sharing your risks with them; they inherently assume more of the integration responsibility.

Match your design to your support processes. You can define operational guidelines and disciplines around your client/server design, or you can define your design based upon your existing support processes. Either way, they must match. Otherwise, when a component in your client/server application fails, it will take longer to diagnose and fix.

Use published specifications to underpin your design. If published specifications or standards exist for a component in your design, consider using them. Published specifications and standards make a larger complement of supporting tools and skills available to your firm. Proprietary capabilities can bring big benefits, particularly in operational reliability, but if a specific proprietary component doesn't bring specific business benefits, avoid it in your design.

Don't believe the hype about management tools. Many firms get bogged down evaluating, and arguing about, systems management tools. Tools are the most concrete expression of systems and network management disciplines, so it's easier to debate them. Automated management tools help, but if your support processes aren't effective already, or if these tools don't match your support processes, they won't help much. Besides, your staff may have many changes to absorb without learning new tools with dozens of nifty features.

First, consider refining the human side of your operational equation. Then, decide what tools can help your staff to become more effective. Of the six major areas of systems and network management, perhaps you will only choose to buy automated tools for one or two at first. Later, as your system grows, you may decide to add more automation tools for other areas.

Managing Distributed Networks

In the 1980s, as IBM's customers increasingly decentralized their computing, systems and network management took on greater urgency. Suddenly, the tools and disciplines of the "glass house" no longer seemed to apply to this new world. Of course, the definition of what needed to be managed simply broadened; the data center's disciplines still apply even if the tools and procedures change. Responding to these needs, IBM has embarked on an ambitious plan to manage many of the systems and networks throughout a customer's enterprise.

IBM isn't the only organization working on systems and network management. ISO, CCITT, X/Open, the Object Management Group (OMG), and others are working to define appropriate specifications for systems and object management. Because the devices and software to be managed are diverse, no single scheme accommodates everything; an amalgamation of several approaches is needed. Those that are completed have become the basis of IBM's systems and network management architecture, called **SystemView**.

On the networking side, the Internet Activity Board (IAB) and the Internet Engineering Task Force (IETF) have defined two versions of a protocol called the **Simple Network Management Protocol (SNMP)**. SNMP is the most commonly implemented network monitoring protocol in client/server environments today. It has deficiencies, but the market has embraced it. A more elegant solution is CCITT's **Common Management Information Protocol (CMIP)**, but this is heftier than SNMP and has achieved less acceptance. It still remains important, though, because carriers often use CMIP.

How Management Frameworks Work

Most management frameworks, including SystemView, divide the tasks of managing resources across a network into two components. The first part, called the **agent**, resides on the managed device. It takes commands and requests from the second component, the **management system**, and carries them out. Figure 6.7 shows an agent interacting with a management system. Agents exist for hundreds of hardware and software products, although they don't all work the same way. Some expect to talk with a management system using SNMP; others expect to use CORBA or CMIP. These management protocols can all be considered "open," since all are published specifications.

SystemView accommodates SNMP, SNMP version 2, and CMIP along with SOM and DSOM as valid ways to pass information from agents to management systems. It can use three transport networks, TCP/IP, SNA, and OSI. If an agent uses SNMP over a TCP/IP transport, however, the management system also must use SNMP over TCP/IP, not CORBA over SNA. SystemView also accommodates IBM hardware and software that uses an earlier, IBM-developed scheme called **NMVT**. NMVT is richer and

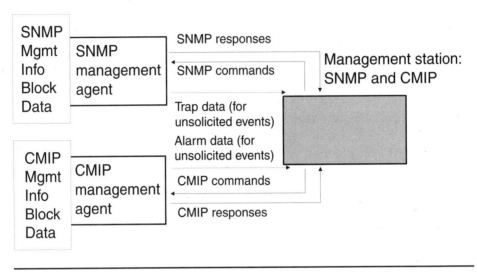

Figure 6.7. How a management station interacts with agents.

more secure than SNMP, and some firms still prefer the features NMVT provides for their mission critical applications.

How SNMP Works

SNMP version one is the simplest such protocol, and since it is common, we'll describe it briefly here. It relies on a Management Information Base (MIB) to store information about the managed device. The earliest MIBs were specific to TCP/IP networking. Since then, vendors and user groups have specified standard MIBs for SNA, DECnet, AppleTalk, and other networks. MIBs also exist for common devices, such as simple network hubs. To manage something outside a standard MIB, an agent must use an enterprise-specific MIB extension. For example, the IBM Hub Management Program for AIX takes advantage of a MIB extension in the hub to get information about port status.

Each SNMP request from the management system to the agent is supposed to contain a password, called a community name. Unfortunately, no encryption of the community name occurs, and most shops use the default community name. Because SNMP's security is poor, many devices only allow a management to monitor, not change, them. SNMP also only operates on one MIB variable at a time, which can generate lots of network traffic. SNMP version 2 (SNMP2) resolves SNMP's problems, but it's not commonly deployed today.

Common SNMP operations include GET, which gets a MIB value, SET, which sets one, and TRAP. Agents generate **traps** when they want to tell the management systems about events as they occur. A management system listens to traps, and might or might not take action. An event that could trigger a trap might be, say, an unauthorized login attempt. Other management protocols call unsolicited messages, like traps, **alerts** or **alarms**.

SystemView Disciplines and Processes

We've talked about agents and management protocols, but the managing system makes most of the decisions. Usually, a managing system is a software platform onto which tools can be integrated. These tools share common data, and the management platform provides common services such as presentation and data management. Thinking in terms of a three-tiered client/server system, the management platform provides presentation services, data management services, and some core "business logic" services. This business logic, however, can be extended by other products, perhaps from other vendors. Defining these core rules clearly is important in providing an extendible technology for a management platform. SystemView defines the disciplines and processes the management platform might undertake.

SystemView covers six main disciplines. Each covers several areas or processes important to managing a large enterprise, its computers, and networks. You may not want to automate some of these disciplines in your firm, or you might want to automate a few processes in each.

Problem Management. The most common discipline for firms to automate is **Problem Management**. Problem Management in SystemView includes several components:

- Problem prevention

- Problem correlation and determination

- Problem analysis and diagnosis

- Problem bypass and recovery

- Problem resolution and verification

This list isn't exhaustive, but it covers the key processes within the discipline. Not every shop may want to automate all of these processes immediately. The larger and more complex the environment, the greater the need for automation. Problem prevention, in particular, seems hard to automate. On the other hand, speeding problem diagnosis, providing automated bypass methods, and correlating multiple alerts seem useful in even middle sized organizations.

Change Management. The next most commonly automated SystemView discipline is **Change Management**. It also includes several components:

- Entering, assessing, and approving changes

- Planning and scheduling changes

- Distributing changes

- Synchronization

- Installing, activating, testing, and rolling back changes

- Monitoring and tracking changes

- Postinstallation analysis

Automated change management is absolutely necessary in large systems. For example, automating software distribution is the only way to correctly distribute, install, and activate a new version of an operating system to 500 systems worldwide during a four-hour period on a weekend. Automating change management eliminates the mistakes that well-meaning but tired humans can make at funny hours of the morning. It also reduces the length of any disruptions to service.

Performance Management. The next discipline within SystemView is **Performance Management**. It includes

- Performance monitoring

- Performance tuning

- Capacity planning

Sometimes, users want computing services providers to provide specific responsiveness to their actions. For example, they may want assurances that they can copy a 1 MB spreadsheet file from a file server to their machine in no more than 30 seconds, or they may want 90% of their online transactions to finish in less than 2 seconds. This quantitative discipline and the processes that accompany it are more common in the mainframe world than in client/server computing environments today. As more software is written using client/server techniques, however, performance management is becoming more important in these environments as well.

Configuration Management. **Configuration Management**, the next SystemView discipline, includes

- Configuration planning

- Configuration design

- Physical configuration

- Maintaining a configuration library

Maintaining accurate configuration records helps support staff do their job more efficiently. It can help them to detect problems that are likely to affect others quickly. With a good configuration library, problem correlation becomes much simpler. If you want to have "proactive" systems and network management rather than reacting to problems as they occur, you will need tools for configuration management.

Operations Management. The next SystemView discipline includes most of what shared system administrators would consider as "systems management." **Operations Management** consists of

- Operational monitoring

- Media and print control

- Data and storage management

- Database management

- Systems availability management

- Disaster recovery

Here, shared systems have a huge advantage over, say, file servers, because their tools for operational management are well developed and robust.

Business Management. The final SystemView discipline, **Business Management**, includes the following subareas

- Inventory control and asset management

- Security management

- Customer service

- Service-level agreements

- Financial support

- Administrative support

- License monitoring and management

Again, you probably would want to automate a few of these areas, especially at first. Asset management is a popular process for automated assistance today, as organizations struggle to keep accurate records of the desktop and laptop computers throughout their organization. Security management is also a hot topic, particularly with the Internet's rise in popularity.

Meet IBM's Systemview Family Of Products

IBM provides over 150 products that have system or network management capabilities built into them. Most of these products simply include agent software and perform other functions such as TCP/IP for OS/2. Others manage databases (e.g., DataHub).

Describing all of these products is beyond the scope of this book. We'll discuss IBM's key management products, the SystemView Family, we'll cover IBM's NetView products in some depth, and we'll then discuss several sample applications that implement parts or all of one SystemView discipline, such as Change Management. Many of these products run on many different hardware and operating system platforms, so it is more convenient to discuss them this way. Finally, we'll see how SystemView's ancestors worked together to solve specific problems at the Enterprise Management Summit, held in winter, 1994.

Common SystemView Family Characteristics

The SystemView family integrates and simplifies IBM's systems and network management products, while also making them more object oriented. Before, firms had to integrate pieces from IBM and other vendors into a completed management solution. This caused problems when products came out on different schedules.

With SystemView, IBM has announced similar capabilities on four operating systems: AIX, OS/2, MVS, and OS/400. Over time, it will use a shared infrastructure across these platforms. IBM also expects to deliver more sophisticated agents on other, non-IBM platforms, such as Microsoft's Windows NT or Hewlett-Packard's HP-UX UNIX operating systems.

This sharing permits IBM to deliver common services across these four platforms. Common system and network management also becomes more scalable, from a small workgroup managed by OS/2-based software to an enterprise managed by MVS-based software. This increased consistency between platforms means you can choose which management platform to use, place it where you wish, and change it if you see fit.

Over the last year or so, IBM has simplified SystemView's packaging. If you were to buy SystemView for AIX, say, you'd receive a single CD-ROM with all of SystemView's possible separate features and documentation on it. IBM has tested all of these features prior to release, so your staff has much less integration work to do.

IBM has also aligned SystemView disciplines with its products. When an operator starts SystemView, the software gives a single view, called the **Launch Window**, on a client system. From this view, an operator can click on a discipline and bring up the SystemView features installed for it. For example, on an MVS-based SystemView system, the operator might click on "Change Management" in the Launch Window. This might bring up the mainframe version of the **NetView Distribution Manager**, IBM's automated change management software.

Unlike human operators, who take a few seconds or minutes to finish a task and turn their attention to a new problem, SystemView responds in milliseconds. Shortening the time to diagnose a problem and automating a response to the problem dramatically reduces the time a problem or an outage affects your users' productivity. SystemView's automation platform provides a responsive system for responding to problems round the clock. This can free your operations staff to spot recurring trends, formulate more effective approaches, and provide better customer support.

SystemView is also becoming more object oriented, using a Common Object Data Model for storage, somewhat as RODM does for NetView for MVS today (we'll discuss RODM later). SystemView is changing to exploit common services, especially SOM and DSOM. This object orientation will permit SystemView to become more independent of specific APIs over time. This simplifies managing environments with products from many vendors.

Finally, SystemView expects to manage systems and networks as well as agents, data, and applications. Such comprehensive function is unprecedented in the industry. Indeed, SystemView is the "backplane" of IBM's Open Blueprint; it manages the resource managers that the Open Blueprint contains. No other vendor has the breadth, the experience, or the will to tackle the challenge of managing and automating complete enterprises.

SystemView for MVS

SystemView for MVS is IBM's enterprise management product family for mainframe users. SystemView for MVS provides several features unique to MVS and the S/390 processor. It supports and automates MVS-specific consoles, such as JES or VTAM. Its configuration management discipline supports mainframe specific hardware features, such as ESCON and parallel channels. If you want to run a CICSplex, its management applications work with SystemView for MVS. SystemView also supports applications that are specific, say, to configuring and managing an MVS Sysplex.

SystemView for MVS features are built upon the foundation of earlier systems and network management products for MVS. This minimizes disruptions for existing users. We can't cover all of the products, such as performance monitors, configuration management utilities, and so forth, that fall within the scope of SystemView for MVS, so we'll cover the main support features of SystemView for MVS. Besides the base SystemView for MVS product, the supported features include Network Management for MVS and System Automation for MVS.

Network Management for MVS

SystemView's Network Management for MVS is based upon NetView for MVS. NetView for MVS was originally designed as a good SNA network manager, monitoring the network and automating tedious operational tasks. Using NetView, after a failure occurred in an SNA network, diagnosis and recovery went faster.

Today, a mainframe-based NetView is both an "element manager" and a "multisystem manager." You can license and configure it to directly manage SNA, TCP/IP, OSI, APPN, and other protocols. It can manage token-rings along with LAN Network Manager, and it can manage NetWare servers. NetView has gone far beyond its roots as an SNA element manager, becoming an enterprise manager. Today, it is especially suited to the needs of large organizations.

NetView for MVS includes IBM's **Resource Object Data Manager (RODM)**, an object oriented storage facility for enterprise management information. RODM follows ISO guidelines for storing information about objects, and it automatically discovers much about your systems and networks. Because RODM is object oriented, it doesn't care if an object belongs to an SNA network, a TCP/IP network, or a Novell NetWare server. The rest of NetView for MVS depends on RODM for its knowledge of the network's topology.

NetView for MVS comes in three forms. The first, called the Procedural System Option, provides those functions appropriate for simple, subarea SNA networks. It does not include a graphical user interface or APPN management support. It does, however, include RODM and all of NetView's automation capabilities. This option is appropriate for firms or divisions of firms that want to use NetView, but at a slightly lower cost.

The second option is the Remote Unattended System Option. When a system runs with this form of NetView, a staff, located somewhere else, can manage that system. This mode of operations is sometimes called "lights out." If your firm has distributed S/390 processors, it makes sense to automate as many operations as possible. Using the Remote Unattended System Option can reduce your software costs while automating these operations at these sites.

The third option is the Enterprise System Option. It includes the **NetView Graphic Monitor Facility (NGMF)** and an APPN Topology and Accounting Manager. This is IBM's premier offering to manage subarea

SNA and APPN networks. With it, a single operations point can monitor the network's topology, status, inventory, and problem history. Your staff can control your networks, down to individual terminals or PCs, from a graphical NGMF station.

Correlation and Automation in NetView for MVS

NetView's correlation and automation capabilities aren't the kind of features IBM can splash across a glossy brochure. As a result, sometimes they're dismissed, although they are more powerful than most of the sexier, GUI-based SNMP systems on the market today. A simple example showing the difference between NetView and other management approaches should explain why we appear so impressed.

Let's say that a remote RJE station on an MVS system failed earlier, but the phone company has fixed the affected line. Your operator doesn't want to go to the VTAM console to start the line and then go to the JES3 console to restart the workstation, flush the spooled information, and start any waiting jobs. She'd rather just say "restart this" and let the system figure out the dependencies along the way. That's what RODM, NetView's object oriented correlation facilities, and its automation platform allow: a series of simple, automated routines that respond to your system's and network's needs. Although we used a mainframe-based example, NetView isn't constrained to automating mainframe activities.

Long before network "management" systems with icons that turn from green to red became popular, NetView set the gold standard for large system users. Even when an automation routine isn't available, NetView provides its operators with better diagnostic information than many of its counterparts. When a fault occurs, for years NetView has not only reported the fault, but listed probable fault causes and recommended operator actions to remedy the fault.

NetView for MVS as an Element Manager

Element managers manage parts of an enterprise network. For example, most SNMP-based management systems are element managers. If an SNMP manager received traps or alerts from a PBX, it probably wouldn't know how to handle them. NetView is an element manager for SNA, APPN, OSI, and TCP/IP networks, using the NMVT, CMIP, and SNMP protocols respectively. So, when NetView receives an NMVT alert from an IBM modem saying the line has gotten unacceptably noisy, it is acting as an element manager.

NetView can also manage other systems and network devices, indirectly, using a **NetView Service Point**. A service point manages something that NetView doesn't know how to manage directly. A service point takes the information from the non-NetView world, wraps it in the NMVT protocol, and transports it through the SNA or APPN network up to NetView. There, automation routines that your staff plugs into NetView respond to changes as required.

NetView can also help to manage a voice network. With the **IBM Network Interconnect Carrier Manager**, NetView even gives your firm access into your carrier's management facilities, such as AT&T's AccuMaster and British Telecom's Concert. NetView also manages PBXs and other voice elements, sometimes directly, sometimes using a NetView Service Point as an intermediary, depending on the specific device. Most major PBX manufacturers include NetView support in their products, but some don't.

As an element manager, NetView isn't limited to MVS. NetView versions also exist for VM and VSE. However, the MVS version is the only one supported directly by SystemView today.

NetView for MVS as a Manager of Managers

As a manager of managers, running the **NetView MultiSystem Manager (MSM)** application, NetView can also receive alerts from and send commands to other managing systems. MSM agents on IBM's **NetView for AIX**, IBM's **LAN Network Manager**, and Novell's NetWare servers work together with corresponding features of NetView MSM. NetView MSM thus can provide a consolidated view of the resources these element managers manage. As you do for other parts of SystemView, you buy only the features for NetView MSM that you need. If, for example, you wanted to manage TCP/IP networks, say, using NetView for AIX, MSM along with the Topology Feature for Internet Protocol would fill the bill.

All of the information NetView MSM receives goes into the Open Topology Manager. The Open Topology Manager works with RODM, which gives your operations staff an accurate view of your enterprise. An NGMF operator or an automation routine can receive alerts and send commands to these MSM agents. So, from a single NGMF station, an operator can see the lobe failure in the token-ring LAN that caused a TCP/IP station to go offline. So can automation routines. Figure 6.8 shows one possible MSM environment. To extend NetView MSM, IBM provides an API, the Open

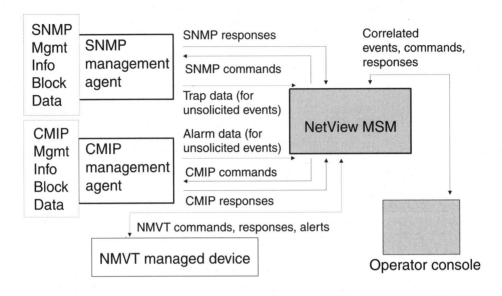

Figure 6.8. A NetView for MVS multisystem manager environment.

Topology Interface, for the Open Topology Manager. So, your staff or your vendors can support protocols or devices that IBM does not support directly.

NetView can be a multisystem manager for some protocols and devices and at the same time be an element manager for other protocols. So, NetView can become the intersection point for a large network. Overall, NetView for MVS provides industry-best management for SNA networks and an unmatched automation platform. It also provides comprehensive services for the most complex multivendor networks.

System Automation for MVS

Earlier, IBM provided several products that create common, automated interfaces in a large systems environment. Now, these have been combined into one optional SystemView for MVS feature, System Automation for MVS.

Automated Operations Console/MVS (AOC/MVS) provides automation for functions normally performed by console operators. AOC/MVS can start, recover, restart, and shut down applications and subsystems within an MVS system; AOC/MVS is an automation platform. It cannot automate everything without help from your systems programmers. That's because AOC/MVS has no built-in knowledge of your site's specific operations processes. However, your staff can customize it to suit your particular needs.

Automated Network Operations/MVS (ANO/MVS) provides similar automation services for token-ring LAN, subarea SNA, APPN, and TCP/IP networks. IBM **Operations Planning and Control/ESA (OPC/ESA)** handles job scheduling on networked mainframe systems. Again, these automation platforms are fully integrated with NetView for MVS, including RODM. So, if the results of one console operation affect another MVS subsystem, your staff can customize these platforms to enter commands to the target subsystem automatically.

SystemView for AIX

IBM's most widely used SystemView platform runs on IBM's RISC System/6000 systems. It began as an outgrowth of IBM's **NetView for AIX** products. Firms used to mainframe NetView wanted the nifty GUI that NetView for AIX provided, but they also wanted the automation capabilities they had grown fond of. Over time, NetView for AIX grew in capabilities and IBM added products to this platform that addressed other systems management disciplines. This base then became SystemView for AIX.

Like the other SystemView products, SystemView for AIX comes on either tape or CD-ROM. The CD ROM version includes all of the related SystemView features and product documentation. To use a feature, you buy it, and IBM provides a key that unlocks that feature on the CD-ROM. Your staff can then install the feature's code.

SystemView for AIX also includes the SystemView Launch Window. Like the Launch Window in SystemView for MVS, the controls and products are arranged by disciplines. Whereas SystemView for MVS uses a client/server approach with an OS/2 client for the Launch Window, SystemView for AIX uses X-Windows. SystemView for AIX does not support the "roving user" capability as MVS does. Otherwise, the Launch Windows work similarly. One caveat: X-Windows over a dialup WAN link is horribly slow. Don't expect a technician to dial in from an X-Windows-capable laptop to a centralized SystemView for AIX machine and solve a problem quickly.

NetView for AIX

NetView for AIX began as a port of Hewlett-Packard's OpenView SNMP management station product. Since those days, NetView for AIX has grown beyond HP's original code to become a solid SNMP and CMIP managing system. Because of its SNMP base, NetView for AIX is well suited to managing networks with many vendors. IBM has also introduced products that link NetView for AIX with a mainframe-based NetView. So, some firms use NetView for AIX as their primary management system for TCP/IP, SNA, APPN, and other networks.

Also, in August 1993, Digital Equipment Corporation selected NetView for AIX as the technology base for its management systems, called **NetView POLYCENTER**. Digital uses NetView to manage products based upon its proprietary products, such as DECnet and LAT. Both IBM and Digital are charter members of the **NetView Association**, a consortium of vendors with systems and network management applications based on NetView for AIX. Today, the NetView Association has 196 members, and the number continues to rise. In recent years, NetView for AIX has achieved broad marketplace acceptance, especially with medium-sized to large customers.

NetView for AIX gives your operations staff a graphical user interface, based on X-Windows. It automatically discovers TCP/IP devices and assesses whether they are capable of SNMP or not. Of course, if you're attached to the Internet, you don't want NetView for AIX discovering the entire worldwide network, so you can also limit its autodiscovery to a range of IP addresses. If you use other IBM programs or third-party software, they also may be able to automatically discover devices. If so, they can put their information into NetView for AIX's multiprotocol topology database.

NetView for AIX automatically defines and dynamically maintains a number of "views," or maps for its operators. One map might show the devices attached to a token-ring or Ethernet segment in an IBM 8260 hub. Another map might show DECnet nodes on an Ethernet segment, and a third might show how TCP/IP routers interconnect. With IBM's optional **AIX SNA Manager/6000** software, NetView for AIX, along with NetView on a mainframe system, can monitor and manage an SNA network. As changes occur in the network, NetView for AIX updates all the affected maps dynamically.

NetView for AIX also provides a capability called distributed discovery. This reduces SNMP polling traffic, which sometimes can overwhelm low-speed WAN links. With distributed discovery, a Mid-Level Manager (MLM) monitors devices local to it, usually on the same LAN segment. Usually, the MLM would be at a different physical site than the main NetView for AIX managing system. It filters SNMP traps and other information, and forwards crucial information to the managing system. For networks with several sites, using MLMs can hold down your line costs, although you should weigh this against added support costs before making a decision. By distributing intelligence throughout your network, the main managing system can also manage a larger, more complex network.

You can use NetView for AIX' built-in structures for storing topology, device, and asset information, or you can use a relational database, such as DB2/6000. If you don't need relational database interfaces with NetView for AIX, then a lower-cost version of NetView, **NetView Entry for AIX** might be better suited for you. It doesn't provide relational database support, and it supports a combination of up to 32 workstations, routers, and hubs.

With additional products from IBM or the NetView Association, you can monitor and manage hubs, switches, routers, bridges, NetWare servers, and DECnet nodes. Usually these additional products interact with specific agents. We don't have the space to discuss all of them here. As examples, though, IBM's **Intelligent Hub Management Program for AIX** runs with NetView for AIX; it lets you monitor the status and security of IBM 8250 and 8260 hubs. IBM's **ATM Campus Manager** manages all of IBM's ATM products, except for the WAN oriented Nways 2220 Broadband Switch. You can also manage Novell NetWare servers with NetView for AIX; NetWare Management Agents can simultaneously report faults to Novell's NetWare Management System and NetView for AIX.

Like NetView on a mainframe, NetView for AIX can manage, with some help, devices and protocols that aren't based upon SNMP. For example, with IBM's **LAN Network Manager for AIX**, you can also monitor and manage IBM 8230 hubs and all token-ring network devices. The original **LAN Network Manager** runs under OS/2. It interacts with IBM token-ring bridges and with agent software on every token-ring adapter IBM has shipped. Together, they build a topology of a bridged token-ring LAN.

Since this protocol isn't SNMP, NetView for AIX can't directly interact with these devices, except for the newest hubs, which support SNMP. So, LAN Network Manager provides an interface for NetView for AIX. When both programs are present, NetView for AIX sees all the token-ring devices present, and integrates this information into its topology database. LAN Network Manager also can forward this information to a NetView on a mainframe, if needed.

NetView for AIX provides an automation platform, although it is slightly less sophisticated than NetView on a mainframe. It lets your staff set thresholds for alarms and filter alerts and events as they occur. As specific events occur, NetView for AIX can trigger SNMP actions or AIX scripts in response. Your staff configures and programs these automatic responses as they see fit. Finally, if your main NetView for AIX system goes down for any reason, you can also specify a backup system. This way, when you perform ordinary tasks, like adding new releases of NetView for AIX, you still can monitor and manage your environment.

If you have mainframe NetView installed, you may want to use it to manage your SNMP environment, using NetView for AIX as an agent. Installing IBM's **AIX NetView Service Point** software allows NetView for AIX to convert SNMP traps into NMVT alerts and forward them to host NetView. AIX NetView Service Point also responds to host NetView RUNCMDs, commands for the service point to run, and sends the output from these commands back to the mainframe. You can use host NetView's correlation and automation facilities to detect if a "down SNMP device" was caused, say, by a failing transmission line that host NetView manages through an interface to a carrier. Finally, NetView for AIX can send its topology information up to the NetView on the host, giving your operations staff a consistent view of all your networks.

Additional SystemView for AIX Applications

Next, we consider several optional SystemView for AIX applications that have a particular affinity for the AIX systems and network management platform. These applications automate other SystemView disciplines, such as Configuration Management and Problem Management. Many more SystemView for AIX applications exist for operations management and performance management, but we simply can't cover them all.

LMU for AIX. Although NetView for AIX provides comprehensive network and device management, it needs help to look at PCs. If you have Novell NetWare servers or IBM LAN Servers in your network, then **AIX LAN Management Utilities for AIX (LMU for AIX)** will work along with NetView for AIX to manage these servers and their client systems. You can thus collect memory, disk drive, adapter card, and software configuration information for many of your PCs. If your NetWare servers have Apple Macintosh clients, then LMU for AIX can also determine their status. LMU for AIX also monitors for thresholds, forwards alerts to NetView for AIX, and schedules jobs or commands to run on LAN attached workstations and servers.

LMU also comes in an OS/2 version, **IBM LAN NetView Management Utilities for OS/2 (LMU for OS/2)**. LMU for OS/2 provides functions similar to LMU for AIX; of the two products, it was the original. LMU for AIX works by itself, with NetView for AIX, or hand in hand with host NetView. LMU for AIX also scales better; it would more easily allow you to centralize the management and administration of a large network of servers.

Distributed SMIT for AIX. An important SystemView for AIX application provides relief for a common complaint about UNIX-based systems: They are hard to configure and understand. As we mentioned in Chapter 4, when AIX first came out, one if its advantages was SMIT's system management interface. SMIT uses a simple X-Windows or menu-driven user interface instead of the more traditional, cryptic UNIX commands, such as grep, awk, and ex.

IBM's **Distributed SMIT for AIX (DSMIT)** extends SMIT's ease of use to multiple systems. While SMIT configures one AIX system, DSMIT can configure many IBM AIX, HP-UX, or SunOS UNIX systems. You can use one or more DSMIT servers in a network. This works well if you distribute system administration responsibilities to specific workgroups. You might use one DSMIT server to manage the configuration tasks for workgroup A while workgroup B uses a second DSMIT server. Of course, you could also centralize these configuration management functions, say, within a campus.

Trouble Ticket for AIX. Finally, a useful problem management application, **Trouble Ticket for AIX**, can run by itself, or along with NetView for AIX. It integrates systems inventory information, problem tracking, and notification and escalation into a single package. A trouble ticket tracks a problem from first report through resolution. Trouble Ticket for AIX can monitor how well your systems and networks comply with service-level agreements. When problems occur, it can automatically generate and track trouble tickets and set priorities for problem resolution. Your operations staff is then freed from the paperwork associated with problem tracking, and they can solve problems more quickly.

Managing Systems with SystemView for OS/400

The AS/400 is competent both as a managing system and as a managed system. It is a managed system because IBM's customers often use OS/400 systems in mainframe or UNIX-based environments. It is a managing system because many sites use an OS/400 system to serve and manage one or more workgroups. Finally, it manages large networks of distributed OS/400 systems well, where it must perform both roles.

SystemView for OS/400 is very much like SystemView for MVS. Its Launch Window also uses an OS/2 client, the Launch Window's content is comprised of the SystemView disciplines, and the Launch Window manages sessions and security automatically, using OS/400's security and authentication methods. Like SystemView for MVS, which works with all MVS/ESA systems, SystemView for OS/400 and the Launch Window work with all models of AS/400 systems.

SystemView for MVS, SystemView for AIX, or older versions of NetView for mainframe systems can manage OS/400 systems. Generally, host NetView will provide more capability if you have a large subarea SNA or APPN network. This is because IBM has provided a strong relationship between centralized mainframe systems and distributed systems, such as AS/400s. Large customers prefer to manage many distributed systems from a single point. These SNA-based services are proven and widely adopted by IBM's customers.

OS/400 itself exhibits several characteristics that enable robust systems management. First, it is tightly integrated, allowing simpler problem diagnosis. For example, if a performance problem exists, IBM's **Performance Tools/400** and **Performance Investigator/400** can analyze the OS/400 integrated database as well as watch CPU and memory usage patterns. In other, less tightly integrated environments, you'd usually need one tool for the operating system and another for the database. The object-based nature of OS/400 also aids distributed systems management because it causes a consistent view of management data, such as problem records, hardware information, and the like. You can use OS/400 alone to verify asset management in a large network of AS/400s; hardware and software objects both record their status for further use. If you have PCs running Client Access/400, OS/400 can also determine their configurations, storing this information on the AS/400 for later use. Larger groupings of AS/400 systems can use OS/400 to notify a central operations group of events requiring attention.

Besides OS/400 itself, the main tool for using the AS/400 as a managing system is **SystemView System Manager/400**. If your AS/400 is a managed system, then you'd use **SystemView Managed System Services/400**. Between them, they handle most tasks within SystemView. SystemView System Manager/400 provides problem management compatible with host NetView, NetView Distribution Manager (DM)–compatible change management, and operations management compatible with NetView remote operations. SystemView Managed System Services/400 contributes NetView DM and NetView remote operations agent services. As a result, a NetView system on a mainframe or another AS/400 can manage an AS/400 system running SystemView Managed System Services/400. Similarly, if a managed system can send alerts and information up to host NetView, it can also use SystemView System Manager/400 as the managing system.

To automate operations, **SystemView Automation Center/400** can monitor over 350 system attributes and respond to specific triggers. For example, SystemView Automation Center/400 can submit jobs, end a job, move some spooled files to manage disk space, and so forth. If you purchase the complete automation package, you can use a component called **OMEGAVIEW/400** at a central site. It gives your staff a graphical view of the devices and problems being monitored and also provides a "visual" programming language to ease the task of building automation routines to respond to specific conditions.

The OS/400 systems management products are like OS/400 itself: There are fewer parts, and they are tightly integrated. For example, on most IBM systems, NetView Distribution Manager (NetView DM) provides software distribution, installation, and version control services. AS/400 customers get this function included in the base products, System Manager/400 and Managed System Services/400. Like OS/400 itself, IBM designed these tools for great deployment flexibility and, once deployed, minimal intervention. Along with OS/400, they make an already easily managed system even more economical to operate.

SystemView for OS/2

The latest SystemView platform is SystemView for OS/2. SystemView for OS/2 today is optimized for use in workgroups or in smaller businesses. SystemView for OS/2 improves the availability of your servers and networks while reducing PC administration costs. IBM has also announced its intention, over time, to extend SystemView for OS/2 to be an element manager in a larger, enterprise configuration. Such a larger environment might be managed by, say, SystemView for OS/400, AIX, or MVS.

SystemView for OS/2 can manage servers, mobile systems, and desktop systems. It monitors system resources continuously, and warns your staff when problems are likely to occur. This is especially useful, say, when your server's disks are nearing their capacity. With SystemView for OS/2, your staff can monitor capacity and other thresholds, and take appropriate action before a problem or an outage occurs. The software can also take an alert, convert it into an SNMP trap and forward it to another management system for action.

With SystemView for OS/2, your staff can also schedule events, like backups, to occur at specific times. SystemView for OS/2 can collect hardware and software inventory information, manage licenses, track assets, and make automated responses to common alerts. It performs software distribution within a workgroup. Finally, SystemView for OS/2 contains "remote control" software, so your help desk can use your network to effectively see and resolve users' problems.

SystemView for OS/2 works within a single LAN. This LAN might be be bridged or switched, containing several segments. Within this logical LAN, it can discover devices automatically, adding them to its inventory list. It can also gather information on which hardware and software products are installed on a given device; SystemView for OS/2 understands how to identify over 3000 commonly used software packages. IBM has promised a SystemView for OS/2 release for later in 1996 that would provide software metering services in addition to inventory and license management.

SystemView for OS/2 can monitor and manage devices running OS/2 and Windows. If you use OS/2 Warp Server software, SystemView for OS/2 software is included in that package. SystemView for OS/2 runs over NetBIOS, TCP/IP, and IPX using asynchronous serial or LAN datalinks. It can also run over asynchronous serial lines without a "network layer" protocol. This is useful, for example, for helping mobile computer users. In a larger enterprise, you might choose to deploy multiple SystemView for OS/2 Managers by task; for example, one SystemView for OS/2 Manager might control inventory while another handles remote control of workstations. Or, you might decide to deploy them geographically, having each manager provide all services to an assigned workgroup of managed systems.

SystemView for OS/2 can track information in ordinary OS/2 files, DB/2 databases, or Lotus Notes databases. It also provides a simple software preparation and distribution facility, suitable for use in a LAN environment. Unlike NetView Distribution Manager, it does not yet attempt to reduce WAN traffic during software distributions.

Along with SystemView for OS/2, IBM offers several systems management packages today. Each provides services that are unique, but likely will be "folded into" SystemView for OS/2 over time. NetView Distribution Manager/2 offers a industry leading software distribution, installation, and configuration platform, like the other NetView Distribution manager products. LMU for OS/2 provides services very similar to LMU for AIX; if you have NetWare servers or Macintosh computers in your network, LMU's capabilities may be superior to SystemView for OS/2 today. NetFinity can manage Windows 95 systems directly; SystemView for OS/2 can manage NetFinity systems, but has not yet shipped direct support for Windows 95.

So, in the short term, your environment might require SystemView for OS/2 in combination with these other systems and network management products. In the long term, though, SystemView for OS/2 will be IBM's premier workgroup management offering.

Applications That Automate Specific SystemView Disciplines

We've already discussed applications to monitor and manage the state of networking devices, for example, intelligent hubs. These are the most common management applications. However, each platform also uses system and network specific applications. First, we'll examine just two areas in detail, security and performance monitoring. Then, we'll look in detail at one family of management applications, IBM's NetView Distribution Manager.

Open Sesame: Authentication and Security with RACF and NetSP

For security, IBM has traditionally supplied its **Resource Access Control Facility (RACF)** on mainframes. RACF provides comprehensive security for all IBM supplied subsystems on MVS, VM, and VSE. RACF is recognized as one of the most difficult authorization and security systems to "crack," or break into. It also allows a single signon to mainframe applications when used in conjunction with other IBM software. With IBM's newly announced "OS/390," the DCE Security Server and RACF will be integrated, providing a single signon for both traditional mainframe applications and DCE cell-based applications. Of course, IBM also supports the DCE Security Server throughout its product line.

IBM's security products also deal with a new threat: intruders from the Internet. IBM's **Internet Connection Secured Network Gateway** provides a firewall between your TCP/IP networks and outside networks such as the Internet. A firewall system protects your data and systems from unauthorized access in several ways. The Internet Connection Secured Network Gateway is built using the same technology that has protected IBM successfully for over seven years. Fortunately, it also gives your users transparent access to programs and files on other TCP/IP networks, while protecting your assets.

Customers historically look to IBM for help in securing their information assets. IBM invented the Data Encryption System (DES), which is the standard for security within the United States. However, the U.S. government prohibits its export. IBM also makes other encryption schemes that are suitable for international use. RACF, NetSP, and the NetSP Secured Network Gateway are the latest products in a long line of security products and services for businesses around the world.

Monitoring and Managing Performance

We don't have space to cover all of IBM's performance management software here. So, we'll cover a few representative examples of the tools available to help you monitor and manage the performance of a multivendor, enterprise network.

IBM's **NetView Performance Monitor (NPM)** runs on mainframe systems. It monitors, analyzes, and displays real-time performance information from Ethernet LAN segments, token-ring LAN segments, NetWare servers, and VTAM. As a result, you can tell that you are achieving subsecond response time to 3270 Terminal Display users in Peoria. At the same time, you can see how many NetWare connections are in use on a file server in Los Angeles. NPM doesn't require NetView on a mainframe system, but once you find a problem, you may want to use NetView's diagnostic capabilities to diagnose it.

As another example, **Systems Monitor for AIX** works with NetView for AIX to monitor UNIX system specific information. You can watch the CPU utilization on a specific system or paging space use on another. Besides supporting AIX systems, IBM supplies Systems Monitor agent software for other UNIX systems. These systems include Hewlett-Packard's HP-UX, Sun's Solaris, and UNIX for AT&T Global Information Systems (NCR). So, if a Solaris system in your network runs out of space on a file system, your NetView for AIX system can point it out to you.

System Performance Monitor/2 (SPM/2) provides similar functions, but it only works with OS/2 systems. You can run SPM/2 on the same system as NetView for OS/2. SPM/2 agents collect information regarding CPU, memory, file, disk, and communications device usage on an OS/2 system and send it to the main collection point, either a local or remote system. For example, you can check the effectiveness of a disk's cache on a remote OS/2 system quite easily with SPM/2.

To monitor traffic on specific LAN segments, IBM provides an implementation of the TCP/IP-based Remote MONitoring (RMON) protocol. **RMONitor for AIX** is the managing application in this case, and it is part of SystemView for AIX. Several vendors, including IBM, supply RMON agents, either incorporated into specialized hardware devices or as software additions to existing systems or servers. With RMONitor software, you can set thresholds and monitor the performance of both token-ring and Ethernet LAN segments.

Automating Change Management with NetView Distribution Manager

Sometimes, a software product's qualities make all the difference. This is the case with **NetView Distribution Manager (DM)**. Although many packages support software distribution, few automate the Change Management discipline as effectively as NetView DM. Once NetView DM agents are installed in the target systems, a NetView DM managing system can schedule, distribute, install, test, and back out software. "Software" here can include application software, operating systems, or even microcode. It manages this without attention by staff. If you need to update dozens, hundreds, or thousands of systems over a weekend, NetView DM can help.

Like NetView itself, NetView DM started in the mainframe arena, supporting MVS as the managing system. NetView DM distributed new configurations and microcode to 3174 Establishment Controllers, IBM 4690 Store Controllers, and remote VSE mainframe systems. It would schedule the installation, distribute the software, install the software, restart the device with the new software, and track the process. If a mistake or problem occurred, it could back out the installation, restoring the device's earlier state. It can still do all of these things, but with new configurations such as client/server environments, it changed to meet new needs.

Today, NetView DM still supports MVS as a managing system, and it still supports traditional SNA and APPN controllers and hosts. It distributes code to OS/2-, DOS-, and Windows based PCs as well. Besides code, it can also distribute arbitrary user files to target agents. So, if you need to install a new version of the OS/2 operating system, a new Lotus 1-2-3 macro, and a new version of APPN software on a LAN Server, NetView DM/MVS can handle this. If you need to update a TCP/IP configuration on a DOS/Windows system and reboot it to take effect, NetView DM/MVS manages this as well. If specified tests after installation fail, it can back the whole change out, restoring the system's earlier state. NetView DM/MVS is considerate of your WAN as well: It can compress and decompress files for transmission automatically.

If you need to manage and distribute software to many remote workstations, you might want to add **NetView Distribution Manager Software Profile Management Facility MVS/ESA**. With this software, your staff maintains profiles of all their systems, and updates them accordingly. For example, let's say your warehouse managers all use the same software configuration on their DOS/Windows systems. This configuration differs from that used by your sales staff, which differs from the one used by executives. With NetView DM Software Profile Management Facility, you'd update all the "executive" PCs by profile, instead of specifying which machines to change. It makes administration simpler.

So far, we've discussed two-tier software distribution. NetView DM/MVS also supports three-tier change management. To do this, it works alongside other NetView Distribution Managers on various shared system and server platforms. The members of the NetView DM managing system family are found in Figure 6.9.

When considering three-tier software distribution, NetView DM/MVS or another managing system distributes changes to another managing system, such as NetView DM/2. Then, NetView DM/2 actually distributes, installs, and tests the change on the target system, say, a PC running DOS. NetView DM/MVS maintains a knowledge of servers and all of their clients, so it knows the "path" between itself and the final target system. This is desirable for several reasons. Mainly, though, it saves telecommunications bandwidth; only one copy of the changes need traverse WAN links even if multiple targets exist at a site.

We've already discussed SystemView System Manager/400, and we won't consider it again here. NetView DM/2 manages OS/2, DOS, and Windows distributions automatically. It uses IBM's NetBIOS protocol to distribute software and data throughout a networked environment. Between servers, it uses NetBIOS, and it uses SNA to communicate with NetView DM/MVS when needed. Depending upon your configuration, you might use one of several IBM products to provide the NetView DM/2 agent or managing system functions needed on the OS/2 system. These can coexist on the same system. Also, NetView DM/2 can reside on the same system as a LAN Server. This makes it convenient for branch offices, for example.

If your file server of choice is NetWare, then NetView DM for NetWare can accommodate similar functions. Unlike NetView DM/2, it uses Novell's IPX and TCP/IP protocols over LANs and SNA and TCP/IP between servers. The software is a port of NetView DM for AIX, discussed later, and runs as native NetWare applications in the servers. The **NetView DM Agent for NetWare Distributed Feature** is the agent software, and **NetView DM for NetWare** is the managing application.

NetView DM for AIX is slightly different. It supports TCP/IP networks and NFS, AFS, and compatible file systems. IBM supplies NetView DM Agent software for HP-UX, SunOS, and Solaris systems, along with OS/2, Windows, and DOS. As a result, if you have a heterogeneous UNIX

Software	Family Member	Platform
NetView	DM/MVS	MVS/ESA
SystemView	System Manager/400	OS/400
NetView	DM/2	OS/2 systems and LAN Servers
NetView	DM for NetWare	Novell NetWare servers
NetView	DM for AIX	AIX/6000

Figure 6.9. The NetView DM managing system family.

environment that includes AIX, you might consider using NetView DM for AIX as its software distribution managing system.

Bringing It All Together: The Enterprise Management Summit

In 1994 and 1995, the Enterprise Management Summit conducted a "shootout" between the leading vendors of systems and network management software. The sponsors required each vendor to complete 13 scenarios in 90 minutes, with an optional 14th. Each scenario covered common systems and network management issues, such as automatic discovery, asset and inventory management, security, performance management, and software distribution. Most of the scenarios judged apply to complex environments, including complex client/server computing systems. The judges were taken from analysts and users from large enterprises and from software applications vendors.

IBM used several products in its bid for this competition. Most were from IBM; some were from the NetView Association. Because Digital was a fellow competitor, IBM used DNM software from Ki Networks for the DECnet scenario instead of Digital's PolyCenter software. Here are the products IBM used:

- NetView for AIX

- Trouble Ticket for AIX

- NetView for MVS/ESA

- NetView MultiSystem Manager for MVS/ESA

- LAN Management Utilities for AIX

- LAN NetView Management Utilities for OS/2

- DB2/2

- SNA Manager/6000

- DMN (from Ki Networks, Inc.; manages DECnet networks)

- PATROL (from BMC Software)

- IBM DataGlance (a network monitor/analyzer)

- Systems Monitor for AIX

- Systems Monitor for HP-UX

- ADSTAR Distributed Storage Manager for AIX (ADSM for AIX)

- ADSM for HP-UX, for Windows, for OS/2, and for SUN

- Job Scheduler for AIX

- NetView DM for AIX

- NetView DM Agent for AIX

- NetView DM Agent/2

- NetView DM Agent for HP-UX

The scenarios were comprehensive, so the solutions demanded this complexity. Platforms included OS/2, Windows, Novell NetWare file servers, an IBM mainframe, DEC VAX/VMS systems, and UNIX systems from several vendors. Contestants used software from several database vendors, although the scenario requiring a relational database demanded that contestants use database software from Oracle Corporation. One of the scenarios required the management station to control several related tasks running on multiple UNIX systems. Another scenario required the vendor to find the cause of poor performance within the systems or networks. Again, many of these scenarios came from the sponsors' experience with large, complex client/server systems.

Overall, in 1994, IBM won 5 of the scenarios and was the only vendor to participate in all 14. Of the other scenarios, DEC won 4, Hewlett-Packard and Computer Associates won 2 each, and Bull won 1. IBM had the highest composite score, both in 1994 and in 1995. Because different sessions were judged by different people, the scoring isn't scientific, but it does show that NetView for AIX and the NetView Association has much to offer.

The summit also illustrates the challenges associated with an open, multivendor, client/server system. Because of the high degree of automation the system management tools provide, you'd expect costs to be lower than if the same environment were without these management tools. However, simplifying the system and reducing the number of vendors involved would probably produce greater savings.

IBM Services For Open Client/Server Computing

If your staff should find they need help in designing, building, or operating your new client/server applications, IBM, and its wholly owned subsidiary, the Integrated Systems Solutions Corporation (ISSC), can help. IBM and ISSC provide services from management consulting to building and operating your I/S infrastructure for you. Most firms use these services to lighten the load on their staff for specific projects. IBM and ISSC's people can augment your staff's knowledge, relieve them of daily operational tasks as they build a new application, and reduce the risks of adopting a new technology.

ISSC's management consultants specialize in business transformation. These consultants could help you to, say, redesign your business processes, revise your product and marketing strategy, or evaluate your firm's viability in particular markets. Their strength is in business operations and strategy, more than in I/S technologies.

Other ISSC consultants and specialists define technological architectures and design and deploy new applications. This is the largest segment of ISSC's consulting arm; they understand technological products from IBM and other firms. Many of these consultants came to ISSC from other companies, including other computer vendors. Because they design and build systems constantly, they are aware of the latest design trends, tools, and reasons for success. Because ISSC also must often operate the designs they conceive, they are aware of the operational and financial implications of their design decisions. Firms use these services mostly to augment their staff. Using ISSC often improves an application's quality, reduces its deployment time, and lowers its ongoing costs.

The most heavily publicized of ISSC's offerings is managed operations, sometimes known as outsourcing. This is where ISSC comes in and runs a firm's I/S operations. ISSC might also assume analysis and design responsibilities as part of a managed operations contract. Some firms prefer to outsource this; others view I/S analysis and design as strategic to their business interests. To date, most of ISSC's managed operations contracts are with large firms, with hundreds or thousands of employees, although ISSC expects this to change in the next few years.

A key tenet of outsourcing is this: Your firm should decide if it wants to be in the business of operating computer systems. If systems operation is a "core competency" of your firm, then outsourcing isn't for you, but if systems operation is a cost, not a competitive asset, you should contact an outsourcer, such as ISSC, to see if an outside firm is more efficient or provides a more reliable, consistent service. Perhaps an outside company can reduce your exposure to data loss, theft, or alteration. Sometimes, firms find their I/S staff provides a highly competitive service at a good price; other times, they choose to outsource.

If you should outsource all or part of firm's I/S duties, you should retain a consultant to help you write the outsourcing contract. You should also retain a staff sufficient to ensure that your vendor delivers the promised level of service. Some firms go one step further; outsourcers get paid more if they exceed certain operational goals and less if they fail to achieve them. Such risk sharing benefits your firm and should be written into outsourcing contracts where possible. Some firms even include such risk sharing clauses in design and deployment contracts, where a consulting firm helps to design or deploy a specific application. Clauses like these help to separate quality service providers from "lowballers," who quote low prices, but whose designs don't meet your business objectives over time.

IBM also offers many packaged services that firms considering client/server computing might find helpful. For example, IBM's **Systems Validation Services** can help you to decide how your design will perform, and what hardware is needed to support it. IBM's **NetReview** services can review your network's design and tell you what delays the network will cause in your application's responsiveness. IBM's **Open Systems Centers** around the world can prototype your new system for you, testing your design's concept, and assessing its costs and performance over time. IBM services, such as these, can help you to make better informed decisions as you assess an application's viability or a design's performance and costs.

Today, IBM and ISSC are the industry's premier provider of I/S services, both for client/server and for traditional applications. Surprisingly, services is the second largest component of IBM's revenue stream today, accounting for over $12 billion in 1995 alone. This part of IBM's business is growing at double digit rates as firms concentrate on their core businesses.

Revisiting Our Examples: Tying the Threads Together

In summary, we'll look one last time at Global Plumbing Supplies, SpeedyTix, Acme Roadrunner Traps, Jones' Happy Travel, Cripple Creek Community Hospital, and Five and Dime Imports. These hypothetical firms have needs that illustrate different ways of using client/server computing. A technician reading this might think of other ways to answer the same design problems; more than one answer exists. Your business needs, staff experience, and costs will vary, and so a "cookbook" approach can't apply to everyone. That's why Acme's answer differs from the approach Five and Dime used.

Global Plumbing Supplies, Inc. (GPSI)

Earlier, we listed many of the components of GPSI's client/server system. We also discussed many of the decisions GPSI made in building their new application. Here, we'll provide a quick component listing.

Because GPSI wants to encourage mobility over time, the client software runs on IBM ThinkPad 755 laptop computers. The ThinkPads have 24 MB of memory and use the OS/2 operating system. They use LAN Requester, VisualAge, and CAE/2 software to communicate over an Ethernet to a LAN Server system, and a LAN Server Ultimedia system. The LAN Server system also contains the DDCS/2 database gateway software. These servers run on IBM PC Server 720 computers, equipped with RAID disks and tape drives. The San Francisco site, though is much larger, and it runs the LAN Server on an IBM 9672 Model R63 mainframe with the MVS operating system. LAN Server for MVS provides San Francisco users with file, printer, and multimedia services, as the OS/2 systems do in New York and Rome. The mainframe also hosts the database, which uses DB/2 software.

GPSI's network uses SNA and NetBIOS protocols. IBM supplied the Token-Ring hardware, using IBM 8238 Nways Token-Ring Stackable hubs for New York and Rome. The ThinkPads use IBM Token-Ring Auto 16/4 Credit Card Adapters to attach to their LAN segments, and the OS/2-based servers in New York and Rome use the IBM Triple LANStreamer PCI Adapter. Each Token-Ring segment uses Category 5 unshielded twisted pair for wiring.

In San Francisco, GPSI chose to use 4 IBM 8260 hubs for their 20 Token-Ring segments. They use 8260 switching modules today, and the 8260 gives them the option to migrate to 25, 100, or 155 Mbps ATM to any desktop at a later date. Using Integrated 8281 ATM Bridge modules now gives GPSI an ATM backbone for segment-to-segment traffic, running at 155 Mbps. To attach these Token-Ring segments to their 9672, GPSI uses 4 Open Systems Adapters. Over their WAN lines, they use IBM 2210 routers to bridge data between sites.

GPSI manages this network using SystemView for MVS and SystemView for AIX. SystemView for AIX handles most of the network, file server, printer server, and PC management tasks. SystemView for MVS automates mainframe operation, management of the main DB/2 database, and SNA network management. For this, GPSI uses the Enterprise System Option for NetView for MVS, along with the MultiSystem Manager option. An operations staff member can use his or her desktop OS/2 system to see how the whole system operates, since GPSI configured SystemView for AIX to forward alerts and status to SystemView for MVS.

Acme Roadrunner Traps

Acme has a simpler problem to solve, and their application is thus less complex. All of Acme's staff had existing PCs attached to an existing Ethernet network, and they continued to use this hardware. Fritz Payling and Fred Brewer use PC-DOS and Microsoft Windows on their machines. Their client software is Lotus Notes for Windows and Lotus cc:Mail. All of the forms needed for the application reside on the Notes server, so no additional software is required here. As discussed earlier, cc:Mail is the way the process-driven application keeps people informed of changes in a request's status. Will Warner's PC runs OS/2. So, he uses Notes client software for OS/2 along with cc:Mail for OS/2.

Acme's existing network runs the TCP/IP protocol over Ethernet. Their staff is already familiar with UNIX systems, and if the pilot works, they want to deploy it throughout the firm. So, an IBM RISC System/6000

Model 590H, running AIX seemed to them a good choice for a server platform. It gives them plenty of growth, since the transaction volume for ordering office supplies isn't high. Lotus Notes server software, the Flowmark for AIX workflow manager, and CICS for AIX software runs here as well. To manage the system, Acme uses SystemView for AIX, running on the same RISC System/6000 hardware.

Jones' Happy Travel

Jones' Happy Travel is another straightforward example. They removed single-use terminals owned by the Computerized Reservation Systems (CRSs), and replaced them with PCs that had more function. They also added a traveler's profile to their software, giving them a more customized and consistent service.

Jones' management approached the CRS owners, and found they could return the single-use terminals, trading them for the hardware and terminal emulation software needed for each PC. Because the CRS owned this hardware and software, they retained responsibility to support it and repair it if needed. Jones' also used this to ensure the compatibility of their plans with the CRS' needs. The hardware boards provided by the CRS assume an AT bus in the PC, and the software assumes the PC uses Microsoft Windows, either by itself or under OS/2. Jones' chose to use OS/2 on each PC.

With the need to use an AT bus, the agency bought an IBM PC 300 for each agent. They didn't opt for the latest, greatest, and fastest model, since their performance needs were modest. They also didn't buy a large disk for each machine, since they decided to use the database server as a code server as well. Each agent's PC runs VisualLift for OS/2 software along with the terminal emulation and communications software provided by the CRS. In addition, each PC runs NFS software to access the file server, and CAE/2 software to access the profile database. Each agent has a printer directly attached to their PC; printer sharing wasn't needed.

Jones' uses three 16 Mbps token-ring LANs, over UTP category 5 wiring, provided by IBM 8238 Nways Token-Ring Stackable hubs. Their server system, a RISC System/6000 Model J30 with 4 processors, runs AIX, along with DDCS/6000 and DB2/6000 software. The DDCS/6000 software works with CAE/2 as a gateway to DB2/6000, which simplifies the client systems. To attach to their token-ring LAN, the agents use IBM Auto 16/4 ISA Adapters. The RISC System/6000 server uses three IBM Auto Token-Ring LANstreamer 32 MC Adapters, feature code #2972, to attach to the token-ring LANs.

When Jones' designed the system, they looked to IBM to verify the size and performance of their server, and of their LANs. Using IBM's Solutions Validation Service (SVS), they discovered their original choice for a server, a RISC System/6000 Model C20, was underpowered for the expected load if the agency grew as expected. They also noted that using two token-ring LAN segments for their 120 users would result in excessive network loads first thing in the morning. So, they added a LAN segment, and increased the server's performance to compensate for the predicted bottlenecks. Because the J30 is an SMP system, the agency can add processors as needed to keep up with its anticipated growth.

Cripple Creek Community Hospital (CCCH)

CCCH decided to use X-Windows devices throughout the hospital to speed access to their existing applications. Because X-Windows is an openly specified protocol, a client system can use AIX, OS/2, Windows, or almost any other operating system. CCCH decided to support three possibilities: RISC System/6000 computers running AIX and AIXwindows, PCs running Microsoft Windows with a third party X-server package, and IBM Xstations.

Most locations in the hospital, including bedside terminals, use IBM Xstations. This eliminates the need to update software on these devices. It also implies that CCCH's network traffic will be greater than, say, if CCCH used PCs instead. Areas of the hospital where speed is critical, like the emergency room, use RISC System/6000 Model 390 desktop systems. Physicians at home or at their office typically use PCs running Microsoft Windows.

CCCH's network is built for responsiveness and reliability, using four IBM 8260 intelligent hubs with ATM as a backbone technology. Each "user device" on the network, such as an Xstation, is attached to an IBM 8271 Nways Ethernet LAN Switch. This gives each device the appearance of a dedicated 10 Mbps Ethernet link. Each 8271 includes an ATM "uplink" Universal Feature Card, which attaches to an ATM port on the 8260.

Four RISC System/6000 model 590H computers, each with two IBM TURBOWAYS ATM 155 MC adapters, also attach to the ATM switches. Each ATM switch has two main computers attached to it, for redundancy. These four RISC System/6000 computers act as X-Windows clients, running software on behalf of the users. They also download software to the X-servers should they request it, say, after a power failure. TCP/IP is the network's main protocol, although DECnet also flows between the RISC System/6000 systems and a Digital Equipment Corporation VMS system at the hospital.

CCCH's WAN design relies upon ISDN for fast, dialup service from physician offices and homes. Unfortunately, it isn't yet available to CCCH for another year, so CCCH uses ordinary analog lines. At the hospital, they use an IBM 8235 for dialup access to their Ethernet and ATM LAN. Most of their physicians use IBM ThinkPad laptops, so IBM WaveRunner Credit Card Digital Modem adapters work well for them. These devices can operate at 28.8 Kbps over analog lines and, when ISDN arrives, support ISDN as well. Physicians with desktop systems use IBM WaveRunner Digital Modem adapters, typically with an ISA bus system. Later, when ISDN becomes available, CCCH will use the IBM 7845 ISDN Network Terminator Extended to give each physician an ISDN BRI connection. At that point, they'll also upgrade to the newest model of 8235, so it too will be ISDN capable.

SpeedyTix

When we left SpeedyTix, they couldn't justify their new application because it entailed too much operational risk; their staff was unfamiliar with client/server technology. So, they hired ISSC to review their application's design and suggest ways to reduce their operational costs. The design review's goal was to eliminate $1,000,000 in risk and ongoing cost, using up to $500,000 of funds to do so. This would save $500,000, thus justifying the application.

The design review recommended that SpeedyTix purchase SystemView/400 and use this to automate common operations. This recommendation helped SpeedyTix streamline operations in their existing applications, not just for the kiosks. The design review also recommended that SpeedyTix outsource the design, coding, and integration of the kiosk's software instead of building it in house. SpeedyTix personnel would be members of the team but wouldn't take responsibility for the software's timely completion. Instead, they concentrated on the AS/400 software at the central site. SpeedyTix asked ISSC to design and write the kiosk's software and to write the automation routines for the AS/400.

So, SpeedyTix' server is an AS/400 system, running CICS/400 and DB2/400 software. Because of higher expected transaction volumes, SpeedyTix upgraded their AS/400 hardware from an older E60 model to a 9406 Model 510 processor. This added capacity also allows SpeedyTix to experiment with other kinds of client access, such as customers using World Wide Web browsers over the Internet. The AS/400 runs SystemView/400, SystemView Automation Center/400, and ADSM/400 software, which monitors the kiosks and automates common processes like backup.

Each kiosk contains an IBM PC Model 300, equipped with a touch screen, running IBM's OS/2 operating system. ISSC's application for these systems uses CICS/2, communicating with CICS/400, as a transaction processor. A DB2/2 database contains current event information, while arena seating charts and images depicting views from specific seats reside in ordinary OS/2 files. Because the data in the kiosk is "read only", no backups need occur here. To receive updated software and data, NetView Distribution Manager/2 also resides in the kiosk.

SpeedyTix' WAN is based upon ISDN, using IBM's LAN Distance server software running on a PC 300 at the central site and on each client system in the kiosk. Each kiosk uses IBM 7845s and IBM WaveRunner Digital Modems. In addition to the LAN Distance software, each kiosk runs Communications Manager/2 software, and the main communications protocol is APPN. At the central site, SpeedyTix uses an IBM token-ring LAN, which attaches the central site LAN Distance system to the AS/400 system. The LAN Distance system uses the IBM Auto 16/4 ISA Adapter to attach to the main 16 Mbps ring, and the AS/400 uses the token-ring feature number 2619. Other central site users use Client Access/400, attaching to rings that are bridged into the main ring using IBM 8229 token-ring bridges. These users don't use the same AS/400 token-ring card as the kiosks; instead, they get better performance via an AS/400 FSIOP.

Five and Dime Imports

Our final hypothetical firm is a large company, Five and Dime Imports. Until recently, it used an IBM ES/9000 9021 Model 711 mainframe running MVS for all of its business computing. Now, it uses a client/server approach to promote regional autonomy and customer responsiveness; Five and Dime now uses the mainframe heavily to analyze market trends. Five and Dime's batch volume, especially batched invoicing, prevents it from using IBM 9672 processors for now; at some point, when the CMOS machines have greater throughput, they expect to replace the water cooled processor.

To move computing power out to the regions, Five and Dime installed AS/400 9406 Model 500 processors at each regional facility. These systems run OS/400, DB2/400, and DataPropagator Relational software. Users at these facilities have PCs, connected to the AS/400s using token-ring LANs and Client Access/400 software. The AS/400s attach to the token-ring LAN using the high-performance feature #2619 adapter. Devices, such as bar code readers, attach using SDLC lines. Many of these devices were attached to the mainframe before; now, 3174 controllers, terminals, bar code readers, and bar code printers all attach to the regional AS/400s.

At the central site, the 9201 Model 711 continues to support Five and Dime's batch and transactional workloads, such as batched invoicing. Most of this data now resides in a DB/2 database, although some still exists in older, nonrelational file structures. Clerks at the central site use CICS as a transaction monitor to direct transactions to the main DB2 database. DataPropagator Relational software handles the replication of relational data to and from the AS/400 systems. Also at the central site, an OS/2 system running DataHub monitors and manages the timing and integrity of data replication operations.

Five and Dime's network is built mostly upon APPN, although recent requests for Internet access haven't been ignored. The WAN uses frame relay lines, attached to an IBM 3746-950 at the central site, and to IBM 6611 Network Processors at each of the regional sites. The WAN directly supports APPN and TCP/IP. The 3746 has token-ring interfaces for users at the central site and T1 WAN interfaces for the frame relay lines. Similarly, the 6611s have token-ring LAN interfaces and a single WAN link for the frame relay line. As part of its redesign, Five and Dime eliminated subarea SNA from its network to reduce administration time and costs. Users gain Internet access through the central site, using an IBM Secured Network Gateway firewall system, located on the central site's token-ring LAN.

Five and Dime manages this environment using SystemView for MVS. It automates common mainframe tasks, such as batch job scheduling, database backups, and so forth. It also includes NetView for MVS; Five and Dime uses the Enterprise System Option to manage the main network. Unlike GPSI, Five and Dime doesn't use SNMP to manage their 6611 processors, so they don't need the MultiSystem Manager software.

This firm is an example of client/server computing without requiring PCs; data replication occurs between the AS/400s and the mainframe without a user's explicit action or awareness. So, even if Five and Dime used only ordinary terminals, their application would still be an example of client/server computing.

A Glimpse into the Future

As we finish our exploration of IBM client/server computing, I would be remiss in ignoring recent events in our industry. Already, some are hyping the "next great trend" in computing, the Internet. Shares in Internet companies, like Netscape, soared in 1995 as analysts looked for the "next Microsoft." The trade press calls client/server applications less than a year old "legacy applications." Oracle trumpets a $500 "Internet appliance" that pundits say will replace the PC. Worried executives already believe they are somehow "behind" the trend.

Does this sound familiar?

Computing using the Internet, whether within or between firms, is a subset of client/server computing. A World Wide Web server is a server, and a browser is a client. If Cripple Creek Community Hospital wanted to be cool, they might have used WWW technology instead of X-Windows to identify and launch their textual and X-Windows applications. Instead, CCCH was prudent, and didn't jump on the latest bandwagon.

Firms that use WWW servers and browsers for internal purposes have developed what writers call an **intranet**; writers call applications designed for use by people outside a firm **Internet applications**. Much of the recent hype surrounds two developments. The first, **Common Gateway Interface programs**, (CGI programs) permit WWW servers to execute commands on a user's behalf. CGI programs are nifty; in the North American Open Systems Center, we built a CGI presentation program for SystemView for AIX. Now, we can monitor and control our lab from anywhere within IBM.

Another example of a CGI program is on IBM's WWW home page. There, you would find a hypertext link called "Search." If you clicked on this link, your browser would present you with a form into which you would type search words. When you submit the search, a CGI program on IBM's WWW server performs the search for you, and returns a hypertext document with the answer. With CGI programs, a user can interact with a WWW server, instead of merely browsing its contents. Some believe this enables interactions like credit card purchases. They see WWW servers as automated sales reps, marketing accepting orders at low cost.

The second recent development is a programming language from Sun Microsystems, called **Java**. Ordinarily, a WWW browser can display text, hypertext links, and images. Sometimes, with **helper applications**, a browser can play audio and video clips. Until Java, a browser's capabilities were fixed. Java is an elegant, object oriented language, designed for use over the Internet. A Java programmer can define a region of a WWW document as an **applet**, a small application. A Java applet can manipulate this region as it sees fit. So, instead of a static image, a Java applet might animate graphics. Some Java applets can also can retrieve data from servers around the

Internet as they run. IBM has licensed Java from Sun; shortly, Java applications and applets will find their way into IBM's products.

Compared to today's PC applications, computing using Java applets or CGI programs holds appeal. Instead of putting, say, database middleware on everyone's PC, an intranet design might only place this middleware on a WWW server. The WWW server would also hold any Java applets or CGI programs required. According to this view, the user's PC only needs a browser and networking software, simplifying the chores of software configuration management dramatically. Instead of managing a desktop on a user's PC, I/S staff would manage HTML documents on a web server. Intranets might make client/server computing less expensive.

This view of an intranet is similar to three-tiered client/server computing. The browser is a remote presentation interface. Business logic resides on the WWW server, whether it executes there or not. Data access is split between the WWW server and other database servers. What's new is the notion of a common presentation method for internal and Internet users. Instead of building an application's presentation using a GUI builder for internal users and a WWW server for external users, I/S organizations can use one interface for everyone.

That's why folks are excited. By simplifying the desktop device, you save support costs, and by using a single user interface, you save software development and maintenance costs. Users also might be happier with such an arrangement; they'd need to understand a point and click browser instead of several different products.

Today's reality falls short of these promises, though. Due to the nature of the HTTP protocol WWW servers and browsers use, you can't just "log in" to a WWW server and do useful work. Each request to the server is handled as an independent unit of work, not as one request in a stream of several, possibly related, requests. Using a WWW server as a front end to high volume transaction processing is difficult today. Also, the notion of enterprise security and intranets are still difficult to reconcile. The OSF and other organizations are currently working on techniques to help, but these efforts won't bear fruit until later in 1996. Synchronized collaboration and workflow, available easily with Lotus Notes, isn't a possible WWW application today. Few people and organizations understand how a network of servers will service millions of HTTP requests, along with CGI gateway, database gateway, and Java applet requests. Even if the technology is ready, many I/S organizations don't have the capacity to assimilate it productively.

For you, though, an intranet is just one more client/server tool. You justify a new intranet application the same way you'd justify a client/server application. Your staff's design methods don't change. They may learn about some new products or technologies, but the process doesn't change. You can still use Resource Sharing or Data Staging or Process-Driven Designs along with an intranet. Intranet computing doesn't suddenly make existing investments in shared system or client/server software worthless. Indeed, most firms will embrace this technology one application at a time, using it where it produces business results.

Internet appliances won't appear on everyone's desktop for a while because the application suite that users have grown to know won't exist right away. When new, say, spreadsheet applets do arrive, users will still need access to existing data. So, PCs, being the chameleons they are, are more likely to become Internet appliances than be displaced by them.

Even in an Intranet, a single huge web server won't service the needs of a large organization. Web servers will need to talk with each other, using client/server technology. In fact, because Java is an object oriented language, some are hoping for CORBA to reassert itself as applets talk amongst themselves. Client/server databases will still exist, though the client will reside on the WWW server instead of in a PC. Process oriented designs will continue to proliferate, because they reflect common business processes. Their forms, though, might originate on a WWW server instead of using an application on a client's PC.

Intranet and Internet technology bears watching, because it may well reduce development, support, and maintenance costs. But as with any new tool, use it appropriately. Follow a rigorous justification and design process. Don't hesitate to call on others for help. Consider your operational needs, including your data integrity requirements. Then make an informed decision.

Client/server computing is here to stay, whether in the guise of intranets, Internets, data warehouses, or some other form. The fundamental idea of client/server computing is too compelling to ignore: It harnesses teams of specialized processors to deliver business value to your customers, stakeholders, and employees. I hope our journey together has helped you to know how client/server computing can help your business.

Index

Reader Feedback Sheet

Your comments and suggestions are very important in shaping future publications. Please photocopy this page, jot down your thoughts, and fax it to (904) 934-9981 or mail it to:

Maximum Press

Attn: Jim Hoskins

605 Silverthorn Road

Gulf Breeze, FL 32561

_____

_____

_____

_____

_____

_____

_____

_____

_____

_____

_____

_____

_____

_____

_____

_____

_____

_____

Dr. Livingstone's
On-line Shopping
Safari Guidebook
by Frank Fiore
$21.95
ISBN: 1-885068-07-7

How to Increase
Small Business Profits
With Technology
by Jonathan Strum
$22.95
ISBN: 1-885068-08-5

Exploring IBM
Client/Server
Computing
by David Bolthouse
$32.95
ISBN: 1-885068-04-2

Exploring IBM's
New Age
Mainframes
by John L. Young
512 pages, 125
illustrations, $34.95
ISBN: 1-885068-05-0

Exploring IBM's
Print-on-Demand
Technology
by Jim Wallace
$22.95
ISBN: 1-885068-06-9

Exploring the IBM
PC Power Series
by Jim Hoskins and
David Bradley, Ph.D.
300 pages, $29.95
ISBN: 0-9633214-5-5

Marketing on the
Internet
by Mike Mathiesen
$39.95
ISBN: 1-885068-01-8

Real World
Client/Server
by Steve Krantz
344 pages, $29.95
ISBN: 0-9633214-7-1

To purchase a Maximum Press book, visit your local bookstore
or call 1-800-989-6733 (US/Canada) or 1-609-863-1030 (International).
For more information or online ordering visit our homepage:
http://www.maxpress.com/books/maxpress/435

*What About
ProductManager?*
by David Curtis
200 pages, $34.95
ISBN: 0-9633214-4-7

*What About
MAPICS/DB?*
by Ken Blackshaw
221 pages, line
drawings, $29.95
ISBN: 0-9633214-2-0

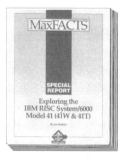

*Exploring the IBM
RISC System/6000
Model 41*
by Jim Hoskins
47 pages, photos and
line drawings, $19.95
ISBN: 0-9633214-8-X

*Exploring the
IBM AS/400
Advanced 36,
Second Edition*
by Jim Hoskins and
Roger Dimmick
105 pages, $19.95
ISBN: 1-885068-11-5

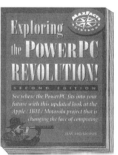

*Exploring the
PowerPC
Revolution!
Second Edition*
by Jim Hoskins and
Jack Blackledge,
165 pages, photos
and line drawings,
$22.95
ISBN: 1-885068-02-6

*IBM Personal
Computers,
A Business
Perspective,
Eighth Edition*
by Jim Hoskins
320 pages, photos
and line drawings,
$29.95
ISBN: 0471-04795-3

*IBM RISC
System/6000,
A Business
Perspective,
Sixth Edition*
by Jim Hoskins
320 pages, photos and
line drawings, $29.95
ISBN: 0471-12959-3

*IBM AS/400,
A Business
Perspective,
Sixth Edition*
by Jim Hoskins
368 pages, photos and
line drawings, $25.95
ISBN: 0471-048-08-9

To purchase a Maximum Press book, visit your local bookstore
or call 1-800-989-6733 (US/Canada) or 1-609-863-1030 (International).
For more information or online ordering visit our homepage:
http://www.maxpress.com/books/maxpress/435